SATHER CLASSICAL LECTURES

Volume Forty

MYTH

MYTH

ITS MEANING AND FUNCTIONS IN ANCIENT AND OTHER CULTURES

by G. S. KIRK

Professor of Classics, University of Bristol

CAMBRIDGE
AT THE UNIVERSITY PRESS

UNIVERSITY OF CALIFORNIA PRESS
BERKELEY AND LOS ANGELES

1971

PUBLISHED BY THE SYNDICS OF THE CAMBRIDGE UNIVERSITY PRESS
BENTLEY HOUSE, 200 EUSTON ROAD, LONDON NWI 2DB
AND
UNIVERSITY OF CALIFORNIA PRESS
BERKELEY AND LOS ANGELES

LIBRARY OF CONGRESS CATALOG CARD NUMBER: 72–628267

INTERNATIONAL STANDARD BOOK NUMBERS:
CAMBRIDGE 0 521 07854 7
CALIFORNIA 0 520 01651 3

FIRST PUBLISHED 1970
REPRINTED 1971

PRINTED IN GREAT BRITAIN
AT THE UNIVERSITY PRINTING HOUSE, CAMBRIDGE
(BROOKE CRUTCHLEY, UNIVERSITY PRINTER)

Preface

THIS BOOK attempts to come to grips with a set of widely ranging but connected problems concerning myths: their relation to folktales on the one hand, to rituals on the other; the validity and scope of the structuralist theory of myth; the range of possible mythical functions; the effects of developed social institutions and literacy; the character and meaning of ancient Near-Eastern myths and their influence on Greece; the special forms taken by Greek myths and their involvement with rational modes of thought; the status of myths as expressions of the unconscious, as allied with dreams, as universal symbols, or as accidents of primarily narrative aims.

Almost none of these problems has been convincingly handled, even in a provisional way, up to the present, and this failure has vitiated not only such few general discussions as exist of the nature, meanings and functions of myths but also, in many cases, the detailed assessment of individual myths of different cultures.

The need for a coherent treatment of these and related problems, and one that is not concerned simply to propagate a particular universalistic theory (the very notion of which is in my opinion chimerical), seems undeniable. How far the present book will satisfactorily fill such a need remains to be seen. At least it makes a beginning, even if in doing so it risks the criticism of being neither fish nor fowl. Sociologists and folklorists may find it, from their specialized viewpoints, a little simplistic in places; and a few classical colleagues will not forgive me for straying far beyond Greek myths, even though these can hardly be understood in isolation or solely in the light of studies in cult and ritual. Others may find it less easy than anthropologists, sociologists, historians of thought or students of French and English literature to accept the relevance of Lévi-Strauss to some of these matters; but his theory contains the one important new idea in this field since Freud, it is complicated and largely untested, and it demands careful attention from anyone attempting a broad understanding of the subject. The beliefs of Freud and Jung, on the other hand, are a more familiar element in the situation and have given rise to an enormous secondary literature, much of it arbitrary and some of it absurd. I have tried to isolate the crucial ideas and subject them to a pointed, if too brief, critique; so too with those of Ernst Cassirer.

The myths of savage societies enter the discussion not only for their own sake and in relation to Lévi-Strauss, but also as essential data for interpretations by other anthropologists, Kluckhohn, Boas and Malinowski in particular. Such 'primitive' myths are of course a critical factor, not least because they can occasionally be seen functioning in a natural and non-literate environment. Nevertheless the main emphasis of the book is on ancient Near-Eastern and Greek myths. The former, the oldest known to us, are deeply fascinating and generally neglected. They also provide a surprisingly good proving-ground both for structuralist and for other kinds of interpretation, and not merely for the ritualistic theories that have recently tended to dominate the Near-Eastern scene. Both they and Greek myths exemplify the effects of passage from an oral to a literate but still deeply traditional milieu. In many respects, however, Greek myths, far from being the exemplar they have always been taken for, constitute a very special and rather impure case. Neither the handbooks nor the detailed studies of individual myths make this plain, and so I have concentrated (in the earlier part of the fifth chapter) on trying to isolate the generic characteristics of Greek mythology and the basic interests that persist even through a long and distorting process of schematization.

Other special emphases, apart from that on ancient myths, will become clear as the book unfolds, but may usefully be outlined here. Most important, my main interest has been in exploring and to a degree rehabilitating the role of many myths as in some sense speculative, as concerned with problems in society or incompatibilities between culture and nature. Lévi-Strauss has already brought that role into prominence, admittedly in an exaggerated form, and has more than compensated for an earlier anthropological tendency to focus exclusively on myths as charters or as effective re-enactments of the creative and determinative past.

These latter functions are correspondingly unstressed in the present context, at least until the final chapter. So too, for different reasons, is that of myth as the accompaniment of ritual, a genuine role that has been heavily inflated in the past forty years. Among specific topics to receive less than their fair share of attention by encyclopaedic standards are Amerindian myths of the Plains and Southwest, because of their almost impenetrable syncretism, and the non-legendary mythology of Homer, perhaps because I have been too closely involved with other aspects of his poetry. On the other hand I have felt free to advance detailed and quite long interpretations of myths that particularly engrossed me, like those of Enki and Ninhursag, Gilgamesh, the birth of a great god from Kumarbi/Kronos, and the Centaurs and Cyclopes. Finally the question of 'modern myths' is entirely omitted. I am convinced that, because of the crucial part in their formation played by sophisticated values and extreme literacy, Franz Boas was mistaken in his assertion that 'we have no reason to believe that the myth-forming processes of the last ten thousand years have differed materially from modern myth-forming processes' (*Tsimshian Mythology*, 1916, 809). This is not to deny that the correct understanding of bastard modern forms may be helped by the study of the real thing.

I have been careful not to overload the text with learned references or to multiply footnotes for mere scholarship's sake, especially since I prefer to regard the book as an essay in interpretation, or a critical venture into the history and philosophy of thought, rather than as a work of agglomerative learning. Anyone who labours in this field has to plough through a good deal of stubble, and there seemed little advantage in piling up allusions to the extensive literature of myth and religion in the late nineteenth century or sociology in the mid-twentieth. I am no less anxious to avoid the implication of having exhaustively covered the bibliography of this vast subject. At a few points my reading has been highly selective. It should also be plain that I have no direct knowledge of either Sumerian or Akkadian, not to mention the languages of the Bororo, the Tsimshian, or the Trobriand islanders. For the translation of their texts or reports of their myths I have to depend on experts in these tongues. Those who believe that this completely disqualifies one from making judgements about content—a quite mistaken view in my opinion—need go no further.

In a few places the connexion between the book and the Sather lectures obtrudes itself—a connexion that I have not tried to disguise completely. The book was written with the lectures in mind, and each of its chapters corresponds, although on a much larger scale, with one of the six lectures. I am grateful to the Berkeley audience for their feeling that other forms of irrationalism in the environment were less interesting than myth itself.

I have particularly benefited from some long discussions in Cambridge with G. E. R. Lloyd, on Lévi-Strauss, and Mrs Stephanie (Page) Dalley, on ancient Near-Eastern literature. Others who helped me over the same topics (and who of course bear no responsibility for the results) are Louis Orlin, W. Heimpel, and W. G. Runciman. To these, and also to Adam and Anne Parry, Hugh Lloyd-Jones, Simon Pembroke and Moses Finley for other contributions, I am most grateful. Michael Grant should also be mentioned here, because I think it was his *Myths of the Greeks and Romans* (1962) that originally sharpened my interest in these matters. I am doubly in the debt of G. E. R. Lloyd, since he also read through the proofs and suggested many improvements of the kind that could be made at that stage. At Berkeley the forthright and amiable criticisms of Alan Dundes and his folklore seminar were immensely useful, and Joseph Fontenrose offered some valuable comments on the text as a whole. The members of the Classics Department there and their wives, and above all Professor and Mrs W. K. Pritchett, helped to make the delivery of the lectures and the final preparation of the book an exceptionally pleasant task. In this last respect I must thank also, and very warmly, two classical graduate students, Christopher Gill at Yale and Mrs Caroline Dewald at Berkeley, who contributed much more in the way of perceptive criticism than I had any right to expect. Finally I should express my gratitude to the two university presses for a rapid and accurate transatlantic operation.

G. S. K.

Cambridge
October 1969

Abbreviations

The following are abbreviations of frequently cited or unwieldy titles:

AES *Archives européennes de Sociologie* [The article cited from this source is now reprinted in E. R. Leach, *Genesis as Myth and other Essays* (London, 1970), pp. 25 ff.]

ANET² *Ancient Near Eastern Texts Relating to the Old Testament*, ed. J. B. Pritchard (2nd ed., Princeton, 1955)

BP *Before Philosophy*, ed. H. and H. A. Frankfort and others (Penguin Books, 1949), the English edition of *IA* below

CC Claude Lévi-Strauss, *Le Cru et le Cuit* (Paris, 1964); vol. I of *Mythologiques*

Essay Ernst Cassirer, *An Essay on Man* (New Haven and London, 1944)

GgrR³ M. P. Nilsson, *Geschichte der griechische Religion*, vol. I (3rd ed., Munich, 1967)

HTR *Harvard Theological Review*

IA *The Intellectual Adventure of Ancient Man*, ed. H. and H. A. Frankfort and others (Chicago, 1946), cf. *BP* above

JAFL *Journal of American Folk-lore*

JCS *Journal of Cuneiform Studies*

JNES *Journal of Near Eastern Studies*

MC Claude Lévi-Strauss, *Du Miel aux cendres* (Paris, 1966); vol. II of *Mythologiques*

Mythologies *Mythologies of the Ancient World*, ed. S. N. Kramer (Garden City, N.Y., 1961)

OMT Claude Lévi-Strauss, *L'Origine des manières de table* (Paris, 1968); vol. III of *Mythologiques*

PSF   Ernst Cassirer, *The Philosophy of Symbolic Forms*,
             vol. II: *Mythical Thought* (Eng. trans., New Haven,
             1955)

Python   Joseph A. Fontenrose, *Python, a Study of Delphic Myth
             and its Origins* (Berkeley, 1959)

SA   Claude Lévi-Strauss, *Structural Anthropology* (Eng.
             trans., New York and London, 1963)

SDFML   Funk and Wagnall's *Standard Dictionary of Folklore,
             Mythology and Legend*, ed. Maria Leach (New York,
             1949–50)

SSMT   *The Structural Study of Myth and Totemism*, ed. Edmund
             Leach (London, 1967; A. S. A. Monographs, vol. 5)

Contents

I

Myth, Ritual and Folktale

1 : Introductory

If a classical scholar chooses the nature of myths as his subject,
it is reasonable to expect that he will devote the greatest part of his
effort to the discussion of Greek myths. It is therefore necessary to
begin by explaining why I am not going to do precisely that, and
yet remain within the true scope of the Sather lectures from which
this book originated. To be brief, Greek myths must share our
time and attention with others, because in the end more can be
learned about them by an indirect approach, by considering the
nature of myths in general, than by a frontal attack on problems
that have proved hopelessly unyielding in the past. Moreover the
general problem of the nature of myths is in itself at least as
important and challenging as any narrowly classical application.

It will be plain from the title that I shall not be primarily concerned with tracing the growth of individual myths at different
periods or in different authors, nor with comparative mythology
as such, nor with the elaboration of literary uses. This is not to
deny that the detailed study of mythical themes in the literature
of the classical period in Greece is essential for the understanding
of the whole culture. It would be absurd to criticize the persistence
and devotion that have been applied to this special task over the
last hundred years—not to speak of the ancient world itself, in
which the learned study of myths, the recording of different
applications in different authors, and the association of specific
myths with particular cults, peoples and places, were already
enthusiastically pursued. Theories about the meaning of myths
were propounded at least as early as the sixth century B.C., and

later found influential if tedious expression in the works of Euheme-
rus and the Neoplatonic allegorists. There was plenty for modern
scholars to build on; and if the results have been—to take a broad
view—both wilful and pedestrian, the fault belongs partly to the
pedantry of the ancient tradition, and partly also to the daunting
complexity of the mythical variants themselves. Yet it must be
admitted that the qualities needed to find one's way in the mythical
and poetical jungle of the Hellenistic and Roman world are not
necessarily those that facilitate an imaginative yet flexible conception of the nature of myth as a whole.

The importance of working towards such a conception should
not need any special defence. Myths concern us not only for the
part they play in all primitive, illiterate, tribal or non-urban
cultures, which makes them one of the main objects of anthropological interest; not only for the grip that versions of ancient
Greek myths have gained through the centuries on the literary
culture of the western nations; but also because of men's en-
dearing insistence on carrying quasi-mythical modes of thought,
expression, and communication into a supposedly scientific age.
From all these points of view it is essential to have a clear idea of
what myths are and what they are not, and, so far as possible, of the
ways in which they are likely to operate. The *ways*, in the plural—
for I regard it as axiomatic that myths do not have a single form,
or act according to one simple set of rules, either from epoch to
epoch or from culture to culture.

Many intelligent people feel that myth is not a matter of the
learned and the reasonable, but rather of the poetical, the symbolic and the beautiful. In reality, of course, myths are often
none of these things—many of them are prosaic, utilitarian and
ugly. Yet what really matters for most of us, perhaps, does lie
closer to that poetical view of myths, and to the kind of value they
accumulate in their literary uses. Even so, the historical, analytical
and philosophical approach must be taken first. In the vital area
of definition, of deciding what myths are, what are not myths,
what makes one symbol mythical and another not, analysis
must precede intuition—and hundreds of pathetic and pretentious essays by amateurs of literature prove that to be so.

The classical attitude to myth, after being rescued by Mannhardt from Creuzer, by Andrew Lang from Max Müller, has been
dominated in this century by the trends initiated by J. G. Frazer.

Frazer's commentaries on Pausanias and Ovid, as well as *The Golden Bough* itself and other works of broad scope, seemed to open up unknown vistas in the interpretation of Greek religion and of the myths and rituals that accompanied it. Gilbert Murray in Oxford, Jane Harrison and A. B. Cook and F. M. Cornford in Cambridge, applied the new knowledge of comparative anthropology to the study of myth and religion; and the idea that the motives of custom and myth in primitive societies could illuminate those of more developed cultures, including that of the ancient Greeks, became the driving force behind works of manifold learning and amazing ingenuity. There was a store oi disparate and often incoherent ancient information about Greek religion and myth, especially in the iconography and in antiquarian authors of the Greco-Roman world like Plutarch and Pausanias; and this store was ransacked to provide supporting evidence for intuitions about scapegoats, fertility-spirits, year-demons, and sacred marriages, as well as mana, orenda, totem, taboo, and all those fascinating new concepts whose authority seemed to stretch from Polynesia and Peru to the Acropolis at Athens itself.

At its best the anthropological approach brought a fresh vitality to the study of classical religion and myths, and enabled its followers to recover from the lethargy that had overtaken them once the nineteenth-century fallacies of the animists, the symbolists, the nature-myth school, the pan-Babylonians and the pan-Egyptians had been exhaustingly laid to rest. It also freed them from the tyranny of Christian inhibitions and preconceptions in matters affecting the investigation of the sources of religious feeling; and opened up an immense range of new comparative material, some of which undeniably gave the clue to longstanding puzzles in the religion and sociology of classical antiquity. The results appeared in immense works like A. B. Cook's *Zeus*, which suffered from the example of Frazer's wide learning without manifesting quite his acumen; or two shorter books that have retained their influence longer, Jane Harrison's *Prolegomena to the Study of Greek Religion* (Cambridge, 1903) and *Themis* (Cambridge, 1912). Miss Harrison had an almost physical passion for the ancient past. Her books are lively, learned, yet unpedantic— and utterly uncontrolled by anything resembling careful logic. In this she was, to some extent, only following the precedent of

Frazer himself; since, as anthropologists of today are fond of pointing out (as they complacently trample on this fallen colossus), Frazer tossed in catalogues of vague similarities drawn from a dozen different cultures in apparent support of highly dubious theories, much as textual critics of the old school used to fling in huge lists of supposedly parallel passages selected on the most arbitrary and superficial principles. That was a heritage of Germanic scholarship in its least attractive aspect; but Frazer also exemplified the special shortcomings of the comparative method when applied to social institutions and systems of beliefs: that such complexes may present certain aspects which resemble each other, while their essential core remains completely distinct. Even by the indulgent view of the comparative method that then prevailed, this sort of thing was rather reprehensible—although no one reached the point of successfully reprehending it. More recently, under the guidance of men like Bronislaw Malinowski and A. R. Radcliffe-Brown, the whole idea of considering phenomena like myths or cult-practices in isolation from the social complex as a whole has seemed, to anthropologists at least, time-wasting and repellent.

Frazer was not the only powerful influence on Jane Harrison, Murray, and Cornford: Durkheim and Lévy-Bruhl (as well, in Miss Harrison's case, as Bergson) were their mentors in the concept of group beliefs and emotions and in the idea, itself developed from E. B. Tylor, of a special kind of 'primitive mentality'—an idea that has now been drastically revised by Lévi-Strauss in his *La Pensée sauvage* (Paris, 1962). The results can be clearly seen in Cornford's early book *From Religion to Philosophy* (London and New York, 1912), in which a people's 'collective representations', founded on principles of social organization, were held to be gradually rationalized so as to become the earliest concepts of philosophy. Such a view of the development of Greek thought has persisted in some quarters until the present day.

Generally speaking this brilliant and confident little group, the so-called 'Cambridge School', who applied the novel intuitions of the French sociologists to the cross-cultural data supplied by Frazer and the new ethnography, gained a surprising influence, at least among classical scholars. Even now there is a widespread feeling that these people, although they used a new method to excess, were in most important respects correct—that they advanced the study of Greek religion and myth to a point from which it has made little further progress. In a way this is true. Comparatively little has been done since, and no Andrew Lang has risen to denounce basic fallacies in the method. Martin Nilsson in his history of Greek religion[1] adopted a cautious attitude to the idea of the Year-Spirit, one of the most heavily emphasized and dubious concepts of Gilbert Murray and Jane Harrison; but much of the free-ranging comparative urge of these authors survives even in the sober pages of the empirically minded Nilsson. That cannot be said, perhaps, for his follower H. J. Rose, best known for a *Handbook of Greek Mythology* (5th ed., London, 1953) that is still widely used in the English- and German-speaking world. Rose, essentially a folklorist, adopted a commonsense approach and rejected much of the excitable speculation of the anthropological school; he was openly critical, moreover, of certain other one-sided attitudes like that of the myth-and-ritual school. And yet the very matter-of-factness of his method—his adherence to the intention of reporting the myths first and foremost, in a reasonable chronological and geographical order, with the least possible interpretation and theorizing—has left many people (including myself) with the idea that there must be a great deal more to Greek mythology than that. The common reaction has been to resort to the 'exciting' presentations of Harrison and Cornford on the one hand, and the more modern efforts of prolific writers like Karl Kerényi and Mircea Eliade on the other. It was precisely the feeling that Classicists and others had little to turn to, on the subject of Greek myths, beyond the erratic Harrison, the factual Rose, the Jungian Kerényi, the repetitive Eliade, or even the brilliant but in this field totally misguided Robert Graves, that encouraged me to carry the investigation a little further.[2]

[1] *Geschichte der griechischen Religion*, 1 (3rd ed., Munich, 1967).

[2] The names I have mentioned so far are primarily of those whose work is available in English; but the position is no different in other languages, so far as the nature of myth is concerned. Naturally a vast mass of specific information is available, for example in W. H. Roscher's *Ausführliches Lexikon der griechischen und römischen Mythologie* (Leipzig, 1884–1937), much of which is distorted by obsolete naturistic assumptions, and in Preller–Robert, *Griechische Mythologie* (Berlin, 1894–1926), of which the second volume, on heroic myths, is by Carl Robert himself and is still of great value. In French, Francis Vian has written extensively and enlighteningly on the Theban myths, but at the crucial points he limits himself by his adhesion to Dumézil's theory of Indo-European organization (see p. 210). The most spectacular progress in the study of

6   Myth, Ritual and Folktale

In the strictly anthropological sphere the results of an energetic and continuous study of myths are little less disappointing. Nearly all modern anthropological work on myths suffers from its smallness of scale, which prevents it from adequately considering the essential preliminaries of classification and definition, even where a particular author shows himself aware of them. This error of scale seems to be the result of the propensity of anthropologists for writing short papers, more or less in the scientific manner, rather than full-length books, and for putting up with collections of random reprints, or so-called symposia, rather than requiring a unified and systematic treatment of essential concepts. In the case of field-reports that do amount to books, the tendency is to divide up the subject into separate and sometimes artificial topics, of which myths may form one—and this in spite of the extensive modern opinion which insists that social structure should be seen as an integrated whole.[3] Then there is a curiously naive quality about the theoretical discussions carried on by many social anthropologists. Philosopher-sociologists of the Durkheim–Marett type are often derided; but conversely the empirical qualities most needed for observation in the field tend to have counter-balancing deficiencies on the theoretical side. Moreover the positivistic strictures of an Evans-Pritchard, although of the greatest value in puncturing the wild theories of the origins of religion and magic that were popular until recently, have inclined to inhibit necessary generalizing over more viable problems.

Anthropology owes much to Bronislaw Malinowski, whose methods are nowadays found rather primitive, but whose views on the subject of myths have continued to exercise a powerful domination. I shall have more to say about him later, but it is relevant here that in seeing the prime function of myths as the

Greek religion (rather than myths) has been made over cults and festivals, especially by L. R. Farnell, M. P. Nilsson, L. Deubner, and now W. Burkert. Some light on mythology is certainly reflected from that direction; but it is bound to be a distorting light so long as the broader understanding of myth remains defective. Another promising approach is by way of the Near East; recently M. L. West's valuable commentary on the *Theogony* (Oxford, 1966) and P. Walcot's interesting *Hesiod and the Near East* (Cardiff, 1966) have opened up this question still further, although the discussion is still too narrowly confined to the Babylonian Creation Epic, the Hurrian Kumarbi and Ullikummi sequence, and (in Walcot's case) the Egyptian wisdom-literature. I hope to extend the range of possibilities in chapters III and IV.

[3] Compare A. R. Radcliffe-Brown's criticism of attempts to define totemism in short formulas: *Structure and Function in Primitive Society* (London, 1952), 131.

recording and validating of institutions, and in totally rejecting their speculative aspects, he has succeeded in restricting the vision of far too many anthropologists of the Anglo-American tradition. Recently the balance has been redressed in the most startling way from the periphery of the quite different and more theoretical Gallic tradition. Claude Lévi-Strauss's theory entails that all myths are speculative, or problem-reflecting, when properly understood. Proper understanding requires concentration on an underlying structure of relationships, rather than on their overt content or any narrowly allegorical interpretation. Whether or not the large claims he implicitly makes for the theory turn out to be justified, it is plain that his contribution, which is still continuing, radically alters the theoretical aspect of the subject, just as his work on kinship has radically modified the excessively mechanical appearance that this important topic was beginning to assume. I am not sure that Lévi-Strauss is going to have a very direct effect on our understanding of most Greek myths, for reasons that will become clear later; but the fecundity of his ideas, however arcane their expression, compared with the sterility of nearly all other recent treatments of myths in their theoretical aspects, justifies the devotion of a complete subsequent chapter to the exposition and criticism of his thought.

In one respect Lévi-Strauss is clearly in error. In implying that all myths in all cultures have a similar function, namely to 'mediate' contradictions, he is needlessly aligning himself with a series of interpretative movements (like the nature-myth or the myth-and-ritual movement) that have reduced their chances of being fairly assessed just because of the excessive generality of their claims. There is no one definition of myth, no Platonic form of a myth against which all actual instances can be measured. Myths, as we shall see, differ enormously in their morphology and their social function. There are signs that so obvious a truth is becoming more widely accepted; and one of the purposes of the present work is to examine the nature of myths in different aspects and against the background of more than one type of culture.[4]

[4] Even Mircea Eliade, who has prolifically urged a view of mythical function derived primarily from Malinowski, prefaced a recent definition (in *Encyclopaedia Britannica*, 15th ed., s.v. Myth) with an admission that myth is an extremely complex cultural reality. Multiplicity of functions is emphasized in an interesting short study that appeared while the present work was in the press, Dr Percy S. Cohen's Malinowski Lecture on 'Theories of Myth', *Man*, N.S. IV, September 1969, 337–53, especially p. 351.

2: Myth, religion and ritual

Etymology is a traditional point of departure, but in this case an unhelpful one. For the Greeks *muthos* just meant a tale, or something one uttered, in a wide range of senses: a statement, a story, the plot of a play. The word 'mythology' can be confusing in English, since it may denote either the study of myths, or their content, or a particular set of myths. For Plato, the first known user of the term, *muthologia* meant no more than the telling of stories. The ambivalence of the modern term is doubly unfortunate, since it tends to persuade us that we are partaking in a scientific study when we say that we like Greek mythology—as we might claim to enjoy palaeontology—when all we mean is that we find the stories entertaining; or it encourages us to talk about 'systems of myths' and the like, when with most cultures what we experience is a sporadic collection that may not form a system at all. In the case of Greek myths, as it happens, we do possess something like a system—and that is part of the trouble; for the system was established at a relatively late stage (in comparison with the probable antiquity of the mythical tradition as a whole) by people like Homer and Hesiod, the tragedians, the Hellenistic cataloguer-poets, and the schematizers and summarizers of the Greco-Roman world.

Nearly everyone thinks he knows what he means by a myth: something like one of the Greek myths, he will say, in a manner that would have infuriated Socrates—something like the tale of Perseus and Medusa, or Odysseus and the Cyclops, or Oedipus and Iocaste, or Hermes and the cattle of Apollo. Yet these examples leave many types unrepresented, and even they are confusing in their admixture of what might otherwise be called folktale, legend, theology, or even sociology. The truth is that Greek myths provide no better an instance of what myths quintessentially are than any other extensive cultural set. In some ways they are less informative than most, for reasons to be discussed in chapter v; and yet we have been brought up to regard them as composing a paradigmatic system that can be used as a central point of reference for the whole study of mythology. It is paradoxical that this attitude still persists even when anthropologists and ethnologists have recorded many other different sets of myths from other cultures, some of them manifestly possessed of qualities, and fulfilling functions, not exemplified by the Greek materials. And yet even ethnologists and anthropologists tend to be ecstatically happy when they can cite a (usually misleading) Greek parallel.[5] It is no part of my purpose to diminish the role of Greek studies in the understanding of culture as a whole, or to deny the charm, the nostalgia and the brilliance of the Greek myths; but I consider that everyone would do better, if they are studying the nature of myths in general, to regard the surviving Greek examples as constituting just one important chapter in a long and varied volume.

It is salutary, all the same, to use Greek myths, among others, to control the theories that have been primarily founded upon them. Perseus and Medusa, Odysseus and the Cyclops, for example, bring us into immediate conflict with two basic propositions that are commonly made in differing degrees of directness. The first is that all myths are about gods, or derived from rituals; the second that all myths are either quite distinct, or quite indistinguishable, from folktales. The consideration of these propositions and their elaborations will take up the remainder of this chapter.

The dogma that all myths are about gods can be easily disposed of in that form, if we agree that the stories of Perseus and Medusa (or Andromeda for that matter), and Oedipus, Laius, and Iocaste, really are myths: for neither is 'about' gods, if 'about' means 'primarily concerned with'. Perseus may be directed or protected by Athena, just as the actions of Oedipus are determined by an oracle of Apollo; but the second tale is essentially about a man moving in a human environment, and the first concerns a being, a hero, who may be something more than a man but falls far short of true divinity. These examples could easily be reinforced by others from other cultures—by Gilgamesh, for instance, who was certainly treated for the most part as a king and not a god, and who, in spite of a divine mother, was to become the arche-

---

[5] 'A first-hand acquaintance with the classical literatures is an indispensable condition for the student of folklore' (A. H. Krappe in *SDFML*, 1, 404) is the kind of remark that is often made about myth, too. Even C. Lévi-Strauss felt that he should bring Oedipus into the range of his theory (*SA*, 213–17). Nor am I entirely satisfied with the reverse position, asserted most clearly by Bronislaw Malinowski: 'In the study of myth the classical scholar must learn from the anthropologist' (*Myth in Primitive Psychology*, London, 1926, 122). Malinowski's own theories show that merely observing primitive societies is not enough.

type of royal mortality. That the general proposition, easy as it is to refute, has been seriously held over a long period, can be shown by a few quotations. As Ernst Cassirer stated, naming two of the most influential figures in the study of myth in the last century, 'For Schelling, who depended principally on Georg Creuzer's *Symbolik und Mythologie der alten Völker* (1810–23), all mythology was essentially the theory and history of the gods'; or as L. Radermacher put it, mythology was the equivalent term (*Deckwort*) under which classical scholarship during the nineteenth century spoke of Greek and Roman religion.[6] In the twentieth century the view persists: Rudolf Otto, the author of the curiously influential *Das Heilige* (1917), regarded myth (together with magic and the belief in souls) as 'the vestibule at the threshold of the real religious feeling, an earliest stirring of the numinous consciousness', whereas Northrop Frye states baldly, if rather emptily, that a myth is 'a story in which some of the chief characters are gods'—that being an attempt to state the essential quality of a myth. That I am not choosing eccentrics is confirmed by the opinion of a reputable anthropologist, E. W. Count: 'on only one point have scholars agreed: myths are a form of literature…about gods or demigods'.[7] Count himself, it should be noticed, does not share this view.

It is a virtue of classical scholars that they are not so prone to make this kind of generalization, at least in its simplest form; no doubt because the heroes, who play so large a part in Greek myths, are obviously not gods. Even so, Hesiod's *Theogony*, partly because it is the earliest surviving document of Greek literature devoted mainly to mythological topics, has occupied the most prominent position in many accounts of Greek myths, and so placed a strongly divine colouring on the mythology as a whole. W. K. C. Guthrie, for instance (in his chapter on 'The Religion and Mythology of the Greeks' in the revised version of *The Cambridge Ancient History*, vol. II), makes it plain from the scope of his treatment that he regards mythology, at least in the earlier period, as an aspect of religion. In this he could count on support from another powerful scholar in this field, Angelo Brelich, who

    [6] E. Cassirer, *PSF*, 15; L. Radermacher, *Mythos und Sage bei den Griechen* (Vienna and Leipzig, 1938), 43.
    [7] R. Otto, *The Idea of the Holy* (Eng. tr., London and New York, 1950), 122; N. Frye, *Fables of Identity* (New York, 1963), 30; E. W. Count in *Culture in History*, ed. S. Diamond (New York, 1960), 595.

believes that different modern approaches have shown that 'mythology has gradually revealed that it cannot be reduced to factors outside religion, and today it is generally considered on the same plane as the other fundamental forms of religion, if not indeed as their ultimate source'.[8]

Even this implication that all myths are associated with religious beliefs, feelings or practices seems misleading. Many myths embody a belief in the supernatural, and for most cultures that will involve polytheistic religion; but many other myths, or what seem like myths, do not. Apart from the case of Oedipus (which seems to me an irrefutable instance of an acknowledged myth only superficially associated in its primary episodic structure with religion or the supernatural), there are the types of myth that are often called legend and folktale. I shall consider these more fully later, but for the moment merely observe that it is imprudent to ignore, in the early stages of definition, tales like that of Paris abducting Helen, or Achilles killing Hector; or of the woman who puts off her suitors by a trick, or the other woman (or her father) who chooses her husband by a contest. The first two of these instances might be called 'legend', the second two 'folktale', but the truth is that they all come within the range of what most people mean by 'myth', and yet seem to have no serious religious component whatever. But suppose we leave such cases on one side —and ignore for the moment the different case of Oedipus, which contains folktale elements but is not a folktale in essence: is it the fact that all the rest are religious? I believe not. If we look outside Greece, there are many myths of savage societies that have no known or probable connexion with cult, and concern beings who, although they may exist outside historical time and perform fantastic and supernatural actions, are not gods and have nothing to do with religion: they are men, often the first men, who established customs and practices and are classified by outside observers as 'culture-heroes'. Most of the South American Indian myths that Lévi-Strauss has examined are origin-myths in one sense or another; they explain the origin of cultural phenomena like cooking or painted pottery, or natural phenomena like animal

[8] A. Brelich, *Gli Eroi Greci* (Rome, 1958), 23 f.: 'la mitologia è venuta gradualmente rivelando la propria irreducibilità a fattori extrareligiosi, ed oggi è generalmente considerato sullo stesso piano delle altre forme fondamentali della religione, se non addirritura come fonte ultima di queste altre forme'. Classical scholars, he thinks, have not yet fully come round to this approach.

species and particular star-groups; their characters are both human beings and animals, who sometimes have strange powers—but there is no reason for associating most of them, either now or in the past, with worship or propitiation, the true external marks of religion. To argue that they, and the stories about them, are in a restricted sense 'sacred' is another matter.

Still less can the narrower position that all myths are associated with ritual be defended; or the narrowest of all, that they all *originated* from rituals, for which they offer a motive or cause. This theory has had an astonishing vogue from the time when it was first acquired (from Robertson Smith and Frazer for the most part) by Biblical scholars, who saw that it had a certain attraction in relation to the myths and rituals of the Near East, and in particular could make theologically acceptable sense of some of the Hebrew material. It is undoubtedly the case that many myths, perhaps especially in the Near East, were associated with rituals, and that some of them may have been created to account for actions whose purpose was no longer apparent. Yet it is often difficult to tell, from the form of the myth and the ritual alone, which came first, and caution is necessary. For example, Frazer's confidence in a statement like the following is unjustified: 'the story that Attis unmanned himself under a pine-tree was clearly devised to explain why his priests did the same beside the sacred violet-wreathed tree at his festival'.[9] It is possible that this was so, but not certain. The words of a careful critic, R. de Langhe, are salutary: 'while the study of the myths and ritual practices of so-called primitive peoples has in some cases revealed a close relationship between the myths and the rituals, it is equally true that it has also shown the existence of myths which are unaccompanied by any ritual performance. Between these two extremes many intermediate types can be attested.'[10] Both on the evidence of other cultures and on the Near-Eastern evidence itself, particularly that of the Ugaritic myths on which he is expert, de Langhe rejects the thesis that all myths are associated with, let alone derived from, rituals. And, to go directly to the Mesopotamian fountain-head of the western Asiatic mythical tradition, Samuel Noah Kramer believes that 'Sumerian myths have little if any connection

---

[9] J. G. Frazer, *Adonis Attis Osiris* (London, 1906), 169.
[10] R. de Langhe in *Myth, Ritual and Kingship*, ed. S. H. Hooke (Oxford, 1958), 131.

with rite and ritual in spite of the fact that the latter played so important a role in Sumerian religious practice'.[11]

Many of the excesses of this myth-and-ritual school have been ably dealt with by Joseph Fontenrose in his recent *The Ritual Theory of Myth* (Berkeley, 1966), which exposes, among other things, the weakness of Frazer's ideas about the 'King of the Woods' who forms the central theme of *The Golden Bough*. Among modern exponents of the theory Fontenrose concentrates on Frazer, Raglan, Hyman and Gaster;[12] I would now like to see him direct his critical attention to Near-Eastern experts of the Hooke school, who would (I predict) collapse like the proverbial house of cards.

One of the school's most influential allies was F. M. Cornford, who, like Gilbert Murray and Jane Harrison, had always found something peculiarly fascinating and peculiarly valid in old, half-forgotten rituals. His attitude deserves our closer examination. His French admirers, like the highly intelligent Jean-Pierre Vernant, still cite Cornford's *From Religion to Philosophy* (1912) with respect, partly because it is Durkheimian, but also because it suggests an alternative to the view of Greek religion advanced by the unsociologically-minded Nilsson. Cornford himself came to regret the book, and it is more helpful to consider his later views, which are in a way a refinement of those earlier and rather naive attitudes. A paper not published in his lifetime, which must now be among the most cited of all his articles, claims to show that 'the bulk of the episodes [*sc.* in Hesiod's *Theogony*] fit into the pattern of a very old myth of Creation, known to us from eastern sources and ultimately based on ritual'.[13] That this Greek Creation myth was aetiological, and derived from a New Year ritual, is conclusively proved, as Cornford thought, by the Babylonian

---

[11] S. N. Kramer, *The Sumerians* (Chicago, 1963), 144.

[12] For a succinct statement of Theodor Gaster's view see his article on 'Semitic mythology' in *SDFML*, II, 989: 'Semitic myths are embodied in poems designed originally to be chanted or recited at religious exercises. Their object was to provide an interpretation of ritual in terms of connected stories. In course of time, however, many of the underlying rituals fell into disuse, so that the myths survived as purely literary compositions, to be modified or elaborated at will. It is mainly in this developed form that they have come down to us...' In spite of its confident tone, this passage presents a mere hypothesis (at least in so far as many Semitic myths are concerned), and not an established fact.

[13] 'A Ritual Basis for Hesiod's *Theogony*', *The Unwritten Philosophy* (Cambridge, 1950), 95 ff.

evidence.[14] And what is this conclusive evidence? It is that the Babylonian Epic of Creation, the *Enuma Elish*, which described how Marduk eventually overcame the monstrous Tiamat and formed earth and sky out of her body, was recited at the New Year Akitu festival; or as Cornford put it more dramatically, 'on the fourth day of the New Year festival of the spring equinox, this hymn was recited, from beginning to end, by the high priest, shut up alone in the sanctuary'. Cornford writes as though this were the central act of the ceremonies; but in fact, as Fontenrose has pointed out with admirable thoroughness, it was nothing of the sort.[15] It was just one episode in a whole series of prayers, purifications and ritual actions which took twelve days in all. Its description, in terms less emphatic than those used by Cornford, accounts for less than a fiftieth part of the late ritual text, of the Seleucid period, that describes these procedures.[16] A whole series of curious things were said and done over the period of the festival; and in the course of an interminable performance whose purpose was to inaugurate the king at the beginning of the natural year, and to strengthen his command over nature on behalf of the god he represented, it was inevitable that the popular *Enuma Elish*, describing Marduk's initial ordering of the world, should form a part of the proceedings.

Cornford's theory does not require that every part of *Enuma Elish* can be shown to have ritual affiliations; but it does claim that the happenings at the Akitu festival *prove* that the whole Babylonian cosmogonical myth about Apsu, Tiamat and Marduk had a ritual origin; and therefore, since the Hesiodic Typhoeus-episode among others reflects that cosmogony, that the Greek creation-myth is ultimately derived from ritual. It proves nothing of the sort. Parts of the Babylonian poem may for a long time have had ritual associations, and it certainly cannot be excluded that they arose out of ritual in some way. Yet that is only one possibility. For Cornford, strangely enough, it is the only one—he simply could not conceive of a story like that of Marduk splitting Tiamat to form earth and sky arising in any other way than as a misunderstanding of a ritual, in which one priest representing the king overpowers another wearing a dragon-mask and representing the forces of disorder. 'No one but a lunatic under the influence of

---

[14] *Op. cit.*, 110.   [15] *Python*, 436–46.
[16] The surviving part of the text is translated by A. Sachs in *ANET*², 331–4.

hashish', he wrote, 'could ever arrive at the theory that they [sc. earth and sky] were originally formed by splitting the body of a dragon in half.'[17] Why Cornford resorted to this untypical derision of acts of imagination and fantasy one will never know, and perhaps is not very important now. But even on his own premise the argument does not stand up; for if a dragon-mask can be suitable wear for a priest representing disorder within a ritual, why cannot a dragon itself represent a condition of primeval disorder outside the ritual? If, in addition, the primeval figure represents water as well as disorder, as Tiamat certainly did, why should not the idea of dividing the waters from the waters (as Genesis puts it) assume the form of dividing the dragon itself? Cornford's early dedication to the attractions of primitive ritual led him to ridicule the possible symbolic and explicative powers of myth; in combating Frazer's assessment of the dragon-fight myth as one that 'for crudity of thought deserves to rank with the quaint fancies of the lowest savages', he descended to an assessment almost equally crude, by which tangibility is advanced as the best criterion of credibility—for what excited him (as he wrote in a revealing note found attached to this article after his death) was the idea that 'early philosophic cosmogony is not only a transcription of mythical cosmogony, but finally has its roots in *ritual*, something tangibly existing...'[18]

Fontenrose's own position, at any rate when he wrote *Python*, was that 'It is simpler to suppose that a well-known type of story was introduced in many places to serve as the primeval precedent of the rituals than to believe that in so many places the rituals spontaneously generated a uniform pattern of myth.'[19] This is surely right as against general theories of the type advanced by Theodor H. Gaster in his *Thespis* (New York, 1950). Yet Fontenrose's concentration on combat-myths, which are more obviously connected with rituals than many other types (for example paradise-myths), persuaded him to overrate, at first, the association of all or most myths with rituals, and led him to statements like the following: 'It is undeniable that myths are closely attached to rituals. In fact, if a story has not been associated with cult or ritual, explicitly or implicitly, it is better not to call it myth, but

[17] *Op. cit.*, 111.
[18] *Op. cit.*, 116. The quotation from Frazer is from *The Dying God* (= *The Golden Bough*, pt. III, vol. IV) (London, 1911), 106.   [19] *Python*, 461.

legend or folktale.'[20] More recently he has modified this view, at the same time emphasizing his approval of the idea that the term 'myth' should be restricted to 'traditional tales of the deeds of daimones'.[21]

Even where myths *are* associated with rituals, the relations are complex and varied, as some well-known Greek instances show. The first concerns the octennial festival of Charila at Delphi. At this festival, according to Plutarch, the 'king' distributed barley to the people on each occasion, but refused it to a doll called Charila and struck her with his shoe.[22] The doll was taken to a ravine and buried, with a rope round its neck, near the traditional grave of a person named Charila. Such was the ritual. The myth recounts that the real Charila was an orphan who was refused barley during a famine and was ignominiously struck by the king, whereupon she went off and hanged herself out of chagrin. Plague was now added to famine, and the oracle enjoined the ritual propitiation of the dead girl in order to stop it. Clearly Charila was in origin not an ordinary girl, orphan or otherwise, but a demoness of famine (as Fontenrose believes) or a spirit of fertility that had to be renewed. One way or another, the doll is a typical scapegoat device. At a second octennial festival at Delphi, the Septerion, a straw hut was ritually burned, and a boy with a group of young companions fled to Tempe, purified himself, and returned later in triumph. All this was associated at Delphi itself with the story of Apollo slaying the dragon Python, the monster who previously had possession of the sanctuary. Yet Plutarch rightly makes one of his characters express reserve about this association of the myth and the ritual, on the grounds that the burned hut seems to represent a king's abode rather than a dragon's lair, and that the flight of the boys represents a purification of some pollution rather than the logical response of an Apollo to victory over the monster.[23] Whether the boy was precisely a scapegoat (as Fontenrose concludes after Halliday) is debatable; but at least the ritual is cathartic in type, whereas the myth that became associated with it is not. In a third case, described by Pausanias, the ritual held

[20] *Python*, 434.

[21] *The Ritual Theory of Myth* (Berkeley, 1966), 54.

[22] Plutarch, *Moralia* 293 B–F; J. Fontenrose, *Python*, 458 f.; L. R. Farnell, *Greek Hero Cults and Ideas of Immortality* (Oxford, 1921), 32–4.

[23] Plutarch, *Moralia* 418 A–B; cf. J. Fontenrose, *Python*, 453 ff.; W. R. Halliday, ed., *The Greek Questions of Plutarch* (Oxford, 1928), 66 ff.

every six years or less at Plataea in Boeotia, and called the Daedala, required that the Plataeans should make a wooden image out of an oak tree designated by sacred crows.[24] The image was dressed as a bride and carried in a cart to the top of Mount Cithaeron. Every fifty-nine years all the images that had accumulated, from other neighbouring towns as well as Plataea itself, were burned there in a holocaust. This is a typical fertility-ritual, akin to the kindling of 'new fire' on hill-tops, although with some obscure features and special political overtones. Yet the myth that became attached to it as an *aition* or explanation is as follows. Hera had quarrelled with Zeus and left for near-by Euboea. Zeus, desolated, was advised by Cithaeron, king of Plataea and a noted sage, to make a wooden image and place it in a cart, pretending that it was his new bride, Plataea, daughter of Asopus. Hera was furious, tore away the veil, and then was so relieved to discover that her rival was of less than flesh and blood that she made up her quarrel with Zeus. The festival, it was held, commemorated this reconciliation.

Each of these three myths is deployed somewhat differently. The Charila tale involves a simple transposition of the actions performed in the ritual into a bare and uninteresting story, with no other mythical or folktale associations. Here is one way, a derivative and unimportant one, in which a myth may be invented. The Plataean tale, on the other hand, makes use of the familiar mythical tradition about the precarious marital relations between Zeus and Hera—also of a folktale ingenuity-motif, how to make your wife jealous by producing an imaginary rival. In this case pre-existing mythical and folktale materials are re-grouped to form a new story in the light of the ritual. In the second Delphic instance (the Septerion at Delphi and the tale of Apollo and Python) an existing myth has been crudely applied as an *aition* for the ritual, although it has little correspondence with it beyond that of a common locality.

Other familiar cases in which there is a clear association of a ritual with some kind of story confirm that there is no simple and universal relationship between the two. In the Attic festival of the Aiora girls swung in swings suspended from trees. Ostensibly this was in memory of Erigone, who hanged herself when her father, Icarius, priest of Dionysus, was killed for making the men-folk think they were poisoned—when they were only gloriously

[24] Pausanias, IX, 3, I ff.; Plutarch, fr. 157, 6 Sandbach.

drunk. Swinging is a vegetation-charm, associated in this case no doubt with the vine-harvest. The connexion with the hanged girl is not a straightforward one, and the myth makes use of an independent narrative theme of the origins of wine. In another fertility myth, from the island of Lemnos, the women were cursed by Aphrodite with an evil smell that kept their husbands away; Georges Dumézil in a brilliant early essay showed that this was connected with a ritual abstention from sexual relations as part of an annual ritual of purification and renewal of fire.[25] I am not sure that this is the whole answer, since the stranding of Philoctetes because of his noisome foot, also on Lemnos, suggests that there may have been special reasons for connecting this island with bad smells; but certainly in this case a quite complex myth, culminating in the murder of the women's husbands and their eventual marriage with the Argonauts, gradually developed out of an annual act of marital abstention. A similarly complex development, but arising out of a probable initiation-ritual rather than the promotion of agricultural fertility, is seen in the tale familiar from Euripides's *Medea* of the killing of Medea's children at the temple of Hera Akraia facing Corinth. In the ritual, seven Corinthian boys and seven girls spend a year at the sanctuary, at the end of which a goat is sacrificed and the children are allowed to depart. According to the myth, the children themselves were sacrificed either by Medea or by the Corinthians—elaborations of the theme continued to the time of Euripides and beyond.[26] As Nilsson remarked, the aetiology of specific cults is often formed very mechanically on the basis of existing myths.[27]

In none of these cases does the ritual determine the real significance, or even the basic narrative core, of a substantial myth. On the contrary, the association with ritual is nearly always trivial and casual, and has no effect on the essence of whatever narrative themes are used. It is preferable, therefore, to assess the narrative elements independently of their ritual associations—unless these can be shown to be notably closer and more significant than in the instances I have discussed. And yet these instances were not selected at random, but are mentioned because they are, in the

[25] G. Dumézil, *Le Crime des Lemniennes* (Paris, 1924); the theme is developed by Walter Burkert, *Classical Quarterly*, N.S. 20, 1970, 1 ff.

[26] See above all Walter Burkert, 'Greek Tragedy and Sacrificial Ritual', *Greek, Roman and Byzantine Studies*, VII, 1966, 117 ff., with the literature there cited.

[27] *GgrR*[3], 28.

whole range of known Greek myths and rituals, among the plainest examples of a connexion between the two.[28] Such cases are few in comparison with the number of Greek myths that have no evident or plausible ritual connexion whatever. It is barely conceivable that they indicate the genesis of all the rest, but there is nothing to suggest it, and much to suggest the contrary.

Apart from routine acts of propitiation and sacrifice, rituals tend to be either *rites de passage* or connected with agrarian fertility. The continuation of social and natural regularity in more general ways accounts for other types. *Rites de passage* involve isolation, reversion to a raw state, combat, and testing; fertility rites involve scapegoats, floggings, purifications, burning, sexual intercourse, and various transparent manipulations of plants and animals. Transvestism and other reversals of the natural or cultural order are common to both. These, then, are the sort of acts that are performed in most rituals that lie beyond routine sacrifices and offerings. Interpreted in mythical form, they tend to give rise, naturally enough, to particular kinds of narrative involving, precisely, isolation, flogging, marriages, transvestism, various uses of fire, manipulation of plants and animals. Where we find these elements strongly emphasized in an otherwise inexplicable and unusually disjointed myth, we may well suspect a ritual origin or reference. But these are not the only themes of myths, or the most common. The others are unlikely to have anything to do with ritual; they may sometimes bear on problems like fertility which are also the subjects of rituals, but in distinct ways.

The classing of all myths with rituals, then, is a special and no more attractive manifestation of the widespread opinion that myths are about gods, or are associated with religion, or are necessarily sacred. Without tracing the opinion back to its ultimate scholarly sources—an easy but unenlightening task—I should like to consider one influential figure in the comparatively recent scholarly tradition, namely Malinowski. He devoted particular attention to the nature of myths, especially in his fascinating *Argonauts of the Western Pacific* of 1922 and in some lectures

[28] See also W. Burkert on the Cecropidae, *Hermes*, 94, 1966, 1 ff. Other examples occur in Pausanias's account of Arcadia, where many obscure customs persisted into the Roman period. Most of the tales associated with them (like that of Scephrus of Tegea, Pausanias, VIII, 53, 3) look as though they were invented or adapted in a quite rough-and-ready fashion, and some of them have a clearly Hellenistic appearance. The process of explaining rituals by mythical precedents went on continuously.

published in 1926 under the title *Myth in Primitive Psychology*. His views were based on a long study of the Trobriand islanders off the coast of New Guinea, and on the evidence of his own rather uncomplicated intuitions. According to Malinowski the Trobrianders distinguish folktales told for entertainment, together with legends of a historical or quasi-historical character, from myths, which are sacred in essence. Yet even on his own evidence it is plain that there is no essential difference between some of the 'folktales' and some of the 'myths' that he describes. I shall consider in §3 the difficult question of whether there is any viable dividing-line between myths and folktales. In the present case the truth seems to be that these islanders classify as 'serious' those tales that overtly deal with such solemn subjects as the origins of clans and sub-clans, the annual feast of the return of the dead, or the loss by mankind of the power of rejuvenation; they apply a different term to other tales whose subjects are less openly of public or tribal concern—tales about agrarian fertility, which is not necessarily a matter of survival in this part of the world, about garden-magic, about the remarkable ceremonial system of the interchange of ornaments known as the *kula* (which also, significantly, enters into some of the 'serious' myths). Yet often enough this latter class has a serious or speculative reference, if an indirect one. In short, they are not really 'play' tales, told purely for entertainment, and are not radically distinct in form, structure or purpose from the 'serious' tales.[29]

Even Malinowski's chosen examples of *lili'u*, sacred myths, in his *Myth in Primitive Psychology*, have no explicit connexion with specific rituals. Those that concern spirits, witches, and so on, are associated with magic, which plays a great part in Trobriand life; but so also are many of the fertility tales that are classed as non-sacred and unserious. Tales of the origin of clans in particular localities (for men are supposed to have emerged from the earth) are used to justify a clan's claim to autochthony and the possession of certain lands and prerogatives, or perhaps to disguise the obvious falsity of such a claim; and they are the best example of what Malinowski named 'charter myths'—a term still much used by anthropologists. Some such myths are recited on important ceremonial occasions to reassert and confirm local rights, loyalties

[29] Not all of these 'serious' tales, incidentally, have a connexion with ritual or religion, although many of them obviously do.

and beliefs. Yet such repetitions of a myth are not really 'ritual' or 'sacred' in the specific sense, and provide little justification for separating these tales from those of fertility or the origin of the *kula*-exchange.

Malinowski, who held that abstract ideas were entirely absent from myths in every savage community, including those of Melanesia, was not well qualified to make judgements about serious or non-serious categories.[30] His view was that myths do not 'make intelligible' any of their contents. That might be so, but, in his anxiety to combat the excessive view of myth as a kind of primitive science, he added that they have no underlying meaning at all. Given this stringent and untested dogma, it is hardly surprising that he should seriously misrepresent the tone of some of the tales that he himself had collected. This is a severe criticism to make of one whose qualities as an observer in the field were in so many ways admirable. Perhaps he misinterpreted his field notes when he came to form his general theory, much as an archaeologist might (and as Sir Arthur Evans did in a few minor respects at Knossos). Thus in one book he quotes as an amusing folktale the case of 'a happy family, a father and two daughters', who sail to the rocky islet of Gumasila.[31] The father lies down on a platform and is eaten by an ogre, who then mates with one of the daughters; the other escapes, and in the end they both kill the ogre and settle down in the island. Yet it can be seen from a fuller account by Malinowski himself that this is a variant of a highly important myth.[32] Actually the 'happy' father has no hands or feet; his daughters leave him on the platform so that they may gather food from the gardens. The tale is a form of the story of the culture-hero Kasabwaybwayreta, or the parallel story of Tokosikuna, with the ogre as an additional motif. These stories are concerned with the origin and functioning of the *kula*, the interchange of ornaments between a ring of islands, and in particular with the question why it is that the people of Dobu (a larger island close to Gumasila) are such mean *kula*-partners. They also connect the practice of beautifying oneself before approaching one's *kula*-partner with the powers of rejuvenation that men once possessed but then lost. Our variant, the one described by Malinowski as a folktale, implies but does not emphasize the

---

[30] *Myth in Primitive Psychology* (London, 1926), 41.   [31] *Op. cit.*, 27 f.
[32] *Argonauts of the Western Pacific* (New York and London, 1922), 307 ff.

decrepit condition of the hero, who has to be carried on the *kula*-expedition by his daughters or, in the Kasabwaybwayreta version, by his son and grandson. Moreover it is significant that the daughters leave him to go to the gardens, since Gumasila was famous for its garden-magic. The consideration of all three known variants side by side enables one to see (especially in the light of Lévi-Strauss's methodology, to be described in the next chapter) the underlying structure and implicit polarities of the basic narrative: old and young, hostile and friendly, normal and abnormal direction for the *kula*-circuit, destruction and rejuvenation, *kula*-magic and garden-magic. That these oppositions are significant and serious can hardly be doubted. If so, then Malinowski's dismissal of the 'happy family' as a mere entertaining fairy-tale, quite different from true myths, is erroneous and misleading.

Malinowski's influence on anthropology has been enormous, and his books on the Trobrianders are still fascinating. Many of his methods and ideas have been abandoned or modified; and yet, just because he paid so much attention to myth, formulated some facile rules-of-thumb for its classification, and devoted a special little book to the subject, this part of his thought seems to have achieved a kind of orthodoxy that in my opinion it does not deserve. Some of his ideas about myths are valuable; in particular the function of certain myths as a charter of customs, beliefs, rights and institutions is obviously an important one, not least for the cultures of the Pacific. It is not the unique function of all myths, as Malinowski implied it to be, but one that happens to be underemphasized in surviving Greek instances. On the other hand the categorizing of tales as folktales, legends, and proper myths, simple and appealing as it seems, can be seriously confusing. It was based in Malinowski's case on terms used for different kinds of story (or for stories told on different kinds of occasion) by the islanders themselves. Similar distinctions are drawn for other cultures, particularly between tales believed to be true and those recognized as fictitious—for example among the Tsimshian Indians of the Pacific Northwest, where Franz Boas reported that the distinction is primarily between tales of the time when animals appeared as humans, and tales of the subsequent 'historical' period.[33] Yet these native distinctions do not of themselves imply that one class is 'myth' and the other not. Moreover

[33] Franz Boas, *Tsimshian Mythology* (Washington, D.C., 1916), 565.

they are sometimes unreliable, since they often depend on the superficial appurtenances of a tale, for example an appended aetiology, rather than on any analysis of its basic implication or structure. Furthermore Malinowski's assumption that the only tales that can be called 'myths' are sacred tales that accompany rituals, apart from its illogicality, is founded on the tendencies of a single culture. In a society in which magic plays a prominent part it will naturally be mentioned in many myths; it will also be often associated with ritual—for the fashionable idea that magic is necessarily individual and not social is fallacious. Yet the consequent convergence of myths and rituals is in such an instance almost accidental; and even in such a culture one can point to many cases where a myth concerns an aspect of a subject that lies outside the range of magic and ritual.

Yet the Malinowskian dogma continues—has even been made more severe by so acute a critic as E. R. Leach, who has asserted that 'myth, in my terminology, is the counterpart of ritual; myth implies ritual, ritual implies myth, they are one and the same...

Myth regarded as a statement in words "says" the same thing as ritual regarded as a statement in action. To ask questions about the content of belief which are not contained in the content of ritual is nonsense.' Or, a page later, 'ritual action and belief are alike to be understood as forms of symbolic statement about the social order'.[34] In a way this is a revival, based on modern rather than ancient evidence, of Durkheim's and Jane Harrison's view that myth is the *legomenon*, the thing said, ritual the corresponding *drōmenon*, the thing performed. Another, earlier, and more elaborate statement of the doctrine occurs in a much-cited article by Clyde Kluckhohn, 'Myths and rituals: a general theory'.[35] Kluckhohn rejected the idea that myth is derived from ritual or vice versa, but concluded that the two are, nevertheless, closely and essentially associated, even if each can appear independently of the other. There is an 'intricate interdependence of myth... with ritual and many other forms of behaviour' (*op. cit.*, 54). Kluckhohn believed that all cultural phenomena must be seen as functional parts of a complex system; he applauded Malinowski

[34] E. R. Leach, *Political Systems of Highland Burma* (London and Cambridge, Mass., 1954), 13 and 14. The second quotation illustrates the kind of oversimplification that can arise from a structuralist approach to society.

[35] *HTR*, xxxv, 1942, 45–79. The emasculated version of this article in John B. Vickery, ed., *Myth and Literature* (Lincoln, Nebraska, 1966), should be avoided.

for showing so vividly how myths were part of the whole social and cultural amalgam of the Trobriand islanders. This innocuous and indeed correct belief led him to the error (as I conceive it) that myths and rituals must spring from the same psychic motivation. 'The myth is a system of word symbols, whereas ritual is a system of object and act symbols. Both are symbolic processes for dealing with the same type of situation in the same affective mode'; they are interdependent because they both 'satisfy a group of identical or closely related needs of individuals'.[36] The nature of these needs is complex;[37] generally speaking, myth and ritual are found to be responses to men's need for regularity, especially in conceptual and emotional regions of greatest potential anxiety (66–8). Essentially 'myth and ritual have a common psychological basis. Ritual is an obsessive repetitive activity—often a symbolical dramatization of the "needs" of the society...Mythology is the rationalization of these same needs...' (78). They provide 'a cultural storehouse of adjustive responses for individuals' (65). This is first advanced as a hypothesis, then found to be proved by observation of the Navaho Indians, on whom Kluckhohn was the acknowledged authority. One swallow, perhaps, does not make a summer—or a general theory; and it is significant that, even among the Navaho, Kluckhohn discovered, rather as it seems to his surprise, another function of myths ranging from 'simple entertainment' to 'intellectual edification' (64).

Much of Kluckhohn's argument seems inadequate. Why, for instance, when it is conceded that myths and rituals can and do frequently occur independently of each other, should we accept that their 'very intimate association' is such that it must imply a common origin in the alleviation of a rather motley collection of psychic needs? Why should we not say instead, for instance, that the association of myths and rituals in certain social conditions is due to the propensity of men, especially in uninhibited and savage societies, for *acting out* any event or description whatever, whether real or fictitious?[38] Such an argument would not need dressing up

[36] *Op. cit.*, 58 and 65.

[37] It includes the sublimation of aggressive and antisocial tendencies (*op. cit.*, 71, 74), or 'their discharge in socially accepted channels' (64, citing A. M. Hocart); the overcoming of anxieties particular to the culture (57, 71); and the reduction of the anticipation of disaster (69) by 'reaction-formation' (71).

[38] One of the best and most vivid illustrations of such a propensity is given by Francis Huxley in his description of life among the Urubu Indians of Brazil: *Affable*

in the pretentious terminology of *logos* and *praxis* to make it a powerful alternative to the 'general theory' offered by Kluckhohn —a theory that once more adds little, apart from a few simple Freudian concepts, to the old idea of the *legomenon* and the *drōmenon*. The truth is that myths seem to possess essential properties—like their fantasy, their freedom to develop, and their complex structure —that are not reproduced in ritual, and suggest that their motive and origin are in important respects distinct. This will be further considered in the final chapter. Meanwhile dubious comparisons between verbal and action symbols had better be left on one side, as had 'adjustive responses' which, if they exist in any sense, provide only a small proportion of the total reasons for making, telling and listening to myths.

Kluckhohn's opinion about the actual occurrence of myth and ritual is independent of the merits of his 'general theory'. 'Generally speaking', he wrote, 'we do seem to find rich ritualism and a rich mythology together. But there are cases (like the Toda) where an extensive ceremonialism does not appear to have its equally extensive mythological counterpart and instances (like classical Greece) where a ramified mythology appears to have existed more or less independent of a comparatively meagre rite-system.'[39] On the rarity of Greek rituals, even apart from their association with myths, he undoubtedly exaggerates; but he is able to cite the Mohave Indians and the South African Bushmen as firm examples of rich myth with poor, or virtually no, ritual. This is enough to refute total assertions that myths are derived from rituals—indeed a single instance is adequate, formally speaking. There are far more than that available; apart from Oedipus, Gilgamesh, and other instances from the ancient world, the extensive repertory of Tsimshian myths recorded by Franz Boas suggests that most of these were kept utterly separate from rituals, even though they mostly concern the creative era; conversely the most conspicuously ceremonial aspect of Tsimshian social life, the potlatch, is ignored in all but a small minority of the myths. A similar impression is given by the vast number of South American myths assembled by Lévi-Strauss, of which some instances will be considered in the next chapter. Some of these myths must have

Savages (London, 1956), especially chapters 17 ('Myth and the world') and 18 ('A cannibal tale').

[39] *HTR*, xxxv, 1942, 48.

had, in the past, closer ritual associations than their content now suggests, but even so the majority are probably independent.[40]

It is worth looking at a cultural complex notorious for its wealth of rituals to see what is the state of myths there: that of the Australian aborigines. As usual one has to gauge the preconceptions not only of the natives but also of their observers. R. M. and C. H. Berndt, for instance, the authors of a generally excellent recent survey, are true followers of Malinowski in one respect: they define 'myth' as a sacred or religious story, and classify every other kind of tale as something different—in this case 'oral literature'. They identify two modern applications of the word 'myth' and two only: first as 'a narrative or story, or series of songs, which is of religious significance; a sacred story', and secondly as a false belief.[41] The second usage is rightly rejected as trivial, but from this point on the Berndts accept the first as embodying a complete and valid delimitation of the range of myth. And yet the truth is that modern popular usage, for what it is worth, does not restrict myth to sacred stories at all. Ancient Greek myths, for example—and they are usually the conscious or unconscious exemplar—often, as has been seen, have non-sacred subjects. The analogy between the Berndts and Malinowski extends further; for they, like him, include in their non-myth category (and under a section headed 'Oral Literature' in a chapter called 'Art and Aesthetic Expression') tales that are certainly not casual folktales told simply for amusement, but probably possess as much 'significance' as many of those classed as sacred and discussed under the heading of Mythology.

One such instance is the tale of the cannibal giant Guruwelin, which the Berndts do not count as a myth.[42] Long ago, in the Dreamtime (that is, in the creative period of the world), there

---

[40] *Contra* Lévi-Strauss, whose opinion will evidently be clarified in a forthcoming article about the Mandan and Hidatsa. In a 1956 article republished in *SA*, at p. 232, he stated that 'Regardless of whether the myth or the ritual is the original, they replicate each other; the myth exists on the conceptual level and the ritual on the level of action'. He then developed a curious argument to the effect that where no ritual association is perceived within the culture it may be found, in an inverted form, in a neighbouring culture; a theory based apparently on an interpretation of a Pawnee myth that has rightly been called into question by Mary Douglas in *SSMT*, 60–2. In the third volume of *Mythologiques* (*OMT*, 1968) he mentions ritual fairly frequently, but seems to assume that it is normally based on myth rather than vice versa.

[41] R. M. and C. H. Berndt, *The World of the First Australians* (London, 1964), 199.

[42] *Op. cit.*, 341 f.

were two sisters, the elder one pregnant. They climbed a tree to gather nuts. Guruwelin threw a huge yam at them, killing the elder and stunning the younger. He then put them both in his bag and took them to his camp. The younger sister escaped, but the giant cut up the elder one and cooked her over one fire, and her foetus over another. He ate the meat and stacked up the bones, but got violent diarrhoea—and built shelter after shelter, as he moved along, in which to relieve himself. The younger sister tracked him down with the help of different birds; then her relatives arrived and, after heavy losses, succeeded in killing him. A native doctor assembled the bones of the other girl and her baby and they came to life again. Now people have to dig deep for their yams in this region (on the northeast coast of Arnhem Land), just like Guruwelin.

The apparently irrelevant aetiology at the end, about the yams, is merely incidental, perhaps a casual addition; but anyone who has read Lévi-Strauss, at least, will recognize that the myth (for that is what it quite palpably is) has more serious implications. It is remarkably similar in important respects to that of the Trobriand 'happy family' described by Malinowski—the two girls and the ogre, and their association with gardening. The possibility of diffusion between north Australia and Melanesia cannot be discounted; be that as it may, in the Australian myth the pregnant girl and her resuscitation are probably connected with fertility, and the putting together of her bones with the continuation of the spirit after death. On the score of content this is just as much a true myth as that (for instance) of the Djanggawul sisters who initiated childbirth in the same region; and the only reason why the Berndts class it as oral literature and not as myth seems to be that it has no ritual connexion. They concede that 'The division between sacred mythology and ordinary stories is not easy to make', and that the ordinary stories, as well as being told for pleasure, 'occasionally...serve other purposes too. They may be admonitory or instructive, pointing a moral, or imparting information in an agreeably easy way.'[43] Even this diminishes the type of serious intention implicit in a tale like that of Guruwelin and the two sisters; and the recognized difficulty of separating sacred and non-sacred tales should have alerted the authors to the possibility that there is no further generic difference. It may be true, as they

[43] *Op. cit.*, 327 and 329.

claim, that 'almost every ritual, like almost every important action in everyday life, can be referred back to some myth, which provides a sufficient reason for it so that there is no need to look further';[44] but this must not be taken to imply its converse, namely that every myth refers to a ritual. Even among the aborigines, whose whole life was dominated by rituals, many of them both messy and long-winded, myths sometimes extended beyond the range of rituals. Here, if anywhere, Kluckhohn's theory that 'myths and rituals satisfy a group of...closely related needs' is applicable; yet even here—and this is the point—many myths have to be artificially classified as 'oral literature' in order to avoid the conclusion that some myths do not have ritual associations, that myths and rituals overlap rather than being interdependent.

What I have tried to point out in some of these modern field studies is not, of course, an error in observation, but rather the persistent and distorting application of a false preconception, namely that 'myth' is a closed category with the same characteristics in different cultures. Once one sees that myth as a general concept is completely vague, that it implies no more in itself than a traditional story, then it becomes clear that its restriction to particular kinds of tale, 'sacred' ones or those associated with rituals, is precarious and misleading; especially if the tendencies of one culture in this respect are assumed to be analogous to those of all other cultures at roughly the same material and social level. It is, indeed, important to remember that different cultures *are* different—that the common preoccupations of mankind (with birth and death, food and sex, war and machines) do not express themselves in the same way or the same proportion from culture to culture. 'General theories' of myth and ritual are no simple matter. The contradictory customs and beliefs of even neighbouring groups or cultures have been dramatically explored from Herodotus onwards. It is an undeniable fact that the Zuni Indians of the Pueblo culture of the American Southwest were utterly different in their quiet and obsessively ceremonial life from their Indian neighbours of Mexico, California, and the Plains, who indulged in crude sexual imagery, violent rituals and brutal self-torture.[45] To use another of Ruth Benedict's famous examples, the

---

[44] *Op. cit.*, 226.

[45] Ruth Benedict, *Patterns of Culture* (Boston and New York, 1934), chapters IV and V.

Dobuans are not ethnically distinct from the near-by Trobrianders (or others who share in the ceremonial exchange-system of the *kula*-ring), and yet, unlike them, they are cruel, suspicious and ruthless in their attitudes, and quite different in many of their social habits. Even if most myths of a particular tribe were closely associated with rituals, it would not follow that the same would be the case with all neighbouring tribes, even in a cultural area which, like Australia, is particularly ritual-conscious—in which ritual action is almost a way of life. And in other regions, for example parts of North and South America, the place of true ritual may be subsidiary even where many public myths are more or less ceremonially re-told at special times of the year.

Where ritual is conspicuous, it is a function of many other aspects of social life. A powerful priesthood can sometimes develop for reasons other than an ethnic predisposition to ritualism; but there rituals will follow. Enforced leisure can be a factor in the proliferation of rituals, as it certainly has been in Australia; and the nature and concentration of settlements is another factor. Certain relatively secular cultures, like those of the ancient Greeks, the early medieval Teutons, the African Bushmen, or the Brazilian Indians, do in fact possess as many myths as the more hieratic cultures. In the latter case it is natural that many, perhaps most, myths are associated with rituals, or more generally with religious practices and occasions; in the former, that relatively few will be so associated. It is possible that myths will be told on certain occasions, or at certain seasons when men are free from work; but that is hardly ritual. Admittedly the term is an ambiguous one, but the kind of ritual we are discussing implies a closely controlled set of actions performed in an established sequence for a specific supernatural end. I hope that enough has now been said on this narrow but fundamental topic to show that there is neither logic nor other virtue in trying to confine the term 'myth' to tales associated in some way with sacred rituals.

On the other hand, and to return to the broader question, it would be foolish to deny that many important myths in many cultures are associated in some degree with *religion*. In polytheistic religions it is natural that the gods (whether anthropomorphic or theriomorphic or mixed), since they are distinct individuals, will have relations with each other, and often too with humans, and that these relations will tend to find expression in continuous narratives; the most successful of these will tend to become traditional, and so be classifiable as myths. And yet it has often been felt that myths have more than that kind of mechanical or incidental connexion with religion; that they are one form of expression of the religious sense itself. Ernst Cassirer, indeed, wrote as follows: 'In the development of human culture we cannot fix a point where myth ends or religion begins. In the whole course of its history religion remains indissolubly connected and penetrated with mythical elements. On the other hand myth, even in its crudest and most rudimentary forms, contains some motives that in a sense anticipate the higher and later religious ideals. Myth is from its very beginning potential religion.'[46] These words seem wholly unjustified. Cassirer's reasons for making such statements concern the nature of myth and religion as forms of expression. He believes that the myth-maker works on a substratum not of thought but of feeling. The feeling according to him is both passionate and sympathetic; 'primitive man' perceives the solidarity of life with the natural world and views them synthetically, not analytically. Lévi-Strauss's *La Pensée sauvage*, with its demonstration of the elaborate systems of categories constructed by natives on the analysis of natural species, is adequate refutation of this last idea; and the whole position, smacking as it does of Lévy-Bruhl's 'primitive mentality', is open to Evans-Pritchard's 'if I were a horse' objection—his exposure of the illusion of modern academics that they can think themselves into the position of any other animate being whatever.[47]

One point in Cassirer's association of myth with religion deserves fuller investigation: the assumption that both involve a passionate response to the world, that they are united by a special *intensity* of feeling.[48] It is undeniable that some myths reveal such an intensity: the Epic of Gilgamesh, for example, or the first chapter of Genesis. These as it happens are literary developments, although they certainly contain much that is pre-literate. Yet in hundreds of

[46] *Essay*, 87

[47] C. Lévi-Strauss, *La Pensée sauvage* (Paris, 1962), Eng. tr. (as '*The Savage Mind*'), 1966, ch. 1; L. Lévy-Bruhl, *La Mentalité primitive* (Paris, 1922), Eng. tr. (as *Primitive Mentality*), 1923, *passim*; E. E. Evans-Pritchard, *Theories of Primitive Religion* (Oxford, 1965), 24, 43, 47. On Cassirer see also pp. 263 ff.

[48] And so, for example, for similar reasons, Leroy E. Loemker in *Truth, Myth and Symbol*, ed. T. J. J. Altizer *et al.* (Englewood Cliffs, 1962), 122: 'A myth is a story which offers answers...athrob with the sense of the sacred...'.

other myths, whether oral or literate, no special intensity is detectable. Most Amerindian, Australian, Melanesian, Polynesian, and African myths fail to reveal any special intensity of feeling. But how could such an intensity be disclosed? Either, I suppose, by purely literary embellishment, or more surely by the mode of narration and by accompanying gestures such as can be observed only by the anthropologist. My impression from anthropological reports is that some myths are recited in a state of high excitement, others are not. Once again it depends on the particular culture, the particular reciter and his audience, and (one might conjecture) the subject of the particular myth. Some myths are concerned with subjects that arouse strong emotions, like death and disaster or paradise and good fortune, and these are most likely to reveal a special intensity of feeling; others, less obviously concerned with emotive issues, tend to be less emotional in their expression.

To religion, on the other hand, intensity of feeling might be conceded as an essential property: feeling of the divine, the supernatural, the *mysterium tremendum*. In short, myths are not connected with religion any more by a universal emotional intensity than they are by their subject-matter—for, as has been seen, whereas some myths are about gods, others are not. Therefore it will be wise to reject from the outset the idea that myth and religion are twin aspects of the same subject, or parallel manifestations of the same psychic condition, just as firmly as we rejected the idea that all myths are associated with rituals.

3: The relation of myths to folktales

One head of Cerberus, growling its insidious dogma, has perhaps been silenced; that still leaves another, barking out that all myths are quite distinct from folktales—or, alternatively, that there is no difference whatever between the two. Once again no abrupt denial will help; the problem is a complex one, simple in appearance but hard to resolve, and yet of extreme importance for the whole enquiry into the nature of myths.

It may be helpful to draw a preliminary distinction between myths and folktales taken together (whatever their relation may be) and legends of a historical or historicizing nature—tales, that is, that are founded, or implicitly claim to be founded, on historical persons or events. The distinction is one that is often made in illiterate cultures themselves, although I have already commented that the categories drawn by unsophisticated peoples can be confusing. The Trobrianders, so Malinowski reported, divide *libwogwo*, 'old talk', into tales of the indefinite and creative past on the one hand, and historical tales of voyages, shipwrecks, the exploits of particular chiefs, and so on, on the other. The Oglala Dakota Indians of the Sioux family are said to distinguish 'tales of the tribe', which are held to have actually happened, to be 'true', from amusing stories about the trickster Iktomi; and the Haussa of northern Nigeria distinguish saga-type tales from imaginative myths.[49] Unfortunately it is easy to confuse this distinction between legends and myths with another distinction also made by tribal peoples, between sacred myths, concerning the most obviously solemn and fundamental matters, and non-sacred ones, which may be no more historical and no less fantastic. Some of these peoples apply a term meaning something like 'true' to their sacred myths alone, whereas others use such a term of legends as distinct from imaginative myths of all kinds—a difference of analysis and criteria that has confused many modern critics (including Pettazzoni). I suspect that the terms translated as 'true' by Malinowski, Boas and other anthropologists have a variety of meanings none of which quite corresponds with our word, even if it is extended to mean 'significant'.

It really is safer to turn to the Greeks at this point. There we can see the differences between legend and myth undisturbed by any terminological confusion, since Greek, far from having too many words for different kinds of tale, has too few. Much of the *Iliad* is obviously historicizing in content. How far legend has exaggerated and distorted history is irrelevant—there is certainly a great deal of exaggeration, but even those least confident in the existence of a 'Trojan War' concede that some attack took place, and that some Achaeans were among the attackers. The point is that the story is based on some kind of memory of the past, and that its progress is described in largely realistic terms. The prime exception is the role of the gods. Obviously the statement that Patroclus hurled himself three times at the Trojans, and killed nine of them each time (a statement which involves mere exaggeration), is of a different order from the statement that he was

---

[49] These two instances are adduced by Raffaele Pettazzoni, *Essays on the Histories of Religions* (Leiden, 1954), 12 f., citing M. W. Beckwith, *JAFL*, XLII, 1930, 339 and C. K. Meek, *The Northern Tribes of Nigeria*, II (London, 1925), 147, respectively.

then struck violently in the back, and knocked out of his senses by the invisible Apollo.[50] The gods of Homer belong to myth; they certainly do not belong to the essence of legend or saga, which is always in some sense rooted in actuality; and therefore they represent in the *Iliad* the metaphysical aspect of a primarily legendary narrative. The idea of gods who determine human events, and who can have heroic progeny like Achilles, was no doubt deeply rooted in the Greek narrative tradition, and before that in the Achaean. The fact remains that the *Iliad* is mainly concerned with presenting a great heroic *geste* that actually resulted in the capture and burning of Troy; and even the *Odyssey*, in which other non-historical elements (folktale and fairy-tale) are added to the participation of the gods, is largely set in the purportedly historical world of the Peloponnese and the western islands.

Any traditional tale is likely to present some kind of mixture of actuality and fantasy; even a 'sacred' myth in Hesiod's *Theogony*, about the birth and development of a god, will contain some elements drawn from life; but it is still legitimate and useful to distinguish between elements and tales that are primarily actual and those that are primarily fantastic. Most critics, if asked the question 'Are Helen, Paris, Priam, Hector, Achilles, Agamemnon, Diomedes, Odysseus, part of Greek mythology, or are they not?' would reply with an unequivocal 'Yes'; and I cannot disagree. Yet most of these characters are involved in events which, although they may be ostensibly controlled by gods and goddesses, are in essence human, take place in human environments, and moreover have few of the special qualities associated with the word 'myth' outside the context of Greek mythology. Even the gods, one might argue, are presented with as little fantasy as possible; they are supermen and superwomen with special powers of instant travel and remote operation—an extra dimension of action and a dramatic source of motivation. According to this view the *Iliad* should be classed as legend rather than myth.

On the other hand the gods are responsible for much of the magnificence of the two poems, especially the *Iliad*; they cannot be treated simply as an 'apparatus' (*Götterapparat*), or mentally subtracted from the poems without affecting their essence, since they contribute a kind of intensity and other-worldliness that pervades even the most ostensibly human, historicizing and

[50] *Iliad*, XVI, 784–92.

realistic episodes. In short, it would be wrong to treat the Homeric poems just as legends, and exclude them from the consideration of myth as a whole. Many human episodes in (or implied by) the poems have acquired archetypal mythical status largely because of the special texture impressed upon legend by the presence of the gods: episodes like the rape of Helen, the choice of Achilles, his friendship with Patroclus, the death and mutilation of Hector, the impending ruin of Troy, the return and vengeance of Odysseus, the endurance of Penelope. These have become mythical paradigms in subsequent thought and literature, and I would no more refuse them the label of 'myth' than deny it to Clytemnestra's murder of Agamemnon, simply because that was a primarily human and realistically possible event. It has been given a poetical and symbolic value, but not so much by Homer as by Aeschylus; it has become myth by a secondary process of development, acquiring in the course of tradition those overtones of fantasy that many other myths possess from the beginning, by virtue of their subjects themselves or of the essential involvement of supernatural powers.

The Homeric example shows very clearly that legend and myth cannot always be separated in practice, even if entirely non-fantastic and historicizing legends are theoretically possible. Yet it is still useful to be able to distinguish primarily legendary components from other, more imaginative ones; and, since the emphasis of the present work is on the implications of myth in general, rather than on the consideration of all possible quasi-mythical expressions of a particular culture, I shall tend to leave the more legendary aspects of Greek and other myths on one side, at least where they are not inextricably associated with other aspects.

It is now possible to approach the main distinction between myths and folktales, a source of unbounded confusion in nearly all discussion of myths. Is it really feasible to separate the two? One preliminary difficulty is that there is no greater agreement on the nature of folktales than on the nature of myths. Something more precise might have been expected, since the study of folklore has developed during the last century into a kind of quasi-science. There is a recognized class of academics known as folklorists, and there are highly respectable journals like *The Journal of American Folk-lore*; and folklorists agree that folktales form one important part of their field of study (their interests also range to customs, songs, games, and other manifestations of popular culture). Yet surprisingly little light has been cast on the real character of folktale and its relation to myth, even though prodigious energy has been expended on attempts to solve just this problem. The definitions of folklore itself propounded by some twenty exponents, some of them eminent, in the reputable *Standard Dictionary of Folklore, Mythology and Legend* (New York, 1949–50), edited by Maria Leach, exemplify the confusion that reigned twenty years ago, at least.[51] One school of thought denied any firm distinction between myths and folktales—an attitude that had some support from anthropologists. Ruth Benedict, for example, in her article on 'Myth' in *The Encyclopaedia of the Social Sciences* (XI, 1933, 179), had written that 'For the purposes of study mythology can never be divorced from folklore', and that myths and folktales 'are to be distinguished only by the fact that myths are tales of the supernatural world'. Moreover 'A story passes in and out of the religious complex with ease, and plots which are told as secular tales over two continents become locally the myths which explain the creation of the people and the origin of customs and may be dramatized in religious ritual'. Here we recognize a familiar assumption: that myths necessarily concern gods, and are associated, for the most part if not always, with rituals. The distinction between supernatural myth and secular tale is one that Ruth Benedict derived directly from Franz Boas, who based it on the practice and terminology of the Tsimshian Indians. Her remark about the 'ease of passage' of a narrative theme from a secular to a religious context, also influenced by Boas, refers primarily to Amerindian cultures and is of the highest interest.[52] Yet that similar themes may occur in myths (as she defined them) and folktales does not by itself prove that myth and folktale are distinguishable merely by the presence or absence of the supernatural. The whole tone and purpose of the two may be distinct, and that themes can pass from one to the other no more suggests that one cannot be studied without the other than the passage of professors from Oxford to Cambridge or Stanford to Berkeley suggests that these institutions are inseparable.

Somewhat similarly Stith Thompson, the well-known folklorist

[51] If there is frequent reference to encyclopaedia articles in this section, it is because it is mainly there that anthropologists and folklorists, by force of circumstance, have been prepared to state unequivocally their views about basic questions of definition and scope.

[52] Cf. F. Boas, *Tsimshian Mythology* (Washington, D.C., 1916), 879 ff.

and compiler of the vast *Motif-Index of Folk Literature* (Bloomington, 1955), finds the distinction between myth and folktale quite artificial; although his reasons for this are less precise, and more typically reflect the comprehensive claims of folklore studies, than those of the two anthropologists. In *The Standard Dictionary of Folklore, Mythology and Legend*, under 'folktale', he wrote that 'There is little agreement in the use of the term myth. But it certainly can be regarded as one branch of the folktale. It concerns the world as it was in some past age before the present conditions were established. It treats creation and origins, and therefore may be identical with creation and origin legends. When it handles adventures of the gods, it may well be identical with the fairy tale. Many divergent theories as to the nature of the myth have been held in the past. All of them contain a grain of truth but none give entire satisfaction.' This is surely inadequate, even allowing for its coming from an encyclopaedia article. Elsewhere Thompson does somewhat better in expressing his feeling that the origins and functions of myths are a topic of great obscurity and little interest.[53] Many other folklorists follow his lead, without adding much in the way of argument. Indeed, since their interest lies primarily in the regional distribution and sequential structure of variant versions, it is not surprising that the more philosophical aspects of myths—which have admittedly attracted some rather wild exponents—should be played down or avoided.

One possible way out of the dilemma lies in assigning myths and folktales to different social classes, rather than to different intentions or occasions. E. W. Count has supported the idea of referring compendiously to 'myth-tales' (rather like Wilhelm Wundt's *Mythenmärchen*) by arguing that the whole concept of the folktale, and not merely its name, was a nineteenth-century invention.[54] The fascination of the already decaying peasant cultures of Europe had just been discovered, and their importance suggested by the high quality of the popular epics and ballads that excited Goethe and the romantics. Yet these illiterate tales seemed a quite different phenomenon from what was then accepted as myth, which consisted almost exclusively of the aristocratic mythology of the ancient Greeks. The traditional stories of the European

[53] E.g. in *Myth: A Symposium*, ed. T. A. Sebeok (Bloomington, 1958), 108 f.
[54] Earl W. Count, 'Myth as World View', in *Culture in History*, ed. S. Diamond (New York, 1960), 596 f.

villager and peasant farmer seemed to require separate names like *Hausmärchen*, fairy-tales, and folktales, and a separate status—a piece of intellectual snobbery that according to Count has greatly complicated the assessment of myth today.

This observation seems to me both acute and relevant. Yet I do not believe it justifies the total abolition of the concept of something like the folktale as a distinctive species, at least, of myth, and possibly as a kind of tale which, despite overlaps, deserves for methodological purposes a separate name. The difference lies partly, but not entirely, in the emphasis on supernatural elements; but that is not satisfactory as a criterion, for there are often fantastic, magical or miraculous elements in folktales, just as we have seen that there are accepted myths from which supernatural elements are substantially missing. I would offer a preliminary and incomplete definition of folktales, independently of their association with any type of society or level of culture, as follows: they are traditional tales, of no firmly established form, in which supernatural elements are subsidiary; they are not primarily concerned with 'serious' subjects or the reflexion of deep problems and preoccupations; and their first appeal lies in their narrative interest.[55]

Let us provisionally accept that definition and see if it can stand elaboration. Among such tales there are different varieties, more or less stressed in different cultures. One variety is the fairy-tale in its precise form, especially in Europe; unfortunately the title has been stretched to include all sorts of folktales, and 'Grimms' Fairy-tales' is a curious misnomer. Another is the animal fable, and we can see from Hesiod, Stesichorus and Aesop that the genre was well established in Greece, as indeed it had been in Mesopotamia. In ordinary folktales that cannot be assigned to such specialized genres, witches, giants, ogres and magical objects are all quite frequent; they represent the supernatural, but the hero or heroine is a human being, often of humble origin, who has to achieve his or her human purpose in spite of, or with the help of, such fantastic forces. Sometimes the theme is a contest or

---

[55] This last part of the definition is again, by itself, of limited value as a *differentia*, since the primary appeal of many myths, also, for many audiences at least, lies in their attraction simply as stories. The Malinowskian view that folktales are told for entertainment, whereas serious myths are told on ceremonial occasions, simply clouds the issue. All traditional tales are told partly for entertainment, with the exception of those that survive in a purely ritual context.

trial, for instance to defeat a monster or win a bride. Sometimes it will be of a more familial nature, the circumventing of a malicious stepmother or a jealous brother or sister; in these cases there may be some reflexion, never profound, of recurrent social dilemmas. Tales such as these are common enough, as the Grimms' collection or Thompson's motif-index shows; and certain types of theme, like the contest for a bride, are familiar from developed mythologies like the Greek (for example Pelops and Hippodameia, Melanion and Atalanta). One special ingredient requires emphasis, and that is the use of trickery and ingenuity. Often the main point of a tale is precisely the ingenious way in which a difficulty or danger is overcome, or the solution to a problem or *impasse* discovered. Herodotus's story of the two brothers who rob a royal treasury, until one night one of them is trapped—and the other cuts off and removes his head to avoid recognition—is a typical folktale, known not only in Egypt (where Herodotus places it), but elsewhere.[56] Similarly there is a strong emphasis on ingenuity in the tale of Perseus, not only in his magical equipment but also in the manner in which he avoids being petrified (see pp. 181, 183). Indeed I would be inclined to suggest that the use of ingenuity is the most striking and consistent characteristic of folktales, one that tends to occur whether or not magical or supernatural elements are present. In a way, magic is just a special case of ingenuity, and exploits a similar feeling of satisfaction at the neatness and finality with which an awkward situation is resolved or an enemy confounded. Neither in magical nor in other kinds of ingenious solution are realism and probability strongly germane (even decapitated bodies can be identified, for instance).

Folktales often exemplify, in addition, a kind of wish-fulfilment fantasy that Ruth Benedict and Franz Boas wished to ascribe to myths in general. Tales of the Cinderella and Prince Charming type obviously embody the longings and aspirations of ordinary people; here one cannot avoid the distinction between essentially aristocratic tales like the Greek hero-myths, and popular tales like the Grimms' *Hausmärchen*. The discovery of treasure, or the winning of great rewards for apparently small actions (but often

[56] Herodotus, II, 121; the same tale is told by Pausanias (IX, 37, 4) of the Boeotians Trophonius and Agamedes. Herodotus's Egyptian tale continues with more and more extravagant devices for catching the surviving brother, and on his part for overcoming them.

highly moral ones: morality is one quality left open to the under-privileged), are again more typical of European peasant tales than of the myths either of aristocratic societies or of primitive ones—since the former have no lack of wealth, the latter no developed conception of it as possibly fortuitous. The wishes of savage societies take a different form, but they too express themselves in some of their tales, sometimes in a complex manner. So in myths concerning the Melanesian *kula*-exchange the recurrent theme of rejuvenation, of how a character suddenly casts off old age and becomes more beautiful, reproduces the desires of listeners and narrators alike, not only for a renewal of youth in general, but more particularly for success in the operation of the formalized exchange of ceremonial goods.

Many folktales do not give particular names to their characters, but generic or typical names like 'Jack', 'the Giant', 'Red Riding-Hood', 'Little Claus', 'Epimetheus'. This practice reflects at once the range of their appeal, their lack of specific local reference, and the importance of situation at the expense of character. Where a set of folktale themes is gathered round a single hero, there a specific personality and name begin to emerge, as with Perseus, or the folktale hero is identified with a legendary hero. One may compare the process by which in an oral legendary tradition minor historical personalities, like Marko Kraljević in late-fourteenth-century Serbia, manage to attract to themselves many anonymous anecdotes and eventually emerge as picaresque or trickster-type heroic figures.

What are usually termed 'myths'—apart, for the moment, from Greece—tend to behave differently. The characters, particularly the hero, are specific, and their family relationships are carefully noted; they are attached to a particular region, although the region may vary according to where the myth is being told. The action is complicated, and often broken up into loosely related episodes. It does not usually depend on disguises and tricks, but rather on the unpredictable reactions of individuals, personalities rather than types. Indeed one of the distinguishing characteristics of myths is their free-ranging and often paradoxical fantasy; this will be further investigated in the final chapter, but meanwhile it is obviously a quality that sets many traditional tales apart from those that specialize in neatness and a kind of logic. This curious lack of ordinary logic operates quite apart from the consequences of supernatural components, which apply both in myths and in folktales. In the latter, however, one event leads naturally to another (given the initial assumptions, for example that one speaking character may be an animal); whereas in myths the supernatural component often produces drastic and unexpected changes in the forward movement of the action. In addition, myths tend to possess that element of 'seriousness', in establishing and confirming rights and institutions or exploring and reflecting problems or preoccupations, that has been mentioned although not so far fully discussed. Moreover their main characters are often superhuman, gods or semi-divine heroes, or animals who turn into culture-heroes in the era of human and cultural creation. For myths, specific though they may be in their characters and local settings, are usually envisaged as taking place in a timeless past. Certain details of contemporary life may intrude, but they are superficial, unless the myth has been strongly complicated by legend. The action of folktales, on the other hand, is assumed to have taken place within historical time, in the past often enough, but not the distant or primeval past. Such tales are no more specific about period than about persons, but 'once upon a time' implies historical time and not the epoch of creation, or of the first men, or of a golden age.[57]

The attempt to define a special class of traditional tales seems viable, and I believe that the term 'folktale' should be accepted as a useful one. Nevertheless Boas and Benedict were right in emphasizing that there is mobility from one genre to the other, especially from folktale into myth. It is not that entire folktales are somehow upgraded into myths by the discovery of some serious or fantastic quality; rather folktale motifs—minimal episodic elements like the solving of a riddle, or the wearing of something that ensures invisibility, or even narrative devices like the performance of a similar action several times over in an ascending climax—tend to be used in the progressive elaboration of myths. Few myths are entirely devoid of such motifs, which in their broader aspects are simply typical applications of the principles of narrative and suspense. Yet only a tale to which we incline to

[57] This kind of chronological distinction has become the chief criterion of myths and folktales among many folklorists, including William Bascom (e.g. *JAFL*, LXXVIII, 1965, 3 ff.). In my opinion its usefulness is mainly at the formalistic level, and those whose primary interest is in the meaning and function of tales will find other criteria, for example in terms of fantasy or the use of ingenuity, more rewarding.

assign the name of folktale rather than myth will be predominantly composed of such elements. On the other hand myths present a very different appearance according to the prominence or absence of such motifs; and in determining the status of a complex myth like the Perseus story it is helpful to apply the concept of folktale or folktale motif, once it has been roughly defined—to be able to use a distinctive term to suggest the absence of certain important qualities (like a serious aetiological intention) or the presence of others (like an overriding interest in ingenuity or disguise). I agree that in practice it will often be difficult to apply one term or another exclusively—for example, the Perseus story is a myth with strong folktale components, whereas many Amerindian trickster tales are (by the present definition) folktales with occasional mythical references or implications. Yet to argue that there is no distinction between the concepts primarily associated with the two terms, or that their overlapping robs the distinction of any usefulness, is to be needlessly defeatist, and needlessly undiscriminating in a subject in which linguistic and conceptual discriminations are all too few.

No binary categorization of traditional tales is likely to be satisfactory; but it emerges that the distinction into sacred and secular tales (the former being called 'myths' and the latter classed as mere entertainment or 'oral literature') is more misleading and less helpful than that into myths, both sacred and secular, and folktales. Myths often have some serious underlying purpose beyond that of telling a story. Folktales, on the other hand, tend to reflect simple social situations; they play on ordinary fears and desires as well as on men's appreciation of neat and ingenious solutions; and they introduce fantastic subjects more to widen the range of adventure and acumen than through any imaginative or introspective urge. Both genres are to different degrees controlled by the laws of story-telling, which operate more prominently—more crudely, perhaps—in folktales than in myths. In practice, as we have seen, the two often overlap, and that argues for keeping 'myth' and 'mythology' as inclusive terms, both for myths in the more special sense and for folktales. My own usage will be clear in any particular context, and in any event my concern is not so much with complete folktales (which I leave to the folklorist) as with the ability to distinguish folktale motifs in imaginative myths.

II

Lévi-Strauss and the Structural Approach

1: An outline of the theory with some preliminary questions

There have been three major developments in the modern study of myths. The first was the realization, associated especially with Tylor, Frazer, and Durkheim, that the myths of primitive societies are highly relevant to the subject as a whole. The second was Freud's discovery of the unconscious and its relation to myths and dreams. The third is the structural theory of myth propounded by the great French anthropologist Claude Lévi-Strauss. It is to the understanding and evaluation of his rather complicated ideas that this chapter is devoted.

The essence of his belief is that myth is one mode of human communication—economic exchange, and kinship exchanges by means of women, being others. It is a product of language, which itself, together with music and rhythmical sound, forms a fourth or auditory mode. Just as the elements of language—sounds or phonemes—are meaningless in isolation, and only take on significance in combination with other phonemes, so the elements of myth—the individual narrative elements, the persons or objects— are meaningless in themselves, and only take on significance through their relation with each other. But it is not the formation of mere narrative as such that is significant; rather it is the underlying structure of relations that determines the real 'meaning' of a myth, just as it is the underlying structure of a language that gives it significance as a means of communication. Variant versions of a myth may show changes in the surface meaning, but the structure and basic relationships will often remain constant— indeed may even be emphasized by the alteration of the overt symbols and by consequent inversions or other forms of transformation. Yet this significant structure is usually, in tribal societies at least, an unconscious one—which does not prevent it from reflecting popular preoccupations with social or seasonal contradictions, like those presented by sisters-in-law or by the growth and decay of vegetation and men.

Already serious problems arise. The linguistic analogy, so heavily used in structural studies in general and by Lévi-Strauss in particular, is ambivalent and confusing in its application to myth. The function of language is to convey content, not to convey its own grammatical and syntactical rules—its own structure, that is.[1] Therefore it is wrong to imply (as Lévi-Strauss does) that the meaning of myth is conveyed by its own structure, corresponding with syntax in language. If the myth–language analogy is valid, then myths, like language, will convey messages distinct from their own structure. And in practice Lévi-Strauss, although he formally maintains that the content of myths is irrelevant, does often rely on specific content for his ultimate interpretation. It would be preferable to say that the message conveyed by a myth is a product of its overt contents and the relations between them: not merely a structure, but a structure of particular materials, and one that is partly determined by them.

Within a myth, according to Lévi-Strauss, a structure can reveal itself at different levels, or by means of different codes. Among South American myths he distinguishes a sociological, a culinary (or techno-economic), an acoustic, a cosmological, and an astronomical code. Any one myth may contain all or most of these. If so, then its 'message', and the significant relationships that compose it, will be reproduced more or less analogously in each of the separate codes—assuming, that is, that the myth is complete. And yet Lévi-Strauss is not altogether consistent on this point. In 'The Story of Asdiwal'[2] he writes of 'reaching rock bottom' at the sociological level of meaning; and in his provisional interpretation of the Oedipus myth he uses the sociological code as a means of revealing something about the origins of men on the cosmological level.[3] His interpretation of the myth's implication is summarized in these words: 'Although experience contradicts

---

[1] On this point see Mary Douglas in *SSMT*, 50 f.
[2] 1958; Eng. tr. by N. Mann in *SSMT*, 1 ff., especially 27.
[3] *SA*, 213 ff.

theory, social life validates cosmology by its similarity of structure. Hence cosmology is true.'[4] Similarly his analysis, in the same article, of the Pueblo creation myth claims to reveal a message concerned with the relation of life and death: namely that some mediation is possible between the two, in this case through the concept of hunting as a way of getting food. Hunting is a mean between agriculture (which furthers life by producing food without killing) and warfare (a special kind of hunting which causes human death). This mediation is confirmed by a further one: for if grass-eating animals are on the side of life, and predatory animals on the side of death, there is a third kind, namely carrion-eaters, which mediate between the two because they do not kill, but eat raw animal food all the same. In other words, a kind of logic is being elicited from certain relationships in nature—one that makes death appear as an acceptable element of human experience.

This idea of a mediation between two polar extremes, which Lévi-Strauss sees as the central characteristic of all myths, often looks curious in relation to a particular example. It becomes especially hard to accept when the message (or relevant mediation) is not conveyed by the identification of a 'rock bottom' or 'privileged' level, of a basic code which is cracked by the determination of analogous codes derived from other levels of reference—but when, in a more severe mood, Lévi-Strauss insists that the message of the myth is conveyed by its structure as a whole, or by the amalgam of relationships (and mediations) at all levels. In this case, presumably, the message conveyed is very abstract, in tune with his own pronouncement that 'mythical thought always progresses from the awareness of oppositions toward their resolution'. He admits that in most cases the authors or reproducers of myths will be unconscious of the kind of meaning he, Lévi-Strauss, attributes to them. Mythical analysis, he writes, cannot have for its object the demonstration of how men think; he does not claim to show how men think in their myths, but 'how myths think themselves in men, and without their awareness'.[5] This is a typically Lévi-Straussian paradox, which might seem to signify little more than that men allow their subconscious preoccupations to emerge from the way they arrange the elements of

[4] Op. cit., 216.

[5] 'Nous ne prétendons donc pas montrer comment les hommes pensent dans les mythes, mais comment les mythes se pensent dans les hommes, et à leur insu': CC, 20.

their stories. That he means more than this is shown by what he writes at the end of the next volume of *Mythologiques*, that all his analyses 'demonstrate that the differential distinctions exploited by myths consist not so much in things themselves as in a body of common properties that can be expressed in geometrical terms, and transformed into each other by means of operations that are, already, a kind of algebra'.[6] If this process towards abstraction really belongs to the myths and not to the mythographer, then, he continues in a very Platonist mood, we have reached the point where 'mythical thought surpasses itself and contemplates, beyond images still clinging to concrete experience, a world of concepts... (defined) no longer by reference to an external reality, but according to their own mutual affinities or incompatibilities manifested in the architecture of the spirit'.[7]

At precisely this point, where we desperately need elucidation of the concept of *esprit*, Lévi-Strauss behaves like any other anthropologist and starts talking about the ancient Greeks. This is the stage, he says (obviously quite wrongly), at which Greek mythology turned into philosophy. By 'spirit' he seems to mean the very structure of the human mind, which is the same all over the world, among illiterate tribesmen and the supposedly civilized: an innate tendency to work in certain ways, notably by a process of binary analysis. In this respect, he concludes, the meaningful content of myth is entirely abstract; it can be expressed algebraically, it is not 'about' any particular aspect of the world or human life— about sociological problems or contradictions, for example; rather it is 'about' the human mind as such, and man's general qualities as an entity involved in an environment. Now if the myths of primitive peoples are really going to reveal that kind of truth about the nature and workings of the human mind, then they are valuable indeed, and their study should be pursued at all costs. Unfortunately Lévi-Strauss cannot seem to say more than that, and the algebra he talks of[8] boils down to relations between different 'codes' that *are* usually interpreted as having a significant bearing on some external content.

[6] *MC*, 407.

[7] 'non plus par référence à une réalité externe, mais selon les affinités ou les incompatibilités qu'ils manifestent les uns vis-à-vis des autres dans l'architecture de l'esprit': *MC*, 407.

[8] Often reduced in the three volumes of his *Mythologiques* to figures and symbols that he himself advises us not to take too seriously: *CC*, 38 f.

On the one hand Lévi-Strauss is anxious to repudiate the approach of Durkheim, by which myths reflect the collective 'representations', or ideas, of the social group; on the other he keeps finding that the message conveyed by the myths he analyses tends to concern the difficulties of social or economic life. This tendency to discover an ultimate significance of myths in the social level is demonstrated by his summary, at the end of *Du Miel aux cendres*, of the results both of this book and its predecessor; for he writes that 'In this case too[9] the link with economic and social life is manifest. First, because the myths about cooking concern the presence or absence of fire, meat, and cultivated plants *in the absolute*, while the myths about the processes bordering on cooking treat of their *relative* presence or absence, in other words of the abundance and want that characterize one or the other period of the year. Secondly, and more important... the myths on the origin of cooking refer to a physiology of marriage alliance whose harmonious functioning is symbolized by the practice of the culinary art... Correspondingly, the myths about the processes bordering on cooking develop a pathology of marriage, one whose germ is symbolically disclosed by culinary and meteorological physiologies...'[10] In short, many of the myths treated in the first two volumes of *Mythologiques* 'refer to' various tendencies and strains in the system of matrimonial exchanges adopted by these tribes: a result that accords well with Lévi-Strauss's view of kinship and 'totemism', but not so well with his profession that what the myths contain is a kind of algebra. In the third volume,[11] an important Tukuna myth (which is treated as a second 'mythe de référence') presents a converse situation. Lévi-Strauss finds its sociological level—a set of matrimonial experiences undergone by the hero—superficial; deeper and deeper levels are investigated, and the final, rather anti-climactic, discovery is of a comparative evaluation of hunting and fishing as ways of life. Once again, there is a basic level of meaning that is not abstract or algebraic; its significance is determined by the structure of the myth as a whole, but in itself the meaning is one of content rather than structure.

Something of the same ambiguity runs through Lévi-Strauss's treatment of the operations of 'the savage mind' even outside the

---

[9] *Sc.* as well as in the myths discussed in *CC*.
[10] *MC*, 405.   [11] *OMT*, 26 f.

sphere of myth. In the introduction to *Le Cru et le Cuit* he wrote that
'The purpose of this book is to show how empirical categories,
such as those of "raw" and "cooked", "fresh" and "corrupt",
"moist" and "burnt", etc.... can nevertheless serve as conceptual
tools for disengaging abstract notions and tying them down in
propositions'.[12] This establishes the connexion with the theme of
his preceding book, *La Pensée sauvage*:[13] that the elaborate categorizations of plants, trees, animals and so forth that anthropologists have shown to be characteristic of 'primitive' societies are
motivated by a need to construct an all-embracing system of
cross-reference between different aspects of experience. The system
then allows the formation of a general (and rather abstract) view
of the total structure of life. To use language which Lévi-Strauss
does not permit himself (because it is too simple?), man has a
tendency to reduce the manifold world of his experience to an
orderly system whose operation he can to some extent predict.
The system adopted by the kind of men who used to be called
savage or primitive is based on a minute distinction of the properties
of each single part of the environment, so as to relate it with all
other congeries of properties in terms both of appearance and of
function. The apprehension of analogies between apparently
distinct relationships, in particular, is indeed sophisticated; but
whether it is really helpful to talk about 'algebra' and the 'disengaging of abstract notions', as though the purpose of these
operations were irrelevant to the empirical world, is doubtful.
Rather it seems to be true that these people are firmly rooted in the
world of concrete experience, that they have subjected its phenomena to a fantastically close (and fantastically limited) scrutiny,
and that the elaborate system of resulting categories, although it
displays an almost Linnaean power of discrimination, is nevertheless designed to function upon concrete experience and nothing
else. Lévi-Strauss sometimes, but not always, writes as though the
actual purpose of the categorization is irrelevant; his interest in
the process is aroused by the observation that it involves considerable powers of abstraction or generalization, powers he
considers to be just as great as those directed, in a scientific society,
upon problems that are themselves abstract.

One of the difficulties is that Lévi-Strauss appears now as a

[12] *CC*, 9.
[3] Paris, 1962; Eng. trans., *The Savage Mind*, London and Chicago, 1966.

philosopher, now as an ethnologist.[14] In one remarkable passage he asserts that it does not matter whether the complexity of structure is actually and objectively present in the myths, or whether it exists rather in the mind of the modern interpreter (in this case, Lévi-Strauss himself); for what we are interested in is the nature of the human mind, the *esprit*, and this shows itself as the result of contact or communication between one mind (or set of minds) and another—so that a structure that can be determined *a posteriori* by the imposition of a kindred structure (existing in the critic's mode of thought) is still implicit in the original circumstances. This is an interesting idea, but one that must be clearly labelled as irrelevant if not whimsical. For much of the time, however, Lévi-Strauss's own approach is ethnological and scientific, and he describes the empirical categories under discussion as 'définissables avec précision par la seule observation ethnographique et chaque fois en se plaçant au point de vue d'une culture particulière'.[15] Therefore it does matter whether the structure belongs to the ethnologist or his subjects. It would really be more helpful if Lévi-Strauss would announce when he was going to change roles, rather than bundle together two quite distinct approaches: that of a scientific observer on the one hand, and that of a philosopher or epistemologist on the other. There is room for both in the study of myth and myth-making peoples; but they should not be confused, and their roles, which are sometimes distinct, should not be compounded.

I propose, from now on, to concentrate on Lévi-Strauss's non-philosophical—one might almost say non-mystical—side; to assume that his theory of myth can be adequately summed up by his statement (in his preliminary article, 'The Structural Study of Myth') that 'the purpose of myth is to provide a logical model capable of overcoming a contradiction'.[16]

Within these limits, two main questions require an answer: (1) Is Lévi-Strauss's analysis of the myths of the South American Indians (mostly in the first two volumes of *Mythologiques*) and of certain North American tribes (in the third) broadly correct? In other words, is their structure on the one hand as complex, on the

---

[14] Although in his dialogue with P. Ricoeur, 'Réponses à quelques questions', *Esprit*, N.S. xi, 1963, 631 ff., he claims to be all scientist—'Pour moi la signification est toujours phénoménale' (636)!

[15] *CC*, 9.   [16] *SA*, 229.

other as homologous, as he finds it to be? (2) If the answer to (1) is 'yes', then do other kinds of culture behave in a similar way? To these questions we might add a third: (3) Can the myths of ancient Greece be seen to behave in that way?

My own provisional answer to (1) will be that Lévi-Strauss *has* revealed a previously undetected facet of the myths of certain tribal societies; that they are much more systematic than had been supposed, and that many of them do individually contain different levels of meaning in which the same structural pattern is reproduced. Yet there is usually, as Lévi-Strauss himself admits, a 'privileged' level, and they also retain other qualities (as narratives, charters, overt or allegorical explanations, and so forth) that are associated with their content and not their structure, and yet cannot be ignored (as they often are by Lévi-Strauss) in the assessment of their ultimate significance. The answer to (2), to which I shall return at the end of this chapter, will depend on one's reaction to a criticism first made by Paul Ricoeur in his article 'Structure et herméneutique', and since much repeated, that Lévi-Strauss's examples of mythical thought 'have been taken from the geographical areas of totemism and never from Semitic, pre-Hellenic, or Indo-European areas'.[17] Ricoeur felt that Sumero-Akkadian, Hebrew, Egyptian, Mycenaean, Iranian and Indian myths might behave quite differently: that, as E. R. Leach expresses it, Lévi-Strauss's myths are those 'in which there is a notable confusion between human beings and animals but which are characterised by the absence of any setting within an historical chronology, real or imaginary. Ricoeur suggests that there may be a fundamental contrast between "totemic" myths of this kind and the mythologies of civilised peoples'.[18] This, too, deserves fuller examination than it has so far received; my own conclusion will be that myth-systems from which the close interrelating of men and animals is absent do behave somewhat differently, but that nevertheless the preoccupation discovered by analysis of the 'totemic' types, and also some of their structural procedures, sometimes lurk behind more 'civilized' types and are in any event worth testing for.

As for (3) and the Greeks, I believe that Lévi-Straussian analyses recently tried out by E. R. Leach,[18a] as well as Lévi-Strauss's own published effort on Oedipus, have been largely

[17] *Esprit*, N.S. xi, 1963, 607.   [18] *AES*, vii, 1966, 60.   [18a] *Lévi-Strauss* (1970), 68 ff.

unsuccessful, although they have brought out some interesting contrasts, parallelisms, and inversions. Greek myths, as I shall argue later, are quite heavily polluted in the form in which we know them. They show many marks of progressive remodelling, and in particular of the exaggeration of folktale elements at the expense of speculative or explanatory elements. Structuralists would reject the implication that we cannot therefore trace the 'meanings' or messages of many Greek myths, in accordance with Lévi-Strauss's theory, which is partly accepted by Leach, that 'the myth consists of all its versions' and 'remains the same as long as it is felt as such';[19] therefore its structure survives even in a learned exegesis, or in a new interpretation such as was proposed by Freud for the Oedipus myth. I find this theory wrong, for simple reasons to be given later, and believe that progressive literate interference can and often does completely alter the purport of a traditional myth. Indeed Lévi-Strauss himself is not clear about it, since he sidestepped Ricoeur's objection about Old Testament myths by claiming that they have suffered from redactors and intellectual interpreters, and therefore their 'résidu mythologique et archaïque' has been overlaid.[20] If I am correct, then the Lévi-Straussian kind of analysis will only rarely be revealing for Greek myths—which are not therefore to be counted as non-mythical, although there are other reasons, to be considered later, for viewing them as a special case.

2: A relatively simple example—the tale of Asdiwal

I return to a more detailed consideration of question (1) above, about the general validity of Lévi-Strauss's analysis of primitive myths. It was his treatment of a Tsimshian myth of the north-west Pacific coast, in the article entitled 'La Geste d'Asdiwal' (1958),[21] that first seems to have convinced other anthropologists that there really was something in his method of analysis, that primitive myths can reveal a complex and significant structure almost independent of their apparent content. It will be remembered that the attitudes of anthropologists towards myths were, before this point, conservative, and were strongly influenced by Malinowski's conception of the function of myth as providing a charter

---

[19] *SA*, 217; cf. E. R. Leach in *AES*, vii, 1966, 64 ff., 99 f.
[20] *Esprit*, N.S. xi, 1963, 631 f.
[21] Translated as 'The Story of Asdiwal' in *SSMT*, 1 ff.

for beliefs and institutions. The tale of Asdiwal was collected in four versions by Franz Boas; in its number of known versions it is surpassed by many of the Bororo and neighbouring myths, but our knowledge of the social, material and ecological background of the Tsimshian Indians, although very incomplete, is superior in certain respects to that of the South American tribes. Moreover the Asdiwal tale has the advantage of having been subjected to recent critical discussion. For these reasons I propose to examine Lévi-Strauss's analysis of this myth first—encouraged also by the fact that his treatment is simpler and more manageable than in the case of the larger and more complicated set of myths considered in the three existing volumes of *Mythologiques*.

The Tsimshian Indians lived around the Skeena and Nass rivers in British Columbia, near the southern border of Alaska. In winter they inhabited regular villages, but in the early spring they all congregated on the Nass river, the northernmost of the two; for this river, which flows roughly north-east to south-west and whose name means 'Stomach', is chosen as a spawning-ground by the candlefish for about six weeks from March the first on. Once the candlefish season was over, the Tsimshian who came from round the Skeena river would move back there to await the arrival of the salmon in June and July; the salmon, unlike the candlefish, entered both rivers. So the Skeena Tsimshian, at least, would move up and down the coast each year as well as up and down each river; but another group, the Nisqua, stayed in the vicinity of the Nass.

In the fullest version of the myth, a mother and daughter, both widowed by famine as winter ends, leave their dead husbands' villages and move to meet each other, from downstream and upstream respectively, along the Skeena river. They have nothing to eat but a rotten berry, but then they are visited by a young stranger who is also a bird; he gives them food and marries the daughter. A child, Asdiwal, is born, and his supernatural father gives him magic weapons, snow-shoes, and a cloak, before he himself disappears. The child grows up and his grandmother dies; the survivors move downstream to the mother's birthplace. There Asdiwal captures a white bear and follows it up into the sky, where it turns into a beautiful maiden, daughter of the Sun. Asdiwal marries Evening Star, as she is called, after overcoming all sorts of trials set him by his prospective father-in-law. He becomes homesick for his mother, and he and his wife descend to earth, where he deceives Evening Star with a mortal woman, is killed by her in retribution, but is revived by his father-in-law. A second time he returns to earth, where his divine wife finally leaves him. He takes up with another mortal woman, and in early spring moves up towards the Nass river with her and her four brothers. There he quarrels with the brothers about the relative merits of hunting by land and by sea (the Tsimshian do both at different times of the year), and infuriates them by making a good catch in his land hunting, with the help of his magical weapons, while they catch nothing at sea. They take their sister and leave him, but he immediately meets another group of four brothers and a sister, and takes up with this sister as with the previous one. After a successful fishing season they return south for the late summer and winter. Now Asdiwal boasts that he can hunt seals better than his brothers-in-law. They go out to a reef, which is so sheer and slippery that only Asdiwal can climb up it by using his magic shoes. Rather justifiably by Tsimshian standards (for they are very susceptible to loss of face, as is shown in the extraordinary custom of the potlatch) they strand him there. He survives by various magical tricks, and then goes down to the home of the seals under water, heals the wounded ones, and begs from them a boat to take him back ashore; the boat is made out of the seal-king's stomach. His wife and new son are waiting for him, and the wife plots with him to destroy her brothers. In spite of this tie Asdiwal's wander-lust eventually reasserts itself, and he abandons his wife to return to his childhood haunts far up the Skeena river. His son joins him; during the winter Asdiwal goes hunting up a mountain, but leaves his magical implements behind. As a consequence he is stranded and turns into stone, where he and his dog can still be seen.

This myth was described in full by Boas between 1895 and 1916, and Lévi-Strauss saw in it a fit subject for structural analysis. Not only are there journeys west and east and north and south, but Asdiwal makes one magical journey upwards, to the sky, and another downwards, to the depths of the sea. His adventures can be seen as 'a series of impossible mediations between oppositions which are ordered in a descending scale: high and low, water and earth, sea-hunting and mountain-hunting, etc'.[22] The same is true

---

[22] Cf. *SSMT*, 16.

of the geographical wanderings: he starts from a point halfway between up- and down-river, and ends at a point which is up-river but, on the vertical plane, halfway up a mountain, where his mobility (which sought a mediation between spatial extremes) is finally ended. There are other inversions and paradoxes too: the great mountain-hunter is almost brought to grief on the reef, a minute sea-mountain; and the slayer of animals becomes their healer in the case of the seals. The myth also has a sociological level, and Lévi-Strauss is right to observe that the relationships between Asdiwal and his mother and grandmother, as well as with his various wives and their kin, are carefully specified, as are their local connexions. There is, finally, what he calls a techno-economic schema, in that the myth is based on a typical seasonal cycle of famine and plenty associated with movement to the different fishing and hunting grounds: it begins with famine and ends with prosperity. But the real 'meaning' of the myth is found to be concerned with the sociological level, after all. By illustrating the tensions between patrilocality and matrilaterality (both seem to have existed in Tsimshian society in the past), yet showing the failure of theoretical alternatives, the myth is trying to mediate or palliate a contradiction at the root of Tsimshian social life.

Many of Lévi-Strauss's interpretations of the ultimate meanings of myths, from the South American Indians as well as these of the Northwest, end up with this question of the tensions brought about by different systems of giving in marriage, or the exchange of women; and there is no doubt that in exogamous tribes, especially matrilineal ones, the proper interchange of women is a subject of abiding interest and enormous potentiality for social stress. But I wonder whether Lévi-Strauss does not overdo this particular interpretation[23]—quite apart from the paradox, already noted, that he rejects Durkheimian social explanations of the functions of myth, maintaining that their true 'message' is nothing to do with content as such but a piece of algebra about the workings of the human spirit in the abstract. Examination of his detailed arguments about the Asdiwal story does nothing to allay suspicion. He begins by adducing a variant form of, or appendage to, the myth, which describes the adventures of Waux, Asdiwal's son by his first human marriage. Waux acts as a kind of doublet of Asdiwal, but with some interesting differences. Forced by his uncles to separate

[23] Which reflects his earlier *Les Structures élémentaires de la parenté* (Paris. 1949).

from Asdiwal, he nevertheless hunted on his father's hunting ground (and thus combined elements of patrilocality and matri- laterality). He married a cross-cousin at his mother's instance. They had twins, who were killed up the mountain where he hunted. Later he forgot to take his magic lance and was himself trapped halfway up the mountain. He shouted to his wife down below to offer fat to the gods, but she could not hear him properly, and thought he was telling her to eat the fat. This she did to such an extent that she burst, and became flint, which is still found in the valley. Waux himself could move neither up nor down, and turned to stone, just like Asdiwal.

Lévi-Strauss finds this a weakened version of the Asdiwal story, among other reasons because twins are weaker mediators, in Amerindian mythology generally, than, for instance, a single trickster figure; and because Waux forgets his magic spear, a stronger and more useful instrument than the snow-shoes forgotten by Asdiwal. His argument at this point, and his comment that 'The weaker mediator loses the stronger instrument of mediation and his powers are doubly diminished as a result', show him at his least convincing and most arbitrary.[24] A more significant difference is the addition of the theme of his wife's misunderstanding and possible greed, which is perhaps relevant to her being Waux's cross-cousin. One is sharply reminded of the myths about the 'fille folle de miel' treated in *Du Miel aux cendres*, sometimes in association with the theme of misunderstanding of speech.[25] Greed (for food or sex) is there associated by Lévi-Strauss with neglect of a wife's duty to her husband's kin—which does not seem to be the case with Waux's wife, however.

The method of closely comparing different versions of a myth is one that Lévi-Strauss has usefully emphasized; but his capri- ciousness in its operation is further exemplified in the conclusions he draws from a third variant, this time derived from the Nass region. Here again two women move to meet each other from points upstream and downstream; but instead of being mother and daughter as in the Skeena version they are sisters, one un- married, the other married and accompanied by her daughter. Moreover the unmarried and nubile one, who attracts the super- natural stranger, now comes from downstream and not up. The child who is born, called Asi-hwil in this version, performs much

[24] *SSMT*, 23.   [25] *MC*, 87 ff. See also pp. 70 f. below.

the same feats as Asdiwal (although he only gets halfway to the sky); but he marries only one mortal wife, with whose brothers he quarrels in the seal episode as before, and whom he does not, this time, abandon. One other difference: instead of travelling empty-handed and then sharing a single rotten berry, the women bring a handful of berries (from downstream) and a piece of spawn (from upstream). This is made by Lévi-Strauss the basis of an improbable and highly complex piece of analysis, leading to the conclusion that this Nass version of the myth is a weakened one, and there-fore, by a rule of his own that has caused much difficulty, that some of its values are transformed. That is why the nubile woman comes from downstream, not upstream. Moreover he thinks that the alteration of the rotten-berry motif also represents a weakening, and that the spawn and the berries brought in the Nass version neutralize each other.

I would suggest the following quite different considerations.[26] That the more strongly emphasized woman travels up rather than down corresponds with the different movements of the Nass and Skeena peoples in early spring: many of the latter have to move *down* the Skeena river before they can go up the Nass, the former go straight *up* the Nass—and this is a Nass variant. The food they carry is not just neutral; it may well reflect a dispute about the relative merits of (men's) fishing and (women's) berry-gathering, or about their seasonal sequence, just as Asdiwal's disputes con-cern the relative merits of different kinds of hunting. That would be a theme of evaluation, comparable with Sumerian myths (for example) concerning the relative merits of herding and agricul-ture and the like. The single rotten berry of the Skeena version may well be intended to emphasize simply that there was no other food available, because the fish had not yet arrived; for in that version the river is specified as still frozen, whereas in the Nass version it is not—the spawn is already available, although in short supply.

On one point I agree with Lévi-Strauss: that the various versions of the Asdiwal myth do reveal an interest in cousin-marriage—although I should not be inclined to argue, on the available evidence, that this is the essential 'message' of the myth (rather than messages about the difference between the ways

[26] And thus invalidate such conclusions as are expressed by the following (*SSMT*, 38): '[West:East] :: [sea:land] :: [water:land (earth)] :: [river:bank]'.

of life round the two rivers, or the advisable proportion of time and effort to be devoted to different kinds of hunting and food-gathering). But I would treat even this theme rather differently. The crucial facts are the following:

Asi-hwil (avoids marrying a cousin) marries a stranger and lives happily.[27]

Asdiwal marries a stranger whom he typically deserts (or is deserted by), and dies by his own error.

Waux marries his cross-cousin, stays with her, and dies by her error (as well as his own).

The outcome of the three versions, seen in this way, is that it is only by avoiding cousin-marriage, and marrying a stranger and then sticking to her, that the hero lives on happily. Marrying a stranger but then deserting (or being deserted by) her, as in the case of Asdiwal, leads to a bad end; so does marrying a cross-cousin and sticking to her (since she reveals herself as both stupid—or somehow inadequate—and greedy). Now this view of the possible sociological purport (among others) of the myth is not a structural one at all. In this respect it accords with certain criticisms marshalled by Mary Douglas.[28] Dr Douglas is especially sceptical about Lévi-Strauss's notions on transformation and inversion; she questions the idea that the difficulties of cross-cousin marriage, in a prestige-society like that of the Tsimshian, lie at the heart of the myth, and exposes as artificial the interpretation of all the marriages in the longest Asdiwal version as matrilocal. There are other positive elements of Tsimshian life, she thinks, that may be reflected in the myth, directly and without difficult assumptions about inversion: the comparison of men with women, the dangers of excessive gift-giving or shaming, and an ambivalent attitude towards successful shamans. Here I am doubtful (over the particular suggestions, not the approach); since these themes, although perhaps present, are not nearly so strongly marked in the versions we know as is the theme of

[27] A word of explanation is necessary about Asi-hwil: by claiming that he avoids marrying a cousin I am placing a possible but conjectural interpretation on the fact that his aunt (his mother's married sister) brings her daughter with her to the meeting-point. Thereafter nothing is heard of this girl, and Lévi-Strauss feels that she is merely a weak reflexion of the Skeena version, where one of the two women is a *daughter* (of the other). In a matrilineal exogamous society the girl is excluded as a possible match for Asi-hwil, but her presence may symbolize the dangers of cousin-marriage in general.

[28] In her valuable article 'The meaning of myth, with special reference to "La Geste d'Asdiwal"', *SSMT*, 49 ff., cf. especially 58 ff.

marriage. In fact in its broadest lines the myth links the seasonal movements of the Tsimshian fisher and hunter with various marriages contracted by the hero; and Lévi-Strauss may well be right in connecting the fuller form of the ending (seen in the Waux version), in which the final wife is immobilized by greed or repletion, with an underlying association between movement and hunger, rest and satiety. Yet once again this is hardly a structural observation, and any implications it may have for the Tsimshian are part of the myth's content and not its structure.

In spite of her reservations, Dr Douglas comments that 'Some may have doubted that myths can have an elaborate symmetrical structure. If so, they should be convinced of their error'—that is, by Lévi-Strauss's analysis of the Asdiwal tale.[29] And this has been the general response to the Asdiwal article. Yet I believe that Dr Douglas may have relaxed her scepticism too soon, if what she accepts is the idea of an elaborate symmetrical structure *in the myth itself*—that is, as belonging to myth as a mode of expression. The truth is that the Skeena river natives did carry out this elaborate seasonal movement, from east to west to north to east to west to south to east, and they did so because of certain facts of nature that are not structural but contingent in essence: *that the Skeena and Nass rivers run roughly parallel, and that the candlefish spawn up the northern river and the salmon up both.* Moreover certain reduplications in the myth, especially the successive marriages to a girl with four brothers and the quarrel with the brothers after an imprudent contest, are narrative doublets, just as the Waux ending (despite its claim to be chronologically subsequent to the Asdiwal ending) is a doublet. There may be a kind of correspondence between Asdiwal's visit to the sky and his visit to the bottom of the sea; but that could be due to empirical tendencies in the narrative deployment of commonly available themes, rather than to an unconscious urge to create a symmetrical and significant structure.

I am not denying that the Asdiwal myth is fairly complex in its episodes, and manifests some interesting parallelisms and repetitions. That is partly why Lévi-Strauss selected it, *untypical as it is,* from the large mass of Tsimshian tales recorded by Boas. But it is important to recognize that many of the symmetries derive from the peculiar life and environment of the Tsimshian, and from

[29] *SSMT*, 56.

the ordinary symmetrical and antithetical tendencies of simple narrative, rather than from any general tendencies towards the expression of structures in the human mind. Only in the facts that marriages of different kinds crop up at different points in the geographical cycle, and that the reaction of the wife is different in the two four-brother episodes, do we see a persistent structure extraneous to those likely to be imposed by narrative art and geographical background; and here I think Lévi-Strauss is right in recognizing one major sociological interest (although it is not necessarily the exclusive one) in the myth. Mary Douglas complains that, although the application of T. S. Eliot's lemon-squeezer type of criticism to poetry produces unsuspected meaning 'in rich cupfuls', when applied to myth it tends to produce a new theme but a paltry one: 'the machine seems to spring a leak'.[30] But is it the machine that is at fault, or is it that the underlying preoccupations of tribal societies *are* very often, in our eyes, 'paltry'? Actually, the complaint is misplaced, and I do not believe Dr Douglas really means quite this. Obviously the rules about the availability of women, and the tensions they tend to produce in a society, are far from paltry; they are of very great importance—rivalling the themes of life and death, or of food-production, as the central concerns of life. More to the point is the criticism that Lévi-Strauss often identifies this marriage-rule dilemma as the ultimate meaning of other myths, in which the detectable references to marriages or in-laws, either in content or in structure, are far slighter than they are in the tale of Asdiwal.

3: The South American material

Any consideration of Lévi-Strauss's *Mythologiques* will be both less thorough and more provisional than that applied to the myth of Asdiwal.[31] That tale was noted in only four versions, and even this number is unusually large for surviving Tsimshian myths. Moreover Lévi-Strauss's analysis, extravagant though it is in places, is not unclear. With the predominantly South American volumes the situation is different. He deals with a hundred and eighty-seven myths in the first volume, almost as many again in both the second and the third. All these myths are held to be

---

[30] *SSMT*, 62 f.

[31] *Mythologiques* consists of three volumes so far: *CC* (1964), *MC* (1966), and *OMT* (1968).

interconnected in one respect or another, so that the interpretation of any one of them can only be understood in relation to the unfolding interpretation of the rest. On no occasion can we assess Lévi-Strauss's analysis of a limited and well-defined quantum of mythological material; at every point he seems to say 'here is half an interpretation, which leaves obvious gaps and difficulties— but we shall try to overcome them by looking at a series of related myths, which will be relevant to the first myth provided that gaps in *their* interpretation can be filled by a provisional interpretation of a third set', and so on. In the end the cycle is closed—or so it is implied. But this interwoven structure, and the assumption that each level of meaning refers to another level, just as each myth refers to other myths, have the result that no special significance can be found for any one myth; rather they all together signify that *esprit* 'which elaborates them by means of the world of which itself is part'.[32] Here the objection to which I have already drawn attention (that there is a contradiction between the frequent assumption in practice of a privileged plane of meaning, and the theoretical claim that the meaning is a purely abstract one about the mode of operation of the human mind) is supplemented by a more practical one, that on his own premises we can never subject Lévi-Strauss's analytical methods, in the broader context of his *Mythologiques*, to detailed verification—unless, that is, we can take all the material together in as much detail, and with as synoptic a vision, as he does.

Part of the fault lies with Lévi-Strauss himself. There have been murmurings in the past from some of his English and American admirers about the luxuriance of his rhetoric, and a metaphysical quality in his thought, that make it difficult for empirically minded Anglo-Saxons and the like to keep up. Edmund Leach, one of his chief followers, professes that Lévi-Strauss often manages to give him ideas even when he doesn't really know what the master is saying. But that is not good enough: if Lévi-Strauss wants to be taken with the seriousness that his brilliance and industry warrant, then he must abjure this Sibylline tone and make certain concessions to the rules of ordinary discourse. Nor is this merely a dull Anglo-Saxon plea; for there is little evidence that many French critics understand him (or succeed in reproducing his ideas in detail) more clearly than those overseas do. It

[32] *CC*, 346.

is significant that so few professional criticisms have appeared even of the first two volumes of *Mythologiques*, although their importance is freely conceded; and that those which have appeared tend to concentrate on paraphrasing certain unusually concise summarizing passages from the introductions and conclusions. That is partly because of the difficulty of extracting from a continuous act of analysis such as I have described above; but it is also because the author makes absolutely no concessions, only rarely points up his argument as it proceeds, and ruthlessly continues a seemingly endless fugue of allusion in which the clearest parts are the summaries of the myths themselves.

All this does not alter the importance of the South American material and Lévi-Strauss's detailed treatment of it. It happens that a great many myths of these Indian tribes (some of which have now died out) have been recorded, chiefly by Jesuit and Salesian missionaries, over the last four hundred years. The tribes of the Gé and Tupi language groups, which are spread over much of Brazil, were culturally related in the distant past, and many specific myths recur among groups that are now widely dispersed. Congeners of many of the myths are to be found further south, in the Chaco, and to the north in Guyana, and Lévi-Strauss has felt free to draw on these distant versions where necessary. In the latest volume the search is extended to the Plains Indians of North America, and in the fourth volume it will evidently reach the Tlingit and Tsimshian of the Pacific Northwest. The layman might feel that Lévi-Strauss finds his examples where he may, without too close attention to the possibilities of evolution or diffusion; but Lévi-Strauss is confident that these tribes, too, are fragmentary representatives of a continuous culture in the past. In any event the undoubted existence of so many variants within and beyond the borders of Brazil is extremely important; for according to Lévi-Strauss every detail in a myth must be taken as significant and, where there is a difference between variants, then the difference will also be important—will point to a distinct but homologous episode in other allied versions. More striking still, where a number of variant versions retain an apparently unimportant detail unchanged, that detail can be seen to be essential in some way to the structure of the myth.

Why, within a single broad culture, is a limited (but large) number of myths recounted over and over again, with variations that can usually be found significant within an expanding structural scheme? Lévi-Strauss answers this question in a narrow but ingenious manner, making no reference either to the tendencies of oral transmission or to the frequence with which certain specific themes tend to show up in quite separate traditions, in part because of their narrative usefulness and dramatic power. His answer is that any effective communication system makes use of *repetition*, partly to show (as in linguistic reduplication) that there is a significant message, partly to ensure that the message ultimately comes through complete. A particular version of a myth may have become distorted, but by superimposing it on other versions, themselves probably distorted in different ways, the whole of the original structure can be reconstituted.

This is the kind of operation he has undertaken on more than three hundred myths (or versions) considered in the two exclusively South American volumes; and it is important to recognize that such an operation could only be satisfactorily carried out where a large set of variants survives. That is why the mythology of these South American Indians, about whom in many respects so little is known, forms one of the best possible subjects for experiment in this method of analysis. Yet, in order to show the closed nature of the supposed system of myths, it is surely necessary to construct a summary of *all* myths and variants recorded from the whole area from which examples are drawn in the reconstitution of the system. That is what Lévi-Strauss has so far failed to do, and his omission is an important element in the impression of sleight-of-hand that many readers derive from his treatment. What is needed is something like Franz Boas's survey of myths and themes in Part IV of his *Tsimshian Mythology* or, more simply, and if it were possible, a statement that all important myths or themes known from the area have been brought into consideration. Sampling of some of Lévi-Strauss's most important sources[33] suggests that this would not be entirely the case, and that a limited degree of selection (even among 'true' myths) has occurred.

Provisionally, however, I am inclined to accept Lévi-Strauss's opinion that there is a more or less closed system of myths in Brazil and its bordering regions, and his implication that he has given a reasonable sampling of it, starting from myths concerning

---

[33] See under C. Albisetti, A. Colbacchini, A. Métraux, C. Nimuendaju in the Bibliography to *CC*.

the origin and symbolic position of fire and cooking as mediators between nature and culture. In his second volume he passes from cooking to consider the cases of honey and tobacco, which represent substances respectively this side of and beyond cooking, in that the one is prepared artificially but at the same time naturally, by bees and wasps, without cooking, while the other has to be over-cooked, or rather burned, in order to be ingested. The range of reference extends to other codes as well as the culinary, but the underlying mediation continues to be that between nature (the interactions of plants, animals, the soil, the seasons) and culture (the interactions of humans, among themselves or with the outside world, according to tribal rules and customs). That is the privileged or dominant theme, and the different codes—culinary, astronomical (in which the position of the Pleiades as markers of the seasons is conspicuous), or acoustic (in which noise and silence, or continuous and discontinuous noise, are applied as mediations between contradictions like those represented by eclipses in the field of cosmological events or by the *charivari* in abnormal sexual unions)—all seem to be relevant to this over-riding polarity.

In *Du Miel aux cendres* Lévi-Strauss proceeds not only to operations on the borders of cooking, which he sees as analogous to equivocal figures, like the seducer friend or the brother-in-law, on the borders of the family, but also to the consideration of more generalized mythical symbols, not concrete qualities like raw and cooked, hard and soft, fresh and corrupt, but more abstract ones like full and empty, continuous and discontinuous, containing and contained. There was a marked local polarity, especially in terms of 'up' and 'down', even in his earlier analyses; but more recently he has moved on to consider the more complex spatial and figurative implications of, for example, hollowed-out trees, which are of great importance for many of these Indians because they serve either as a place for bees' or wasps' nests (on the side of nature) or, when the hollowing is done artificially or culturally, as canoes, as receptacles for the fermenting of brews made out of manioc or honey, or as sacral drums. At this point, as at many others in Lévi-Strauss's detailed analyses, I feel that the significant relationship between these different uses can be expressed in simpler and less abstract terms than those used by him; yet it should not be forgotten that in *La Pensée sauvage* he was able to adduce many instances to show that primitive peoples are not only aware of semi-abstract properties like hollowness, but are also accustomed to relate subjects by their possession or otherwise of such properties, which in many cases strike us as incidental, unimportant, or simply weird. Conversely, their simple technology means that a single object or operation—like the hollowed-out tree, or the act of hollowing it—has many different uses, and so brings out unusual connexions between different categories.

The reservations felt about the analysis of the myth of Asdiwal apply equally to Lévi-Strauss's detailed procedures in the later works, although, as I have suggested, it is harder here to pin him down. The looseness of his concept of transformation by inversion, and the extreme freedom with which he moves from direct parallelisms to those that have to be found in metaphor, synecdoche, or supposedly chiastic arrangements, continue to be alarming. Yet it has been said that when one turns from Lévi-Strauss to any other attempt to analyse these myths, the results look old-fashioned and unconvincing; and I too find this to be so. Even if one does not accept his theory in all its details, even if one rejects many of his specific arguments, the broad outlines remain attractive: that the myths form a system, and that they embody certain structural forms that are as important as their overt content; that they operate simultaneously on different levels (in what Lévi-Strauss terms different codes), but in an analogous process; that, where there is a privileged level, it is to be elucidated by comparison with other levels; that the myths tend to emphasize polarities or contradictions, for which they offer progressive (but often ultimately frustrated) mediators; and that they are constantly preoccupied with the contrast between nature and culture, for which the culinary code, among these Indians at least, is an important means of exploration.

4: Geriguiaguiatugo and related myths

In summarizing three related myths of the Bororo (from the first volume of *Mythologiques*), I want to illustrate Lévi-Strauss's method in action, and also to give an example of myths that are remote as could be in cultural background from those of ancient Greece, but are obviously real myths all the same—not least in the eerie, almost poetical quality that, despite their often crude subjects, they seem to possess. This is the myth (M_1) from which he starts, and which forms the basis for a fantastic voyage of exploration ranging over hundreds of related and interlocking tales:

Long ago a young man called Geriguiaguiatugo followed his mother into the forest, where she was going to collect special leaves for the initiation of young men after puberty. He raped her, and his father, discovering by a trick that his son was the culprit, sent him on a deadly mission to fetch various kinds of ceremonial rattle from the lake of souls. The young man's grandmother advises him to enlist the help of a humming-bird, which obtains for him the object of his quest. Other missions aided by other kinds of bird are also successful, so that eventually his father takes him on a parrot-hunting expedition and strands him halfway up a cliff, hanging on only by a magic stick given him by his grandmother. Father goes away, but son manages to climb the cliff. On the isolated plateau above he kills lizards and hangs some of them round his belt as a store of food; but they go rotten, and their smell makes the young man faint, then attracts vultures who devour his posterior as well as the maggoty lizards. The sated vultures turn friendly and convey him to the foot of the cliff. The young man is now hungry again, but the wild fruits he eats go straight through him, devoid as he now is of fundament. Remembering a tale of his grandmother's, he fashions a new posterior out of a kind of mashed potato. He returns to his village, which he finds abandoned; but eventually discovers his family, after taking the form (according to the main version) of a lizard. He appears to his grandmother in his own shape; during the night a terrible storm extinguishes all the fires except hers; the other women, including the father's new wife, come for embers the next day. Father pretends that nothing has happened between him and his son, but the son turns into a stag and casts him with his antlers into a lake, where the father is devoured by cannibal piranha fish. His lungs rise to the surface and become the origin of a special kind of floating leaf. The young man then kills his mother and his father's second wife.

There is an explicit but minor aetiological function in this myth, in the origin of the leaves floating on the lake, and an implicit one in the origin of sacred rattles. According to its original collector it was also meant to explain the origin of storms (or wind) and fire—certainly the grandmother is left as the sole possessor of fire in the primeval village. But the examination of variants, and many of the details of the myth itself, show that its function is more complicated than that—that it goes beyond simple aetiology. In another Bororo myth, Lévi-Strauss's M_2, a boy follows his mother into the forest, where she is going to gather fruit, and sees her raped by a member of her own moiety—in an exogamous society, a kind of incest. He tells his father, who kills the offender and also his wife, whom he buries secretly under her hammock with the help of four different kinds of armadillo. The boy searches for his mother, but father misleads him; in order to continue his search the boy turns into a bird, which drops excrement on the father's shoulder. The excrement grows into a tree, which is so inconvenient that father, whose name is Birimoddo Baitogogo, leaves the village. However, he notices that wherever he stops to rest a lake or river springs up (there had been no terrestrial water before) and the tree diminishes—finally, indeed, disappears. Life becomes so pleasant that he resigns his chiefdom and is joined by his sub-chief, which explains why nowadays the two chiefs belong to the other moiety. They make ornaments and decorations, the symbols of culture and tribal life, which they present to the villagers in their new role of culture-heroes.

In a third Bororo myth (M_5) a young man refuses to leave his mother's hut and frequent the men's hut, as he should do just before puberty. His grandmother punishes him with her intestinal vapours, crouching over him as he sleeps. The youth becomes ill, but eventually finds the trouble and kills his grandmother by thrusting an arrow up her anus; he secretly buries her under her hammock with the aid of four species of armadillo, named in the reverse order to those of M_2. Now there is an expedition to catch fish by suffocating them—a method used by the Indians—and on the following day the women of the village return to the river to collect the final victims. The young man's sister wants to leave her child with the grandmother so that she can accompany the other women, but when she cannot find her she places the child in a tree, where he turns into an anteater. The sister stuffs herself with dead fish, suffers horribly, and exhales evil vapours that are the origin of all diseases; her brothers kill her and throw pieces of her into two particular lakes.

There are plainly some important thematic connexions between these three myths, and not the sort that are due to the recurrence of narrative elements for their own sake, as in folktale—although there are obvious folktale components in these as in most other myths. Each of the three has overt aetiological features, but the most striking thematic similarities are not directly concerned with them. Each begins with a form of incest—for in the last of the three the boy clings to his mother in a quasi-incestuous way, and enrages his grandmother who enters into a kind of inverted incestuous relation with him. Curiously, in two out of the three myths the originator of the incestuous relations does not suffer, but rather initiates a new term that mediates the disjunction caused by his initial action. In M_2 the son turns into a bird, and his excrement causes a tree to grow on his father, producing water: according to Lévi-Strauss the mediation between sky (bird) and earth (tree) is terrestrial water, and it provides a link between living and dead because a lake is the proper abode of souls, denied to the mother by her secret inhumation. In M_5 a different mediation between life and death is achieved by the creation of diseases, which arise from an excessive relation to water (or rather to the poisoned fish), corresponding with the defective relation implied by the unnatural burial of grandmother; but a similar polarization between high and low had been suggested by the placing of the child up the tree and his transformation into an anteater, which is confined to the earth. In the original myth (M_1) the incestuous youth is placed in a similar relation to earth and sky when he is stranded, hanging in mid-air, halfway up the cliff. In this instance, however, no obvious mediating term appears (like the diseases in M_5 or the ornament made of feathers in M_2; these are given by the two chiefs to the tribe, and, being natural objects used for cultural purposes, serve as a mediator between nature and culture). This leads Lévi-Strauss to consider in great detail a whole new set of related myths from tribes beyond the Bororo. In the end nearly two hundred are brought to bear, and they reveal that the mediation in M_1, which has been lost or suppressed, must be connected with its implied aetiology of domestic fires. Indeed the mediation turns out to be achieved by means of cooking, a prime symbol among these Indians, as we have seen, for the interrelation of nature and culture; for it is by fire (which is artificially created and preserved by men, once it has been shown them) that raw food is most satisfactorily civilized and made digestible. The use of fire establishes a link, in many of the myths, not only between *le cru et le cuit* but also between earth and sky, nature and culture, and life and death.

Let me cite a fourth myth (Lévi-Strauss's M_7, collected from the Kayopo tribe 500 miles to the north of the Bororo, and representative of a group of Gé myths), to show that the origin of cooking is indeed connected with the group of three myths considered so far. An Indian takes his young brother-in-law to catch parrots up a cliff; they quarrel, and the boy is left stranded like Geriguiaguiatugo in M_1. He is there several days, and is forced to eat his own excrement to keep alive. Then he is rescued by a jaguar who is walking past carrying a bow and arrow—for most of these tales are set in the period when men and animals lived together, and when some animals had both human and superhuman qualities. The jaguar takes him home for a cooked dinner, for jaguar alone has the gift of fire and cooking at this stage. Jaguar's human wife does not like the boy, who is eventually forced to murder her with the bow and arrow; he runs back to his village, taking with him a piece of cooked meat. Then he shows the villagers jaguar's lair, and they capture an ember and so learn about fire and the art of cooking; but the jaguar becomes man's enemy for this betrayal. So, as man moves towards culture by the discovery of domestic fire and cooking, jaguar moves away from culture and becomes the embodiment of raw nature; and just as in the Greek Prometheus-myth man has to pay for the gift of fire by the loss of automatic agriculture, so here he pays for it by the hostility of animal life in the jungle.

The stranding of the boy up the cliff is common to M_1 and M_7; but in the former, the Bororo myth, there is no mention of a jaguar, or explicitly of the origin of fire and cooking. Yet, if jaguar is master of fire among tribes of the Gé language-group, the vulture fills this role among those of the Tupi group, with which the Bororo have close contact.[34] Thus in M_{65} a culture-hero named Nianderu gives men fire after a disastrous flood; he does so by pretending to be dead, attracting the vultures to his corpse, and then seizing an ember from them as they build a fire to cook him on. As Lévi-Strauss observes, there is a significant difference between the concept of jaguars and of vultures as masters of fire: the one eats meat raw, the other eats it corrupt. He suggests that the Gé tribes are more interested in the contrast, on the side of

[34] *CC*, 151 f.

culture, between raw and cooked, the Tupi tribes in the contrast, on the side of nature, between raw and rotten. Corruption is in one sense nature's way of cooking. The Bororo myth (in which the vultures who turn helpful may reproduce another motif of M_{65}, that the vultures disguised themselves as shamans, and pretended to be friendly, in order to gain access to the corpse) falls to some extent between the two attitudes, and Lévi-Strauss suggests—rather remarkably for him, since it introduces a historical explanation of a mythical structure—that this could reflect a 'refusal or incapacity' to choose between them. I would suggest rather that the Bororo version, with its uncompleted themes, is the result of a process of mythical accretion and degradation that depends more on the tendencies of oral narrative than on any unconscious logic of structure. This suggestion may suitably serve as transition to a reconsideration of the Bororo and related myths summarized above, in which the possibility of different structures, or of important non-structural motives, will be explored.

On p. 69 I offer a schematic analysis of the main incidents of the four myths. It shows how some incidents but not others are reproduced from myth to myth, and how the superimposing of one on another often reveals a significant structure; also how certain themes are reversed—for example the benevolent grandmother of M_1 becomes the hostile grandmother of M_5, who is drawn into the theme of corruption represented by excrement or its associated vapours. This reversal is associated, according to Lévi-Strauss, with the fact that the four species of armadillo that help with the burial are named in reverse order in the second myth—the trivial reversal is a signal, as it were, of a more significant inversion. The main reversal also accords with the aetiological conclusion, which in M_5, alone of the four, concerns the origin of something undesirable rather than desirable (although disease is part of culture all the same).

According to Lévi-Strauss the group of myths begins with an 'immoderate conception of family relationships': over-close in M_1, M_2, M_5, over-distant in M_7.[35] That we may accept. This lack of measure brings about the 'disjunction of elements normally connected', for example isolation of the youth up the cliff (M_1, M_7), hostility between him and his grandmother (M_5) or father (M_1, M_2), or exclusion of the dead from their normal (ultimate) abode

[35] *CC*, 71.

M_1	M_2	M_5	M_7
youth rapes mother	youth sees mother raped	youth clings to mother's hut	
			man quarrels with young brother-in-law
father tries to kill him	father kills wife and assailant	grandmother tries to kill him with gases; youth kills her	tries to kill him
by sending him to lake of souls, then stranding up a cliff			by stranding him up a cliff
grandmother protects youth		(grandmother tries to kill him)	
	buries her in hut youth turns into bird to seek mother	buries her in hut his sister seeks her	
he reaches top of cliff			he reaches top of cliff
kills lizards, some of them rot (he cannot hold food)	drops excrement on father's shoulder	(gases)	has to eat his own excrement
they attract vultures which eat his fundament			
vultures rescue him, he cannot hold food, makes new fundament	(drops excrement)		jaguar rescues him
	excrement turns into a tree (youth turns into bird)	places her child in a tree it turns into anteater	
he returns to grand-mother, makes (?) storm and rain; fires quenched except grandmother's	tree makes lakes and rivers	she goes to river, eats too many fish	
		she exhales rotten vapours, origin of diseases	
youth kills father, stepmother, mother		her brothers kill her	he kills jaguar's human wife
grandmother redistributes fire	father invents ornaments for men	(she originates diseases)	shows men how to cook meat, use fire

[Motifs in parentheses are repeated from elsewhere in the myth.]

in rivers or lakes (M_2, M_5). That is possible, but the analysis is not certain. 'Conjunction is re-established by the introduction of an intermediary term whose origin the myth sets out to retrace': for example water (sky^earth), ornaments (nature^culture), funeral rites (living^dead), illness (life^death). But I am not sure that these terms should *necessarily* be seen as a means of resolving these particular disjunctions. Moreover certain disjunctions may have non-structural causes. When the youth in M_2 turns into a bird, it may be not to establish a polarization between sky (represented by the bird) and earth (father, with the tree growing out of him), but rather to explore a new way of introducing excrement into the story. Actually the matter is more complicated than that; the tree plays some significant role, as M_5 suggests:

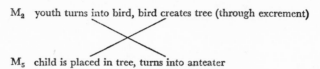

M_2 youth turns into bird, bird creates tree (through excrement)

M_5 child is placed in tree, turns into anteater

It must be conceded that the tree is associated with transformation (into bird/high and anteater/low), but that is because it is itself a mediator; and in M_2 we have the sequence excrement → tree → terrestrial water (the last being associated with culture and the proper place for burial). In fact the bird-dropping *turns into* the tree, and the tree seems to *turn into* water, since it diminishes as the lakes and rivers spring up. I suspect that the other transformations associated with trees, into bird and anteater, are mainly a by-product or signal of the more important transformation-role, of turning excrement into (cultural) water. In M_5, where the reversed role of the grandmother and the reverse order of the armadillos suggest that other values and relationships, too, have suffered inversion, the water is harmful, not beneficial. That is partly because this version introduces a totally new theme (known from many other myths and explored by Lévi-Strauss in *MC*, 87 ff.), that of the greedy girl or 'la fille folle de miel'; but partly also because, as Lévi-Strauss suggests, this girl in a way stands for the grandmother: the grandmother's excessive resentment of the young man causes her to emit corrupt vapours from her anus, while the sister's excessive passion for eating fish causes her to emit corrupt vapours from her mouth. Moreover the grandmother commits a kind of reverse incest, and sexual greed is closely allied, in the greedy-girl set, with ordinary greed. Here the tree does not itself produce excrement or corruption, and so water; rather the leaving of the child in the tree is a means towards its mother approaching the river, and therefore stuffing herself with fish and producing corruption. Undoubtedly the role of the tree has been somewhat distorted in this version; but it is still associated, although by inversion and less directly, with corruption, or rather with its transformation into cultural (or in this case anti-cultural) water.

Up to this point I have been speculating in typically Lévi-Straussian terms—suggesting an analysis somewhat different from his, yet dependent on a free assumption of significant transformations. Like him, too, I have used content as well as structure, and have assumed certain symbolical values (for example bird suggests 'high', excrement suggests 'corruption'). It seems to me, however, that the 'meaning' of the myth is to be found, not in any algebra of structural relationships, but quite explicitly in its *contents*, seen in terms, no doubt, of certain significant relationships that have analogies at different levels. This small group of myths is obviously concerned with family relationships, in particular with the young man who clings for too long to the womenfolk and resists initiation into the world of men, and with the excessive reaction against him (and the women) by the father; also with certain specific aetiologies and, most persistently and curiously of all, with the fact of corruption and the role of excrement and decay. Doubtless there were tensions between women and men in a matrilineal and matrilocal society, and especially between women and youths at the point where the latter were about to leave the womenfolk and live in the men's hut. The substitution of a quarrel between a man and his young brother-in-law in M_7 merely broadens the general theme, which may also include counter-tensions when a young man sets up house with his wife's lineage on marriage. But how does this bear on the prominent and persistent theme of excrement or decay?

Here is a simplified matrix of the group: social and inter-sexual tension caused by puberty, initiation and matrilocality leads to the 'disjunction' of the hero, or isolation from his normal locale and/or family connexions. This isolation is accompanied by his involvement with excrement and the process of natural corruption. The restitution of excremental norms leads to the production of, or his beneficial association with, cultural water (or cultural fire in M_7). Therefore social excess on the side of nature is associated with excrement and natural decay; but this kind of decay is itself associated with (sweet) water and the uses of culture, and the balance is restored. Therefore corruption is a mediator between nature and culture, and natural decay (for example in stagnant marshes, in the fermentation of honey or manioc and water, or in the human and animal process of digestion and excretion) is therefore acceptable—but not in excess, as used by the grandmother or the greedy sister in M_5. Indeed it is necessary and inevitable, as is shown by the loss of the youth's fundament, and consequently of his powers of absorbing food, in M_1; it is a necessary mediation between man's animal or natural aspect and his civilized or cultural aspect. Maladjustment of the social balance causes a counterbalancing excess of his natural functions; yet these natural functions are themselves allied with cultural uses, since corruption is the natural analogue to cooking, and is also associated with (sweet) water, which has cultural associations—especially because it is where spirits dwell. One might go further and suggest that the jaguar's human wife in M_7, and the fact that in many Indian myths vultures have sexual relations with girls, imply a comparison between sexual relations and excremental and natural decay. Sex, the conjunction of humans like animals, is associated with corrupt discharges; but these, which like digestion and excretion reproduce rotting in nature, are acceptable and even necessary as part of culture, since natural corruption is paralleled by cultural cooking.

This interpretation is still very Lévi-Straussian in aspect, and relies on many of his procedures. Yet it is not exactly his interpretation, in fact it is a much simpler one which openly accepts content (sometimes interpreted symbolically) as equally significant with structure. The emphasis of the interpretation is placed on the most striking and persistent overt themes of the myths, namely inter-sexual stress, excrement and corruption, and the consequent establishment of cultural benefits. In a sense the interpretation accords with Lévi-Strauss's dictum that 'the purpose of myth is to provide a logical model capable of overcoming a contradiction';[36] the contradiction implied by the opposing tensions of the men's and women's world, and their respective needs,

36 *SA*, 229.

is palliated (rather than overcome) by the observation in mythical terms that apparently harmful excess in the direction of nature, provided it does not go too far, is counterbalanced by a beneficial excess in the direction of culture. This last excess is presented as an episode in the past, and it is hard to see how it could be represented in ordinary life; but perhaps the provision of the mythical model is enough.

5: Some desirable modifications

If the interpretation of these four myths still seems rather unsatisfactory, Lévi-Strauss would say (I conjecture) that this is because they have been treated as a closed group and not seen in relation to many others that reinforce their structure at different points; and also because the element of structure has been degraded too far in relation to that of content. Yet I feel that his own interpretations, or rather his understanding of what is happening in the process of telling and developing myths like these, are too imprecise and too inconsistent in their formulation to be acceptable. Let me recapitulate the ways in which I have departed from his methods. First, I have laid no stress on his theory that the final significance of myths is that they reflect something about the working of the human mind. Secondly, I have abandoned his theory that every detail in a myth has significance and must be worked into the analysis of its structure. I am sure that theory is wrong, because Lévi-Strauss thereby totally (and presumably deliberately) disregards the facts and circumstances of story-telling, or what is commonly known as oral literature—of which myths in a non-literate society must form a part. Every time a poem or a tale is sung or recited, unless there is a written version—or in rare cases an oral one so sacrosanct that it is known virtually by heart—its form is slightly altered. That is a generalization derived chiefly from the study of the oral heroic epic and from the Serbo-Croatian information provided, sometimes in a rather inflexible form, by A. B. Lord on the basis of his work with Milman Parry.[37] But it is a generalization that seems valid wherever it can be checked among non-literate societies, whether primitive or not, and one which seems to accord with several distinct human capacities and limitations.

[37] A. B. Lord, *The Singer of Tales* (Cambridge, Mass., 1960). For a summary account see my *Homer and the Epic* (Cambridge, Eng., 1965), ch. 2.

If, then, myths are traditional tales, then their telling is subject to the rules of all traditional tales: they will be varied in some degree on virtually every occasion of telling, and the variations will be determined by the whim, the ambition or the particular thematic repertoire of the individual teller, as well as by the receptivity and special requirements of the particular audience. Themes will be suppressed, added, transposed, or replaced by other apparently equivalent themes. Admittedly these changes will often be minor, and they will not utterly transform the appearance and possible implication of a myth over a length of time—at least in many societies, where the oral tradition is fairly strict, they will not do so. Yet any version of a myth that is collected and recorded by a literate observer, that is 'fixed' once and for all and then becomes an object of theoretical study by a Lévi-Strauss, is likely to have certain details, gaps or excrescences which depend, not on the essential structure of this myth at all, but on the habits and interests of some obscure individual, a particular singer or teller. Admittedly his alterations on any one occasion will be in some degree consonant with the content and arrangement of the myth as he has heard and told it before. But they will not necessarily be completely harmonious with the underlying structure, especially if that structure is, as Lévi-Strauss claims, a highly abstract affair of which most myth-tellers are largely unconscious. Indeed any observation of story-tellers or oral poets in action, or any study of first-hand reports of their methods, reveals that some of them can be quite careless over matters of inner consistency and relevance. I am convinced that the tellers of myths, who are after all story-tellers, are no exception, and that many individual recitals of a myth will include illogicalities or make omissions that affect its over-all structure; just as any scholar or exegete is liable to distort that structure in the process of offering personal and learned interpretations. I have said before, and I repeat now after this fuller statement of my reasons, that I find Lévi-Strauss's theory, especially as accentuated by Leach, that the structure of a myth necessarily maintains itself through all vicissitudes, that 'a myth is made up of all its variants', quite fantastic. It depends, presumably, not on any ignorance on the part of these scholars of the habits of non-literate story-tellers (which they have both observed), but in Lévi-Strauss's case on the idea that the structure of all myths is identical with that of the human mind, which is invariable, and in Leach's case on an over-elaborate comparison with communications-theory. I prefer to approach the general problem from empirical observation of the behaviour of story-tellers rather than from *a priori* convictions about the mode of operation of human minds, about which it is hardly necessary to say that we know very little; or about the transmission of radio messages, which are in important respects quite distinct from myths.

Lévi-Strauss's rule that every detail of a myth has to be taken into account leads him to overlook other ways in which the narrative aspect of myths controls, or encroaches on, any assumed structural meaning. Thus he rejects the possibility that an apparent oddity in a myth may be due to the accidental conflation of two versions. That, he says, would be to make light of 'an absolute rule of structural analysis: a myth is not subject to discussion, it must always be accepted *as it is*'. If a narrator assembles into one myth episodes otherwise found in different ones, that is because 'there exists between these episodes a link which it is incumbent on us to discover, and which is essential to the interpretation of each'.[38] By 'link' here Lévi-Strauss does not mean a narrative link, but a structural one; in other words, he is prepared to exclude (for example) one simple form of narration in which essentially disparate adventures are attached paratactically, one after the other, to a specific hero. Yet many myths, including a few Brazilian ones, have every appearance of being formed in this way.[39] Clearly, in this form of composition, one adventure or another may be added or omitted from time to time, and the method leaves a great deal of flexibility to the narrator. Yet the only structural link between episodes might be that they are all held to be compatible with, or roughly suitable for, the particular subject—a particular hero, perhaps. That is not sufficient to make the details of each episode structurally significant to the whole in the way suggested by Lévi-Strauss; which confirms my belief that he should have second thoughts about excluding the rules of story-telling from the study of those traditional stories that we call myths. If the next volume of *Mythologiques*, to appear probably in 1971, is really to be called *Du Mythe au roman*, then the distortion may be corrected there—although I am not hopeful.

[38] *MC*, 101 f.

[39] Certain paratactic myths ('récits à tiroirs', *OMT*, 164, cf. 26) form a closed system, but naturally many do not.

In short, one should be prepared to find that the following parts of a myth may contribute little or nothing to its underlying meaning or structure:

(i) Realistic details drawn from the life of the society to which the myth belongs—some such details will be extremely significant, others not at all. Thus climbing trees and cliffs to find parrots' or bees' nests is part of everyday life for the Bororo Indians, and strandings of tiresome male relatives are naturally put into that kind of context. Lévi-Strauss finds it significant that in M_1 the youth kills the lizards with an improvised bow and arrow, and that the jaguar in M_7 is carrying a bow and arrows when he happens to pass by; but is the relevant fact rather that the bow is the natural weapon of these Indians, and that whenever they wander outside the village they take one with them?

(ii) Common narrative motifs, or what we have elsewhere called folktale motifs, are likely to be inserted almost automatically. So the father in M_1 finds his wife's assailant by a trick or device twice repeated; he then sends his son to fetch three different kinds of object from dangerous surroundings, just as Perseus, Heracles or Jason is despatched on adventures that are planned to lead him to his death; the son is helped by three different kinds of bird—and so on.

(iii) Transformations of human beings into animals or birds are not necessarily significant, at least among peoples whose myths are mostly set in a time when men and animals were not yet rigidly distinguished. In the fullest version of M_1 the young man adopts the form of a lizard in order to spy out the land when he returns to his grandmother. There might conceivably be some significance in the choice of a lizard, since lizards were so strongly involved in the earlier episode of the vultures; but Lévi-Strauss makes nothing of this (although on his principles he should), and I think he is right: changing into a bird or animal was so common a means of disguise in these myths that any one transformation, unless it is emphasized or consistently repeated in several different versions, is unlikely to be significant.

(iv) Finally, the simplest type of aetiology often seems to be a mere appendage to a myth. This is especially obvious with Melanesian, Polynesian and Australian instances, where geographical aetiologies ('that is why there is that cave over there') are often appended to a story that seems otherwise irrelevant to that particular natural feature. The story of Guruwelin mentioned on pp. 26f. does not really explain why yams in that part of Australia grow so deep. It seems as though aetiology is one natural domain of myth, and that superficial or trivial *aitia* are thrown in by the handful—whereas an essential *aition* often lies concealed and is not so brashly identified. In the Waux variant of the Asdiwal myth considered earlier (pp. 53–7), Waux's wife is turned into flint at the bottom of the mountain when she bursts through eating too much fat. Yet the episode of her gluttony certainly has a significance beyond the aetiology of flints in a particular valley, and it is possible that the detail about those particular flints is an accretion or afterthought, and not one that would be significant for the total structure of the myth.

6: The limits of the structural approach

I have now listed some Lévi-Straussian theories that I reject in the assessment of these tribal myths, and identified some narrative properties that in many cases will be irrelevant to the determination of a myth's significant structure. We are now in a better position to reconsider two basic questions: Is 'structuralism' either significant or useful in the study of myths? and Has the particular structure that Lévi-Strauss professes to find in all myths, namely one that offers a series of mediations of contradictions, any validity?

The concept of structuralism as a special doctrine has been questioned more than once in its short history; recently, and with considerable success, by W. G. Runciman in his article 'What is Structuralism?'[40] Runciman asks whether 'structure' in this context really means more than 'system'. In relation to social structure as a whole that is a pertinent enquiry. For the special applicability of structuralism to myth it is less relevant, since what we primarily want to know about myths is whether they do represent a system, or structure, or whatever we may choose to call it. With society as a whole we know that a system or systems are involved, and the chief question is what kind of system it is. In relation to myth, however, according to Runciman 'the essence of "structuralist" method seems to lie in the construction of deliberately abstract models by the artificial breaking-down of the object under study and its subsequent reconstitution in terms of

[40] *The British Journal of Sociology*, 20, 1969, 253–65.

essentially relational properties'; and he wonders whether this is different from scientific method in general. Even if it were not, we perhaps should not mind, since any justification of a 'science of mythology', the application of scientific method in any relevant guise, would be welcome; but Runciman goes on to cast doubt on whether Lévi-Strauss really does dispense with content and the question of motive (what purpose if any a myth was created to fulfil)—that is, whether its structure is, after all, particularly significant. Roughly this coincides with the doubts expressed by Mary Douglas, which, as has been seen, I to a large extent share. All the same, the structuralist approach to myth, even if it cannot constitute the kind of scientific approach that Lévi-Strauss claims for it, is always worth adopting *among other approaches*. Attention to a myth's structure will sometimes bring palpable rewards, as I hope to show with certain Mesopotamian and even one or two Greek myths.

The second question can be rephrased as follows: Is it indeed the purpose of all myths (or even of those treated by Lévi-Strauss) to construct a model by which contradictions in men's view of the world can be mediated? For Runciman this question lay outside his immediate concern with structuralism, but he nevertheless observed that the view that 'human thought is essentially binary, and that this fact can in turn be related to the binary neurophysiological mechanisms operating in the brain...is neither a necessary nor, for that matter, a very significant assumption'. It is, I believe, questionable whether the brain always or for the most part works (as Leach at least supposes) like a binary computer; and such Hegelian processes as Lévi-Strauss sees operating in myths could be due to other causes. Admittedly, binary analysis is one obvious mode of thought, and it is doubtless encouraged among peoples of an anthropomorphizing and exogamous bias by their application of left and right, up and down, male and female, we and they, as categories into which many aspects of experience can be conveniently sorted.[41]

[41] One may cite the importance of opposites in early Greek philosophy, recently stressed by G. E. R. Lloyd in his *Polarity and Analogy* (Cambridge, 1966). They constitute only one type of analysis, although a prominent one (analogy is another, as Lloyd points out); and in any event they would not imply that Greek myths, in their earlier and pre-literary forms, must all have been concerned with polarizations and subsequent mediations, or indeed that they contained any kind of analysis or synthesis whatever.

The system of myths uncovered by Lévi-Strauss certainly reflects some tendency to binary analysis (as one might particularly expect with tribes organized on a moiety principle), although he equally certainly exaggerates it—as in some of his 'up and down' polarizations and in such curious contentions as that the ears must be the orifices that represent the polar opposite to the anus, since they are the nearest to being 'above' and 'in front' as opposed to 'below' and 'behind'. . .It is also a system that reflects a continuous concern with the problems of kinship and communal living, as well as with methods of food-production and hunting and the limits and determinants of the seasons of the year. Some of these problems, but not all, can be posed in the form of polar alternatives. Two that can, and are of broad scope and intense interest in themselves, are those concerning life and death and nature and culture; and one of Lévi-Strauss's most brilliant successes is to have shown the dominant position of the second of these pairs in the thought and imagination of the central Brazilian Indians and their neighbours. Many, perhaps most, of their myths are concerned directly or indirectly with this problem, and Lévi-Strauss has shown conclusively that the contrast between the raw and the cooked is the model through which the problem is most commonly stated, and fire, cooking and natural processes of corruption the means by which it is elucidated.

The awareness of the contrast, and often the apparent contradiction, between village and jungle, between men's ways and animals' ways, between nature's mode of action and the human mode, reinforces the tendency imposed by physiological and social dualities to see things in terms of polar extremes and the tensions between them. Yet it is important to remember that more specific concerns (with hunting, food-production, the seasons), even where they can be subsumed under the nature–culture contrast, are not in themselves so susceptible to simple binary analysis; indeed the same is so even with certain concerns about social life, which cannot all be reduced to tensions between ego's group and the rest, or between mother's line and father's line, and so on. How far they can be so reduced in any one culture depends on the stress laid on binary divisions in its social rules on the one hand, and in its myths and traditions on the other. My own impression of the social and mythical structures of the South American Indians is that binary divisions are fairly prominent but by no means universal. In maintaining that it is the function of all their myths (or even of all those that he takes into account) to set up a model capable of overcoming a tension between polar extremes, Lévi-Strauss exceeds the evidence; or rather he merely shows that it is susceptible to one kind of analysis, without showing that much of it would not also be susceptible to another.

Mediation, moreover, is something that follows from the application to a binary system of the general assumption that myths attempt to resolve problems; since resolving problems of contradiction means either revealing one or both poles as false (that is, the original analysis is quite wrong—a kind of demonstration that is hardly a likely role for myth), or offering a mediation or conciliation between the two poles. The result is that, of the two assumptions being made (that all mythical thought reflects polar analysis, and that it is problem-solving in some sense), the first has already been found exaggerated, and the second is shown to be so by the consideration of many undoubted myths, from other cultures, whose intentions are clearly distinct, whether they be charter myths or ritual myths or whatever. The South American myths seem unusually inclined in the direction of reflecting or solving problems—but that is partly because Lévi-Strauss has omitted from his survey certain myths whose function seems different, for example to record and confirm an institution or a rite.

One is inclined to ask at this point a question that has wider implications. Can the Bororo Indians really have derived much comfort, conscious or otherwise, on occasions when they were worried about the passage of young male initiates from the womenfolk to the menfolk, from retelling the myth of the young man who was half-eaten by vultures, or from reflecting on the ambivalent status of human excrement? That depends among other factors on one's assessment of the working of the unconscious mind. And yet the intensive interest applied by people at the tribal level to subjects like excrement, and the wide range of partial and complete analogies that are discovered for it, may imply that the observation that corruption is nature's way of cooking could be, not only intellectually suggestive, but also emotionally rewarding. That is mere psychological speculation, subject to the Evans-Pritchard 'If I were a horse' critique mentioned on p. 30, and I carry it no further. In any case it is doubtful whether enquiries of this kind are really justified, at least in relation to many of the myths studied by Lévi-Strauss and in the light of the incontrovertible successes (never mind the failures and exaggerations for the moment) of his analyses. If the group of myths about the boy and the excrement or corruption is not concerned with relating, and so palliating, certain contradictions between nature and culture, then what is it about? One cannot réply that it is 'about' nothing except a story, since if it were we should not find the extraordinary persistence of inconspicuous themes and relationships from variant to variant, neither should we find systems of transformations maintaining themselves against all the canons of mere narrative. I have argued that narrative rules are relevant, and that some of the transformations are structurally insignificant; my own analysis of the myths would be less complete, less severe and less structural than Lévi-Strauss's; and yet in its broad lines his approach is the only one that accounts for most of the Brazilian evidence—that is, for themes behaving as they do in different variants, and maintaining themselves in some cases in ways inexplicable by the ordinary tendencies of story-telling. In short, the structural approach to *these* myths is meaningful and helpful, although it should not be exaggerated. Content does count, whatever Lévi-Strauss professes, and many aspects of the myths are determined by the plain rules of narrative and drama —which are not necessarily those of a supposedly polarizing *esprit*.

To end this chapter, I return to a question posed near its beginning: whether the Lévi-Strauss type of structural analysis is only valid (in so far as it is valid at all) for myths of tribal, 'primitive', or 'totemistic' societies. Paul Ricoeur argued that this is so; that in such societies 'arrangements matter more than contents, and thought is indeed *bricolage*'.[42] *Bricolage* is an untranslatable term introduced by Lévi-Strauss in *La Pensée sauvage* as a metaphor for the mode of savage thought. It means something like 'improvising out of random materials'; the *bricoleur* is the handyman who makes things out of what lie ready for use, whether or not they are the best conceivable materials. In his turn Lévi-Strauss derived the idea from Franz Boas, who wrote of mythological universes as 'destined to be dismantled as soon as assembled, for other universes to grow out of their fragments'. The myth-maker, according to Lévi-Strauss, allows the structure of his mind, already reproduced in the structure of society, to find reflexion in

---

42 'Structure et herméneutique', *Esprit*, N.S. xi, 1963, 607.

the structure or interrelationships of the symbols that he puts together in a myth. The value of the symbols themselves is indifferent; what matters is the relation they bear to each other. It is in this way that he works like a handyman, creating a structure out of what comes to hand. It is just this emphasis on matters of arrangement, and an indifference to the suitability of the things arranged, that Ricoeur finds in savage societies and not in developed ones. The result is that the thought of such people 'is precisely that which has most affinity with structuralism'.[43]

Lévi-Strauss could hardly deny this, since it is merely drawing out an implication of his own analysis in *La Pensée sauvage*. In the same volume of *Esprit* he had his opportunity to reply, and evidently could not put forward any compelling defence.[44] At one point he came perilously close to claiming that myths which do not accord with his idea of structure are not true myths. At another he attempted to discount Semitic myths on the ground that they have been subjected to too many intellectual restatements; that one would have to begin by discovering their 'archaic and mythological residue'.[45] Finally he suggested that the structuralist interpretation is best applicable to non-western-type societies precisely because the western observer is not personally involved, can stand outside them and view them objectively—an argument that Ricoeur justifiably found rather weak.

Lévi-Strauss has undoubtedly shown in *La Pensée sauvage* that tribal societies employ a quite different style of logic from that of developed western societies, including those of the Bronze Age. The minute categorizing of animal and plant species according to principles that are either invisible or wilful to the western mind, and the use of those categories for the organization of abstract thought on such subjects as social arrangement, give a quite distinct flavour to 'savage thought', one that moreover bears no resemblance to the old 'pre-logical' and almost half-witted quality ascribed at one stage by Lévy-Bruhl and his followers to the unfortunate 'primitive'. It seems *a priori* probable, therefore, that the operations carried on below the surface of the

[43] *Op. cit.*, 608.

[44] 'Réponses à quelques questions', *Esprit*, N.S. xi, 1963, 630 ff.

[45] *Op. cit.*, 632. This caused Edmund Leach to write his fascinating article on 'The Legitimacy of Solomon', *AES*, vii, 1966, 58 ff., in which he claims to find a structural basis, and a kind of mediation, even in the versions of the surviving hermeneutic tradition of the Old Testament. The article is now reprinted: see p. ix.

myths of such cultures will often differ from those implicit in myths elaborated in the context of developed and non-totemistic societies. It is hard to see, therefore, why Lévi-Strauss persists in his theory that *all* myths mediate contradictions. I have suggested that that is an overrated function even among primitive myths; to this must be added the inability of Lévi-Strauss himself to make any serious defence against Ricoeur's objection. It must be admitted that he had not at that time, and still has not, devoted any serious analytical effort to myths of western type.[46]

Further work and further thought will be needed before a final and credible conclusion can be achieved on these matters.[47] In the meantime it looks as though Lévi-Strauss's theory, not least in its conception of archetypal mind, is as misleading as every other universalizing theory of myths—that they all explain rituals, that they are all nature-allegories, and the rest. What Lévi-Strauss has succeeded in doing is to demonstrate that some myths in some cultures can have a kind of explanatory function that had not previously been suspected. From now on it will always be necessary to consider the possibility that any myth, even in the western tradition, may turn out to provide a model for mediating a contradiction, in terms of structure as well as content—along, of course, with other possibilities, such as that it is a charter myth, or is concerned with fertility and the seasons, or with the representation of fears and beliefs about the world of the dead, or with the nature and function of gods, or with the evaluation of different occupations, materials, or methods of food-production. Sometimes a myth will fulfil several of these functions at once, as well as offering explanations of origin and presenting a story which, partly because of its fantastic or supernatural elements, will have a special appeal to the imagination. The important thing for the modern student of myth, in my opinion, is to be prepared to find any or all of these properties in the myths of any culture; and not to apply generalizing theories *a priori* to a category of human expression and imagination that is likely, after all, to be a broad one.

[46] In this context it is as well to remember that Lévi-Strauss's interesting but erratic analysis of the Oedipus myth in *SA*, 213–17, is explicitly offered simply as an illustration of a technique. I prefer to say no more about it.

[47] E. R. Leach has now published a short book, *Lévi-Strauss* (Fontana, London, 1970), which is valuable for the question of what is structuralism but surprisingly unhelpful over the theory of myth.

III

The Nature of
Myths in Ancient
Mesopotamia

1: Introduction

The literature of ancient Mesopotamia is an enthralling and neglected subject, and it possesses a special relevance to Greek myths and the understanding of myth in general. Influence on Greece from the Near East extends far beyond the striking resemblances to which most critics confine themselves, mainly those between Kumarbi and Kronos and Ullikummi and Typhoeus. These happen to involve Hurrian myths from northern Syria and Asia Minor, but of all Near-Eastern myths it is the Mesopotamian that are the richest and most varied and, indeed, the source of most of the others. They also present special difficulties. Even the verbal meaning, especially of the Sumerian texts, is often in dispute; the language is hard, and the cuneiform tablets are usually damaged or incomplete. For the best-known and most important tales, however, the area of agreement between experts is sufficient to make provisional interpretations and conclusions worth while. The two main protagonists in the interpretation of Mesopotamian myths, Samuel Noah Kramer and Thorkild Jacobsen, have not felt that generalizing on the basis of such materials is unjustified. The debate between them, so far as it went, was fruitful; but discussion has been too closely confined to these two figures.

It appears that many Sumerologists and Assyriologists are deterred from working on the literature and the ideas behind it by

the feeling that materials at present unpublished might frustrate
their efforts and expose them to professionally damaging accusa-
tions of prematurity. Judging by past experience, one is likely to be
severely and even unjustly mauled in the event of even minor
error.[1] I believe this to be a risk that someone outside the field
should be prepared to take. Wider discussion of this fascinating
literature can only help to speed, one way or another, the painfully
slow publication, even the preliminary examination, of the
thousands of still undeciphered tablets lying around in the base-
ments of museums.

Much of what I have said applies primarily to Sumerian texts,
but the Akkadian material has fared little better in recent years.
After a spate of publication on the Epic of Gilgamesh in the 1920s
and 1930s, little has been done to elucidate the meaning and
mythical implications of this great composite poem. Admittedly
we now have a translation that inspires confidence and is of special
value to amateurs like myself.[2] Indeed some Assyriologists have
been as helpful in the publication of translations and popular discussions as others have been dilatory in attacking the real problems raised by the mythical texts themselves. Once again I
would like to affirm that this fascinating literary and mythological material from Mesopotamia should not be left aside by the
rest of the world until some impossibly remote time when there
are no more tablets left to publish and no more textual and
grammatical uncertainties to be resolved.

The most significant difference between texts recorded in
Sumerian (a non-Semitic language of uncertain type) and Akkadian (which is Semitic) is their date. The attempt to distinguish a
Sumerian from an Akkadian *culture* is probably abortive, since
there were Semitic-speaking people living in the river-valleys of
Sumer as early as the beginning of the third millennium B.C., and
Sumerian continued as the learned and written language long
after the Semitic-speaking peoples of Akkad and Babylon had
gained the political ascendancy of the Mesopotamian world. Most
of the surviving myths in Sumerian were written down, on the
tablets we possess, as early as about 1700 B.C., but can be shown on
linguistic and other grounds to have originated by about 2300 B.C.
Many of the surviving Akkadian myths, on the other hand, are

[1] Cf. Joseph Fontenrose, *AJA*, 1962, 189 ff.
[2] By E. A. Speiser in *ANET²*, 72 ff.

known primarily from Neo-Assyrian tablets recovered from the library of Ashurbanipal in seventh-century B.C. Nineveh, but can be shown to go back to the Old Babylonian era before the middle of the second millennium. Some contain still earlier material.

The difference in date between myths recorded in Sumerian and those in Akkadian (to which I shall refer henceforth simply as Sumerian and Akkadian myths) is important; for the whole outlook of the Mesopotamian cities changed radically between 2300 and 1700 B.C. The main political factors were first the rise of the central and northern cities, especially Babylon, and the relative decline of the cities of Sumer (which was retained as the name of the southern parts of the Tigris–Euphrates valley), and secondly the substitution, for a loose nexus of independent city-states, of a national state under the successive hegemonies of Babylon, Kish, Akkad (Agade), and Ur. Both before and after these changes each city had its own god, whose main temple was there and who owned and managed the land and its people through his steward the king. Some of the Sumerian myths reflect the struggles between neighbouring cities through their gods. In a light-hearted tale Inanna managed to make Enki drunk, then removed the great Ordinances, usually manipulated in favour of Enki's city of Eridu, to her own temple at Uruk. And in the Akkadian era the Babylonian Epic of Creation (sometimes called the *Enuma Elish* after its opening words) has the principal purpose of showing how Marduk, the local god of Babylon, was granted the leadership of all the gods by Anu, Enlil, Enki, and the rest, how he ordered the whole universe, and how his great temple, the Esagila, was built for him at Babylon, which now controlled all the other cities and so had to possess a new kind of supreme god.

Thus in spite of a strongly conservative streak in Mesopotamian culture, and the ability of its highly organized literate tradition to preserve certain versions unchanged for a thousand years or more, many of the myths vary in the attitudes they reflect and the purposes they seem to fulfil. This is one factor that makes the study of these poems valuable for the assessment of myth as a whole. It provides, for example, small support for the view that the underlying message of a myth inevitably maintains itself through chronological variations and changes in historical background.[3]

[3] Cf. E. R. Leach, *AES*, VII, 1966, 60–7, 98–101, and p. 50 above.

The question of the literary status of Mesopotamian myths must be broached without delay; for if the definition of myth includes the proposition that it is a traditional tale, there must be an initial doubt whether some of the Sumerian and Akkadian tales really qualify as myths at all. They are known to us, most of them as poetry, in a literate form that is much weaker than that of the Homeric poems, for example, in its internal indications of an underlying oral basis. At the same time, as Kramer puts it, 'A key figure in the growth and development of Sumerian literature was the *nar* or minstrel, who is mentioned sometimes side by side with the *dubsar*, or scribe, in the hymns'.[4] Ultimately in such conditions one's judgement must be subjective, although it should be governed as far as possible both by comparisons with other cultures and by the careful assessment of such historical information as exists. Certain obvious distinctions can be drawn. The Neo-Assyrian tablets from Nineveh, for example, have plainly been copied and re-copied in a fully literate tradition for many centuries, and the scribal colophons often report that a fresh copy is being made. In the transmission of some of the Gilgamesh stories the process is different: not only is there a change of language from Sumerian to Akkadian, so that the accuracy of exact copying would in any event be modified, but there is also a marked alteration of emphasis and detail. It is theoretically possible that the innovations of the Akkadian versions are entirely the result of conscious literary effort, nothing to do with an oral tradition. Yet one can usually distinguish scholarly elaborations. Many of the details of the *Enuma Elish*, and in particular the elaborate listing of Marduk's fifty titles, are undoubtedly learned, literate and un-traditional or at least non-oral in character. But most of the apparently 'new' themes in the developed Epic of Gilgamesh look just like the old—like traditional, oral themes of myth or folktale that have just been shifted from one literary formulation into another. All in all, considering the type of society in which these versions flourished and the wide distribution of a relatively small number of tales over the whole of the Near East, far beyond Mesopotamia itself, it seems likely that there was a broadly based popular tradition of myths, from which the literate and poetical versions we know derived their persistent strength and their capacity for apparently spontaneous variation.

[4] S. N. Kramer, *The Sumerians* (Chicago, 1963), 170.

In considering the Sumerian material it will be helpful to remain aware of the very different attitudes maintained by its two chief exponents in recent years. Samuel Noah Kramer adopts a rather extreme commonsense approach; he thinks that myth is merely a symbolical or allegorical way of expressing rational observations or truths—so that, for example, the myths about the early inter-relations of Anu, Enlil and Enki can be translated directly into physical language: sky and waters were separated by air, and so on. Thorkild Jacobsen, in his long review of Kramer's little book *Sumerian Mythology* (Philadelphia, 1944),[5] objected that there is much more to the interpretation of myth than the removal of what Kramer has termed 'the theological cloak and polytheistic trappings'.[6] These 'trappings', according to Jacobsen—and here I would certainly agree—are part of the whole conceptual apparatus, and it is wrong to think that one can simply rationalize mythical terms by substituting, for example, 'combustion' for 'god-fire'.[7] Kramer defended his position by arguing that what we are confronted with in the surviving form of these myths are the highly literate versions of scribal schools, in which there is a great deal of conscious philosophizing in picturesque terms.[8] That, again, seems to me to be an exaggeration of the position; but in any event it does not meet Jacobsen's objections, or remove the impression that Kramer sees myth as simple allegory: the expression of one set of terms by means of another, each element of which can be decoded into the original by the consistent application of systematic rules.

Jacobsen, on the other hand, distinguishes clearly between what he calls the 'mythological' interpretation of myths and the 'human and psychological' interpretation; by which he means to separate the allegorical interpretation of content from the comprehension of feelings that led to the expression of that content in its mythical form.[9] The real difficulty for modern critics, he thinks, lies in fusing the two kinds of interpretation: in understanding, by a process of sympathy, this content in this form. In the last resort Jacobsen, like Kramer, accepts that myth is in a sense allegorical; but he considers that it contains some additional factor, some emotional overtone, that we have to appreciate before we can

---

[5] *JNES*, v, 1946, 128 ff.   [6] Kramer, *Sumerian Mythology*, 73.
[7] *JNES*, v, 1946, 150 f.   [8] *JCS*, ii, 1948, 39 ff., esp. 40–53.
[9] *JNES*, xii, 1953, 169 f.

understand the content. This idea is slightly preferable to the bald rationalism of Kramer's original position, but it is still unsatisfactory. And yet it is difficult to avoid *something like* Jacobsen's model of a particular and theoretically discoverable content of meaning encased in, or permeated by, a particular set of emotions. Even in Lévi-Strauss's structuralist view of myth, according to which the relations between mythical symbols correspond in some sense with relations between people, institutions, and natural and cultural objects in the real world, there is a degree of allegory —that is, on the assumption that there is a 'privileged' level of meaning. Yet Jacobsen's position, in spite of the perceptiveness of his theory of the emotional aspect of myth, is shown by his specific interpretations to be too simple.

Not only does Jacobsen see Sumerian myths as being in a sense allegorical, but he also sees the allegory as being primarily of one kind; for what these myths seem to him to express are the facts and processes of nature. Superficially he bears some resemblance to a nineteenth-century nature-myth addict of the Max Müller kind; he is actually, of course, very different. His idea, itself Tylorian in ancestry, is that by representing the forces of nature as anthropomorphic gods, and telling stories about their mutual relations in terms of human psychology, the Sumerians were able to understand and accept the workings of the natural world in a manner that would have been impossible on a purely logical and descriptive basis. For some of the general characteristics of elemental gods like Enki he has brilliantly proved his case. His account of the devious ways of water as it is coaxed through the irrigation channels, and the manner in which it sinks into the thirsty earth, enables even us to understand a good deal about the conception of Enki as water-god and god of wisdom, and about his relation to fertility.[10] Yet Jacobsen surely carries this kind of intuition too far when he attempts to interpret almost every motif as though it referred to some part of nature, and almost every myth as though its purpose were to represent, in indirect terms, some kind of natural event, usually a seasonal one. This will become clear, I believe, in the analysis to be undertaken shortly. And yet I do not

[10] H. and H. A. Frankfort, J. A. Wilson, and Thorkild Jacobsen, *The Intellectual Adventure of Ancient Man* (Chicago, 1946), 146 f. (= *BP*, 159 f.). The title of the English edition of this book is *Before Philosophy* (Penguin Books, 1949). Both sets of page-references will be given, i.e. as *IA* and *BP*.

want to give the impression that the Sumerian gods were not connected with nature, or that their myths were not often concerned with irrigation, fertility, the development of farming or herding, and so on. That Anu is the sky and Enlil the atmosphere, whatever else they may be, is beyond dispute, just as it is beyond question that Zeus or Dyaus is a sky-god in origin. Raffaele Pettazzoni has demonstrated at length that the chief deity of most races tends to be a weather-god who represents sky or rain, wind or thunder; for Nilotic peoples he is Jwok, sender of rain, wind or thunder (among the Shilluk), or Kot, wind as well as rain (among the Nuer).[11] These are power-gods, one might say—since the thunderstorm, for instance, is the manifestation of irresistible power; but other aspects of nature like the moon (so beloved of the defunct nature-myth school) are worshipped as creator-gods, as by the Haikat Indians of California.[12] There is nothing surprising in the Sumerian interest in the natural aspects of their chief gods, even if they carried it further (so far as we can tell) than other ancient peoples of the Mediterranean and Near East. Yet Jacobsen makes the interest appear even larger than it was.

2: Irrigation and fertility

Jacobsen's method, and to some extent the dispute between him and Kramer, are exemplified in the interpretation of the Sumerian myth of Ninurta and Asag. Asag is the underworld-demon whose name according to Jacobsen means 'crippler'. Kramer described him as 'the demon of sickness and disease', a fairly standard underworld figure.[13] Jacobsen, however, takes him to represent the cold of winter, whereas his opponent Ninurta, god of the south wind, symbolizes the powers of spring that overcome this cold.[14] A difficulty is that Asag lives in Kur, and this name is applied either to a mountain, or the mountains, on the one hand (from where the enemy, the snows of winter, come according to Jacobsen) or to the underworld on the other, an interpretation here supported by Kramer. What happens in the myth is that Ninurta is told by his weapon Sharur, by a common folktale motif, to attack Asag. He destroys the monster, but the waters of Kur

---

[11] *The All-Knowing God* (Eng. tr., London, 1956), 38.
[12] *Op. cit.*, 365.
[13] So e.g. in *Mythologies*, 105.   [14] *JNES*, v, 1946, 147.

rise up and in some way prevent the ordinary irrigation waters from reaching the fields. There is a famine, which Ninurta over-comes by setting a vast pile of rocks, described as a great wall in front of Sumer, over Kur, and so preventing the waters from rising any further. Then he directs the flood waters back into the Tigris; the canals and ditches are filled once more, fertility is restored. Ninurta's mother Ninmah, the earth-goddess, visits him to express her concern, and for her intrepidity in coming to the 'inimical land' she is made queen of the stone mound and named Ninhursag. This, together with the expression '*over* Kur' and the description of Kur as an 'inimical land', suggests that Kramer may be right in thinking of it as the underworld rather than (as Jacobsen believes) the mountains. Moreover Ninurta is a violent god, a war-god, and the south wind in Asiatic myths is not a gentle wind heralding spring, or a steady breeze holding back the floods, but a violent wind such as sank the boat of Adapa in an Akkadian tale to be considered in § 5.

If Jacobsen's allegory of the seasons is unconvincing, it remains a question what, if anything, the myth does signify. The great pile of stones, together with the reference to the collapse of the irri-gation system, suggests some sort of damming operation. But why over Kur? Perhaps the answer lies in this direction: that when the drainage ditches are neglected in Mesopotamia, water wells up and lies stagnant on the topsoil, so damaging the crops. It might therefore be envisaged as coming from the underworld—whose entrance, incidentally, is reached by way of a mountain in the Akkadian Epic of Gilgamesh. As for Ninurta, perhaps he appears just as a powerful war-deity rather than in his more specific role of the south wind; and the whole story of the stone heap might conceivably be occasioned, rather weakly, by a desire to explain the name of Ninurta's mother, Ninhursag—'she of the stone heap'.

Ninhursag appears once more, this time in her usual role as earth-goddess, in the most fascinating of all surviving Sumerian myths, 'Enki and Ninhursag'.[15] The action takes place, before the creation of man, in the paradise-land of Dilmun, imagined as lying to the south of Sumer, either at the mouth of the great rivers or in the Persian Gulf. Dilmun is 'clean' and 'bright', and that is somehow associated with Enki's lying with his wife Ninsi-

---

[15] Translated by Kramer in *ANET*², 38 ff.

killa, 'pure lady'—an epithet, probably of Ninhursag, that may explain the emphasis on Dilmun's purity. In spite of this purity and the absence of old age and death, Dilmun is still short of water. Ninsikilla asks Enki, the god of sweet water, to supply it, and he does so by calling on the sun- and moon-gods for help, as well as by making it come up from the earth. Then (or perhaps as part of this same water-supplying sequence) Enki impregnates Nintu, 'the mother of the land', who is definitely Ninhursag; she bears a daughter after nine days. Enki has forbidden anyone to walk in the marshes, but this young daughter, Ninmu, does so; Enki catches sight of her, crosses the river in his boat, and impregnates her. She too bears a daughter, Ninkurra, who also lurks around in the marshland with the inevitable consequences; her daughter is called Uttu. But now Nintu–Ninhursag decides to intervene; she tells Uttu to require that Enki bring her, out of the desert, cucumbers, grapes, and some other fruit. Enki irrigates the uncultivated places to the delight of an unnamed gardener, who gives him the fruit. Uttu receives it and now at last allows Enki to impregnate her. But along comes Ninhursag and removes Enki's seed from within Uttu—or so it seems from a fragmentary text; next we are told that eight different plants are growing, and it is probable that Ninhursag has placed Enki's seed within herself —in the earth—to make them grow. Enki catches sight of them and eats each in turn, apparently so that he may know their name and nature and decree their fate.[16] Ninhursag is infuriated; she curses Enki and withdraws from him 'the eye of life', so that he sickens. She disappears, and because of this and the water-god's illness there is a drought(?). The great gods are in despair (a common motif), but the fox says that he can bring Ninhursag back (another common motif, of folktale type) and does so. Ninhursag now seats the dying Enki in her vagina; Kramer misleadingly translates 'in' as 'near', although he identifies the literal sense in a footnote. Enki is diseased in eight different parts, presumably corresponding to the eight different plants he has so destructively eaten; and Ninhursag causes to be born eight deities, one to heal each part. The deities are a miscellaneous lot, chosen solely because their

[16] Kramer in *Mythologies*, 102 f., compares the eating of the fruit of the tree of knowledge by Adam and Eve in Genesis, and also associates Eve's birth from Adam's rib with Ninhursag's birth of a goddess, in what follows, to cure Enki's rib. Sumerian influence on the Biblical myth is not unlikely, but the implications of the two myths seem quite different.

names happen to resemble, superficially, those of the different diseased parts of the body. And so, with Ninhursag's assignment of functions to these deities, the myth ends.

What does it all mean? It presumably has some reference at a level beyond that of the simple narrative, which is too odd, repetitious and inconsequential to have survived simply as a good tale. Naturally it contains folktale motifs, but that is insignificant: they are the building-blocks of any narrative. One motive can be easily identified—the superficial etymologies and aetiologies of the minor deities at the end, and also, probably, of the name Ninsi-killa at the beginning. To the rest Jacobsen applies his allegorical and nature-myth type of interpretation, based on the clue pro-vided (as he thinks) by the names of the three girls Enki seduces. Unfortunately Ninmu, Ninkurra and Uttu are not altogether clear. The first means 'lady who brings forth' and is concerned with vegetation according to Kramer, or river-plants according to Jacobsen.[17] Ninkurra, 'lady of the mountain' or 'lady of the underworld', is associated with dyestuffs according to Jacobsen, stone-working according to Kramer; while Uttu is undoubtedly connected with weaving and is allotted this function by Enki in another myth described by Kramer (see p. 99 n. 23).

Jacobsen begins his analysis plausibly enough: Ninmu (whom he reads as Ninsar) is 'born of the marriage of soil, Ninhursaga, and water, Enki. But, as the waters of the yearly inundation in Mesopo-tamia recede and return to the river bed before vegetation comes up, so Enki does not stay to live with Ninhursaga as her husband but has already left her before the goddess of the plants is born. . . The goddess of the plants gives birth to a daughter representing—we would guess—the plant fibres used in the weaving of linen. Such fibres are obtained by soaking plants in water until the soft matter rots away and only the tough fibres remain. They are, therefore, in a sense the child of plants and water.'[18] Now it is quite plausible that the Ninhursag–Ninmu sequence symbolizes the recession of the flood waters and the subsequent growth of vegetation in the fertilized land; but the later stages suggested by Jacobsen are both more doubtful in themselves and raise greater difficulties in relation to the meaning of the Sumerian names. Ninkurra is the most obvious stumbling-block: even if a goddess connected with Kur were to be associated with dyes, which Kramer obviously

[17] ANET², 37; IA, 157 = BP, 171.   [18] IA, 157 = BP, 171.

does not accept, do dyes really belong to this process of vegetation? Some dyes come from plants, others from minerals mixed with water—but that is becoming very abstruse. According to Jacobsen 'this myth endeavours to trace a causal unity among many disparate phenomena';[19] but what would be the purpose of tracing a unity in terms of water between plants, dyestuffs, and weaving (which is in any case different in that it does not directly entail the use of water), when the unity of the process from flax, for example, to finished linen is obvious in any case? The argument should not be pressed too hard, since, as Lévi-Strauss has pointed out in *La Pensée sauvage*, in tribal societies all sorts of interlocking relationships are carefully established whose purpose is not immediately clear to western minds. Yet this is not noticeably characteristic of Mesopotamian myths. On the contrary, they seem to specialize in arbitrary links by means of trivial etymologies, as we have seen; and I would guess that the association between the three young goddesses is more likely to be of this kind than to represent a systematic allegorization of the type proposed by Jacobsen.

Nevertheless the first stage of his reconstruction, with plants born from the soil after the annual flooding, seems persuasive; and Enki's disappearance after being cursed by Ninhursag, since it is followed by drought, obviously represents, by a very direct transference of symbols, the drying of the soil either in summer (as Jacobsen thinks, and as would best accord with the annual-flooding idea) or on some special occasion in the past.

Yet such an explanation would entirely fail to take account of much of the action, and in particular of Enki's fetching of the fruits for Uttu, the removal of his seed from her, the eight plants that he swallows, the eight diseases he incurs, and the method by which he is healed. Jacobsen does not deal with these events, which in addition can only be partially explained by the aetiology of the eight deities. I would like to propose a different interpretation that takes the whole myth into account. Obviously its first part is concerned with irrigation in some form; and I wonder whether the impregnation of the successive young goddesses does not represent the steps by which (in an alternative and more graphic version of what is stated at the beginning, that Enki gave orders for fresh water to appear in Dilmun) Enki fills different parts of the river

---

[19] *IA*, 158 = *BP*, 172.

and its canal system. At verses 67 f. Enki 'causes his phallus to water the dikes, Causes his phallus to submerge the reeds' (in Kramer's supplement of a text that is not quite certain), and this action is associated with his impregnation of Nintu–Ninhursag. In other words, if the reading is correct, irrigation is here definitely associated with sexual activity. The further acts of impregnating Enki's daughter, grand-daughter and so on might well be simply a dramatic elaboration with some unknown etymological significance, rather than an attempt to represent new and specific stages in irrigation. Yet the case of Uttu brings us back to that theme: for Enki 'filled the uncultivated places with water' (verse 155) in order to grow the cucumbers, grapes and other fruits required by Uttu—in other words he was compelled to extend irrigation further afield, towards the desert (cucumbers and vines, incidentally, will grow in arid conditions with a little irrigation; 'apples', an improbable conjecture for the other fruit, will not). Moreover Enki's eventual impregnation of Uttu has special effects, for his seed seems to be removed from her womb and sown in the earth—returned to Ninhursag, in a manner of speaking— so as to grow the eight plants. Unfortunately the names of these plants are missing, fragmentary, or otherwise obscure; but the cassia-plant, the thorn-plant and the caper-plant at least are probabilities, and these all grow in or near deserts.

Ninhursag's plot had been to draw Enki's irrigation further and further towards the desert, to extend her own region of fertility. This worked well with the intermediate regions where vines and cucumbers grow; but the planting of Enki's seed at the very edge of the desert was foiled by Enki himself, by his impetuosity in eating the plants so as to be able to decree their fates. This impetuosity is punished by earth, and Enki becomes sick. As a consequence of trying to force irrigation beyond its natural place, and of Enki's over-violent reaction, water perhaps fails, and there is a drought that has to be corrected by action of the great gods. Enki has carried thoughtlessness and unnatural sexual activity too far; in swallowing the eight plants he was swallowing (although perhaps he did not know it) his own offspring, just as Kronos swallowed his children and, a closer parallel, just as in the Hurrian congener of the Kronos myth Kumarbi goes to excess by swallowing the male member of his father, the sky-god Anu whom he has displaced; subsequently he becomes pregnant with three 'terrible gods' (see pp. 214 ff.). Just as Kumarbi is in pain with his unnatural progeny, so it seems is Enki. It is important to notice that in his cure he is seated within, and not just near, Ninhursag's vagina. That is because he thus becomes implicated through her in the very process of birth—a natural birth, of the eight gods that eventually heal him, because from the mother, and as a result (it may be inferred) of the original, straightforward impregnation of Ninhursag by Enki himself.

So understood, the myth survives the question that may be asked of many allegorical interpretations: what then is the point of all this complex transposition from one code to another? There may be a simple point, of course, if the allegorical code has special associations or makes a striking or poetical impact that the original code (the direct meaning) could not reproduce. Yet Mesopotamian myth does not seem to be working primarily in this direction. Jacobsen would justify simple allegory by saying that by representing earth, water, and so on as persons acting according to a human psychology, men were enabled to come to grips with them better. But what is Enki's psychology in his multiple incest, and why are some details of the myth, like the sowing of the plants, inexplicable in these terms? My suggestion is that the various forms of sexual activity are not just accidental, nor added to make the narrative striking or shocking, or to make Enki's behaviour as water more easily intelligible; neither is the interest in irrigation, and the apparent reporting of various simple facts about its limitations, simply naive or tautological. Rather it is precisely by the interrelating of these two topics that a new insight is gained into each of them.

In a sense this is a structural interpretation, one that places emphasis on relations rather than on their particular subjects— although the nature of the subjects will no more be irrelevant in practice than it is, for all the abstraction of his theory, for Lévi-Strauss himself. So let us look at the myth once more in this way. Enki lies with his wife in Dilmun, and so causes purity there, together with the absence of old age and disease. He also grants abundant fresh water, first by non-sexual means, but then by directing his seed into his wife, the earth. The result is the birth of a daughter—perhaps, as Jacobsen suggested, with symbolic reference to the growth of plants as the waters recede. As a result of this daughter wandering in the marshes, which Enki had forbidden, he has sexual relations with her and then with her daughter, and hers again. This irregular use of sex merely wastes the fertile potentialities of the water-god, and in order to fulfil his latest incestuous desires he has to agree to water the uncultivated places so as to grow grapes and cucumbers. But then his wife Nin-hursag in turn behaves in an irregular sexual fashion, by removing the seed from Uttu's womb and apparently planting it in herself. This unnatural attempt to carry fertility still further into the desert is frustrated by Enki, much as she herself had half-frustrated Enki's unnatural union with Uttu. Moreover Enki, by swallowing what is in effect his own offspring, is committing an unnatural act that reverses the attempt at birth by the mother. The whole sequence is one of reversals of natural marital relations and child-birth: the woman Ninhursag removes seed from the girl's womb, whereas it should be placed there by a man and then remain; Enki the father absorbs his children into himself, whereas the mother should discharge them out of herself in childbirth. Enki is made seriously ill as a result of his behaviour, and in order to be made well again, or put into a reverse condition, he has to undergo a reversal of the inverted form of childbirth that caused his disease: the plants he had swallowed are somehow transferred from him, as he crouches within Ninhursag, to her, and are reborn in a regular fashion, this time, almost as parts of himself. That may be doubt-ful; but it is undeniable that in order to be cured Enki has to be absorbed into the very process of regular childbirth. Only so can water be restored to those parts of the earth to which it can fruitfully be applied.

This reversal game can be carried too far, especially when we are dealing with a single myth and not (as Lévi-Strauss usually is) with a set of variants that can be expected to emphasize signi-ficant relationships. But I do not think it excessive to claim that, just as sexual regularity represses diseases in Dilmun (for there is neither old age nor disease there at the beginning of the myth), so does sexual irregularity promote them, and in Enki's own person. Opposing irregularity by further irregularity, as when Ninhursag removes Enki's seed from Uttu, only leads to further trouble, which is only cured by the drastic reversal of irregular roles and the re-establishment of normal processes. That is on the sexual plane; on the geographical or irrigation plane the case is more straightforward, but once again a balance seems to be eventually struck between excessive direction of water into the main canals and excessive efforts to lead it into the desert itself. This is not exactly a mediation in the strictest sense of the Lévi-Straussian term, although there is certainly some suggestion of a middle course being steered between excesses. Rather it is the pursuing of these two topics side by side, as it were, that leads to an acceptable attitude towards both; and implies, to revert to a more genuinely mythical level, that human fertility and natural fertility (which in Mesopotamia depends on irrigation and the annual inundation) are strictly interrelated—one of the key themes of all myth and much ritual.[20]

This is not quite the end of my discussion of 'Enki and Nin-hursag'; other facets will be revealed by comparison with four or five of the other main myths to have survived in Sumerian. These will extend the picture I have presented so far of an interplay between the themes of human sex and natural irrigation. Yet that will remain the main emphasis; and if it appears too specialized to be acceptable, I remind you that all the myths that took shape in the third millennium B.C. are concerned with details—as Jacobsen put it, of creation, organization, or evaluation.[21] The formation of the broad assumptions (about gods, the structure of the world, the position of man) lay in the pre-literate past; so a detailed interest in the origin and natural limits of irrigation is not surprising, especially because the subject was of such enormous importance. To cite Jacobsen again, Mesopotamian civilization crystallized around the middle of the fourth millennium B.C.[22] At this time a large-scale canal system is initiated, the economy of the whole area changes, the villages are expanded into cities, writing is invented, large buildings, temples and ziggurats, appear for the first time...Jacobsen may be compressing a longer process of development, but it is not too much to claim that it was the organization of the canal system, of irrigation, that made the further developments possible; and it is not surprising that this amazing extension of fertility—on the maintenance of which

---

[20] Perhaps I had better defend myself against an obvious criticism by adding that any modern explanation of a myth will falsify it by reducing it to a kind of reasonableness that it probably never possessed. Myths deal in poetry rather than logic; but there is a kind of logic even in poetry, and critics who try to elucidate it do not profess to be dealing with the whole of poetry—just with one of its aspects.

[21] *IA*, 151 = *BP*, 164 f.

[22] *IA*, 128 f. = *BP*, 140 f.

Mesopotamian civilization depended until its ultimate decline—should become one of the principal subjects of myth.[23]

Next I want to consider a story described as 'tender' by Kramer, 'unwholesome' by Jacobsen: the myth of 'Enlil and Ninlil'. Before men were created, Nippur (the city where Enlil's greatest shrine was situated and from which, as it happens, most of the mythical tablets have come) was inhabited by the gods. Enlil and Ninlil are its 'young man' and 'young girl'; Ninlil's mother tells her daughter not to go bathing in the canal, in case Enlil, the 'great mountain', should catch sight of her and make love to her. Needless to say, Ninlil shortly feels an urgent need for a bathe.[24] Enlil sees her and immediately proposes intercourse, to which she replies that she is too young, her sexual organ is too small. With the help of his vizier Nusku, Enlil nevertheless gets her into his boat and rapes her, impregnating her with the moon-god Nanna-Sin. Amazingly, the other gods are deeply shocked, and Enlil is arrested and sentenced to banishment. This means that he has to leave the land of the living and descend to the nether world. He sets off, but Ninlil follows him. Enlil is worried by this, since he knows that Ninlil will soon give birth to the moon-god; and he is not particularly anxious to have the moon-god, who belongs up in the sky, condemned to a life below. The action he takes is at first sight surprising: he persuades the gate-keeper of Nippur to absent himself and not try to make love to Ninlil; then he disguises himself as the gate-keeper and makes love to her himself, impregnating her this time with a god of the underworld. The same thing happens twice more: Enlil disguises himself as the gate-keeper of

[23] Enki, after all, is the third of the great gods, and in some ways the equal of Enlil himself; and he is the god of fresh water. His name means 'lord earth', and it is water that makes the earth viable for gods and men. In a myth already referred to on p. 93, and now translated by Kramer in his *The Sumerians* (Chicago, 1963), 174 ff. (cf. Jacobsen in *IA*, 160 f. = *BP*, 174 f.), Enki passes through the world in his boat, decreeing the fates of cities, blessing the flocks, and giving vegetation. He fills the Tigris with fresh water by mating as a bull with the river as a cow—again the connexion between impregnation and irrigation; then he organizes the marshes and canebrakes, fills the rivers with fish and appoints a supervising deity, and calls down rain. Finally he establishes ploughing and farming, creates bricks and the pick-axe, and appoints deities to look after the mountain region, the borders, and shepherding and weaving (this last deity being the desirable Uttu). In other tales this sort of organizational activity is attributed to Enlil; such accounts are really summaries of functions rather than regular mythical narratives.

[24] Kramer (e.g. *Mythologies*, 96 f.) understands the text differently, and according to him the mother encourages Ninlil to bathe.

the world of the dead, then as the ferryman of the river of death (the Sumerian prototype of Charon), and each time makes love to Ninlil and impregnates her with another underworld deity. The reason for this he states himself: the three new offspring are to be given in exchange for the moon-god, and thus allow him to go to his proper place in the sky. This accords with a rule that was ruthlessly applied by the queen of the dead: no one who enters the underworld can leave, even a god, unless in special circumstances a substitute can be provided.

There is no doubt that this myth is in one important aspect what Jacobsen has termed a 'myth of organization': it explains how it is that the moon-god has three brothers who are gods of the underworld. Here we see myth working to unravel certain details of cult. It is impossible to know how the moon-god first came to be associated with gods of the world below; conceivably there was some special point to it (for example, by an obvious astronomical allegory he was sometimes held to spend the last day of each month in the nether world), but it may equally have been an accident of the agglomeration of local cults, or even have depended on a chance similarity of titles. Moreover Ninlil turns out to be no casual conquest, but Enlil's established and powerful consort in Nippur; Nanna-Sin became the city-god of Ur, and in another myth is depicted as journeying by river from Ur to Nippur to seek Enlil's blessing.

There is a political as well as a liturgical point to our myth. But can these details really account for its most remarkable qualities—even when note is taken of that important element of sheer narrative drama that determines many of the details and sequences of any myth? Jacobsen, who is over-optimistic in his assertion that the myth answers the question 'How did the moon originate?' (since to say that Nanna is a son of Enlil and has brothers in the underworld is no real answer), argues that Enlil's violence provides an acceptable motive for the events described. The myth, he says, seeks their cause 'in Enlil's own nature with its curiously dark and violent strains. It is this element of wildness and violence which makes him break the laws and taboos of society of the world above when he takes Ninlil by force and Sin is engendered.' [25]

That is yet another instance of Jacobsen's favourite kind of

[25] *IA*, 156 = *BP*, 169.

interpretation. The approach taken by the myths, he suggests,
'is a psychological approach: the key to understanding the forces
which one meets in nature is felt to lie in the understanding of
their characters, exactly as the clue to understanding men lies in
understanding their characters'.[26] This is an important idea that
makes greater sense of anthropomorphism in general and illu-
minates certain aspects of Mesopotamian myths in particular.
Nevertheless I agree with Kramer that the whole emphasis on the
universe as a 'Thou', likewise heavily stressed by the Frankforts
in their contributions to *The Intellectual Adventure of Ancient Man*, is
too strong and too simple.[27] Kramer maintains that the Mesopotamian peoples were in reality quite objective in their dealings
with the outside world, as their laws and historical records show.
That may be going too far: a people often manifests a different
attitude in their myths and religion from that which reveals itself
in their practical life. Even so, I share some of Kramer's doubts
over assigning a high degree of animism and child-like subjectivism
to the Mesopotamians on the basis of their myths, which I tend to
see somewhat differently from both these critics.

To return to Enlil and Ninlil: Jacobsen's argument that Enlil's
behaviour can be seen to be motivated by a violent strain in him,
as wind- and storm-god, is unsatisfactory for two reasons. First,
even such a feeling would hardly make sense of (or provide adequate emotional justification for) the whole myth, given that its
ultimate intention was to establish relationships between Enlil,
Nanna-Sin, and certain underworld deities. Far better narrative
structures could be found for this purpose; in particular, structures that did not need to attribute to this powerful god, Enlil, a
pointless violence that brought about his removal to the underworld—a remarkable event that almost needs another myth to
explain it. Secondly, a comparison with 'Enki and Ninhursag'
reveals that Enlil's type of behaviour is not unique to him, and
therefore cannot be explained as the result of his particularly
violent nature. This is a comparison I now want to pursue.

The structural similarity between the two myths is really remarkable, although it has attracted little attention. In each case a
very young goddess is instructed not to approach the water (Enki
forbids anyone to walk in the marshland; Ninlil's mother tells her,
more specifically, not to bathe in the canal—or, if Kramer is

[26] *IA*, 168 = *BP*, 182.   [27] See his review of *IA* in *JCS*, II, 1948, 39 ff.

right (p. 99 n. 24), to bathe there; in either case bathing is stressed). In each case she does so, and is immediately impregnated by the god. In each case this act of impregnation is repeated several times more, the result being another child of each act of impregnation; in the case of Enki it is successive daughters that he seduces, and the number is brought up to four only by counting in his initial fertilization of Ninhursag; whereas Enlil repeatedly takes the same girl, Ninlil, although once in one type of circumstance and the other three times, in a sequence of parallel acts, in another. Even the initial circumstances, and the results, are similar: for it is emphasized that both Dilmun and Nippur are pure and well supplied with sweet waters (at Dilmun we are told how this is done); and in each myth one of the protagonists, Enlil or Ninhursag, goes to the underworld as a result of irregular behaviour. This is explicit in the case of Enlil, who is banished by the other gods; in the Enki myth it is not Enki himself, but Ninhursag, who disappears there.[28]

The use and re-use of narrative motifs (like the discovery by some small or unlikely animal of a god who has disappeared) is common enough, and the triple sequence of impregnations exemplifies a pattern of repetition that can be paralleled elsewhere— most dramatically by the progressive stripping of the goddess Inanna's garments as she passes through the gates of the underworld in a myth to be considered shortly. Yet the emphasis on the excessive youth of the girl or girls, and the parallelism of the different episodes, cannot be explained on purely narrative grounds. What, then, is likely to be the purpose common to each myth? The answer is implicit in my suggested interpretation of the Enki myth, where the interweaving of sexual regularity and irregularity with success and failure in the extension of irrigation (of which Enki was the supreme overseer) was found to cast fresh light on both. In the Enlil myth there is no suggestion that the god's acts of fertilization are connected specifically with irrigation; on the other hand they are undeniably concerned with fertility, even if their most direct purpose is the production of four particular deities.[29] The core of the two myths is as follows: a succession of

---

[28] This is the implication of her threat, which nearly kills him, not to look on him with the eye of life: *ANET*², 40.

[29] Enlil is not primarily a fertility-god, but was sometimes envisaged as carrying out the same kind of organization of farming and fresh water as Enki himself: see

carnal encounters between a high god and a goddess (or series of goddesses), who is really too young for this sort of thing, leads to the birth of several relatively minor deities and, directly or indirectly, to the removal of a major deity to the underworld, with damaging effects (so it can be inferred) on fertility above. Therefore it appears that the pursuit of fertility can be carried to excess; if it is so carried, it tends to result in infertility.

It would be foolish to deny that each myth has other, separate aims: the Enki myth to make a special point about irrigation and what sort of plants can be grown near the desert, the Enlil myth to explain a puzzle in the apparently contradictory nature of Enlil's sons. Yet the similarity of their central structure suggests an underlying meaning of the kind I have proposed. There may, too, be a specific social argument in the Enlil myth, namely that intercourse with minors is wrong; for the reaction of the other gods is both violent and moralistic in tone, whereas in the Enki myth there is no overt condemnation of Enki's acts. That is possible, although it would be surprising in a way, since these great gods, although their behaviour is broadly modelled on human behaviour, were also regarded as a law to themselves. Yet the reason may be this: that in the Enki myth the consequences of irregular fertilization were plainly shown in Enki's sickness and Ninhursag's withdrawal; whereas in the Enlil myth there was nothing except stated disapproval by a third party to point out the evil consequences—since Enlil's visit to the underworld was, in a sense, quite useful, in that he was able to establish the known relationship between his sons.

Moral comment may be incidentally implied in a third myth, 'Inanna and Shukalletuda', which seems to bear a hidden resemblance to the other two. Shukalletuda is a mortal, a gardener who has no success with his garden, because the plants are dried up by the hot sun and wind, until he plants a *sarbatu* tree to provide shade. He has divined the idea of the tree by studying the heavens and their omens and so learning the divine decrees—an unusual theme in Mesopotamian myth, in spite of the important role of divination at least from the second millennium on. One day the goddess Inanna, queen of heaven and of love and human fertility,

---

Kramer in *Mythologies*, 96. Moreover Ninlil is called 'the lordly wild cow' in Ashurbanipal's record of his achievements (*ANET²*, 300); which may well associate her (and him) with rivers (cf. e.g. p. 99 n. 23).

lay down to sleep near Shukalletuda's shady garden, and while she slept he came along and coupled with her. On waking and perceiving what has happened she is determined to find the guilty mortal. She fills the wells with blood, sends strong winds and storms. After each onslaught Shukalletuda goes for succour to his father, who tells him to hide in the cities, the best rule for miscreants then as now. Inanna, baffled, decides to ask Enki for advice...and here, frustratingly, the tablet breaks off. Presumably he was caught in the end, like Dumuzi after a similar chase in another Sumerian myth to be described shortly. And yet we cannot be sure: Shukalletuda's knowledge of the divine decrees puts him in an unusual position, not unlike that of Ziusudra the wise, the Sumerian Noah who escaped the wrath and plague and deluge of the gods; moreover Inanna could sometimes be escaped, as she was (in her Akkadian form of Ishtar) by Gilgamesh.

This tale, like the two already discussed, has a true mythical aura. It is surely no mere allegory, no simple case of transposing one set of terms into another. Part of its force, and perhaps much of its significance, lies in the odd interrelating of its two main themes—the gardener who invents a new technique of cultivation, and the mortal who forces the goddess of love. Apart from this, it is just possible that the myth contains a moral implication: it is wrong to make love to sleeping females, and doubly imprudent to do so to sleeping goddesses. As a matter of fact the Gilgamesh epic tells us what Inanna–Ishtar was likely to do to gardeners, for in Tablet VI Gilgamesh insultingly reminds her that she had made advances to her father's gardener Ishullanu (a minor god this time), and that when he spurned her she turned him into a mole or something like it. Perhaps, then, moralizing is not really to be expected in relation to this goddess and her *affaires*. She is, after all, the love-goddess. But why does she get caught up in sexual imbroglios with gardeners, imbroglios in which one partner or another is unwilling, and the gardener makes or rejects love against the goddess's wishes?

The answer I suggest is that this myth, like the other two, illustrates a connexion between irregular sexual unions and agricultural innovation—on the broader plane, between human fecundity and the fertility of the soil. If one compares its basic structure with that of 'Enki and Ninhursag' and (in items 2 and 3) 'Enlil and Ninlil', the result is something like this: 1. X (the hero) produces plant-fertility; 2. *X* applies human fertility by force; 3. *X* is punished. Naturally, it is possible that a basic narrative idea (that Inanna as love-goddess has an affair with a minor fertility-god) has been subjected to variations that have little more significance than that; some such variations could undoubtedly be due to accidental transpositions of themes in the course of transmission. For reasons given in the preceding chapter, I am far less sanguine than Lévi-Strauss and Leach about the necessary maintenance through all vicissitudes, especially at the oral stage, of the essential form of any particular myth. Nevertheless the persistence of the idea of irregular coupling (by rape, in sleep) is important—although it could be argued that some motive for Inanna's persecution of Shu-kalletuda is needed, and this is as good as any. Judgement should be reserved in view of the loss of the ending; yet there is a distinct possibility that this myth, like the other two, is concerned with more than why a minor deity possesses a certain position or prerogative, or the allegorical restatement of familiar truths about nature and agriculture. The use of vivid sexual situations may be not merely intended to motivate natural events by the ascription to them of human psychological reactions; rather the continuing interplay of sexual action and cultural advance in the realm of agriculture may be a means of exploring and emphasizing certain parallels between human and plant fertility, and their natural limitations.

The last myth in the group is that of 'Enki and Ninmah', and it provides further striking parallels to 'Enki and Ninhursag'—which is almost taking on the status of what Lévi-Strauss calls a *mythe de référence*. Ninmah, indeed, is just another name for Ninhursag, so that the two protagonists are the same in each case. The myth begins with a version of a common, but usually quite incidental, Mesopotamian theme: the creation of man.[30] The gods are tired of work, and they ask Enki, the lord of wisdom as well as of water, to suggest something. Enki instructs his mother Nammu, the primeval ocean, to provide clay, and Ninmah–Ninhursag the earth-goddess (who is also thereby the mother-goddess) to impose on the clay the shape of the gods.[31] The gods themselves celebrate

---

[30] On this myth see Jacobsen, *IA*, 161 ff. = *BP*, 175 ff.; Kramer, *Mythologies*, 103 ff.

[31] In much the same way Ea (the Akkadian equivalent of Enki) created the brick-god Kulla by pinching off a piece of clay in the primeval ocean, in a tale recited as part of the ritual for restoring a temple (*ANET²*, 341). The fuller details of the process, and its closeness to human childbirth, are probably revealed in another Akkadian parallel, 'The creation of man by the mother-goddess' (*ANET²*, 99 f.), which exists

the happy event, and Enki and Ninmah become a bit drunk. Ninmah fashions six further, but odd or defective, creatures, and challenges Enki to decree a place in the world and a fate for each of them—which Enki, ingenious as ever, succeeds in doing. Much is obscure, but it seems that these creatures are anomalies like eunuchs, barren women, and bedwetters—people who exist in real life, and for whom a 'fate' and a place in society can be found.

So far, then, the myth, apart from exemplifying the idea that men's first duty is to serve the gods, has given an aetiology of defective births and recorded the way in which such individuals can be integrated in society. It now proceeds, if a plausible conjecture by Jacobsen is correct, to something even more interesting. Enki takes over the manufacture of oddities to see if Ninmah can do as well as he in providing a place for them; but his second creation is so feeble, so decayed in all its functions, that it cannot even speak or hold out a hand to take the bread that is offered it. Ninmah can think of no use for the creature, whose name means (according to Jacobsen, whose exposition I am here following closely) 'My day is remote', and who is thus a very old man. As a result of her failure Ninmah's city is destroyed and she is forced into exile; she curses Enki, and so drives him down to the underworld—from which, in due time, he must have escaped. Now this part of the myth is surely attempting to account for the existence in the world of old age and disease—conditions which, unlike the other abnormalities created by Ninmah, can be put to no conceivable social use. If so, the myth is unusual. Demons of disease are often mentioned in other tales—the underworld is full of them—and the Sumerian myth of the 'Death of Gilgamesh' makes it clear that death is inevitable for men; but this is, precisely, man's destiny, and no other attempt is known (apart from the Akkadian tale of Adapa) to say how or why this is so. The present myth seems to offer a brilliant solution, whose slightly frivolous nature may conceal a serious argument implicit in the idea that old age and disease are an accident of the very creation of man. To see how the argument would run it is necessary once

in an Old Babylonian as well as a later Assyrian version and was used as a ritual aid in human childbirth. A god is slain and his blood is mixed with clay (a common theme that also occurs in the Babylonian Creation Epic, where Kingu's blood is mixed with clay at Marduk's command so as to make man as servant of the gods); the mother-goddess, here named Mami, produces fourteen 'mother-wombs' in which the clay is formed into seven males and seven females.

again, as I would suggest, to take account of resemblances with other myths, especially with 'Enki and Ninhursag':

Enki and Ninmah	*Enki and Ninhursag*
Ninmah takes creative material (clay from Nammu), makes six odd creatures in an irregular fashion (i.e. in a drunken game)	Ninhursag takes creative material (Enki's seed), makes eight (odd?) plants in an irregular fashion (i.e. by artificial insemination)
Enki finds a fate for them	Enki 'decreed their fate' (verse 217) by eating them
Enki creates a creature for whom Ninmah can find no fate	⟨and so prevented Ninhursag from determining their fate⟩?
Ninmah is furious and disappears, cursing Enki who goes to the underworld	Ninhursag is furious and disappears, cursing Enki who sickens and is close to death
⟨Enki is revived after Ninmah finds a cure for certain diseases⟩?	Ninhursag revives Enki by creating healing deities, involving him in childbirth

Irregular creation, like irregular procreation and the irregular growth of plants, leads to unfortunate results. Mild anomalies can be accepted, although at a cost; but their production leads to major ones that are irreversible, and can be no more than slightly palliated—as by the discovery of healing deities to cure certain ills (and also to bring Enki back to normal life and activity, which implies normal irrigation of the soil?). In the myth of Enki and Ninmah—which admittedly smacks of learned elaboration—the ultimate irregularity is the production of old age and diseases; the final stage of the process is missing, but it may be (as suggested in the table above) that certain diseases are relieved by the very means used to bring Enki back from below.

3: Three myths of the underworld

Finally among Sumerian myths I want to consider three tales that elucidate and carry further the idea of a disappearing fertility deity as well as elaborating one of the main themes of Sumerian as of Akkadian myths, namely the nature and appearance of the world of the dead. The first concerns the death of Gilgamesh's companion Enkidu. It survives as the twelfth and last tablet of the Akkadian Epic of Gilgamesh, but does not properly belong there, and has been shown by Kramer and C. J. Gadd to be a direct translation from a Sumerian original.[32] Moreover the beginning

[32] References in *ANET*[2], 97.

of the same myth, missing from the Akkadian tablet, has survived in its original Sumerian form. What happens, then, is this: Inanna has found a tree floating in the Euphrates and plants it in her garden; enemies interfere with it (the *Imdugud*-bird nests at the top, a snake at its foot, and the vampire Lilith in the middle); Gilgamesh comes to the rescue, and in gratitude Inanna gives him a *pukku* and *mikkū*, evidently a drum and drumstick with cultic or ritual meaning, that she had made out of her tree. Unfortunately Gilgamesh somehow lets these objects fall into the underworld. Enkidu offers to retrieve them, goes down to the nether world, and behaves so obstreperously there (in spite of Gilgamesh's warnings to the contrary) that Ereshkigal, queen of the dead, keeps him for good. In short, he dies. Gilgamesh, distraught, cannot win back his friend, but is granted a temporary visit from his spirit. Enkidu, or rather his ghost—and the comparison with the ghost of Patroclus in the twenty-third *Iliad* is, indeed, almost irresistible—gives a hair-raising account of conditions down below: vermin devour his body, and his fate is compared unfavourably, it seems, with that of those who have many sons to render them funerary offerings. Once again we observe a curious connexion between Inanna and a tree, as in the Shukalletuda myth; once again some irregular act concerning a goddess associated with fertility causes the withdrawal of a chief participant to the underworld, as was the case with Ninhursag, Ninlil and Ninmah. But I do not press these resemblances; the main object of the myth is certainly to clarify the inexorable fate of the dead and the treatment meted out to various kinds of victim in 'the house of dust'.

The second underworld myth, 'Inanna's descent to the nether world', is of special interest because it exists in both a Sumerian and an Akkadian version, separated in the date of their recording by the greater part of a millennium. The main outlines of the myth are common to both versions.[33] Inanna (or her Akkadian equivalent Ishtar) decides to visit 'the great below'. She gains entrance by one means or another, and is progressively stripped of her clothes and decorations as she passes through each of the seven gates on the way. As soon as she comes before her sister Ereshkigal, queen of the underworld and goddess of death, she is killed. Her death becomes known to the gods, and they send a messenger or messengers to rescue her by sprinkling her with life-

---

[33] For translations of which see *ANET*², 52 ff. and 106 ff.

water. She revives and ascends, but on her return to earth a substitute has to be provided, and this turns out to be her husband Dumuzi (Akkadian Tammuz), the shepherd-god.

This bare core is made richer by details over which the versions differ:

	Sumerian version	Akkadian version
Means of entry to underworld:	On excuse of attending funeral of Ereshkigal's husband	By threat to break in and release the dead
How killed:	By a deadly look from the underworld judges	By Namtar, a demon of death, and the 'sixty miseries'
Why rescued:	Because of a plan pre-arranged between Inanna and her vizier	Because the great gods deplore resulting infertility on earth
How rescued:	Enki makes two creatures who carry food and water of life to underworld and sprinkle her sixty times	Ea (= Enki) makes a handsome (?) eunuch, who obtains life-water bag from Ereshkigal as a wish; she curses him; he sprinkles Ishtar
Mode of leaving underworld:	Accompanied by demons of death and disease	By passing back through the seven gates, regaining clothes, etc.

The first difference is rather unimportant; although it is worth noting that the threat to release the dead in the Akkadian version accords with the Akkadian motive for rescue, which again emphasizes the general association of infertility and the dead. The second is only significant because the Akkadian version mentions demons of death and disease, who occur in the Sumerian version as Inanna's companions on leaving. It seems probable that each version has selected one, and suppressed a second, motif in this last connexion, and that in a hypothetical exemplar Inanna both was accompanied by demons of death and disease and passed once more through the seven gates. She may also have been killed by sixty demons (as in the Akkadian version), corresponding with the sixty-fold sprinkling to revive her in the Sumerian; and the same sixty demons may have been those who accompanied her on her release. The difference over the motive for rescue is important mainly because the Sumerian version embroiders this theme at considerable length—Inanna's careful arrangements in case she does not return take up almost a quarter of the 300-odd surviving verses of the poem. This is really a folktale theme exemplifying ingenious precaution, and is similar in tone to Inanna's obviously false excuse (again in the Sumerian version) for entering the underworld in the first place. As against these folktale elements the Akkadian equivalents stress the more serious and relevant topic of the upsetting of the balance between fertility and infertility, the world of the living and that of the dead.

The most substantial difference is perhaps in the mode of rescue—although here we have significant variants on a common theme rather than totally different motifs: Enki/Ea creates a strange creature, or creatures, to sprinkle the water of life on the dead goddess. In the Sumerian version the two creatures, the terms for which suggest that they are minor temple officials, are made from the dirt beneath his fingernails; one carries the food, the other the water of life. In the Akkadian version Ea creates a eunuch by conceiving an image of him in his wise heart—an unusually sophisticated formulation; the eunuch's name is Asushunamir, which Speiser says means 'His appearance is brilliant',[34] but is perhaps more accurately translated as 'His coming-out is bright'. There is some doubt, then, about whether he is very good-looking—but that would at least explain why Queen Ereshkigal is so delighted at his arrival that she offers to grant him a wish. She falls in love with him, that is, for his being a eunuch would not greatly matter to the queen of infertility and death. At all events she is furious when he asks for the life-water bag and she realizes that his real purpose is to restore Inanna, and she curses him with an evil destiny. There is probably an aetiological intention here, concerned with the social position of eunuchs, parallel to that of Enki and Ninmah and the odd creatures they formed; and the wish granted to someone who then uses it against the giver is clearly a folktale motif. The constitution of this scene is in any case complex, and it is admittedly more natural for the life-water to be brought from above, as in the Sumerian version, than being kept below. Yet the idea of the eunuch, and the possibility that Ereshkigal falls in love with him, fits in very effectively with the contrast between fertility and infertility, living and dead, which has been emphasized throughout this Akkadian version. The figure of the beautiful eunuch, and the love that is no

[34] *ANET*², 108, n. 21.

love of the queen of the dead, would make a striking symbol of the whole contradictory relationship between life and death.

All in all the Akkadian version maintains the main theme of the myth more consistently than the Sumerian. It is less marked by folktale digressions, and its dramatic climax comes more accurately at the point where Ishtar is released—since the strong emphasis on Inanna's arrangements with her vizier tends to make the point of climax in the Sumerian version ambiguous. We cannot therefore conclude that it is more genuinely mythical, or earlier in origin, or closer to oral versions, although it may be all of these. Other Akkadian myths, as we shall see, strongly emphasize the fertility theme, and perhaps the Akkadian sources of our version omitted certain minor themes that did not accord with the general plan—a type of rationalizing. The whole question is a salutary reminder that in spite of the venerable antiquity of these documents, and especially the Sumerian (whose origins can be taken well into the third millennium B.C.), we are dealing with myths that have undergone something approaching the degree of deliberate formulation that appears, in the Greek context, in Hesiod. Nevertheless I remain convinced that many of these poems retain an authentic core of myth, and that this is so with the story of which our two versions are variants.

One problem remains over Inanna: why did she want to go down to the nether world, with all its tremendous risks, in the first place? She may, I suppose, be just another instance of the disappearing god, envisaged to account for the withdrawal of fertility whether seasonally or at longer intervals. But other fertility-gods who do this sort of thing, Enki or Enlil or Baal or Adonis or Persephone or Demeter, are assigned a reason consonant with the rest of the mythical narrative. Inanna is assigned none; she did not go to look for someone, for example; it is as though it were a pure sightseeing trip; both versions agree that she simply 'set her mind' towards the world below.[35] Part of the explanation may lie in this: that the ultimate result of her excursion is the downfall of Dumuzi her consort. That is made plain at the end of the Sumerian version, with which the Akkadian, although fragmentary, is not

[35] In a sense she establishes a mediation between the two contradictory aspects of earth and its parts, namely as source of life and vegetation and as recipient of the dead. J. Fontenrose (*Python*, 256) usefully emphasizes this duality; his assumption that Inanna descends in order to overcome death and infertility seems less secure.

inconsistent. The demons who accompany Inanna on her release do so in order to lay hands on a substitute. They threaten successive minor gods, who prostrate themselves and are spared; but when they reach Inanna's city of Uruk, Dumuzi does not prostrate himself, in fact he takes very little notice of them—a fatal error, since they drag him off weeping to the world of the dead. So Inanna's imprudent visit to the nether world might be said to motivate Dumuzi's removal there, rather as Enlil's temporary banishment below explains how three of his sons are underworld deities and the fourth is the moon-god.[36]

Dumuzi's fate, suggested at the fragmentary end of 'Inanna's descent', is the general subject of our third myth of the underworld, represented in two further variants. In 'The myth of Dumuzi's dream'[37] Dumuzi has an ominous dream interpreted for him by his sister Geshtinanna. He then tries to escape from the gallas, the underworld demons who pursue him, but returns to the city when they seize his sister. They beat him up, but the sun-god Utu listens to his appeal for help and turns him into a gazelle (in the ending of 'Inanna's descent' it was evidently a snake; perhaps originally both, one after the other). Even the swiftest of animals cannot escape the demons of death, and Dumuzi finally resorts to his sister's sheepfold, the place where, as shepherd-god, he is most at home. The gallas—there are five of them in this version— break up the fold and kill its tutelary god: 'The holy churn lies (shattered), no milk is poured,/The cup lies (shattered), Dumuzi lives no more,/The sheepfold is given to the wind' (Kramer's translation). In another poem, 'The myth of Inanna and Bilulu',[38] a very different account is given of Dumuzi's death. This time Inanna is not indifferent to him, nor angry; on the contrary she misses her young husband, who is away with the sheep, and asks her mother's permission to visit him. Before she reaches him a messenger, perhaps a partridge, reports that Dumuzi is dead— murdered, it seems (although Kramer doubts this), by the old

[36] The parallel with 'Enlil and Ninlil' goes further, since in both myths the deity performs a succession of similar actions en route: Enlil impregnates Ninlil at three important stages of the journey, while Inanna is progressively stripped at each of the seven gates. But this may signify no more than the use of a common narrative device, especially since the substitutes in 'Enlil and Ninlil' are provided not for Enlil himself but for his son Nanna-Sin (see also p. 100).

[37] Discussed most fully by Kramer, Mythologies, 109–15.

[38] Published by Jacobsen and Kramer together, JNES, XII, 1953, 160 ff.

woman Bilulu and her son Girgire. Inanna breaks into, not exactly a lament, but rather a paean of praise to Dumuzi for being a faithful shepherd. She then hunts down Bilulu and Girgire and kills them; the former is turned into a water-skin, they become spirits of the desert, and their servant stands there to preside over offerings of flour to them. The text as it has survived ends with a lament by Inanna and Dumuzi's sister Geshtinanna.

We may at least conclude that there was no canonical view of the relations between Inanna and Dumuzi. Sometimes the goddess is heartless towards him, as she is to her other lovers in the sixth tablet of the Gilgamesh epic; here she is seen rather as a goddess of fertility in nature, and therefore devoted to her shepherd-lover. Dumuzi himself is also seen in different ways.[39] Sometimes he is simply the shepherd, as in the little myth of Dumuzi and Enkimdu (*ANET*[2], 41 f.), where he stands for herding as against farming, represented by Enkimdu. They compete for the hand of Inanna; the farmer seems to be winning her at first, but withdraws gracefully before the more violent arguments of the shepherd—a typical myth of evaluation, in a Sumerian (not Akkadian) genre that had rhetorical as well as popular appeal.[40] In 'Inanna and Bilulu', on the other hand, Jacobsen has shown that Dumuzi represents the power in the milk itself. His mother seems to be called a ewe, one of his own titles means 'mother milk', in Dumuzi's dream he dies just when the milk-churn is shattered, and he describes himself as 'he who dances on the holy knees, the knees of Inanna'— a reference which Jacobsen convincingly explains by the (for example Bedouin) custom of churning milk by joggling it on the knees.[41] Now Jacobsen goes further: Bilulu is a thunderstorm-deity, as is known from other sources, and the reason she is turned into a water-skin is that the skin both resembles a thunder-cloud and imitates its water-sprinkling function. This seems far-fetched at first, but is supported by the further observation that Girgire, Bilulu's son and accomplice, is elsewhere a god of the lightning-flash (and this explains why in the present myth 'His

[39] Even his status as a god is slightly equivocal: in the Sumerian King List (*ANET*[2], 265 f.) he was king of Bad-tibira for 36,000 years before the flood, but also king of Inanna's city of Uruk (although described as 'the god Dumuzi') shortly before Gilgamesh, i.e. in the 3rd millennium.

[40] Cf. W. G. Lambert, *Babylonian Wisdom Literature* (Oxford, 1960), 150 f.

[41] *JNES*, xii, 1953, 166 and n. 21.

(victims) struck down with the mace he (left) scattered in the fields', verse 94—they have been struck by lightning). Therefore the lightning-flash is the child of the thundercloud. So, concludes Jacobsen, the myth unfolds a 'sequence of events with its interplay of forces in nature', since in Mesopotamia the milking-season comes in the spring when thunderstorms are frequent.[42] As the storms become fewer the milk dries up; therefore Dumuzi's death is attributed to the thunderstorm. This does not work out quite so neatly, since milk and storms in fact fade more or less together; but thunder is the natural enemy of milk, which it tends to curdle and destroy. The thunderstorms cease altogether because they are killed by Inanna in revenge for Dumuzi; the thundercloud becomes a mere water-skin for offering libations to Dumuzi in the desert.

This is all so brilliant and ingenious that one's first reaction is that it cannot be true, yet its consistency is in the end convincing. Jacobsen's further conclusions are another matter. They amount to a reaffirmation of his theory that the purpose of most Mesopotamian myths is to express natural events in human and psychological terms, which enable men to sympathize with nature and so, in a sense, understand it. It may be freely conceded that this particular myth is a striking example of a nature-allegory, not a 'mere' allegory but one in which the relation of the life-giving power in the milk to fertility in general, in the person of Inanna, and the curious association between milk and thunderstorms, are made more dramatic by being stated in human terms. That is an important observation—but is it enough to account adequately even for the present myth, let alone become a general principle of interpretation? The truth is that very little in these events is explained by the human psychology that results from the imposition of anthropomorphic form on natural forces. Bilulu and Girgire kill Dumuzi not because they are human-like gods—they are assigned no motive for the murder—but simply and solely because they symbolize thunder and lightning, and these things are inimical to milk as represented by Dumuzi. It would be more useful to say that the tale points to a relationship between milk and the thunderstorms of springtime that is not as paradoxical as it at first seems: thunder curdles milk, and may even appear to cause the ewes to dry up—but as a consequence Inanna, perhaps

[42] *Op. cit.*, 169.

representing fertility in general rather than the coupling and propagation of animals in particular, ends the thunderstorms and leads the fertility-cycle into a different phase.

In any case the tale of Inanna, Dumuzi, Bilulu and Girgire is different in tone from most of the Sumerian myths considered so far. Apart from paeans and laments its most conspicuous aspect is the very specific and relatively long account of Inanna's seeking out of Bilulu and Girgire, her careful description to them of the transformation they are to undergo and its precise ritual purpose, and the almost identical description of its actual fulfilment. Jacobsen argues, partly on stylistic and rhythmical grounds, that the poem is very old, and he assigns it to a local genre of Dumuzi-myths connected with the city of Bad-tibira. But should not this poem be regarded as a hymn or lament rather than a myth, interspersed by brief details of Dumuzi's life and death to be sure, but with the primary motive of explaining details of his cult and ritual? We shall have to wait for further evidence until Jacobsen publishes his full study of the Dumuzi myths; meanwhile we should be cautious about regarding the present example as typical of Sumerian nature-myths in general. Several of the other myths we considered included etymologies and minor aetiologies of cult or ritual—but not as their main point, with the episodic content kept brief and incidental. The present example, on the other hand, looks like a learned cult-hymn whose truly mythical content may be relatively low.

4: The nature of Sumerian myths

Looking back on the Sumerian myths, I would stress once again that they are known to us through quite elaborate and carefully composed narrative *poems*, which moreover make many excursions into hymnody, the etymology of divine names, and the aetiology of cults and rituals. In some, like 'Enki and Ninhursag', the narrative element is strong and the other elements are slight; in others, like 'Inanna and Bilulu', the position is reversed. Yet the content of the former type, at least, suggests that these poems are dependent on a living tradition, a true mythical tradition. This content is too systematic to be the result of independent literary creation, too diverse to be the product of a systematic theology. I have tried to argue that several of the main myths are closely interrelated, partly by their overt subjects but more conspicuously by their underlying narrative structure, and that this common structure points to the essential concerns that are their main impetus.[43] Among the basic preoccupations are fertility, human and agricultural, and the complex relations between them; the plotting of men's ultimate destiny in the underworld, and the evaluation of death in relation to life and fertility; and the creation and ordering of men, their functions and place in the world.[44] To these must be added, from a broader conspectus of the surviving poems as a whole, the description of the various gods and their organizing and creative activities during the paradise-time before men were created; the competition between different cities and their gods for the possession of power in the form of the everlasting Ordinances; and the origin of evil and diseases, with the attempts made by the gods to put an end to men by fire, plague, war, or flood.

This last theme of a great flood I have deliberately passed by so far. It is familiar ground that the Biblical story of Noah and his ark is simply one version of a widely distributed Near-Eastern myth. In its Akkadian form it is described in the Utnapishtim episode in the eleventh tablet of the Gilgamesh epic, and also as one episode of the more fragmentary Atrahasis epic. In Sumerian it is preserved in a single broken tablet from Nippur which tells how, after the gods had 'lowered kingship from heaven' and the first five cities had been founded, it became necessary to destroy men, preserving only the pious Ziusudra and his wife; he was warned in a dream to build his great boat. The origin and function of this myth, which finds its Greek reflexion in the story of Deucalion's flood, have occasioned much discussion. Yet its origin must be Mesopotamian, and it must be based on experience. Only in Mesopotamia, of the whole Near-Eastern and western Asiatic world, are widespread and disastrous floods quite frequent. That they occurred at intervals in antiquity is shown by the stratigraphy of the great city-mounds. I do not assert that some parti-

[43] For this kind of analysis I am obviously indebted to Lévi-Strauss, although he would disown it as insufficiently abstract. Certainly such an approach could profitably be carried further with Near-Eastern myths, which seem to provide better material for it than most other mythologies outside the world of the 'totemic illusion'.

[44] Compare this with the summary offered by Kramer at the beginning of his chapter in *Mythologies*, 95: 'The extant myths of the Sumerians and Akkadians revolve primarily about the creation and organization of the universe, the birth of the gods, their loves and hates, their spites and intrigues, their blessings and curses'...and so on.

cular flood must have remained in men's memories; rather that floods were so recurrent a feature of history, and sometimes so nearly catastrophic, that the idea of an overwhelming flood must have presented itself as an inescapable variant of the common mythical theme whereby the gods try to destroy mankind.[45] To this theme has been added that of the single survivor, who in this case has to be a man distinguished for wisdom and piety. The resulting complex, with its combination of terror, realism, ingenuity (in the design and building of the boat and the motif of the three birds), fantasy, and moralism, was unusually powerful and therefore achieved the widest distribution. It is an excellent example of a myth that establishes itself in the tradition because of a felicitous blend of narrative qualities rather than because it serves a particular purpose, either speculative or practical.

The more elaborate Sumerian myths are, indeed, remarkable for the unimportance of their operative or charter aspects. Such aspects are more prominent in local tales that did not gain wide currency; but in any event that kind of mythical function was seriously diminished by the rapid advance, in the Mesopotamian cities, of formal and literate records of institutional affairs. On the other hand a unique blend of cosmology and politics was produced by the association of different nature-gods with different cities.

A possibly analogous tendency appears in the productive relating of two subjects by placing them side by side within a mythical framework. Several of the myths, I have suggested, are composed of two at first sight independent episodes (involving, however, the same god or goddess), each more or less complete in itself; and it is the reactions of one upon the other that give the myth its ultimate point. In 'Enki and Ninhursag' Enki's impregnations of the series of goddesses forms the first stage, the growth of the eight plants and their consequences the second. In 'Enki and Ninmah' the creating of men forms one stage, the creating of abnormalities, and the quarrel between the two deities, another. In 'Inanna and Shukalletuda' the mortal gardener's problem with his garden, and his discovery of the shade-giving tree through divination, seems to be an independent episode, joined to what follows by the accident of Inanna happening to go to sleep near by.

---

[45] A theme that once again recurs in Greece—for example in Zeus's plan, alluded to at the beginning of the *Iliad*, to relieve the teeming earth of men.

In the myth of Enkidu's death the opening incidents, in which
Gilgamesh wins the drum and drumstick by preserving Inanna's
huluppu-tree, form the first stage, and Enkidu's descent to the
underworld and its consequences a quite different stage; similarly
Inanna's descent, and the persecution and death of Dumuzi to
which it ultimately leads, seem like different chapters, at least, of
the same book. If this is correct, it appears that many Sumerian
myths of complex structure acquired significance through the
combination of originally independent themes that seem to react
significantly and illuminatingly upon each other. Those themes
often seem simple and obvious in themselves, and their chief
interest lies in their narrative qualities. If so, then an important
and promising principle is suggested: that some myths, at least,
convey a special meaning (or explore a problem, reflect a preoccupation or attitude) by the productive juxtaposition of themes
whose independent interest is primarily as mere narrative.[46]

5: Akkadian myths

Akkadian myths are often similar to Sumerian ones; sometimes,
as has been seen in the comparison of Inanna's and Ishtar's
descents to the world of the dead, they are substantially the same.
In both languages the range of themes includes monster-fights,
gods of pestilence attacking mankind, wise men escaping disaster,
elaborate descriptions of conditions in the underworld, the distribution of fates and their subsequent borrowing or stealing,
whether by a god or by the great bird Zu; all this against a semi-
realistic background of assemblies or feasts of the gods, dangerous
or prophetic dreams, discussions between kings and their advisers,
and so on. Yet there are certain apparent divergences, and these
are worth noticing. Some may simply be due to the accident of
survival; but Akkadian myths in particular are so widely distributed, in both space and time, and so often represented by
several surviving versions from different periods, that it seems
reasonable to conclude that a considerable proportion of the
subjects of the poetical myths, at least, are known to us, if only from
fragmentary allusions.

One does not find in Akkadian (so far at least) the theme of a

---

[46] The observation has something in common with Lévi-Strauss's idea of a *récit à
tiroirs* (*OMT*, 164, cf. 26), although it was formed independently and as a result of
analysing Sumerian myths alone.

high god or culture-hero seducing a goddess or series of goddesses, with some kind of creative or restrictive effect on agricultural fertility; and there is less emphasis on irrigation. Ea, the Akkadian equivalent of Enki, is seen as the god of wisdom rather than of fresh water. On the other hand a new topic in Akkadian poetry concerns a mortal who ascends to heaven to plead with the gods over matters of life and death or the birth of a son; and the attempt to evade mortality, a main theme of the Epic of Gilgamesh, is virtually unrepresented in any of its Sumerian prototypes. That may be accidental; but a more certain innovation in the Akkadian epic lies, as will be seen in the next chapter, in the role of Enkidu as a wild man who crosses into the realm of culture. In the Sumerian poems cosmogony was almost totally neglected; in the Akkadian Epic of Creation, the *Enuma Elish*, it is of course an important initial motif—although this was to some extent for political ends, as part of the effort to increase the antiquity, and so the authority, of the relatively new Babylonian god Marduk. In presumed earlier versions of the poem the main role probably belonged to Enlil, not Marduk, and so the political motive would be less prominent.

More important because more pervasive is a change of emphasis that has been acutely described by W. G. Lambert, away from the gods as aspects of nature, each installed in a separate city-state, and towards a more abstract pantheon.[47] Under the Babylonians and Assyrians the cities of Mesopotamia were more closely linked than before, and the relationships between the gods, minor as well as major, became both more systematic and more artificial. The predominant concern in the second millennium B.C. was with the social order, with administration, with justice; and the myths seem to reflect a decrease of attention to the spread of fertility and culture and the limits of irrigation, and an increased concern with the nature and powers of kingship, the relation between king and priest, and the organizing of the whole Mesopotamian world under one supreme god and city. In some ways this suggests a diminution of the powers of myth, and that is confirmed in the subjects of the cylinder seals that are such a prolific and fascinating relic of Mesopotamian life and beliefs. The elaborate pictures of cult-scenes and mythical episodes common in the Agade dynasty at the end of the second millennium are replaced by mere rows of

[47] *Babylonian Wisdom Literature* (Oxford, 1960), 10 f.

deities, with Shamash, justice, and Ea, wisdom, outstanding, or by anonymous scenes of intercession. Mythological scenes, especially monster-fights, re-establish themselves around 1200 B.C. The effects of mere artistic fashion cannot be discounted; but the political developments and the elaboration of ritual and legal texts are further indications that there was indeed some change of *Weltanschauung* at the turn of the third and second millennia. It should not be exaggerated. Social preoccupations were already implicit in the Sumerian myths (although Jacobsen's emphasis on their nature-allegory qualities has diverted attention from this), and the short Sumerian Gilgamesh poems contain in embryo some of the important themes of the developed Akkadian epic.

Akkadian mythical literature is dominated by two long poems, known in modern times as the Epic of Gilgamesh and the Epic of Creation. Each is many times the length of most Mesopotamian myths, although shorter than what we usually mean by an epic— the term merely implies that they have an unusual monumental quality and are conglomerates, to some extent, of other and shorter poems. The Gilgamesh poem, which is of exceptional importance, is reserved for the next chapter. The Epic of Creation will be discussed rather briefly in relation to its length and undoubted importance. That is mainly because it has been so widely described in the literature of the last half-century—so much so, indeed, as to distract attention from the merits and interest of other and less conspicuous Mesopotamian myths. Discussion has been concentrated on two aspects: the cosmogonical part of the poem, culminating in Marduk's defeat of Tiamat, and its ritual aspects, remarked in the first chapter. Much of the poem is, indeed, of primarily religious interest; that certainly accounts for its redundant and rather unexciting style at many points. Akkadian myths in general, in comparison with Sumerian, have a tendency to fullness, not to say longwindedness. That the tendency increased in the course of the Semitic tradition is shown by comparison of Old Babylonian with Neo-Assyrian versions, where they overlap.[48] The older versions are briefer, more pointed and evocative, sometimes more cryptic—more mythical, in fact. That may be in part due to accident in individual traditions, but it remains true that even the shorter Akkadian poems are more detailed, wordier

---

[48] Compare, for example, in the Gilgamesh epic, *OB*, II, I with Assyr. I, v, 25–vi, 18, or *OB*, II, ii, 5–26 with Assyr. I, iv, 21–41 (all translated in *ANET²*).

and more prosaic than their Sumerian analogues and prototypes. Only the Gilgamesh epic escapes—it is full, even repetitive, but is redeemed by unusual artistry and by the qualities of its subject. The Creation Epic itself is the worst offender, presumably because it has been most closely controlled by a hieratic tradition.

Sumerian myth seems to have had relatively little to say about the first stages of cosmogony, but it was assumed that the world developed out of primeval water. The Akkadian epic makes this assumption explicit: first of all are Apsu and Tiamat, male sweet water and female salt water. From them are born another male–female pair, Lahmu and Lahamu, perhaps some kind of silt, and from them again Anshar and Kishar, probably the earth-aspect and sky-aspect of the horizon. These last two pairs, which are a little obscure, are probably the result of priestly speculation, but from now on we are on more familiar ground: Anshar and Kishar produce the sky-god Anu, and Anu begets Ea (equivalent to Sumerian Enki), the god of the earth and its sweet waters and also of wisdom. Now there is a quarrel between the primeval gods and the younger ones, who by their rowdy behaviour infuriate Apsu and Tiamat. Apsu decides to destroy the offenders and is encouraged by his vizier Mummu—whom Jacobsen, true to his principles, sees as 'perhaps...the cloud banks which float low over the earth'.[49] By a typical narrative motif the young gods are at first dismayed, but then Ea casts a spell on Apsu, kills him, and puts a halter round the loathsome Mummu. Ea takes over the Apsu as his own domain, and in it he and his wife Damkina create Marduk—or originally, in all probability, Enlil, god of the winds and air that separate earth from sky, whom the Babylonian adaptors suppressed in favour of the huge four-eyed and four-eared Marduk. Now Tiamat is persuaded to act on behalf of the older gods; the earth creates monsters to help her, and Kingu is appointed general. Ea tries a spell against them, but this time it fails; even Anu can do nothing; but finally the younger gods persuade the youthful Marduk to be their champion, on condition that he becomes supreme god if successful. Marduk attacks Tiamat, hurls fierce winds into her and then cuts her in half: the upper half he sets as the sky, to hold back the waters that descend as rain, and the lower half becomes earth with the subterranean waters below. Next Marduk proceeds to the organization of the rest of the

[49] *IA*, 174 = *BP*, 189.

universe, the setting in place of the heavenly bodies, the creation of men as servants of the gods from the blood of the slain Kingu, the appointment of the great gods to the sky and the underworld, and the building of Marduk's great ziggurat, the Esagila, in Babylon—the last piece of manual work to be carried out by the gods for themselves. Finally at a banquet they proclaim the fifty ritual titles of Marduk, which takes up about a quarter of the whole poem; it is a curious fact that Enlil's name means 'fifty', and the titles as well as the performance may have been annexed from him on behalf of Marduk.

This myth was of enormous importance in the religion of Mesopotamia and western Asia during the second and much of the first millennium B.C.; and it became so closely associated with the cult of Marduk that it was, as we have seen (and as F. M. Cornford over-emphatically remarked), recited to himself each year in Babylon by the priest at the New Year festival. The idea of cosmogonical differentiation on the lines of human birth and marriage was a fruitful one, familiar also in Egypt and later, of course, through Hesiod's *Theogony*. The hostility of the primeval gods, representing the originative cosmic constituents, and the younger gods establishes a theme that passed into Hurrian and Greek myths. Marduk's splitting of Tiamat is as ingenious as it is dramatic, since it accounts for the division between the two sources, upper and lower, of fresh water. The apportioning of the heavenly bodies and the different younger gods is a possible prototype of Zeus's *diataxis* or distribution, also carried out when all the enemies had been disposed of, in the *Theogony*; but the rest of the poem, recording for all time Marduk's titles and functions, is of religious rather than mythological interest. Indeed the mythical content of the whole poem, although important so far as it goes, is both restricted in implication and relatively straightforward in expression. It will be more rewarding for present purposes to consider a much briefer and more fragmentary pair of myths, each of which seems to have become widely known without ritual support.

Adapa is the subject of a myth known as far afield as Amarna in Egypt in the fourteenth century B.C., although that version must be supplemented by three later but still fragmentary versions from Nineveh.[50] Created by Ea to be wise but not immortal, Adapa looked after Ea's shrine in Eridu, baked bread for him and

[50] *ANET*[2], 101 f.

caught fish for offerings. One day he went out fishing and was sunk by the fierce south wind. As he swims he curses the wind, saying that he will 'break its wing'; at which the south wind really is crippled and ceases to blow. After seven days Anu, king of the gods, asks the reason for this; he is told by his vizier that Adapa is responsible, and summons him. Ea advises Adapa to put on mourning garments and tell the two gatekeepers at Anu's gate that he is mourning for two gods who have disappeared from the land. The gatekeepers are those very gods—one of them, surprisingly enough, is Tammuz, the Sumerian Dumuzi, who is very far in this version from being a permanent corpse—and they are so pleased at this piece of flattery that they say a good word for Adapa to Anu, as indeed Ea had foreseen. Another piece of Ea's advice does not seem to work so well. He had instructed Adapa to refuse food and drink in heaven, since what would be offered him would be the food and water of death. Adapa consequently does so, only to be told by Anu, who seems pleased, that what he has refused was the food and water of *life*. According to two of the Nineveh tablets Anu seems to have been angry with Ea, apparently for trying to thwart Anu's purpose (C2 ff., D4 ff.). Before that, according this time to the Amarna version, Anu had felt that any mortal to whom so much wisdom had been granted (for Ea had revealed to Adapa the 'heart' of the heaven and the earth, B57 ff.) would have to be made immortal, just like Utnapishtim in the eleventh tablet of the Gilgamesh epic. According to the third Nineveh version Adapa seems to have been sent back to earth with certain new decrees concerning the priesthood and the promise that the goddess of healing would attenuate the diseases he had brought with him—but it is not at all sure that this last part does not belong to a ritual or incantatory appendix rather than to the narrative of the myth itself (D 15 ff.).

The myth has undergone certain vicissitudes: the earliest and longest tablet, from Amarna, is in prose, and of the three later ones, from Nineveh, the last two seem to have been somewhat condensed. The first, however, describes Adapa's wisdom, the gift of Ea, in a leisurely and impressive way; then, with Adapa beginning his fishing, it breaks off; but we cannot ignore its emphatic statement that 'To him he [*sc.* Ea] had given wisdom; eternal life he had not given him'.[51] What subsequently seems to

---

[51] A4, tr. E. A. Speiser, *ANET*², 101.

annoy Anu is that Ea should have given his favourite a kind of knowledge that should be reserved for the gods; there is no suggestion that Adapa's impatience in cursing the south wind was the real cause of the trouble—indeed the support of the gatekeeper gods (by a typical piece of folktale ingenuity) seemed to ensure that Adapa would be pardoned by Anu. Anu's offering of the food and water of life may either have been his reaction to a *fait accompli*, the fact that Ea had already endowed Adapa with a wisdom that was almost divine; or it may have been an ironical reversal of what Ea had predicted would happen, in order to emphasize Anu's superiority. But in either case there is a difficulty: why should there have been any question of offering the food and water of *death*? If Adapa had taken it, what would have happened? He himself, presumably, would have died forthwith—there was no question of his earning mortality, because that he possessed already. But if immediate death was the danger, it was hardly being offered as the choice for all mankind; and yet the fourth tablet, whether or not the relevant part of it is myth or interpretation, regards Adapa as the origin of diseases (and presumably death) for men.

The mythical motif of a choice between mortality and immortality is a common one throughout the world; men choose wrongly, by folly or greed or just accident. In other tales, for example several Amerindian variants, it is some animal that makes off with men's chance of eternal life, and indeed a similar folktale motif (for one can almost call it that) occurs in the Gilgamesh epic, where a snake filches the plant of youth. Even so I am not sure that Alexander Heidel was right in asserting that the Adapa myth answers the question 'Why must man suffer and die?' by saying 'Because Adapa had the chance of gaining immortality for himself and mankind, but he did not take it'.[52] Certainly the question was raised, but perhaps only in a rather trivial way to which the light-hearted folktale motif would be appropriate. In earlier forms of the myth I believe the choice must have simply concerned Adapa himself.[53] Moreover there can never have been much probability, in the mind of the hypothetical myth-maker, of immortality being

[52] *The Babylonian Genesis* (2nd ed., Chicago, 1951), 124—a useful book, dealing primarily with the Epic of Creation.

[53] Adapa is not described as the representative or first ancestor of men, as Heidel pointed out (*op. cit.*, 152, n. 33).

granted; Adapa had been fated by Ea to be mortal and, however much Anu may have wanted to shame or rebuke Ea, he would hardly have done so in such an ambivalent way. Anu's position is very much that of Zeus when confronted with the choice of the two portions of sacrifice by Prometheus; and Ea resembles Prometheus in falsely thinking that he can deceive the king of the gods. There may well be some thematic connexion here. In short, our surviving versions of the myth represent a conflation of at least three different stories about a choice between life and death; but I conjecture that this choice was never a serious issue of Akkadian mythical thought, but rather a folktale theme used here to show up other facets of the gods and perhaps also to throw light on the powers and privileges of the priesthood. Just as the Gilgamesh myth has as one of its themes the insistence that even a king must suffer death, so the Adapa myth may emphasize that even the greatest scrupulousness in carrying out the temple rituals cannot be expected to carry so unnatural a reward as immortality.

The second myth is the myth of Etana. Part of it is structurally very similar to that of Adapa, and it likewise concerns a mortal of unusual piety. Etana is the first king among men, and according to the Sumerian King List the first post-diluvian ruler of Kish. The myth consists of two lightly linked stages and a prelude. The prelude relates how the gods chose Etana as the first king, an important event in the rehabilitation of mankind after the great flood. The first stage of the myth proper describes the compact between an eagle and a snake, which ends with the eagle devouring the snake's young and being cast into a pit. The second stage reintroduces Etana: he is childless and prays to Shamash the sun-god for an heir; Shamash sends him to the eagle in the pit, who, he says, will show Etana the plant of birth. After a gap Etana is seen flying up to heaven on the eagle's back. They seem to have reached Anu's gate, but after another gap they are flying still higher—so high that Etana cannot even see the earth. Somehow the eagle and he start plunging downwards—and there, rather typically, the text finally peters out. Some interpreters have naturally felt that the outcome of the quest was disastrous, but I agree with Kramer that in the end, and in spite of this alarming plunge, Etana must have brought back the plant of birth safely to earth. After all, he is under the protection of Shamash, guardian of oaths; the whole point of the myth as emphasized in the prelude is concerned with the establishment of kingship; and Etana has a son as his direct successor in the King List.

The Etana myth is of unusual interest not only for its content but also for its antiquity and its demonstrable stability over a long period. The Neo-Assyrian version from Ashurbanipal's library happens to be the most complete surviving text, but where it overlaps with an Old Babylonian version of a thousand years earlier it corresponds with it very closely, sometimes word for word. A short Middle Assyrian fragment maintains the same accuracy. Moreover the story probably went back at least to the end of the third millennium, since cylinder seals from the Old Akkadian period more than once show a man riding on a bird's back. This repetition of the motif suggests that a well-known tale is being used; and indeed the story may well ascend into the first part of the third millennium, the period when the Gilgamesh legend (which was also concerned with a problem of kingship, namely whether the great king must be mortal) seems to have originated. Finally some of the constituent themes were probably earlier still.

At first sight the structure looks clumsy and incoherent. In particular the episode of the eagle and the snake (which, judging by the scale of the surviving portions, must have been a conspicuous part of the whole) seems extraneous to the main purpose of the myth, to be dragged in merely as one of several possible ways of showing how Shamash makes the eagle available for Etana's journey. And no doubt the quarrel between the snake and the eagle, or in more general terms the compact between two creatures that is broken by one of them, followed by a trick that brings about the downfall of the aggressor, was an animal fable in its own right. Yet its close association over so long a period with the story of Etana's quest suggests some significant bearing upon it. If so, the structure of the whole would have that kind of two-stage character which was discovered in several of the Sumerian myths, and we should expect one underlying point of the myth to arise out of the juxtaposition of the two parts.

The agreement is that the snake will live at the bottom of a particular tree, the eagle among its foliage at the top.[54] Both will

---

[54] Compare the Sumerian tale of the *Imdugud*-bird and snake that occupied the top and bottom of Inanna's tree (p. 108), and see also R. J. Williams, *The Phoenix*, x, 1956, 70–7 and W. G. Lambert, *Babylonian Wisdom Literature* (Oxford, 1960), 150.

beget young in safety, and they will share their food. Shamash
witnesses the agreement but, as soon as the eagle's fledglings can
fly, their ruthless parent descends and eats up the serpent's brood.
The snake returns to find them gone, guesses what has happened,
and calls on the sun-god for vengeance. Shamash responds by
telling the snake how to catch the eagle: Shamash will 'bind' a
wild ox for the snake to kill—the snake is then to tear open its
belly and hide inside it. All the birds of heaven will come to feed
on the carcass, the eagle among them; then the snake is to catch
the eagle, tear off his wings and claws, and cast him into a pit to
die of hunger and thirst. All of this, short of the eagle's actual
death, comes to pass—in spite of advice given by the youngest
fledgling, called 'Exceeding wise', who had also warned his
father against the initial crime. This is another motif of animal-
fable or folktale type, but one that does not seem to have any
bearing on the broader context.

A remarkable piece of visual evidence may help to illuminate the
significant emphasis of the animal fable. The most striking of the
cylinder seals believed to represent Etana belongs to the period of
Sargon, in the later part of the third millennium B.C.[55] It shows a
man being lifted skyward by a great bird; two dogs beneath watch
his departure, as does a shepherd with his sheep who raises his
right hand in apparent valediction. Between the rising figure and
the shepherd stands a conspicuous tree; a bird is hovering in its
branches. At the foot of the tree a lion (not a snake) rears up in a
hostile fashion; a second lion on the other side of the tree has his
head turned towards the earth—in other words, these lions are
not heraldic in posture. The shepherd and his sheep are not so
irrelevant to Etana as they might seem, for Etana was himself a
shepherd, and is so described in the King List: 'a shepherd, the
one who to heaven ascended'.[56] Moreover an important detail
confirms the association with both stages of our Etana myth; for
the bird in the tree is holding a small animal, something very like
a lion cub, in its right talon. But what about the duplication of the
bird and the lion—why are there two of them? And why in any
event a lion and not a snake? The answer to the first question is
surely that duplication represents successive roles for a single

[55] Illustrated as pl. XXIV (h) of Henri Frankfort's Cylinder Seals (London, 1939), and
described there on pp. 138 f.

[56] Th. Jacobsen, The Sumerian King List (Chicago, 1939), 80 f.; ANET², 265.

figure, no unusual characteristic of this kind of representation. The bird in the tree is the same as the bird, the eagle, that later carries Etana skyward; the lion is at one moment facing the earth, perhaps feeding or even searching for its young, at another rearing in rage against the eagle who has stolen his offspring. Even the shepherd with his raised arm may be Etana himself in an earlier phase, and the arm may signify an invocation of Shamash rather than, as it seems at first, a valediction; although the artist may not have been precise on this point.

That leaves the question: why a lion and not a snake? Artistic convenience may be partly responsible, but there are important resemblances between the two animals that may more fully explain the substitution and give a clue to the meaning of the whole. We know that lions were caught and destroyed by being lured or cast into pits; that is what happened to a lion who became Ishtar's lover according to the sixth tablet of the Gilgamesh epic. Lions were associated with pits, with holes in the ground, just like snakes, who lived underground in holes. If the eagle were to be lured into a pit and kept there to die, that would be the most fitting of all punishments if his victim had originally been a lion rather than a snake; for he finds himself in the most unexpected of places, the place where his terrestrial victim would normally be trapped and done to death. But if that were the original version of the myth, or perhaps just an alternative version, why should the snake be substituted? After all, the snake is not so appropriate a partner in the food-sharing part of the original compact; and the ox he eventually catches has first to be paralysed by the sun-god. As against this, the snake might be a more formidable danger than the lion to the eagle's young. But the reason may also, I think, be connected with the one important quality the snake shares with the lion, his association with the earth beneath its surface. The eagle sits in the top of the tree, as high as possible; the snake lives at the bottom of the tree, but really in the ground beneath it, and so at the polar extreme to the eagle. This polarity of high and low is emphasized by what happens later: the eagle is cast down, not merely from his natural element to the ground, but to a hole or pit below the ground; later still he rises so high in the air, even above the abode of the sky-god, that he begins to crash earthward once more.

Here one is strongly reminded of some of the Bororo and related myths examined by Lévi-Strauss and described in the second chapter, where stranding halfway up a cliff, or the dropping of excrement on the hero's shoulder, from which a tree grows upwards, emphasizes a polarization between high and low that is then seen to be related to the mediation between extremes in a social situation.[57] The Etana myth, as I have interpreted it, responds in a rather remarkable fashion to a Lévi-Straussian kind of analysis. The snake and the lion belong to the earth—even, in different ways, to beneath the earth's surface; the eagle, on the other hand, belongs to the air, and the highest parts of the air. To disregard the lion for a moment, the eagle and the snake each nest in a position symbolizing, by the medium of the tree, this up-and-down relationship. By eating the snake's young, the eagle removes them (inside himself) from their natural position down below to his own natural position up above. As a consequence the eagle finds himself removed to the polar opposite of his natural position, down into the pit. The breaking of the compact, itself a reversal of Shamash's rule of law, has resulted in a complete reversal of the natural relations between eagles and snakes. The balance can only be restored by a subsequent reversal, in which the eagle is first removed to a place unnaturally higher than his normal position, higher than the sky-god himself.

In the complex form of the surviving literary versions the myth is primarily concerned with Etana's search for a successor, to ensure the continuation of the new and vitally important institution of kingship. The restoration of normal relations between high and low, in relation to eagle and snake or lion, may well have seemed relevant, at some level below that of conscious rationalizing, to the achievement of balance in the kingship, namely the removal of the anomaly that the king had no successor.[58]

That may or may not seem plausible in itself; but I am not sure

[57] See pp. 66 and 71–3.

[58] This conclusion is not seriously affected by further speculations one might be tempted to make about missing parts of the myth. For instance the snake may have been introduced in part because it is a symbol of fertility (the intertwined pair of copulating snakes appearing commonly on Sumerian and early Akkadian seals with this significance). Fertility is what is entailed by the plant of birth, too; perhaps the eagle's claim to have access to this, before he is released from the pit, depends on his having swallowed the young snakes. Th. Gaster suggested (SDFML, II, 991, s.v. Semitic mythology) that the eagle was looking for the plant of birth when he plundered the snake's nest, deceived Etana by telling him it was in the sky, and suffered for his deceit by crashing with Etana.

that the implications of myth can often be gauged in this way, namely by apparent plausibility from the standpoint of a modern western man. At least one may ask what the connexion between the two stages of the myth can have been, if this link is excluded. It is true that the sheer narrative appeal of myths, and the steps that might have been taken towards increasing it, must not be underestimated; yet that does not explain the combination of the animal fable with the tale of Etana's search for the plant of birth—since the means by which Etana persuades the eagle to help him are neither dramatic in themselves nor particularly neat. But even if the eagle-and-snake episode has been appended at random, or for some untraceable dramatic and narrative effect, that still leaves the tale of Etana's quest; and there can be little doubt that the folktale motif of the quest for the plant of birth, or of youth, is deliberately used in relation to the succession to kingship. Indeed there is a remarkable similarity of structure between this myth and the Adapa myth, which is likewise unusual in having a mortal, if highly privileged, hero:

Adapa	*Etana*
Adapa is Ea's priest in Eridu	Etana is king (the city-god's steward on earth) in Kish
He suffers misfortune (his boat sinks), depriving the god of fish and other offerings	He suffers misfortune (he cannot produce an heir), depriving the gods of a representative on earth
He curses the south wind	
He is summoned up to heaven (to answer for this)	He flies up to heaven (to obtain the plant of birth)
He returns with rules for the priesthood	⟨Presumably in the end he returns with it⟩
Result: priesthood is strengthened and established	Result: kingship is maintained and the law of succession is regularized

If this analysis is roughly correct, the pair of myths is concerned with two institutions for organizing and regularizing the relations between men and gods and ensuring that men remain both subservient and useful. Each myth shows how a breakdown in one of the institutions (priesthood or kingship) was averted by a culture-hero's direct confrontation with the gods. In the Adapa myth the apparent offer of immortality is a complicating issue, which in the present state of the text we cannot properly understand; and both myths contain other motifs of elaboration that are primarily of narrative value. The Etana myth has a two-stage structure that the Adapa tale could not easily emulate—although it is conceivable that the offer of immortality, if properly understood, would perform an analogous function to that suggested for the snake-and-eagle fable.

These two myths show a typically Akkadian interest in institutions, and are hardly concerned with the natural world at all. They are quite distinct in this respect from many of the Sumerian myths. And yet the theme of mortality and immortality, incidentally introduced in the case of Adapa, is brought in another Akkadian myth into contact with the theme of nature in its relation to the whole of culture. That myth is the Epic of Gilgamesh—totally different in many ways from Adapa and Etana, yet like them concerned with a mortal brought into theoretical conflict with the gods. This represents an Akkadian development of the Sumerian idea of the pious mortal who, like Ziusudra, is simply preserved or rewarded. In this development, and in the generalizing of the concern with death and culture as such, the Epic of Gilgamesh—the initial subject of the following chapter—brings the whole Mesopotamian mythical tradition to its emotional and speculative, as well as its narrative, climax.

IV

Nature and Culture: Gilgamesh, Centaurs and Cyclopes

1 : Gilgamesh

The study of Mesopotamian myths is rewarding not only for their unusual richness in complexity and fantasy and their promising response to a structuralist approach, but also for their influence as a model for Greek myths. Detailed and specific resemblances can be proved only at one or two points, but when Mesopotamian myths are better understood their influence is likely to appear as considerable, if not overwhelming. Therefore the lively discussion of the nature and implications of these myths, even if it is something many Near-Eastern experts do not themselves care to pursue, should be of deep concern to Hellenists. In considering the Epic of Gilgamesh I shall once again be more concerned with its underlying implications, as revealed by apparently arbitrary details of non-folktale type, than with its meaning at a more obvious level (although even that is a profound one). The underlying implication seems to be associated with the valuation of the sometimes opposing ideas of nature and culture— an opposition given modern expression by Jean-Jacques Rousseau, but one that Lévi-Strauss has shown to be of deep interest to the Indian tribes of central Brazil, and one that impinged, as I shall suggest, on ancient Greek culture far earlier than is usually assumed. If so, then the nature–culture relationship is beginning to manifest itself as one of the central and most universal pre-occupations of speculative myths, along with problems of life and death and the relation of different kinds of human, animal, and agrarian fertility. That in itself is relevant to one of the central theses of these studies: that many myths, despite attempts to limit their functions by Malinowski and his followers, or by the myth-and-ritual school, or by a restricted nature–myth approach, are speculative in some sense above and beyond that of straightforward allegory or trivial and concrete aetiology.

The Epic of Gilgamesh is an astonishing poem, and should be read and studied with care by every devotee of Greek culture.[1] It should be studied for its own sake, but also because it reminds one so clearly of what Greek literature and Greek mythology did not attempt. Short as it is in comparison with the scale of the Homeric epics, or even the Hesiodic *Theogony*, it manages to raise, in an extraordinarily incisive and at the same time poignant way, some of the deepest questions of life and death. On another plane it makes a varied and enthralling narrative, told with intense and dramatic vigour. Above all it retains, in spite of its long and literate history, an unmistakable aura of the mythical—of that kind of emotional exploration of the permanent meaning of life, by the release of fantasy about the distant past, that Greek myths, at least as we experience them, so often fail to exemplify in their own right.

The epic is based on stories about Gilgamesh that had existed for many centuries in the Sumerian tradition, although it is, as it stands, an Akkadian composition. The hero was originally a real figure, king of Sumerian Uruk in the first half of the third millennium B.C., who, perhaps because he lived at the beginning of a historical age, attracted to himself many tales of power and resourcefulness. One of the Sumerian compositions about him, 'Gilgamesh and Agga', describes what happened when he was called on to pay tribute to the king of Kish; this is not a myth in the strictest sense, but a legendary tradition that loosely records the decision-making processes of the king, counsellors and free citizens of Uruk. Of the other Sumerian tales, one describes Gilgamesh's death and elaborate funeral, three others are more obviously fictitious. 'Gilgamesh and the Land of the Living' relates how he and his servant Enkidu attacked the giant Huwawa in his cedar forest, and may owe something to knowledge of

[1] For most of us necessarily in translation, preferably that by E. A. Speiser in *ANET*[2], 72–97.

timber-expeditions to the western or eastern highlands; but 'Gilgamesh and the Bull of Heaven'—which like the Huwawa episode is incorporated, in an altered form, in the Akkadian epic— has no such overtones of actuality, and the same is the case with Gilgamesh's drum and drumstick and Enkidu's detention in the underworld (pp. 107 f.). Of the five known relatively complete Sumerian tales about Gilgamesh, therefore, two are quasi-historical, one may have historical overtones but is primarily mythical, and the other two are more or less completely mythical although literate in the form known to us. Of the three mythical tales, two were used for the Akkadian epic compilation, whereas the other gives a quite different version of the death of Enkidu from that of the epic but resembles it both in tone and in the reaction of Gilgamesh.

The process of composing the epic can be tentatively placed at least as early as 2000 B.C. The fullest surviving version is the Assyrian one from the library of Ashurbanipal at Nineveh, and therefore no older than the seventh century B.C.; but fragments from other sources—texts in Hittite, Hurrian and Akkadian from the Hittite capital at Hattusa (Boghaz-Keui), as well as sporadic Old Babylonian tablets—help to fill the gaps and, equally important, prove that the text of the epic did not vary in the course of its transmission over more than a thousand years. It was, indeed, a very widely known poem, probably the most familiar and most scrupulously preserved of all Mesopotamian literary works outside the ritual tradition. In spite of the number of versions that have survived, there are still tantalizing gaps at certain points; only the eleventh and last tablet, which gives Utnapishtim's account of the flood and then describes Gilgamesh's departure and return to Uruk, is almost complete, consisting as it does of over three hundred verses.

The epic was composed quite deliberately. It possesses many of the qualities of myth, but is no more 'a myth' in the sense of a tale passed down in a popular oral tradition than any of the other and shorter Mesopotamian tales examined so far. It is less so, in fact, because, although all of them are literate (which is the condition of our knowing them), this has more clearly been the object of complex processes of selection, compilation, and careful adaptation. The processes have not been completely successful in the technical sense, since one can detect joins and minor inconsistencies—much more clearly, for example, than in the Homeric poems which, although probably composed within a true oral period and with little or no help from writing, are far more finished than the Akkadian work. Partly that is the result of the process of transmission itself, the gradual tidying-up to which Greeks down to the time of Aristarchus subjected the *Iliad* and *Odyssey* (whereas the Epic of Gilgamesh seems to have been treated with something of the veneration of a religious text); and partly it reflects the great technical skill that a complex and developed oral poetical tradition like the Greek demands of its singers.

It is this very rigidity of the Mesopotamian literary tradition, the unimaginative conscientiousness with which scribes copied and recopied works or documents from the past, that may have retained much of the content, not too heavily distorted and over-laid, of unselfconscious myth drawn from an illiterate and popular milieu. The Gilgamesh epic does nothing to diminish the probability that, alongside the literate tradition, there flowed a popular tradition that was essentially oral. Although the poem is in one sense a thoroughly artificial affair, in another it consists of themes of genuinely mythical relevance, and in its totality expresses pre-occupations for which myths are the natural medium. Examination of its content will show more clearly what I mean.

Gilgamesh, king of Uruk, has a mortal father (although he was later held to be a god) and a divine mother. The mortal element is decisive, and he himself, as he eventually comes to accept, is irretrievably human. In Uruk he behaves abominably, sleeping with all the wives and the pretty girls and constantly summoning the young men to corvée duties or worse. The people of Uruk ask the gods for help in their predicament, and the gods tell the goddess Aruru, who in some sense made Gilgamesh, to create his image or double. She does so in a multiple process of conceiving an image within her, washing her hands, pinching off clay, and casting it (or drawing a design on it) on the steppe. It is on the steppe, in the desert wastes, that Enkidu is born (1, 33, 35). His whole body is shaggy with hair, and his head-hair is like a woman's (which was unusual in the third millennium B.C.). He feeds on grass with the gazelles and drinks at their watering-place; he is a wild man. For three days on end a human trapper catches sight of him at the pool; he is terrified at the sight, and his face becomes like that of a traveller from afar. The trapper tells his father, who advises him to report the matter to Gilgamesh in the city and to bring back a harlot as a lure. That is what he does. The harlot displays her charms, and Enkidu falls for them. For six days and seven nights he makes love to her; but when he returns to the animals they run away, and he is now so weak that he can no longer catch up with them.

With weakness, however, comes greater understanding. The harlot, to whom he returns, tells him that he is wise, 'like a god', that he should stop roaming the steppe with the wild creatures and come with her to Uruk, where Gilgamesh lords it like a wild ox. Enkidu wants Gilgamesh as a friend, and meanwhile, back in Uruk, Gilgamesh himself has two dreams, about a star and an axe; he is strongly drawn to them, and his mother interprets them as representing Enkidu, a mighty companion. Now the harlot continues Enkidu's acculturation; she clothes him, leads him to the house of the shepherds, teaches him to take solid food instead of the milk of wild creatures. He drinks strong drink, becomes cheerful, rubs the hair from his body and anoints his skin, and as a final service to his new friends he chases off, or captures, some of his old ones, the lions and wolves. When he hears from a passer-by about Gilgamesh's riotous and immoral behaviour in town he is deeply shocked. Finally he goes to Uruk; the people, recognizing him as Gilgamesh's natural counterpart, feel relieved. That night he intercepts the king on his way to an amorous assignment, and they wrestle. Gilgamesh eventually wins, and Enkidu recognizes him as a true king. They become fast friends.

At the beginning of Tablet III Gilgamesh broaches the idea of making a journey to the cedar-forest of the giant Huwawa (Assyrian Humbaba), there to slay him. Enkidu is appalled—he knew the forest and its guardian when he roamed with the animals— and attempts to dissuade his friend. Gilgamesh is adamant; he is determined to make a name for himself by this heroic encounter, since he perceives, and reminds Enkidu, that 'only the gods live for ever under the sun. As for mankind, numbered are their days'.[2] Axes and weapons are made in Uruk; the elders pray for his safe return; an omen is taken and is in some way unfavourable, for Gilgamesh weeps, but persists. The elders counsel him to let Enkidu lead the way, and to purify himself after the giant is

[2] Translation by E. A. Speiser, *ANET²*, 79.

slain. His mother Ninsun (this supplement comes in the Assyrian version) prays to Shamash for her son's safety, adopts Enkidu and asks him to bring back Gilgamesh safely. In the fragmentary fourth tablet they arrive at the gate of the forest; Enkidu touches it and his hand is paralysed, but Gilgamesh enables him to overcome the weakness. In Tablet v they approach the cedar mountain, then lie down to sleep. Gilgamesh has three dreams, the first two probably favourable, the third sinister; for in it the earth is overcome by fire and lightning. Nevertheless Gilgamesh cuts down one of the cedars, and Huwawa approaches. At first, as is usual in these Mesopotamian monster-encounters, the heroes are panic-stricken; but then Shamash encourages them and sends eight fierce winds that hold Huwawa motionless—not unlike the winds with which Marduk distended Tiamat in the Epic of Creation. The giant pleads for his life and offers to be Gilgamesh's servant, but Enkidu counsels firmness and they cut off his head.

At the beginning of the sixth tablet Gilgamesh has washed himself and put on his crown and clean clothes. He is so magnificent that Ishtar herself, the goddess of love, desires him and offers him the role of husband. Gilgamesh rejects her with extraordinary insolence, pointing out the fate of her previous lovers: Tammuz seems to have been turned into a bird, the lion was cast into a pit, and so on. Ishtar rushes off in anger to her father Anu and demands that he make the Bull of Heaven for the express purpose of laying Gilgamesh low; if not, she threatens to smash in the gates of the underworld (just as she did in the separate myth of Inanna/Ishtar's descent, p. 109). Anu reluctantly agrees, but the Bull turns out to be a bit of a fiasco, since Enkidu easily grips its horns and Gilgamesh rapidly despatches it. They dedicate the heart to Shamash, but Enkidu flings its thigh (which may be a euphemism) at the goddess of love as she stands on the walls of Uruk. Gilgamesh is fêted there as the most splendid among the heroes; but that night Enkidu has a bad dream, and the tablet ends with his fearful question 'My friend, why are the great gods in council?'

In the seventh tablet Enkidu describes his dream, which gave a vision of what had in fact happened. Anu has demanded the death of either Gilgamesh or Enkidu for killing the Bull of Heaven, and Enlil has decided, in spite of the pleas of Shamash, that the victim must be Enkidu. Enkidu accordingly falls ill, and Gilgamesh, who knows that his friend is suffering for them both,

bewails him. Foreseeing death, Enkidu curses the successive stages
that led to his downfall: the gate of the cedar forest that paralysed
his hand, the trapper who first saw him in the desert, the harlot
who seduced him and won him over to civilization. Shamash
points out how unfair this is, since Gilgamesh has raised him up,
given him a name among the people, and will mourn him with
uncut hair, wearing a lion-skin and roaming on the steppe.
Enkidu is persuaded to change his curses into elaborate blessings—
a theme that smacks of a rhetorical exercise. He tells of another
dream in which he enters the underworld, after being carried
there by a great bird, and sees former kings acting as servants.
For twelve successive days his sufferings increase; finally he calls
Gilgamesh and tells him that he, Enkidu, is accursed in the
manner of his death—not like one slain in battle, who is blessed.
At last (although the end of the tablet is missing) he dies.

Tablet VIII begins with Gilgamesh's extravagant mourning for
his friend, 'the panther of the steppe': he refuses to believe that
he is dead, asks what manner of sleep it is, but then touches
Enkidu's heart and finds that it does not beat. 'Then he veiled his
friend like a bride...storming over him like a lion;'[3] he recalls
Enkidu's prowess in the past, and sets up a statue of him; here the
tablet, which is very fragmentary, ends.

The next tablet sees Gilgamesh ranging the steppe in terrible
fear of death: 'When I die, shall I not be like Enkidu? Woe has
entered my belly. Fearing death, I roam over the steppe.'[4] To try
and evade death, it may be inferred, he decides to journey to
Utnapishtim, the only man—and, with his wife, sole survivor of
the flood—to have achieved immortality. He arrives at the
mountain called Mashu, guarded by scorpion-men (a long-
established hybrid in Mesopotamian art and myth, particularly
chosen to guard the boundaries of earth and sky). They recognize
him as one-third mortal and two-thirds divine, and allow him to
pass through the mountain. After twelve leagues of terrifying
darkness he emerges into the brilliant light of a jewelled garden,
originally it seems described at some length. In the tenth tablet
the journey continues. Gilgamesh clothes himself in skins, and
defends his enterprise to Shamash the sun-god; also to Siduri, a
divine alewife or barmaid here envisaged as living near the sea of
death. To her he explains that he would not give up Enkidu for

---

[3] VIII, ii, 17 f., tr. Speiser.   [4] IX, i, 3–5, tr. Speiser.

burial, but mourned him for seven days and nights until a worm
fell from the corpse's nose; since when he has roamed like a
hunter on the steppe. Siduri replies that he is being foolish, since
'When the gods created mankind, Death for mankind they set
aside, Life in their own hands retaining':[5] let him seek the happi-
ness that is the lot of men, dancing and feasting, clean clothes, an
affectionate wife and child! In the fuller Assyrian version Gilgamesh threatens Siduri, who has taken fright at his grim appearance as he approaches; his face, like that of the trapper who
first saw Enkidu, resembles that of a traveller from afar. He reveals that he is indeed Gilgamesh, the vanquisher of Humbaba,
and that his appearance is due to sorrow at Enkidu's death and
his own fear of dying. She tells him he must cross the waters of
death to reach Utnapishtim, and directs him to Urshanabi,
Utnapishtim's ferryman, who is 'picking *urnu*-snakes' (a still
mysterious occupation) in the woods. There is some sort of
contretemps, in which Gilgamesh himself picks the snakes and moreover smashes 'those of stone', evidently two magical statues that
Urshanabi carries in his boat to act as a means of propulsion.
Nevertheless Gilgamesh and he have a conversation that is the
image of the one he had held with Siduri. At Urshanabi's bidding
Gilgamesh cuts 120 sixty-cubit punt-poles; they launch the boat
and abandon each pole after one thrust, evidently so as not to let
the waters of death touch them. When the poles are used up Gilgamesh spreads his cloth as a sail, and Urshanabi gives voice to
this Eliot-like lament:

> Why have the Stone Things of the boat been broken,
> and rides in her one who is not her master?
> He who has come hither is not of men;
> and...
> I peer, but I cannot...
> I peer, but I cannot...
> I peer, but...
>
> (x, iv, 15 ff., tr. Speiser)

Evidently they reach Utnapishtim in the end; Gilgamesh recounts
his hardships, and explains that he is wearing animals' skins
because his clothes were worn out.

At the beginning of the eleventh and last tablet Gilgamesh

---

[5] x (Old Babylonian version), iii, 3–5; tr. Speiser, *ANET*², 90.

comments that Utnapishtim looks very much like himself: what is
the difference—why should the one be immortal and the other not?
Utnapishtim replies with the whole story of the flood; how Ea
warned him to build a great ship, which enabled him and his
family to survive the flood sent by the gods—a flood which by a
typically Mesopotamian change of heart the gods, and especially
Ishtar, regret: 'How could I speak evil in the Assembly of the
gods, ordering battle for the destruction of my people, when it is I
myself who give birth to my people!'[6] On the seventh day the
storm subsides, the ship comes to rest on Mount Nisir, and three
birds are successively despatched; the last of them does not return.
Utnapishtim emerges from his ship and makes sacrifice to the
gods, who crowd round like flies. Enlil is enraged that any mortal
has escaped the ordained destruction, but Ea defends Utnapishtim, and finally Enlil makes him and his wife immortal, to dwell
far away at the mouth of the rivers. But who, asks Utnapishtim, is
going to call the gods to assembly on Gilgamesh's behalf? To
demonstrate his visitor's innate mortality Utnapishtim challenges
him to stay awake for seven days: Gilgamesh immediately falls
asleep. Utnapishtim foresees that Gilgamesh will try to deny it,
and tells his wife to bake a loaf for each day that Gilgamesh
sleeps; the seven loaves are produced when he claims to have slept
for only a moment or two.

Gilgamesh now seems almost to accept his mortality, but is no
less plaintive. Utnapishtim dismisses Urshanabi, but tells him to
escort Gilgamesh home after taking him to the washing place to
wash off the dirt, cast off the skins, and put on clean clothes for his
return to the city. As they leave, Utnapishtim's wife seems to take
pity, and urges her husband to tell Gilgamesh about the plant of
rejuvenation (something less than immortality—its name means
'an old man becomes young') that lies at the bottom of the sea.
Gilgamesh dives and, after seeing a sign whose significance he only
realizes later, plucks the plant, but decides to wait till his return to
Uruk before eating it. Soon he stops to bathe; a snake comes out
of the pool and carries off the plant, sloughing off his skin. Gilgamesh sits down and weeps, but now sees the meaning of the
sign—that immortality, or a second youth, is not for him. He and
Urshanabi continue their journey, and the poem ends with the
king proudly displaying to Urshanabi the walls of Uruk his city.

[6] XI, 120 ff., tr. Speiser.

In one sense this extraordinary poem is a compendium of some of the best-known and most successful stories of the Sumerian narrative tradition: not only the short Sumerian Gilgamesh-tales already mentioned, but also the myth of the flood, and the tale (which likewise looks like an originally independent poem) of Ishtar's passion for Gilgamesh and his violent rejection of her, followed by the successful disposal of the Bull of Heaven.[7] Many other minor motifs, such as the journey through the mountain of Mashu, the jewelled garden, and the crossing of the waters of death, were possibly incorporated from other poems. Yet the whole composition has a life and unity of its own.[8] The main underlying theme, as has long been recognized, is mortality; yet the problem presented is more complex than is suggested by phrases like 'man in his search for understanding of death'. To perceive the proper emphases of a work that is often allusive and obscure even where it is not fragmentary, it is essential to notice the changes introduced in relation to surviving Sumerian poems.

In the Sumerian poem of 'Gilgamesh and the Land of the Living' the hero 'sets his mind' towards Huwawa's precinct in order to establish his own name and the names of the gods. He tells the sun-god Utu that men die in his city, that he has seen their bodies in the river[9] and knows that he too will die; therefore he wants to set up his name, accomplish a deed that will be remembered long after his death.

The main motive, the establishment of a reputation, is the same in the Sumerian and the Akkadian versions; but it is made much clearer in the Sumerian that Gilgamesh accepts the full facts of

---

[7] Admittedly Enkidu's dying, a crucial theme of the epic as a whole, is linked with the slaying of the Bull, but that could be the result of a minor adjustment. His death could, for instance, have been determined by the gods in revenge for the slaying of Huwawa, and there are factors that indicate this. It is Enkidu that insists on the giant's death, and Huwawa is in places envisaged as a guardian of the forest appointed by Enlil himself, not just as an ogre.

[8] Theodor H. Gaster misleadingly implied that there can be no significant unity: 'Despite its heroic framework...the *Epic of Gilgamesh* is, at bottom, a collection of popular Märchen artificially clustered around a traditional figure of legend. The folklorist who recognizes its constituent types and composite nature can but look askance at the conventional attempts to interpret it as an organic whole, e.g. as representing the progressive journey of the sun through the constellations of the zodiac' (*SDFML*, II, s.v. Semitic folklore).

[9] Or rather, as Stephanie Page has suggested to me, '*on* the river', being carried down by boat to the place of burial. It is unlikely that the river, which provided drinking-water, would be regularly polluted by corpses.

death, that he has seen the corpses of ordinary men and is aware that he will suffer the same fate. This detail is suppressed in the Akkadian version, since Gilgamesh's grief and despair at Enkidu's death have to be fully motivated—and the motive offered is that now for the first time does Gilgamesh understand what death really means. And yet the change is not quite so straightforward. In the Sumerian poem on 'The Death of Gilgamesh' Gilgamesh has a dream that portends his own imminent demise. The manner of its interpretation implies that he has not, after all, accepted the inevitability of death for himself as great king of Uruk: 'Enlil, the great mountain, the father of the gods—O lord Gilgamesh, the meaning of the dream is—has destined thy fate, O Gilgamesh, for kingship, for eternal life he has not destined it.'[10] One of the purposes of this poem, or the original that lies behind it, was surely to emphasize that even the king, in spite of his divine associations, must die; and to assert that this was no anomaly reflecting on the king's authority on earth, but the result of a solemn divine decree. Echoes of such an emphasis descended into the Akkadian epic, although it is not there made explicit that it is Gilgamesh *as king* who cannot accept his fate as that of all other men.

In the Sumerian poem about the attack on Huwawa, Enkidu plays a lesser part, as it seems, than in the Akkadian version (although he similarly refers Gilgamesh to the sun-god for help, then tries to deter him from the actual encounter with the giant, and finally insists, as in the Akkadian version, on Gilgamesh killing the giant). Gilgamesh falls into a deep sleep from which he can only be awakened with difficulty, and this appears to correspond with Enkidu's paralysis after touching the gates of the cedar forest in the Akkadian version: he has replaced Enkidu at this point, and Huwawa before he dies emphasizes Enkidu's subordinate position by calling him a 'hired man'. In all the Sumerian poems where he appears Enkidu is the servant of Gilgamesh (perhaps, admittedly, in the sense of the Greek *therapon*), and not his near-equal as in the Akkadian epic. The difference is significant. The whole theme of the creation of Enkidu by the gods as an equal and counterweight to Gilgamesh is unknown in the surviving fragments of Sumerian poetry. It may yet appear, or be present in tablets still undeciphered; it is more probable than not that some rudimentary predecessor of the theme was known before the Gilgamesh epic was

[10] A 33–5, tr. S. N. Kramer, *ANET*[2], 50.

composed. Even so, it is strange that none of our Sumerian Gilgamesh-poems foreshadows Enkidu as the wild man from the desert, the man who was gradually introduced to civilization and culture. In 'Gilgamesh and the Land of the Living' it is made clear at one point (98 ff.) that Enkidu has already seen Huwawa—but that is not explicitly related, as it is in the Gilgamesh epic, to his days as the companion of the wild animals, when he roamed at large through the desert places. It would be a reasonable conjecture that the author or authors of the Akkadian composition at the least emphasized the motif of Enkidu's original wildness, gave it a prominence and a point that it does not seem to have had in earlier versions.

In the Sumerian poem about the death of Enkidu, of which Tablet XII, appended to the Akkadian epic, is a direct translation, the motive of Enkidu's gradual dying, and of his despair at what association with Gilgamesh has turned him into, simply does not exist. There Enkidu's death is caused by his own heedlessness in not following Gilgamesh's advice. He deliberately challenges the underworld, and as a consequence is finally detained.[11] Moreover Gilgamesh's dismay at the news that Enkidu's body is devoured by worms and turned to dust (XII, 93 ff.) is at odds with his acceptance of death in 'Gilgamesh and the Land of the Living', and more in accord with his excessive grief in the Akkadian poem. Even so, it might be explained by details of the Sumerian poem that we cannot properly comprehend; and Gilgamesh's ignorance of the full implications and inevitability of death was probably developed in the later recensions. The Sumerian death of Enkidu is in any case rather mysterious: how did Gilgamesh drop his drum and drumstick into the nether world, why did Enkidu so readily volunteer to retrieve them and then act so imprudently? When not even the goddess Inanna could escape from the House of Dust without the fullest efforts of the great gods above, how could Enkidu, a mere mortal, hope to do so? Conceivably his function is precisely to emphasize that, for a mortal, death is absolutely irreversible. But what is the implication of the refrain 'Namtar did not seize him, Fever did not seize him; the nether world seized him', and so on (e.g. XII, 51)? It is an odd story, part of the purpose of

---

[11] The report of conditions there given by his spirit to Gilgamesh is to some extent paralleled by the dream of the underworld that he reveals shortly before his death in Tablet VII of the epic.

which was to provide another opportunity for a description of the conditions of the dead; but one that confirms the impression that Enkidu's complex role in the Akkadian epic is the result of much new speculation, and does not reproduce a standard Sumerian view.

Out of the incompletely homogeneous Sumerian background the Akkadian authors seem to have created a consistent picture of change and development in Gilgamesh's view of death. At the beginning of the epic he is carefree and extroverted, uncontrolled and autocratic. The provision of a companion and equal turns his mind elsewhere, to the making of a name. He knows that men must die, and determines to achieve a kind of immortality by a deed of prowess. Enkidu, who knows Huwawa, tries to deter him, but Gilgamesh presses forward in spite of an unfavourable dream. When the monster is slain they are both irrepressible, and insult Ishtar; this results in the gods decreeing Enkidu's death. The loss of a close companion, someone he loved, makes death very much more real to Gilgamesh; so do the lingering nature of Enkidu's death and his graphic predictions of what awaits him below. His statement that in the underworld even kings act as servants may have had some special effect, and reproduces a motif outlined in the Sumerian 'Death of Gilgamesh'. When at last Enkidu dies, Gilgamesh cannot understand it until the visible sign of corruption, the worm, appears. Then he behaves like a madman—carries grief to exceptional extremes, and allies it with new fears about his own death. He, too, he now perceives, will completely die; his body, too, will be corrupted. This causes him to set off on the lonely journey to Utnapishtim, to face every kind of danger, despite all warnings that Utnapishtim is a special case who cannot be copied. This message is repeated by Utnapishtim himself; the test of wakefulness, miserably failed, finally persuades Gilgamesh to depart. The unexpected information about the plant of rejuvenation (a folktale-type motif) and his consequent joy and sorrow, together with the sign glimpsed beneath the sea, complete his acceptance of failure in his quest, and he returns to Uruk. The myth exemplifies, through a single legendary figure, the various attitudes to death that humans tend to adopt: theoretical acceptance, utterly destroyed by one's first close acquaintance with it in someone loved; revulsion from the obscenity of physical corruption; the desire to surmount death in one's own private case, either by means of a lasting reputation or by the desperate fantasy that oneself could be immortal. Finally, a kind of resignation—but before that, perhaps, an attempt to delay death by emulating youth.

The interpretation offered so far depends on neglecting several details of the tale that cannot be reconciled with the scheme of consequential action. Closer examination suggests that this kind of more or less literal interpretation is seriously incomplete—that some of the most fantastic and apparently arbitrary components are probably significant, and give the story a more fully mythical (because less directly allegorical and logical) status. In much the same way the underlying implications of the Sumerian 'Enki and Ninhursag' were found to depend on just those details that could not be fitted into any obvious allegorical interpretation.

Leaving aside fantastic elements of fairy-tale or folktale origin— like the garden of jewels, the waters of death and the means found to cross them—which add greatly to the richness of the narrative but little to its central subject, we find that the main unexplained element is the insistence on Enkidu as a wild man from the desert. This at first sight arbitrary theme, inconspicuous in the Sumerian versions, is emphasized, not only in the earlier part of the poem, but also, by reminiscence, up to Enkidu's death. What is its point, does it serve any real purpose in the epic as a whole, and how did it become so prominent a motif in the Akkadian elaboration?

One of the main preoccupations of the Central Brazilian Indians was seen to be the relationship between nature and culture, the untamed and the tamed, the raw and the cooked, and the tensions, contradictions and paradoxes that operated between these extremes. I believe the Gilgamesh epic in its developed Akkadian form to be partly concerned with exploring, consciously or not, something of the same polarity. Men have always been preoccupied with status: with their relations as individuals to families, as families to clans, as clans to tribes—more generally still with their own society's relation to the whole world outside. That world extends from its broadest cosmological aspects (sky and heavenly bodies, for many the abode of gods or spirits) to the immediate terrestrial environment. It is here that the nature– culture contrast is seen at its most striking, in differences between the organization of the village and its surrounding fields or the whole cultivated area and the enfolding forest or desert; between the customs and rules of men and women and those applied between animals; between human cultural techniques and the natural processes they seem either to imitate, as Aristotle put it, or to counteract. Life in Mesopotamia did not present quite that knife-edge division between the Indian settlement and the jungle, the circle of huts and the teeming undergrowth beyond; yet the division between fertile alluvial plain and barren deserts or mountains, or the packed cities themselves and the empty lands beyond, was sharp enough to provoke surprise and thought. I quote Thorkild Jacobsen (whose subject is not quite the same, but the probability of the related Cain-and-Abel motif occurring independently in Mesopotamia): 'The contrast and rivalry of two ways of life, of the desert and the sown, goes through all Near Eastern history: it is of a nature to seek literary expression spontaneously, independently at varying times and places.'[12] I would add that it is of a nature to seek oral expression, in the mythology of the people, even before seeking literary expression. At all events the investigation, in some sense, of the relationship between nature and culture is not improbable for the Mesopotamian peoples, especially since their myths certainly dwelt on the difference between the irrigated and the barren and on the gods who were responsible.

I want now to reconsider the poem, selecting for notice those phrases and actions which suggest that a contrast between nature and culture, primarily through Enkidu but also though his counterpart Gilgamesh, is implicit in the whole composite story; a meaningful contrast, in which positions are being opposed or reversed in order to explore and illuminate their full relationships. First, it is emphasized that Enkidu is created 'on the steppe'; moreover he is shaggy all over, like an animal. And it is as an animal that he lives: he feeds and drinks like animals and in their company; he not only runs with the gazelles, but he also jostles with the wild beasts at the watering-place. But in some ways he behaves more craftily than they, since he tears up the traps set by the hunter. So Enkidu, although a man, is also the very antithesis of man and his works. Then comes the harlot, who introduces him not only to love—which the animals, too, can practise—but also, later, to shelter, company, clothes, cooked food, strong drink, and all the benefits of culture. But first, when he has grown tired of love for the time being, he tries returning to the animals, who reject him and with whose running he can no longer keep pace. The harlot consoles him by telling him that he is now 'like a god'; it is no longer fitting that he should roam the steppe. She tells him, too, of Gilgamesh back in Uruk, who lords it 'like a wild ox'. Enkidu immediately feels the need for a friend, especially perhaps for one with some of his own latent wildness. Already there is an element of mutual reversal of roles: in the desert Enkidu has rejected the animals and become wise like a god, while in the city Gilgamesh, who is king and should be wise, behaves like a wild beast. Meanwhile Enkidu proves that he has indeed 'forgotten where he was born' by taking a weapon and chasing off, or capturing, the lions and wolves, so that the cattlemen and shepherds may rest in peace.[13] He has become one of them, has turned utterly against the world of wild animals, just as they have rejected him.

He wrestles with Gilgamesh and they become fast friends. Now Gilgamesh conceives the Huwawa project; Enkidu (who seems uncomprehending of Gilgamesh's motive) is dismayed, since he had learned all about the cedar forest 'in the hills, as I was roaming with the wild beasts'.[14] That implies that the cedar forest represents the steppe, the wild; and it certainly lies, as is proper for a monster's lair, beyond the civilized world. Admittedly there is probably more to it than that. Why is it called 'the land of the living' in the Sumerian version? To be sure, it belongs to Enlil, who has set the giant there to guard the cedars; but Huwawa himself is hardly a vivifying force, and rather his forest, which lies in the mountains—the Kur, the name that also means the underworld—may represent death, and give a presage of its power by paralysing Enkidu's hand (Akkadian version), or sending Gilgamesh into a death-like sleep (Sumerian version). At all events, in order to make a name, to overcome death in a modified way, Gilgamesh has to move from culture and the city into the mountain wilderness, to overcome the savage Huwawa, and to bring back the cedars to Uruk.

The details of the penetrating of the forest and the slaying of Huwawa are too uncertain to form the basis of further speculation.

---

[13] *ANET*², 77; Tablet II, ii and iii. All translations are again by E. A. Speiser.
[14] *ANET*², 79; III, iii, 14 f.

After the slaughter, Gilgamesh washes himself and puts on clean clothes.[15] In rejecting Ishtar's love he adduces some remarkable reasons; for what the goddess seems to have done to most of her previous lovers is to reverse their position as between nature and culture. The lion, the embodiment of power and freedom, through having been loved by her is liable to be trapped and confined in the hunter's pit; the stallion has been subjected to the whip and spur. Conversely the herdsman has been turned into a wolf, and Ishullanu, Enlil's gardener (who had insultingly rejected Ishtar's love), has been turned into a mole, or some animal that is stuck, perhaps in a burrow, and can go neither up nor down. Being turned into one's opposite is a drastic punishment, and perhaps that is why these pairs seem to fit the nature–culture reversal so well—only Tammuz, changed into a wounded bird, somewhat obscurely, remains apart. Even so the grouping by pairs (nature–culture twice, and culture–nature twice) is remarkable.[16]

Enkidu sickens and curses three instruments of his downfall: the gate, the hunter and the harlot. It is perhaps significant that two of these three are directly associated with his passage from nature to culture. Why does he mention both the hunter and the harlot, when just one of them would have adequately represented that whole stage in his history, and the third curse could then have been directed (for example) at the Bull of Heaven or his own rash hurling of its thigh at Ishtar? I believe it to be a legitimate conjecture that Enkidu takes the main reason for his lingering death to be his passage from the desert into the world of culture; and that is why he stresses the two similar incidents.[17] At least two of these curses, against the hunter and harlot, are eventually reversed under the persuasion of Shamash, who points out the benefits of culture—especially the friendship of Gilgamesh and the lamentations to be received from the whole of Uruk and from Gilgamesh himself, who will let his hair grow, clothe himself in a lion-skin, and roam over the steppe (in other words, will simulate nature in

---

[15] Tablet vi, *init.* This is not only to motivate Ishtar's love for him, for it fulfils a specific injunction given him by the elders of Uruk (back at tablet iii (Old Babylonian version), vi, 38 f.) to observe ritual purity and wash his feet after killing the giant.

[16] Substituting freedom–confinement for nature–culture in the cases of the lion and stallion, as is otherwise feasible, destroys the common quality of the two pairs.

[17] The gate of the cedar forest, on the other hand, may represent the inverse process, from culture back to nature; passing through it was, of course, according to Enkidu, an ill-judged process in itself.

a typical *rite de passage* inversion). At this thought Enkidu grows quiet and changes his curses into blessings. Once again, however, he claims that he is accursed, because he is dying not like someone who falls in battle but, presumably, slowly and from illness.[18] Therefore it is death by disease, as much as dying itself, that Enkidu seems to resent; and disease may well be something he associates with culture and civilization. Is this, then, the reason for his cursing the hunter and the harlot—not so much because they had introduced him to Gilgamesh (the thought of whose friendship, after all, assuages his wrath against them), but because they enticed him into a world of disease and slow death, away from the world of the steppe in which death tends to come suddenly and before the onset of old age and corruption?

Gilgamesh refuses to accept the reality of Enkidu's death—dresses him like a bride (a symbol of culture, or rather fertility: a *rite de passage*, but the wrong passage). Whether or not he hopes to preserve his friend by asserting his connexion with culture, Gilgamesh himself finally responds to the situation by moving over to the world of nature and rejecting culture entirely. First he storms over the body like a lion deprived of its whelps, then he tears his hair and his garment (perhaps no more than regular signs of mourning), finally he does what Shamash had predicted to Enkidu, by roaming over the steppe clad in skins. It is true that any act of mourning is liable to involve an alteration of clothing and of the length of one's hair (either by cutting it off or by letting it grow). The motives are complex, although the rejection of the world of culture by the mourner, and on his own behalf, is probably not part of them. But by any standards Gilgamesh's actions are extreme, and they are heavily stressed in one aspect: he himself, the embodiment of culture, now rejects the cultured world and roams like an animal in the wild—not only like an animal, but also clad in a wild animal's skin.

It is not altogether easy to see why, either in his own mind or in the minds of those who created his mythical *persona*, Gilgamesh resorted to the desert. For at this point in the composite epic a drastic piece of rearrangement takes place. At one moment the

---

[18] This touches on a theme that may have been further developed in the missing part of the end of Tablet VII. Tablet XII, 147 ff. (an Akkadian translation of a Sumerian original) suggests that it was not so much the possible glory of dying in battle, but rather its suddenness, that caused Enkidu to say that he who dies in battle is blessed.

hero is roaming the steppe, clothed in skins because of the death of
Enkidu; at the next he is beginning his journey to Utnapishtim
dressed in ordinary clothes—or so we may infer, since he specifically tells Utnapishtim on arrival that 'I had not reached the
alewife's house, When my clothing was used up'; and that only at
that point did he slay 'the wild beasts and creeping things of the
steppe', eat their flesh and wrap their skins about him.[19] There
is an undeniable change of viewpoint here: clearly the whole
episode of the journey to Utnapishtim has been joined on to the
description of Enkidu's death and Gilgamesh's subsequent grief,
and that accounts for the inconsistency. In its way the conversion
of Gilgamesh's reason for being clothed in skins, from an act of
mourning to an act of necessity, is very neat. Yet it tends to
obscure the significance of his resort to the wilderness, and may
be responsible for a further confusion about what Gilgamesh is
wearing as he crosses the waters of death in Urshanabi's boat; for
he takes off his cloth and uses it as a sail, whereas on any explanation he is dressed only in skins by this point.

In spite of this, those who thrust Gilgamesh upon Utnapishtim
seem to have remained aware, for most of the time, that his
clothing was an important index of his state of mind. So much is
suggested by the emphasis placed by Utnapishtim, in his instructions to Urshanabi, on taking Gilgamesh to the washing-place as
he leaves for his homeward journey, so that he may wash himself
thoroughly and cast his soiled skins into the sea. Utnapishtim
carefully specifies the dirt of Gilgamesh's limbs, the skins that
have distorted them, the need for the sea to carry off the skins,
the putting on of a completely new cloak.[20] One might also ask
why Utnapishtim and his wife tolerated Gilgamesh's foul condition for so long, including his seven days' sleep in their house.
That sounds like an absurd piece of pedantry that pushes the
evidence, and the obviously loose narrative techniques, too far.
Yet there would be no conceivable reason for reintroducing the
motif of Gilgamesh's being clothed in skins, after the natural assumption that on arrival in Utnapishtim's house he would be treated
in the normal way of hospitality, were it not remembered that this

[19] x, v, 29 ff.: compare this with viii, iii, 6 ff. and vii, 3, 47 f., which make it clear
that Gilgamesh would dress in skins immediately his mourning began. This must have
been stated at the beginning of the gap after viii, ii, a verse or so after the words 'tearing
off and flinging down (his) finery'.

[20] xi, 237–55.

was an important part of his characterization after the death of Enkidu. In short, the theme of Gilgamesh's becoming like an animal has been partly, but not completely, overlaid by the accretion of the popular Utnapishtim story.

Why does Gilgamesh withdraw from the world of culture into that of nature after his friend's death? Why is that idea so important that it runs even through the elaborated theme of his visit to Utnapishtim in search of personal immortality? It is not merely an exaggerated form of mourning; it is too emphatic for that, and the stress on the mode of clothing, and its relation to his return to Uruk, too pronounced. Does he hope to restore Enkidu to a kind of life? I doubt it; his concern seems to be more for himself, at this stage, than for Enkidu. It is his own preoccupation with death, as much as guilt for Enkidu, that he is expressing by these means. If so, then I suggest that his rejection of the world and of the appurtenances of culture is a rejection of death itself. Just as Enkidu blamed his acculturation for the manner, if not the inevitability, of his dying, so Gilgamesh rejects the actuality of Enkidu's death by seeking out the world of nature, of the animals who were Enkidu's companions and seemed to symbolize freedom, lack of restraint, lack of corruption—and yet some of them he slaughtered, much as Enkidu had attacked them after his initial assimilation to culture. Later, in returning to Uruk, washed and dressed in clean clothes, he not only signifies his resignation to death, but he also seems to imply that culture is not, after all, to blame for disease and the lingering aspects of mortality—or at least that man cannot avoid them, that there is no point in altering one's life because of them. Culture is in many ways questionable, and in the end it did Enkidu little good; although Enkidu had been comforted by Shamash's listing of its benefits (living like a king, being Gilgamesh's friend) in his own case. Wisdom, too, he had gained, as the harlot told him, like a god. And so this whole myth, revealing a persistent preoccupation that overrides the mechanical complexity of narrative accumulation, explores the relations of culture and nature, resignation and despair, disease and sudden death, mourning and madness. It balances one against the other, investigates ways out of the confrontation, and achieves, as a myth perhaps should, a valuation that is complex, ambiguous, emotional, and personal.

According to the interpretation here suggested, the Epic of

Gilgamesh is something more, on the speculative plane, than an investigation of man's attitude to death; and the investigation of death is itself more subtle than had been supposed. Once again the question must be posed, Is the epic mythical in essence? Incorporated in an ancient setting and touching matters of universal concern, it possesses many of the characteristics of myth. Yet is the underlying speculation, such as it is, 'mythopoeic', conducted by developing intuitive associations and images arising out of the tale itself, or is it primarily the result of more rational processes? No final answer can be given, but I venture one conjecture: that the confrontation between nature and culture at least, with its effects on the assessment of death, is primarily intuitive. The more overt sides of Gilgamesh's obsession with mortality, on the other hand, may suggest a more deliberate elaboration of motifs and attitudes implicit in Sumerian predecessors like 'The death of Enkidu' and 'The death of Gilgamesh'.[21]

2: The Centaurs

The contrast between nature and culture is certainly an old one, and has much in common with the Greek opposition, exploited by the Sophists in the fifth century B.C., between *physis*, nature, and *nomos*, law or custom. If the reader is tired of Lévi-Strauss, and prefers to envisage what I am going to say in these established terms rather than those of the nature–culture contrast, I shall not dissent. As it happens I believe that the modern formulation, because of its freedom from the specialized and constricted values placed on the *nomos/physis* polarization by the Sophists themselves, is more useful. Whichever terminology we prefer, the polarization is an enormously fruitful one that can be made to subsume and

---

[21] S. N. Kramer considers that the whole of the first part of the epic—the tyranny of Gilgamesh, the creation and civilizing of Enkidu, and the struggle between him and Gilgamesh—'form part of a well-knit plot-progression' and are essentially Semitic in invention. He also thinks that the story of Enkidu's death and burial is Babylonian and not Sumerian in origin (since the Sumerian version of his death, given in tablet XII, is substantially different). That may well be so; but I very much doubt whether the death of Enkidu 'was invented by the Babylonian authors of the "Epic of Gilgamesh" in order to motivate dramatically Gilgamesh's quest for immortality, which climaxes the poem' (*From the Tablets of Sumer* (Philadelphia, 1956), 221; Eng. ed., *History Begins at Sumer* (London, 1958), 255). If there really is an undercurrent of contrast between nature and culture—if Enkidu exemplifies, at least as powerfully as Gilgamesh, both the good and the bad side of culture—then the climax of the poem is subtly altered, and Enkidu's death is no longer incidental to it.

illuminate many of the most important problems of life—it is a mode of analysis whose application to human dilemmas can elicit significant and otherwise unsuspected connexions and distinctions.

At the same time the contrast of nature and culture is no more a universal theme of Greek myths than of Mesopotamian. It is largely absent from both the primarily divine and the primarily heroic myths. It would be forcing the facts to claim that Prometheus's role as cultural benefactor to men, for example, is seriously concerned with an opposition between the continuing states of nature and culture; for the process from non-culture to culture must be part of any historicizing or evolutionary view of the world. Neither the ancient Greeks nor their modern interpreters have been able to trace the specific *physis/nomos* contrast far back into the past, although more general contrasts between word and deed, name and object named, or appearance and reality, are familiar in Aeschylus, Pindar, Heraclitus and Homer. Rather it was the curious differences between native Greek culture and those of Egypt and Persia that seem to have crystallized that particular line of enquiry. It arose out of a kind of primitive ethnography, and I agree with the opinion of Felix Heinimann that the polarity 'originally grew out of the Greek national consciousness'.[22] One would not expect the contrast to press itself upon the Greeks as it did on the Bororo Indians of South America or even on the Mesopotamian peoples. The Greeks were not, like the Mesopotamians and Egyptians, living in fertile valleys enclosed by desert nor, like many savage peoples, were they squeezed in by the raw jungle and the hostility of wild animals. Even their climate, on land at least, did not confront them too often with the conflict between human planning and the arbitrariness of nature. Yet there is at least one element of Greek mythology that seems sympathetic to this kind of analysis and is made more comprehensible by it; which is some indication of its validity.[23] I refer to two groups of unusual creatures, neither heroes nor gods, who move in the

---

[22] *Nomos und Physis* (Basel, 1945), 39: 'so ist das Begriffspaar Nomos–Physis ursprünglich aus dem griechischen Nationalgefühl heraus erwachsen'. For a discussion of the general intellectual background of this idea see chapter II of the same book.

[23] For an interpretation of the ephebic initiation-rites at Athens and Sparta in somewhat similar terms (and with some reference to Lévi-Strauss) see P. Vidal-Naquet's fascinating 'The Black Hunter and the origin of the Athenian Ephebeia', *Proceedings of the Cambridge Philological Society*, N.S. XIV, 1968, 49–64.

background of the mythical world: the Centaurs, Satyrs and Silens on the one hand, the Cyclopes on the other.

The first of these groups are part man, part horse. The Satyrs were seen as goatish rather than equine in the Hellenistic age, perhaps somewhat before, but were certainly equine in the seventh and sixth centuries B.C. Probably they were subsequently conflated with an Arcadian goat-demon or Pan-figure. The Silens did not undergo this transformation, but otherwise they are always difficult to distinguish from Satyrs. By Euripides's time the chief difference lies in their age: the young Satyr-chorus of his play *Cyclops* is led by the much older Silenus. Both Satyrs and Silens tend to be envisaged, at least by the classical age, as both lecherous and ithyphallic; the Centaurs, too, share the general characteristic, though its special symptom is rarely shown in their numerous representations in art. The Centaurs, who have the body of a horse and the chest and face of a man (or in Geometric and early archaic representations the trunk of a horse attached to a complete male figure), as opposed to the ears, tail, hooves and facial expression that are the equine characteristics of Satyrs and Silens, differ in a more important respect: they became the chief actors of a few distinct and well-known myths, whereas the others were merely incidental figures and attracted almost no specific mythology.

The names and origins of all these species remain obscure, although the most diverse explanations have been confidently offered. The connexion of the name Κένταυρος, earlier *Κένταϝρος, with Indian Gandharva, Iranian Gandarǝva, strongly urged by Dumézil (who sees most European myths as derived from Indo-Iranian exemplars), has found few supporters.[24] Roscher, who wrote the article on Centaurs in the mythological lexicon of which he was editor, explained them as spirits of the mountain torrents.[25] His allegorical interpretations, such as that they fought with boulders and tree-trunks because these are what are carried down by torrents in spate, or that they were horse-like because torrents are as swift as horses, were typical of the nature-myth school to which he tenaciously adhered. Mannhardt more usefully compared them with the wild men of Germanic folklore, and took

[24] G. Dumézil, *Le Problème des Centaures* (Paris, 1929), ch. II.

[25] W. H. Roscher, ed., *Ausführliches Lexikon der griechischen und römischen Mythologie*, II (Leipzig, 1890–7), 1058 ff.

them to be wind-spirits possibly connected with the Greek word meaning breeze.[26] P. Kretschmer, however, provided some philological support for associating Κένταυρος with words like ἄναυρος, meaning exactly a mountain torrent, and names like that of Πληξαύρη, a water-nymph. That leaves the κεντ-element unexplained. It is hard, nevertheless, entirely to reject the possibility of an original connexion with water; but the connexion certainly does not show in their actions in surviving myths. If it exists, I would trace it back to the dual nature of Poseidon—god of horses, and himself worshipped in equine form as Hippios at Thelpousa in Arcadia, but also god of streams, springs, and the sea. Again, however, he fails to play any significant part in the Centaurs' genealogy.

Mythical ancestors give little help in this case. The Centaurs as a tribe were usually regarded as descended from Ixion, either directly, by his union with the deceptive cloud Nephele, or by the commerce of a son, Centaurus, with some Thessalian mares.[27] Cheiron, on the other hand, who was far the most important of the Centaurs, was son of Kronos and the Oceanid Philyra. There is this to be said for Ixion's union with Nephele: the union was an unnatural one in that his seed fell on the ground; as such it was liable to produce something odd and monstrous rather than fully human. Hephaestus's seed had likewise fallen on the ground when he attempted Athena, and it engendered the snake-man Erichthonius. Admittedly a snake is more obvious than a horse as a product of the earth, and one might be inclined to think that manhorses were not monstrous at all, just charming and pretty. Yet the Greeks thought otherwise, at least in the seventh century B.C.; for, as Ernst Buschor showed, in the art of that period man-horse figures were used to represent all sorts of monsters, not necessarily nice ones. Typhoeus may be a case in point, and Medusa is certainly given a horse's body on a Boeotian relief-pithos from Thebes, since Perseus has sliced her head from an equine trunk and is putting it in his magic wallet.[28] For a time, at least, being shaped partly like a horse had some of the same implications as being shaped partly like a snake.

[26] W. Mannhardt, *Antike Wald- und Feldkulte* (Berlin, 1877), 39 ff.

[27] Both these genealogies look late and rationalistic. P. Von der Mühll suggests that the former depended on a false etymology of κέντ-αυρος, with κεντέω bearing a sexual meaning; for Ixion copulated with the air or a cloud (*Museum Helveticum*, xxv, 1968, 227 f.).   [28] E. Buschor, *AJA*, xxxviii, 1934, 128 ff.

What, then, were the Centaurs? Nilsson, who sometimes fell below his usual standard of acuteness in judging such mythical groups (mainly because of an excessive reliance on the uncritical J. C. Lawson and the often misleading modern Greek parallels), was nevertheless correct in maintaining that they were nature spirits of some kind—'a species of those nature-demons with which the primitive fantasy fills the whole of nature', as he says in somewhat Tylorian terms.[29] Their exact origin he thought unimportant. Well, it would be important it we could determine it, but at least it is wise not to be dogmatic like Roscher. One must be content with the conclusion that the Centaurs were associated with nature, with mountains, trees, caves, and streams. The same is so of Satyrs and Silens, who are the male counterparts of the Nymphs. So at least the Homeric *Hymn to Aphrodite* suggests of the Silens, who like Hermes mingle with the Nymphs in love in the recesses of caves (262 f.); and a Hesiodic fragment (123 M-W) makes the 'worthless and useless Satyrs', as well as the Nymphs, descendants of Phoroneus the inventor of fire. And the Nymphs (in their various special forms of Dryads, Naiads, Oreads, and so on) were beyond question spirits associated with different aspects of the world of nature.

The Nymphs were not conceived as horse-like; why then were the Centaurs, Satyrs, and Silens? Obviously the origin of the males was separate—and the origin of the Centaurs may have been different from that of the Silens and Satyrs. Nilsson described the idea of Centaurs as 'very old', partly because of one or two representations of half-horses in Mycenaean art.[30] Few would have considered them post-Mycenaean, in any case; most of the figures, divine or heroic, of Greek myths known in the classical period are at least Mycenaean in origin—often, in all probability, considerably older. 'Very old' is not, perhaps, an appropriate description of the Centaurs. It could be maintained, on the contrary, that they are comparatively recent; or on the other hand far older than Nilsson probably conceived. Horses are a relatively new phenomenon in the cultures of the eastern Mediterranean and western Asia. They were introduced into Greece to draw chariots, probably around the middle of the second millennium B.C., from Asia Minor. Even there they were a recent import, being first attested around 2000 B.C.; and Egypt acquired them at roughly

---

[29] *GgrR*[3], 231.   [30] *GgrR*[3], 229 f.

the same time as Greece. The ultimate source of all these importa-
tions was Northern Europe, apparently the first homeland of the
domesticated horse, which then passed to the south and south-east
through the Balkans. Wild horses were more widely dispersed;
they were hunted in the Ice Age and the earlier Palaeolithic, as
we know from cave-paintings in France and Spain. It seems
doubtful whether horses could have been seriously regarded as
wild monsters, anywhere in Europe, later than the Neolithic
period; and the idea, if it is not sheer invention, must have been
derived not from Asia Minor (the source of many Greek mythical
concepts) or from Egypt, but from somewhere to the north where
wild horses had actually been known.

That is illuminating so far as it goes; but we are concerned with
mixed horses and men, not wild horses as such. It is possible, then,
that the idea of these mixed creatures as wild nature-spirits was a
Greek invention, the alternative being that it was derived from
further north in the remote past. At least it was no more Babylonian or Egyptian than the wild horse itself. True Centaurs are
extremely rare on, if not totally absent from, the Asiatic cylinder
seals, in spite of the enormous proliferation of mixed demons and
theriomorphic gods; and they are unknown to Egyptian art. Bull-
men are common in mythical scenes on seals of the Agade dynasty,
and might sometimes represent the Bull of Heaven in the Gilgamesh epic or its precursors; but there is no similar indication of
a rich development of Centaur-myths like the Greek. Much
remains uncertain; but whichever choice is made (Neolithic
influence on Proto-Greeks in the Balkans, or Greek imaginative
development of Asiatic horses late in the second millennium),
Centaurs in their developed mythical form look like a peculiarly
Greek phenomenon—and there are few other parts of Greek
mythology of which that can be said.

The Centaurs were chiefly at home in the mountains bordering
the plain of Thessaly. The Centaur Cheiron, 'sage' and 'friendly
to men' according to Euripides and Pindar, 'justest of the Centaurs' according to Homer, lived in a cave on Mount Pelion.[31] The
Homeric phrase is ambiguous: Cheiron and one other Centaur,
Pholus, were just and law-abiding, but the rest of them had
nothing to do with justice, they were anarchic and uncontrollable,

[31] Euripides, *Iphigeneia at Aulis*, 710; Pindar, *Pythians*, III, 5 and 63; Homer, *Iliad*, XI,
832.

wild figures always prone to run amok. That is what they did at the wedding of Peirithous, king of the Thessalian Lapiths, and Hippodameia, and on this occasion Homer referred to them simply as 'shaggy beasts', φῆρας...λαχνήεντας (*Il.* II, 743). They were invited to the wedding feast by their human neighbours of the plain, but being unaccustomed to wine they became drunk and tried to carry off the bride and the other Lapith girls. In the battle that followed, brilliantly represented on the west pediment of the temple of Zeus at Olympia, they were defeated and driven in flight to the Peloponnese. Earlier, they had tried to murder Peleus when he was stranded defenceless on Mount Pelion by Acastus, whose wife had treacherously denounced him after failing to seduce him; but Cheiron came to the rescue. Next the Centaurs (but not Cheiron, who had withdrawn directly to Mount Malea in the far south) clashed with Heracles on Mount Pholoe between Arcadia and Elis. The Centaur Pholus had always lived there, and was entertaining Heracles during his quest for the Erymanthian boar. Heracles was eating cooked meat and Pholus raw;[32] the hero asked for wine and, although Pholus was reluctant to broach a jar that belonged to all the Centaurs in common, hospitality demanded that he eventually do so. Attracted by the bouquet, the other Centaurs rushed up and tried to attack Heracles with their usual boulders and branches or tree-trunks. He routed them with arrows and firebrands, and they retreated to join Cheiron at Malea. The hospitable Pholus inadvertently dropped one of Heracles's poisoned arrows on his foot, and so died; a similar motif was used in connexion with the death of Cheiron himself—Heracles came in pursuit of the others, and shot Cheiron by mistake with an arrow that had passed through another Centaur's arm. Cheiron, although immortal, was in such continuous pain from the wound that he accepted the cunning Prometheus's offer to take over his immortality and allow him to die. After the dispersal of the other Centaurs from Malea some were 'received by Poseidon at Eleusis and hidden in a mountain', as Apollodorus mysteriously states (II, 5, 4). There were two other famous incidents involving Heracles and individual Centaurs. He killed Eurytion (the chief offender at Hippodameia's wedding according to *Odyssey*, XXI, 295 ff.) for trying to rape the daughter of king

---

[32] Apollodorus, II, 5, 4: οὗτος Ἡρακλεῖ μὲν ὀπτὰ παρεῖχε τὰ κρέα, αὐτὸς δὲ ὠμοῖς ἐχρῆτο.

Dexamenus of Elis while his guest; and he despatched Nessus for similarly trying to rape Heracles's own wife Deianeira while Nessus was carrying her across the river Euenus near Calydon. That was the indirect cause of Heracles's death, since (as Sophocles described at length in his *Trachiniae*) the dying but still cunning Centaur persuaded the girl to accept some of his blood as a love-potion. Years later she used it on her unfaithful husband; it turned out to be a corrosive poison, and led to his agonized self-cremation on Mount Oeta.

Cheiron has a totally different role from the others. He is neither fierce and unpredictable nor wild and uncultured. On the contrary, he is the gentle and gifted teacher *par excellence*. Among the pupils who came to live and study with him in his cave on Mount Pelion were Achilles, Actaeon, Asclepius and his sons, Jason (Iason, 'the healer'), and Aristaeus the son of Apollo and the nymph Cyrene. Isolated sources add others to the list, Heracles and Dionysus themselves as well as Medea's son Medeius (according to *Theogony*, 1001) and Teiresias. Membership of the group depended either on association with Cheiron in other episodes, or with medicine or prophecy, or, in the case of Dionysus, with wine, fertility and mountain-roaming (which properly, however, belong to the other Centaurs and not Cheiron). For Cheiron was master of nearly all the arts: hunting, spearsmanship, riding (!), music, prophecy, and in particular healing—certain herbs were named after him and were found in the glades of Pelion near his cave. Needless to say he has none of the *ardeur indiscrète* of the other Centaurs, but is respectably married to the nymph Chariclo (as for example Pindar implies in the fourth Pythian ode, 103); his sons were relatively undistinguished, but his granddaughter was that Melanippe known as 'the wise'.[33] In the later tradition he is seen as a philosopher, and in this respect is closely similar to the wise Silenus. But Silenus, who was never in any case such an important figure, retained more of the qualities of his brothers; in an evidently famous tale alluded to by Herodotus he was captured by Midas, who wished to test his wisdom, by lacing his fountain with wine.[34]

[33] Admittedly Chariclo as a nymph had certain wild associations (p. 156). It is also interesting that Cheiron fed the infant Achilles (who had been over-exposed to fire by Thetis) on the innards of wild beasts according to Apollodorus, III, 13, 6; cf. Statius, *Achill.*, II, 96 ff., 382 ff.

[34] Herodotus, VIII, 138, 3.

In short, Cheiron (and to a lesser extent Pholus) represents the extreme of culture, while the rest of the Centaurs represent nature in its most unpredictable and anti-cultural form. The contradiction has often been noted, never adequately explained. Escher in Pauly–Wissowa suggested that it was Cheiron's rescue of Peleus from the other Centaurs that first set him apart, and that the difference grew as the tradition proceeded: in my view, highly unlikely. Dumézil pointed to a similar duality (as he believed) in the Indian Gandharvas, and also adduced role-reversals at carnival and other festivals; whereas Nilsson observed more generally that some nature-spirits are benign towards men.[35] The reference to reversal of roles is ingenious; Durkheim seems to have been right in arguing that passage from the sacred to the profane and vice versa tends to be marked by a ritual exchange of roles or sexes on the part of priests or participants; but I still do not believe this has anything to do with the problem of Cheiron and the Centaurs. Rather the clue may be given by the simple observation that many aspects of the natural world can be seen either as friendly, or as violent and hostile, according to time and circumstance.

It was some such perception, perhaps, that developed into the extreme contrast between the two types of Centaur. First of all the Centaurs themselves, in that they were half horse, symbolized both the wild aspect of nature (for horses are shaggy, swift, sometimes difficult to control, and obviously potent in a sexual sense) and its more benign side (for they are also friendly to men, impressive and dignified in appearance, contemplative in their glance, and a mark of social standing). That is in their horse-aspect; but they are half men as well, and so the coexistence of nature and culture becomes all the more striking.[36] In order to derive from them a type of sage, to be set in opposition to their more savage aspects, it was necessary to separate off Cheiron, to make him oppose them (as he did by saving Peleus) or remove himself from them (as he did in his isolated cave, frequented by humans, on Pelion; and by retreating, at first alone or just with his family, to Malea). But why bother with a half-horse at all, if a

[35] G. Dumézil, *Le Problème des Centaures* (1921), 136, cf. ch. 1; M. P. Nilsson, *GgrR³*, 232.

[36] It has often been remarked (as Alan Dundes reminds me) that the horse-part is the lower and more animalistic, whereas the human portion is the upper, including heart and head—at least in the developed, classical form.

symbol is needed for the best side of culture? Why not a man, or an ordinary hero? The answer must lie partly, at least, in the superhuman qualities of nature itself: in the wisdom of birds and other wild creatures, from which seers like Teiresias, Melampus and Polyidus learn of the future; in the prophetic oak tree of Dodona; in the signs in the heavens which the Babylonians revered, even if the Greeks, apart from their sailors, were more indifferent. Certain species have always been regarded as wise; the owl is an obvious case in point, and here as elsewhere it is the physical appearance of wisdom or solemnity that establishes the fabular reputation. Few philosophic beasts also have a savage side; the horse serves as well as most—better in fact, because of its monstrous role in the artistic tradition. Because of its comparative novelty it might well have become, at some time in the latter part of the second millennium B.C., an especially evocative symbol.

A second look at some of the details of the Centaur myths confirms this intentional duality. Cheiron is a master of simples, and horses are important in folk-medicine; practically every part of them has its medical uses, and potions brewed from horses' hooves and the like have universal currency. Yet Cheiron cannot cure himself when he is wounded by Heracles; culture means death, and there are conditions to which death is preferable. Most of the Centaurs cannot tolerate culture; they like wine and (human) females, but they run wild, behave bestially, at the first contact with either. They are controlled and punished primarily by Heracles (apart from the Lapiths), a figure who himself combines savagery and gluttony with civilized activities like the inauguration of games, oracles and medicinal springs. Most suggestive of all is the encounter between Heracles and Pholus. I have already mentioned that Apollodorus, who describes the episode, emphasizes that Heracles ate cooked meat, Pholus raw. But is that not rather extraordinary? Horses do not eat raw meat. They are strict vegetarians, and that is as true of wild horses as of domesticated ones. Therefore the emphasis in this myth on Pholus's eating raw meat is no piece of realism, rather it presupposes an effort to stress an important aspect of the Centaurs, that they embody raw nature; even Pholus did so in his eating habits, although in terms of hospitality he belonged to Cheiron's side and to culture. Diomedes, king of the Bistones in Thrace, possessed some man-eating horses, and it was one of Heracles's incidental tasks to capture them; they too suggest that horses could be regarded as fierce monsters, but the Pholus story goes far beyond this possibly folktale exaggeration by combining an (inappropriate) aspect of savage animality with a cultured subject. In the continuation of the tale the same careful opposition persists. Why does not Heracles use his club? Perhaps because it would be too similar to the huge branches or tree-trunks, themselves typifying nature, traditionally wielded by the Centaurs. But why does he use not only arrows (which might be stressed because of their necessary part in the deaths of Cheiron, Pholus himself, and Nessus in some accounts), but also firebrands of all things? It is conceivable that this is because fire is the possession of men and the symbol of culture, and so most strongly opposed to raw nature as represented here by the other Centaurs.[37] At least Heracles himself, with his skins, his hairiness, his club, his poisoned arrows, his treachery and lust and nobility, his association with healing and oracles, makes the ideal heroic counterpart to the Centaurs—exemplifies in one person their duality of role as a species.

3: The Cyclopes

The probability that the Greeks in some of their myths developed a systematic confrontation between nature and culture is further supported by the case of the Cyclopes, the 'circle-eyed' (rather than merely 'round-faced') giants whose first generation were children of Gaia and Ouranos and brothers both of the Hundred-handed giants and of the Titans. The ancient mythographical tradition identified three types of Cyclopes. Hellanicus, for example (fr. 88, quoted by the scholiast on Hesiod, *Theogony*, 139), distinguished those who built the vast walls of Mycenae, then Polyphemus and his group, and finally 'the gods themselves', αὐτοὶ οἱ θεοί, by which he means those mentioned in the *Theogony* as giving to Zeus his special weapons, thunder and lightning, and who are described at 142 f. as like the gods save for their one

---

[37] Three points might be made against the suggestion. First, Heracles's meal has just been cooked for him, so that fire is ready to hand. Secondly, the Centaurs themselves were sometimes represented, from the fourth century B.C. on, as holding torches; but that is irrelevant (the story of Pholus and Heracles being much earlier), since the torches depend on the association, not before the late sixth century B.C., of the Centaurs with the Bacchic rites of Dionysus. Mountainous, fertile creatures were inevitably brought into association with a mountain-dancing cult with strong fertility aspects; the nocturnal dances required the use of torches, which also added to the excitement. The third point is that fire, as in forest-fires, obviously has its natural and savage side.

eye. Their sons, according to the mythographer Pherecydes (cited by the scholiast on the opening verse of Euripides's *Alcestis*) were killed by Apollo for providing the thunderbolt used by Zeus to blast Asclepius.

All sorts of origins and connexions have been proposed for these three types of Cyclopes. S. Eitrem in Pauly–Wissowa (s.v. Kyklopen, vɪ) thought that they all derive from a single type of fire-demon; he adduced some unconvincing arguments, such as that when the wall-building kind are called χειρογάστορες, literally 'hand-bellies', the χείρ element means not 'hand' but 'phallus', and that certain fire-demons are phallic (itself uncertain); or that one-eyed folk have the evil eye, which is sometimes conceived as flashing or fiery. Wilhelm Grimm had gone so far as to consider that the single eye is the sun, whereas Mannhardt thought of the Cyclopes as whirlwinds. A. B. Cook argued that the stake that drilled out Polyphemus's eye was a firedrill and symbolized the invention of fire; Eitrem doubted this, but thought that the firedrill itself was a good idea because fire is the correct way to destroy the evil eye. And so on—this is exactly the kind of uncontrolled speculation I am anxious to avoid. At least this much can be said: the Cyclopes who were imagined as building the great walls of Mycenae were chosen, by a piece of popular lore rather than true myth, because they were giants.[38] There is no special connexion between these Cyclopes and the solitary giants visited by Odysseus, who were no extensive builders. Indeed, if the one type belongs primarily to folklore, the other to myth, no link beyond gianthood need be expected. Polyphemus professed no use for the gods, but there are signs that he and his peers were favoured by Zeus; this might connect them with Zeus's helpers, providers of thunder and lightning, who were specially rewarded in some way. As to these, 'the gods themselves', we are largely in the dark; but for present purposes that does not much matter, since it is Polyphemus and his neighbours that chiefly concern us.

The account in the ninth book of the *Odyssey* is by far the fullest, as well as the earliest, that we possess. It presents a complex picture in which two quite distinct views of these particular Cyclopes seem to be combined, sometimes violently. D. L. Page has dealt amusingly and convincingly with the complexity in so far as it affects

---

[38] The Hundred-handers might have been even better for the purpose, but were known to be in Tartarus guarding the defeated Titans: Hesiod, *Theogony*, 734 f.

the detailed description of the blinding of Polyphemus;[39] he argues for conflation of two or more earlier versions of the myth rather than a plurality of final authors, and is unquestionably right. My concern is rather with the sociological status of the Cyclopes, the contrast between Polyphemus and his neighbours, and their relation as a whole to the possible opposition between nature and culture.

At their first mention these Cyclopes are described as 'over-bearing and lawless', ὑπερφιάλων ἀθεμίστων (*Odyssey* IX, 106); yet in the very next verse it is by 'trusting in the immortal gods' that they need neither plant nor plough, since everything grows for them without sowing or tilling—wheat and barley and vines (from which they make wine), all watered for them by the rain of Zeus (108–11). They have neither assemblies at which they take counsel nor established customs or laws, θέμιστες (112)—this resumes, and somewhat moderates, the description of them as 'lawless' a few lines before (at 106). They dwell on the mountain peaks in hollow caves, 'and they each make their own rules for their children and wives, and pay no regard to each other'—that is, each family ignores all the others.[40] They are lawless, then, only in limiting social life strictly to the family; which some might consider a very idyllic, if primitive, state of affairs.

It is near an imaginary coast that the Cyclopes live their easy if unsociable lives. Offshore, out of reach (since they are not craftsmen and have no boats), lies a deserted island. It is wooded and has countless wild goats, for no hunters go there (Homer seems unaware that woods and goats are incompatible), but is devoid of flocks or ploughland: 'unsown and unploughed for all its days / it is barren of men, but nourishes bleating goats' (123 f.). In being 'unsown and unploughed' it resembles the land of the Cyclopes just across the water; the same phrase, virtually, is used in each case, although, in a formular style, that is not necessarily significant.[41] Yet the reasons and circumstances are completely different: the soil miraculously bears crops for the Cyclopes in spite of being unsown and unploughed—they are like the men of the golden race in Hesiod's *Works and Days*, for whom 'of its own accord the fertile earth bore fruit' (117 f.). The island, on the

[39] D. L. Page, *The Homeric Odyssey* (Oxford, 1955), ch. 1.
[40] *Od.* IX, 114 f.: θεμιστεύει δὲ ἕκαστος / παίδων ἠδ' ἀλόχων, οὐδ' ἀλλήλων ἀλέγουσι.
[41] 109, ἄσπαρτα καὶ ἀνήροτα; 123, ἄσπαρτος καὶ ἀνήροτος.

other hand, is barren, and is quite normal in that crops do not grow because there is no one to work the soil. If the Cyclopes had possessed ships and could have reached it, the poet adds, they would have made it ἐϋκτιμένην (130, literally 'well-established'), because the soil is good and could bear all things in season. There are well-watered meadows by the seashore where numerous vines would grow, and flat ploughland that would bring good harvests since the soil is rich. There is also a wonderful harbour, where it is unnecessary for a ship to lie out at anchor, with a spring and poplar grove at its head (131–41). Into this harbour Odysseus and his shipmates were led by some god in the depths of darkness, seeing nothing until the bows gently grounded on the beach. In one way this island, like the land of the Phaeacians—they had once been neighbours according to *Odyssey* vi, 4–7, but had been forced to move by the Cyclopes's aggressiveness—represents a colonist's ideal landfall, and its affectionate description reproduces a kind of wish-fulfilment dream to which most of the audience might instantly respond. On the other hand it also represents nature in its ideal and benign form, not as opposed to culture, not as savage and repellent, but as waiting to be developed by culture, as its exemplary precondition. The Cyclopes, an extraordinary mixture of the divine and the brutish, are inadequate to carry out this development. Odysseus's men, in a way, begin the process by killing and cooking some wild goats that the Nymphs put up for them (154 f.). As they feast on meat and wine they look across to the mainland, see the Cyclopes's smoke rising, and hear the bleating of their sheep and goats—domesticated goats, we remember, as opposed to the wild ones they have just killed (161–7).

After this vignette, which opposes the island, benign nature potentially acculturated, to the mainland, both ambivalent culture and ambivalent nature, the poet makes Odysseus ask an over-simple but traditional question: whether the inhabitants are 'violent, wild and unjust / or hospitable, with a god-fearing mind' (175 f.). He takes his ship across to the mainland at last, and comes upon Polyphemus's cave. Polyphemus lives apart, in a cave in the most remote part of the island, not far from the sea (182); he does not mix with the others but keeps to himself with a lawless mind (188 f.). The poet is here faced with contradictory needs: to make all the Cyclopes formidable, but to distinguish Polyphemus as in a class on his own in this respect. Yet it cannot be simply for this contrast that the other Cyclopes are treated, for most of the time, as more or less normal people at the family level. Polyphemus, at least, has no resemblance to a 'cereal-eating' man, but looks like a solitary mountain peak (190–2). Both the negative and positive poles of this description are remarkable: what distinguishes civilized men is their eating of cereals (and yet the other Cyclopes eat, but do not have to cultivate, them); whereas the striking comparison with the mountain peak (and yet the other Cyclopes, but not Polyphemus, live on mountain peaks) is designed to strengthen his association with raw nature.

Even Polyphemus is not without contradictions. Until he notices Odysseus and his companions crouching in the shadows of his cave, his behaviour is that of a devoted shepherd and goatherd. He drives in his flocks; inside the cave are pens for the different ages and types of animals, and all the apparatus for milking and cheese-making (219–23, 246–9). Once he has replaced the great boulder that serves as a door he settles down to some quiet and systematic work in the dairy. He has brought with him a pile of wood 'to go with supper',[42] not because he plans to cook anything, but presumably to provide light and warmth (cf. 308). So far, then, we have a picture of a huge, one-eyed, unsociable herdsman: a vegetarian who takes an occasional cup of wine (357 f.) but evidently has no spit for cooking meat in his cave—if he had, Odysseus would have used it, as did the heroes of so many other versions of this almost universal folktale, for putting out the giant's eye. Instead he has to make do with the green stake of olive-wood.[43] Polyphemus is devoted to his flocks, or so at least his pathetic address to his ram at 447 ff. would suggest; evidently he does not eat them. Now comes the change of character, and apart from anything else it is a brilliant dramatic surprise. He sees Odysseus, asks who he is, tells him that his plea for hospitality and invocation of Zeus, protector of strangers, are provincial if not sheer folly (273 f.). And then, when he learns from Odysseus (who tells an automatic but timely lie) that his guests are stranded and isolated, he makes no reply—but leaps forward, seizes two of the companions, shatters them on the ground, and devours them, bones, guts

[42] ἵνα οἱ ποτιδόρπιον εἴη, 234—a slightly strained use of the formula, cf. 249.

[43] I am aware that the stake, when heated, 'glowed terribly' (Od. IX, 379) and therefore might have had a metallic prototype. What is significant is the particular selection of details made from a probably complex tradition by the singers who developed the surviving contrast.

and all, like a wild animal, a mountain lion (287–93). The vegetarian has an appetite for meat after all, and for raw meat, and
human raw meat, at that: worse than the Centaurs! Polyphemus
crowns his uncultured behaviour, a little anti-climactically, by
taking his wine neat, unmixed with water, always for the Greeks
a sign of boorishness, imprudence or greed (297).[44]

Polyphemus's odd flashes of culture are not simply designed to
prepare the *coup-de-théâtre* by which he reveals his cannibal nature,
neither are they mere accidents of his living apart from the others
(and so making do with the life of a solitary herdsman); for they
recur in other places. In a prospective allusion in the opening book
of the *Odyssey* he is described as ruler of all the Cyclopes.[45] At
IX, 275 f. he allies himself with the others in his boast that 'the
Cyclopes pay no regard to aegis-bearing Zeus / nor to the blessed
gods, since we are far stronger'. We might be inclined to wonder
whether at this point Zeus's omniscient mind is wandering, why
he does not smite this blasphemer with a thunderbolt. But then we
remember that the first-generation Cyclopes were Zeus's uncles,
that Polyphemus is Poseidon's son and Zeus's nephew, that the
Cyclopes like the Phaeacians are 'close to the gods' (VII, 205 f.),
that in the struggles against the Titans the giants were stronger
than Zeus, and that the Cyclopes as well as the Hundred-handers
intervened decisively on his side. That is why their soil gave crops
without labour, miraculously; even Polyphemus drinks its wine.
Yet these prodigies, although close to the gods, are not divine; they
are mortal, and in their liability to disease they share the penalties
as well as the benefits of culture. When Polyphemus cries out for
help, says that 'No-man is killing me', they assume he is ill:
'it is impossible to avoid disease from great Zeus'. And with this
concession to culture they reassert their wild and unsocial nature
by leaving him to it, with advice to pray (like any respectable
person) to his father, Poseidon (408–12).

The clearest way to show these departures from uniformity in the
poet's attitude towards Polyphemus and the other Cyclopes is to
arrange them side by side, schematically. The range is from super-
culture, in that the other Cyclopes have crops with no labour, to

[44] Again, the needs of the folktale plot no doubt demand that the giant becomes
drunk; but this may have been adequately foreshadowed by the special strength of the
wine Odysseus offers him.

[45] *Od.* I, 70 f.; that is what the formula ὅου κράτος ἐστὶ μέγιστον, 'whose power is
greatest', elsewhere implies.

super-savagery in the case of Polyphemus's cannibalism. Each of the two groups (Polyphemus, the rest) also veers in the other direction, and at these points, in the two central columns on the facing page, they come relatively close together.

In all this there is a kind of orderly confusion of attitudes that suggests that various aspects of nature and culture are being manipulated into proximity for the purposes of evaluation. In a sense it is this apparent manipulation that turns a folktale topic into myth —that gives it an aura not only of fantasy but of underlying meaning. The basic narrative of the Polyphemus story is compelling and ingenious in its economy and suspense; the conflicting details of status and behaviour seem to add another dimension, and yet they arise naturally enough out of separate elements of the plot. They are too complex, however, and too systematic in essence, to be the accidental result of conflation. Rather one may guess that, in the course of the development of the tale in its Odyssean form, various choices of suppression or elaboration were made by a succession of singers; and that some of these choices were partly determined by some underlying interest in the problem of relating culture to nature—more concretely, in the validity of human customs and the distinction between wildness and innocence. A certain understanding of the problem can be gained even by those who assimilate the myth in its present form: both nature and culture are seen to be ambivalent—and that is surely the key to the general dilemma. Nature can be either savage and hostile (Polyphemus) or beneficent and peaceful (the island)—a romantic view that is rare but not unknown among Greeks of many periods. Culture can be both desirable, in the application of law, humanity, and techniques (the other Cyclopes are ambiguous over the first two, primitive over the third), and undesirable; for culture goes with disease, the consciousness of death, and the abuse of gifts like wine and kinship.

It is not suggested that these opposed aspects are precisely mediated, in a strict Lévi-Straussian sense, in the myth of the Cyclopes, but rather that by bringing them into contact, by combining contradictory elements into a fantastic amalgam, the poets of the tradition gave expression, consciously or not, to ambiguities and complexities inherent in the concepts eventually stereotyped as *nomos* and *physis*, custom and nature. Particularly revealing is the demonstration of the relativity of one element to another. The

Other Cyclopes		Polyphemus	
Civilized or super-civilized	*Uncivilized*	*Super-uncivilized or barbaric*	*Relatively civilized*
'Trusting in the immortal gods' (107)	'Overbearing and lawless' (106)	He is monstrous, lawless, does not mix with the others, is not like a cereal-eating (civilized) man (187–92)	(The others live around him, 399 ff.)
Crops and vines grow for them without sowing or ploughing, watered by Zeus (108–11)		He pastures his flocks alone (187 f.)	
		He seems to live on milk and cheese? (216 ff.)	
They habitually drink wine (357 f.)		He guzzles Odysseus's wine, becomes drunk (361, 373 f.)	He drinks wine like the others (357 f.)
		He commits murder, eats raw human flesh and bones like a wild beast (288–93)	(He normally seems to live on milk and cheese, 216 ff.)
Each family has its own laws (114 f.)	They have no assembly or laws in common (112)	He has no family, no laws at all (188 f.)	
They live 'around' Polyphemus, respond to his cries (399–402)	They live in caves up in the mountains in independent family groups, take no notice of each other (113–15)	He lives by himself in a remote place above the sea (182 ff.)	The others live around him, within earshot (399 ff.)
	They have no ships, do not travel (125–9)		He has a built sheepfold and wrought pails (184–6, 222 f.)
They are 'close to' the gods, like the other Giants and the Phaeacians (VII, 205 f.)	According to Polyphemus they do not respect Zeus or the gods 'since we are far stronger' (275 f.)	He does not respect the gods because he is far stronger (275 f.)	
			He is affectionate to his ram (447 ff.)
		(He does not mix with the others, 188 f.)	His 'power is greatest over all the Cyclopes', i.e. he is their ruler (I, 70 f.)
Disease cannot be avoided (411)			He is prone to disease and should pray to Poseidon for help (411 f.)

other Cyclopes are civilized in relation to Polyphemus, uncivilized in relation to Odysseus and his companions, and in one respect super-civilized, akin to the Hesiodic golden race, in relation to mankind in general. The process is not exactly speculative; rather the tale is told in a way that heightens its piquancy by juxtaposing conflicting values in a region of special human concern. The situation was much the same with the Epic of Gilgamesh. That, too, was a complex myth in which selection and elaboration took place in the course of a long tradition; and it, too, bears testimony to underlying ambiguities in the status of man in society and in his wider environment. These ambiguities are reflected in dramatic ideas which in turn stimulate myths—for example the idea (common to the myths of Gilgamesh and the Cyclopes) that nature, both hostile and divine, and culture can be conjoined in figures like the wild, shaggy man who comes in from the desert, full of natural power and goodness like Esau or John the Baptist, or the king who is so sated with culture that he tries to move outside it, or the man-eating ogre who is both inside and outside a group that veers wildly between anarchy and the simple institutions of the divinely privileged.

No less remarkable than the parallel with Gilgamesh is that between the two Greek phenomena themselves, the Cyclopes and Centaurs. In each case there is a group of fantastic creatures (men-horses, one-eyed giants) with ambivalent qualities of both nature and culture, the former predominant. In each case one figure is set apart—living in or near the mountains in a cave like the rest (for a cave belongs to nature, but is also an embryonic house), but in isolation from the others. Yet the two isolated figures are themselves at polar extremes from each other: one, Polyphemus, has moved in the direction of savage nature and total inhumanity, the other, Cheiron, in the direction of humanity and almost god-like culture. As for the others, each group is to some extent under divine protection: the Cyclopes enjoy crops for which they do not have to labour, the surviving Centaurs are eventually rescued by Poseidon and hidden under a hill at Eleusis, close to one of the great Hellenic centres of fertility and culture. Finally the part of each group that represents raw nature and savagery is brought to heel by a hero, a prominent figure of other myths, who is himself ambivalent. Odysseus, like Heracles, is boastful, at times excessive and dangerous; he, too, is a good shot, and his arrows too are liable to be poisonous.

These correspondences (and their number could be increased) are hardly deliberate. They are neither emphasized in the way in which deliberate correspondences usually were, nor marked by cross-reference between the two groups, nor noticed by ancient mythographers still in touch, even if indirectly, with the oral tradition. Rather they seem to arise naturally out of the underlying attitude towards the problem of nature and culture that I have tried to identify: an attitude of unconscious or barely conscious concern that shaped the narrative formulation of the Cyclopes and Centaurs in a manner that turns out, as will appear in the next chapter, to be quite unusual among surviving Greek myths.

V

The Qualities of Greek Myths

1: The thematic simplicity of the myths

Various approaches to Greek mythology are possible; mine is determined by the need to define its total qualities. It might be described, somewhat pretentiously, as a phenomenological approach, one that achieves an understanding of an inner essence by the analytical description of outward appearances. Several different kinds of analysis must be applied, and that presents a problem in itself—how to do so without becoming unacceptably tedious in the process. I shall inevitably have to omit some aspects and present others in a drastically condensed form. Unfortunately, summarizing is a less acceptable activity with familiar tales than it was with the relatively unknown and unworked Mesopotamian material. Moreover the mere condensation of mythical content, without in most cases penetrating deeply into its sources and development, might seem superficial and unscholarly. Nevertheless, for present purposes it is probably better to avoid controversial *Quellenforschung*, especially because there are few branches of classical studies in which so much learning has been applied with such slight and often deceptive results. Rather than be drawn into that impasse I find it more useful to consider the myths in their classical and pre-Hellenistic form (for that much consideration of source and date is unavoidable) without speculating in detail, at least in the first instance, about their development.

This development was affected by many influences and gave rise to many different variants. Historicizing legend, cult and ritual, the vicissitudes of oral tradition, conscious literary elaboration and refinement: all played their part in shaping stories whose initial impetus, imaginative or practical, lies concealed in the shadows of the past. Provided one remains aware of this complexity, the general qualities of Greek myths are more likely to emerge from a synoptic assessment than from precarious attempts at piecemeal restoration. Ideally this assessment should be supplemented by surveys of all known Greek cults and rituals, in order to determine their possible mythical associations, and of the whole logographical and mythographical literature from Hecataeus to Fulgentius and beyond. Yet the results would be disappointingly restricted in the first case and, in the second, largely irrelevant to the probable earlier forms of myth—always with the exception of Apollodorus, who must in any event be taken into account.

The old dichotomy into divine and heroic myths has its uses, provided the misleading implications of the terms *Göttermythologie* and *Heldensage* are avoided—that only tales about the gods are myths, the rest are saga or oral literature or legend or whatever. Generally speaking, one sector of Greek mythology *is* primarily concerned with the gods, another and somewhat larger one with heroes. Obviously the two often overlap, as when a hero like Odysseus or Jason is aided or persecuted by a deity like Athena or Poseidon or Hera.

The development of the gods is the general subject of Hesiod's *Theogony*, composed by soon after 700 B.C. The poem's particular theme is the successive stages by which Zeus achieved his supremacy; accordingly it is perfunctory over some of the great Olympian gods, and devotes more attention to figures like Kronos, Hecate, Prometheus, and an assortment of giants and monsters of which the Cyclopes, the Hundred-handed giants, Typhoeus and the descendants of Phorcys are the most prominent. Much of our earliest information about the growth of other gods comes not from Hesiod but from Homer, the Homeric Hymns, Stesichorus, Pindar, the other lyric poets and the tragedians.

The beginning of Hesiod's divine genealogy is concerned with the primeval entities Ouranos and Gaia, sky and earth, enfolded and then separated by the dark wastes of Chaos; and with the multiplication of their offspring, whether in the form of local differentiations like Okeanos and Pontos or more anthropomorphically as the Titans, among them Zeus's parents Kronos and

Rhea.[1] The poem devotes great attention, also, to the description of the underworld, its various regions and aspects—a sign that the Greeks were deeply concerned with the condition and physical surroundings of the dead. The same interest is visible in Homer, especially in the underworld scenes of the eleventh *Odyssey*, while Plato's four great eschatological accounts confirm that the elaboration of a detailed and picturesque world of the dead continued as an important element of the mythical tradition.

For the behaviour of the gods, once they have achieved their permanent functions and status, the earliest and in some ways fullest sources are the *Iliad* and *Odyssey*; particularly for Zeus himself and the martial or protective deities like Athena, Hera, Apollo, and Poseidon, who support one side or the other in the Trojan War, or gods with specialized functions like Hermes and Hephaestus. Yet the elaborate divine setpieces—not the scenes of assembly or discussion but the abortive battle of the gods in the twentieth and twenty-first *Iliad* or the love-affair of Ares and Aphrodite in the eighth *Odyssey*—appear to be sophisticated Ionian developments belonging to the latest stages of the true oral tradition. They are not myths in any strict sense, but literary inventions that have something in common with the ingenious mythological elaborations of Euripides. That they occur in Homer should not persuade us that they are as 'archaic' or 'mythopoeic' as many traditional divine episodes of which we happen to hear for the first time in Stesichorus or Hecataeus—or even Apollodorus in the first or second century A.D.; and the same warning applies to many other Homeric details that can be less clearly identified as bastard mythology than these.

The primeval Ouranos and Gaia give birth to the Titans, six male and six female in Hesiod's list, which already shows signs of rationalizing a confused tradition. These Titans are a mysterious group; to suggest that they were originally nature-gods is almost meaningless, and the truth is that we have no idea where most of them come from.[2] By Hesiod's time they include vague figures

---

[1] Strictly Pontos is the offspring of Gaia alone, Okeanos of both Gaia and Ouranos (*Theogony*, 132 f.), by a careful piece of allegorizing—since Pontos is the inner sea, Okeanos the surrounding waters where earth meets sky. This reminds one of some of the detailed nature-allegory of the earliest stages envisaged in certain Mesopotamian myths.

[2] For a sensible discussion of details see M. L. West, *Hesiod, Theogony* (Oxford, 1966), 200–6. K. Kerényi finds most of the Titans 'violently solar but including in their midst the moonlike Prometheus' (*Prometheus* (New York, 1963), 61)!

like Koios, Krios, and Theia, as well as the powerful Kronos and
Iapetus the father of Prometheus and Atlas. Whether or not they
are a Hellenic version of those older gods whose leaders were Apsu,
Mummu, Tiamat and Kingu in the Babylonian Creation Epic, it
seems probable that before Hesiod they existed as one of those
collective and largely anonymous *blocs* of deities or daemons, like
the Giants, the Nymphs, the Oceanids, or the Cyclopes, that
move in the background of the Greek mythological scene and
occasionally throw up individual figures like Thetis the Oceanid,
Polyphemus the Cyclops, or Cheiron and Pholus the Centaurs.
With them might be included the whole group of serpentine
monsters, from which cosmological figures like Ophion and
Typhoeus or genealogical heroes like Cecrops and Erechtheus
emerge into functional individuality.

Thus in addition to the cultic, erotic and martial relationships of
their everyday life the gods have a history of fantastic development
against the wider background of nature-powers and cosmic
differentiations, of the underworld as well as the earth and sky;
and against the chaotic initial opposition not only of monstrous
giants, huge winds, and serpentine prodigies, but also of their own
direct ancestors like the equivocal Kronos.

Through, or in spite of, the protection of Prometheus the race of
men eventually achieves a stable relationship with the gods; and
women, even though descended from Pandora, begin to win divine
favours. The result of such unions is the second main category of
mythical subjects, namely the heroes, ἥρωες, men who had a god or
goddess as one parent or who at least walked the earth when such
figures existed. Here, at once, the word 'hero' reveals its looseness
and ambiguity. Lewis Farnell—whose work on hero-cults appeared
in 1921 and still has value[3]—distinguished seven types of hero:
hieratic hero-gods of cult origin like Trophonius or Amphiaraus; sacral heroes or heroines who are associated with a god,
perhaps as priest or priestess, like Iphigeneia; secular figures who
eventually became fully divinized, particularly Heracles, Asclepius,
and the Dioscuri; epic heroes like Hector, Achilles, and Agamemnon; fictitious eponyms and genealogical heroes like Aeolus, Ion,
and Danaus; functional and cultural daemons, Usener's *Sonder-
götter*, often anonymous and always of secondary or merely local
importance; finally a few real men (that is, men who certainly

[3] L. R. Farnell, *Greek Hero Cults and Ideas of Immortality* (Oxford, 1921).

lived) who were made heroes after their deaths and given minor cults within the full historical period. Popular taste does not change so much: they seem to have been primarily boxers and athletes.[4]

Farnell's division is not ideal, although, as a schematic analysis rather than a practical categorization into which all known heroes can be fitted, it has its merits. Neither Perseus nor Oedipus, each the subject of prominent myths, falls into one particular group. They are neither markedly hieratic or sacral figures, nor epic characters like Paris or Diomedes, nor in many important respects do they resemble Heracles. They are eminent ancestors in the royal lines of Argos and Thebes, yet more than clan or tribal projections. Composed of all these aspects and others, they achieve a complete mythological status of their own. Perseus was propitiated as a hero at Argos and elsewhere, but Oedipus had no cult at Thebes—only in Attica and elsewhere in Boeotia, and then probably at no early date. Possession of a cult became for the Greeks themselves one of the chief marks of a hero; the form of heroic worship was distinct from that of divine cult, for example in the type of sacrifice. Yet Aeneas the son of the goddess Aphrodite had no early cult, and Menelaus and Agamemnon, whose parents were mortal, gained cults at least by the time of Homer and probably before. Amphiaraus, admittedly a prophet, acquired an early and important cult in spite of parents who were not only mortal but also rather undistinguished. The truth seems to be that cultic association and semi-divine ancestry were felt more and more, from the time of Homer and Hesiod on, to be the hallmark of important heroes; but that many heroic figures of myth, and not only in the developed literary forms of the *Iliad* and *Odyssey*, just belonged to aristocratic families that traced their ultimate genesis to a god or goddess. Such heroes would normally have no individual cult, but were nevertheless conceived as belonging to a generation that still enjoyed the protection of the gods and shared, to a varying extent, their supernatural capacities, in favoured cases their very blood. Simple arguments to the effect

---

[4] A good example is Euthymus of Italian Locri, who won the boxing at Olympia in 484 B.C. (for the first time), and whose statue Pausanias saw there six centuries later. This gave Pausanias the excuse to relate how Euthymus freed the city of Temesa of a dreadful ghost known simply as the Hero, who had to be propitiated by a beautiful girl each year. Euthymus fell in love with one of the girls and drove the Hero into the sea; he (Euthymus) lived to a ripe old age and, escaping death, 'departed in some other way' and gained a shrine and a cult thereby (Pausanias, VI, 6, 4–11).

that all heroes were 'faded gods' (a phrase once popular, now obsolete), or conversely that they were all semi-deified men, are a waste of time, since the heroes are as heterogeneous in their probable origin as in their developed qualities. Heracles himself is the best example of heroic diversity. Not, with that name, a god in origin, he certainly became one in the end; his cults were various, widespread, and relatively early; and yet many of his mythical qualities are thoroughly human, more so than those of any other hero—one thinks of his brutality, his capacity for dishonesty, and his voracious appetites of every kind.[5]

He is also easily the most conspicuous single figure in the whole range of Greek myths, and reminds us that, whatever the complexities of the heroes and their types, it is the semi-divine ones, with a few heroes of the great epic adventures (the Seven against Thebes, the Argonauts, the Trojan War), the princely families of Thebes and Argos in particular, that dominate the heroic sector. The others, hieratic, functional, or relatively modern, are unimportant. Even the epic heroes have to be scrutinized for genuine mythical quality; many of them had been promoted from mere names in the course of the developing tradition, and fulfil roles that are essentially secondary or generic. Even the greatest figures of the *Iliad* and *Odyssey*, like Achilles and Hector, Odysseus and Telemachus, must be cautiously assessed; I have already suggested that most of what they are involved in is better described as legend than as myth in its stricter form (pp. 32-4). Whatever the ancestry of the Homeric heroes, whatever their prodigious feats, their acquisition of god-given powers and their occasionally privileged fates after death, such fantastic and imaginative qualities as they possess are rubbed off on them by association rather than being theirs in true essence. Perhaps that is too extreme a statement—yet it is significant that the heroes involved in the myths that seem most typically Greek are not Agamemnon, Menelaus, Achilles, Diomedes, the Ajaxes, Odysseus, and the rest, so much as Pelops, Atreus, Perseus, Cadmus, Oedipus, Jason, and of course Heracles —figures whose power depends on their association with simple episodes that nevertheless seize the imagination, rather than with complex and semi-realistic epics that stimulate more intricate reactions. It is curious and revealing that the second group of heroes belong to an earlier heroic generation than the first; their

[5] On Heracles see also pp. 161 f., 184-7.

adventures are not restricted by a recent tradition from the Trojan War on, but were probably originated many centuries before.

As for the gods, once they have achieved their form and functions most of them are quite limited in their actions. Zeus pursues various amours or dispenses occasional rough justice; he dominates or conciliates the other gods. Poseidon produces monstrous progeny, because he is the horse-god (and horses, as we saw, were once conceived as monsters) and also god of the deep sea; he persecutes those like Odysseus who offend or damage his offspring. Athena disputes the control of Athens with him, and wins; she is guardian of the city and its workers and has a few sensational dealings with the early kings of Athens and their daughters—as well, of course, as with Tydeus, Odysseus, and other hero-favourites. But generally she is a curiously static figure once her remarkable birth has been achieved. The lives of Apollo and Artemis are more eventful: they shoot down Tityus and Niobe's children and defeat the giant Aloadae; Apollo pursues various women—Coronis, Cyrene, Marpessa, Cassandra—as well as Hyacinthus, whom he kills by mistake with a discus. More important, he defeats the dragon Python and becomes master of Delphi. I could go through the other gods, in greater detail, to show that the range of incident in which they are involved, once they have found their developed form, is surprisingly restricted. That may not be altogether unexpected, although it is an observation full of significance for the assessment of Greek myths as a whole. It certainly emphasizes an important truth, that the mythical power of a deity may depend not so much on what he or she does, as on what he or she is; and that, among the range of things done, generic or day-to-day actions envisaged by cult may be as influential on the minds of men as the famous and exceptional actions envisaged by myth. So Hestia, who has no substantial mythology of her own beyond a problematical birth from Kronos and Rhea, remains a force—and elicits a special emotion wherever she occurs as a subsidiary figure —because she represents the hearth, is the centre of the household cult, and plays an important part in the great rituals surrounding birth and coming of age. At this point, it goes without saying, myth and religion overlap.

The prominence of the heroes in Greek myths is itself a standing refutation of the contention (discussed in chapter 1) that all myth is primarily concerned with gods, that it is a facet of religion. Yet the Greeks are a special case. In the mythology of most other peoples, heroes (in the sense of superior mortals placed in the not indefinite past, some of whom acquired a cult and certain supernatural powers after their death) are either inconspicuous or altogether absent. Among ancient myth-systems (to anticipate §§3–6) the Egyptian had little concern with heroes, and the king was the unique intermediary between men and gods; while in Mesopotamian myths they are few in number although important in their effects—Gilgamesh, Etana, Adapa, prototypical kings or priests. The Hurrians, also, had quite elaborate tales about legendary figures like Gurparanzakh and Kenshi. But only Germanic myth, to come nearer to our own day, is at all closely comparable, and there the influence of classical mythology cannot be discounted.

Consider the sort of actions in which first the gods, then the heroes, were involved. Ouranos mates with Gaia, then holds back their children inside her womb, within the earth itself. One of them, Kronos, castrates him, and so allows them all to be born. These are the Titans; they intermarry, and there is a Golden Age under the rule of Kronos. But he, too, brutally prevents his children from growing up, being warned by an oracle that he too will be displaced by one of them. So he swallows them as they are born; but on Gaia's advice his wife gives him a stone in place of the infant Zeus, who is spirited to Crete and grows up there in safety. An emetic causes Kronos to vomit up his other children, and they, under the leadership of Zeus, fight against Kronos and the Titans and despatch them to Tartarus beneath the earth. Zeus is now ruler, and fights off new challenges from Typhoeus and the Giants; he divides up the cosmos and assigns spheres of influence— his brothers Poseidon and Hades are to have the sea and the underworld respectively, while he keeps the sky; earth is to be shared between them. At this stage men and gods live in close contact; but Prometheus deceives Zeus over sacrifices, Zeus responds by depriving men of fire, until Prometheus steals it back, and then inflicting on them women and other diseases. Men become a nuisance and are destroyed by the flood, all except Deucalion and Pyrrha who survive in an ark and re-create men by throwing stones over their shoulders on to the earth (which is not, *pace* C. G. Jung, a way of saying that they defecated). Zeus consorts with a string of goddesses (Metis, Themis, Eurynome, Demeter, Mnemosyne, Leto and Hera according to Hesiod), either to produce further offspring (like Apollo and Artemis from Leto) or to absorb the goddesses' special powers. He continues a long career as a womanizer by impregnating Io, Semele, Europe, Danae, Leda, Alcmene and others to produce some important heroes, the great Heracles among them, and even, in special circumstances, the god Dionysus. The cosmos, with its divine rulers and their favourites, is now more or less complete. Of the actions of other gods only Demeter's search for her ravished daughter has cosmic implications; for Persephone's disappearance to the realm of Hades causes the decay of vegetation, which is seasonally restored by her partial release—as well as by Demeter's lying with Iasion in the thrice-ploughed field and her despatch, with Persephone, of Triptolemus to spread the art of agriculture.

The process of divine emergence and differentiation comprises by far the most important part of the independent mythical activity of the gods—it also contains a high proportion of the most obviously speculative component of surviving Greek myths, of which more later. Primeval nature-gods, the succession-motif, the flood and a kind of golden age are shared with Near-Eastern accounts, and it is primarily in these themes, together with that of Prometheus as trickster and protector of men, that the myths seem to be used as a special mode of conceptualizing. Pure fantasy, on the other hand, is chiefly confined to the idea of the golden age and the violence of Ouranos, Kronos and Zeus. In the rest of the mythology of the gods there is little of either of these characteristics—and they are even less conspicuous in the heroic myths to which I now turn.

These heroic myths revolve around the great centres of Mycenaean Greece and their ruling families—primarily Argos, with Mycenae and Tiryns, and Thebes, then Athens, Aegina, Calydon, Iolcus, Corinth, Sparta and Crete. Let me give a brief sample of the content of Argive mythology. Danaus ordered his fifty daughters to murder their fifty male cousins, sons of Aegyptus, whose attentions were for some reason unwelcome. Only Hypermestra spared Lynceus; their son Abas engendered Proetus and Acrisius, famous kings of Argos and Tiryns who quarrelled even in the womb. Proetus sent Bellerophon to Lycia to try and destroy him, after his own wife Stheneboea (also called Antaea) had failed to seduce him and then accused him of rape—the Poti-

phar's-wife theme that is so commonly used in Greek myths, as
with Peleus and the wife of Acastus and Hippolytus and Theseus's
second wife Phaedra. But Bellerophon succeeded in the dangerous
quests that were set him, just as Heracles did, and settled in
Lycia—from where, indeed, he had probably first entered the
mythical consciousness of the Greeks.

Acrisius, on the other hand, locked up his daughter Danae in a
brazen tower to keep her away from men, because an oracle had
foretold that he would be killed by a grandson; Kronos had
swallowed his children for much the same reason. But Zeus got at
Danae all the same, in a shower of gold (which later rationalizing
interpreters saw as a bribe for the jailer), and she gave birth to the
famous hero Perseus. Acrisius forbore to kill them outright, but
set them adrift in a hollow chest—a surprisingly common sort of
thing to do in Greek and other myths—and they landed on the
rocky isle of Seriphos. Its king was Polydectes, who later desired
Danae and sent Perseus out of the way for the Gorgon's head. With
the help of Athena and Hermes—this is the sort of way the gods
intervene in heroic myths—Perseus blackmailed the Graeae, the
grey-headed sisters, into equipping him with the cap of invisibility,
a pair of winged shoes, and a magic wallet; he did so by stealing
the single eye and tooth that the three old women shared between
them. Then he slew Medusa (taking care to look only at her
reflexion in his shield in some versions, although vase paintings
tend to show him merely turning his head away), and escaped
with her head in the wallet. On the way home he rescued Andromeda, exposed by her father the king of Ethiopia to placate a
sea-monster sent to punish a foolish boast of his wife. Acrisius's
fears were well founded, because Perseus killed him by mistake
with a discus; but Perseus and Andromeda founded the Perseid
dynasty of Argos, and he became eponymous ancestor of the
Persians.

A different dynasty, inconsistently related in time to that of the
Perseids, was started by Pelops, son of the Lydian king Tantalus.
Tantalus had shared the banquets of the gods; later he became a
famous sinner in the underworld (where food and drink tantalized
him by being always just out of reach), either through giving
divine food to men or because he had served up his son Pelops to
the gods to see if they could tell the difference. Demeter absent-
mindedly ate a bit of shoulder; a gleaming ivory replacement made

Pelops so beautiful that Poseidon fell in love with him. The god of horses made him a brilliant horseman, so that when he came to Greece he aspired to the hand of Hippodameia, princess of Pisa, who could only be won by the defeat of her dangerous father Oenomaus in a chariot-race—a typical bride-contest motif. To make doubly sure, Pelops persuaded the king's charioteer Myrtilus to sabotage the chariot; but later he had to kill Myrtilus too, who cursed him and his descendants. It was this curse that started the trouble between Atreus and Thyestes, Pelops's sons; for Thyestes out of jealousy seduced Atreus's wife Aerope, and Atreus in turn served Thyestes with his own children for dinner. Only Aegisthus escaped for a while; he was Thyestes's son by his own daughter, and carried on the quarrel by seducing Clytemnestra, wife of Atreus's son Agamemnon. The consequences are well known. The theme of curses, seduction and incest is continued when this story makes contact with the Theban cycle; for Pelops's youngest son Chrysippus was seduced by Laius king of Thebes, and Pelops's curse (corresponding in its effects to the curse placed on himself by Myrtilus) led to disaster for Laius and his son Oedipus, then for Oedipus's sons Eteocles and Polyneices, who killed each other in the war of the Seven against Thebes—a war in which the Argive king Adrastus once again links the two regional cycles.

This fleeting survey of primarily Argive myths includes many of the main themes of a substantial proportion of Greek heroic mythology. What, then, are the qualities and interests revealed so far? First, the fantastic elements—elements not only remote from real life and the actually possible, but also genuinely imaginative in conception—are few. The Graeae sisters' single eye and tooth, the Gorgon's power to turn to stone, the replacement of Pelops's shoulder, Tantalus's punishment below, some of Zeus's amorous transformations: these are the most imaginative elements, together with the whole conception of anthropomorphic gods who can take part in the affairs of men. Magic in itself is fantastic, but in a limited way, and the particular uses exemplified in Perseus's magic cap and wallet show little beyond routine narrative imagination; the same is so with Andromeda's sea-monster, even though the conception of monsters itself reveals an imaginative extension of familiar hostile creatures. Lastly there are certain unusual acts, like the cooking and serving up of children, that are not physically impossible but are commendably remote from real life.

Much of this material is folktale rather than myth in the strictest sense—I refer to the discussion of these concepts in the opening chapter. Some of its motifs are recurrent mechanisms of Greek mythology as well as being familiar from other folklore: Potiphar's wife, killing a relative by accident, and so on. To these may be added the fifty sons and daughters of Aegyptus and Danaus, as of Aeolus and Priam according to Homer; fifty is a standard number for groups—as for the Argonauts, or the Theban ambush of whom Tydeus let only one escape. This motif of the only survivor is another standard one, as in the case of Hypsipyle, the one Lemnian woman who spared her husband, as well as with the Danaids themselves. I passed over Bellerophon's adventures, but they too, with the exception of the flying-horse idea and in particular the last impertinent flight towards the gods (which may reproduce the Akkadian theme of Etana), are commonplace types, most obviously similar to the adventures of Heracles and Theseus. Sending a hero to his presumed death is extremely common, and is used in the case of Perseus as well as Bellerophon; the most familiar example is Jason, despatched on a seemingly impossible task by the usurper Pelias. The father who tries to prevent his daughter from marrying, or destroy his child or grandchild because of an oracle that foretells his own death or supplanting by such a child, is another well-worn theme: it occurs here with Laius and Oedipus as well as Acrisius and Perseus. The overcoming of a difficulty, for instance in performing a supposedly fatal task, by ingenuity or trick is a further topic endemic in Greek myths, represented by Myrtilus's sabotage of his master's chariot (by inserting lynch-pins made of wax) or Perseus's manner of aiming at Medusa (by looking in his polished shield); and ingenuity is the keynote of other motifs, such as Pelops's testing of divine omniscience or the neat idea of the transferable eye and tooth. Other recurrent themes in our Argive sample are Hera's jealousy itself, which plagues Heracles and motivates many of his actions, the winning of a foreign princess (by Perseus and Bellerophon, compare Theseus and Jason), and the displacement of a hero from one mythical milieu to another by reason of blood-pollution, often through an accident with spear or discus—a displacement that serves to connect different regional cycles as well as to give variety to a hero's life and deeds.

There are other factors: historical reminiscence, not only with

Danaus and Aegyptus but also in the advent of Pelops from Lydia, which might indicate some kind of influx from Asia Minor (although Perseus's Ethiopian adventure probably reflects nothing more than the desire to set certain heroic feats at the exotic confines of the known world); or simple allegory—Io is daughter of the Argive river Inachus and may be turned into a cow because rivers often tend to be represented as bulls. These additional factors are themselves complex and uncertain: Io may be a cow for a quite different reason (apart from the possibility of mere narrative invention for its own sake) connected with the Egyptian cow-headed goddess Hathor or Isis, or alternatively with the waters released by Indra when he slays the serpent Vritra, waters that are envisaged as cattle according to the Rig-Veda. Greek myths, like others, were drawn together from various sources and for various reasons. Occasionally one can detect a special motive for a particular theme—for example an aetiological motive of some kind, or occasionally the reflexion of a serious preoccupation. Yet the schematic qualities stand out. The Perseus myth is well known for its folktale characteristics; the point to be stressed is that the rest of the heroic mythology is not essentially different. This emerges, too, from a further brief survey, this time of the myths about Heracles.

From his birth on, Hera continued her paradoxical hatred of him—paradoxical because Heracles's name would naturally imply her particular protection; drove him mad so that he killed his wife Megara and their children, then subjected him to king Eurystheus of Mycenae for twelve years of expiation. These years, and the twelve labours they contained, do not make him a sun-god. Twelve was a good number, a Babylonian paradigm apart from anything else, and the tradition had some difficulty in filling it out with feats which, whatever their hold over ancient and Renaissance writers and artists, are for the most part feeble and unimaginative. Of the six labours set in the Peloponnese, three are routine monster-slayings (Nemean lion, Lernaean hydra, Stymphalian birds); two involve animal capture (Erymanthian boar, Ceryneian hind); and the cleansing of the stables of Augeias involves either ingenuity or brute strength or both. Of the rest, three are likewise fairly typical heroic exercises (the Cretan bull, another rather tame monster-slaying, the man-eating horses of the Thracian king Diomedes, and the Amazon's girdle, which has a faint tinge of folktale). The remaining three, all associated with the distant west, have a more exotic quality: Heracles brings back the cattle of the triple monster Geryon, crossing Okeanos in the bowl of the sun; then he descends to Hades itself to capture Cerberus; finally he wins the golden apples of the Hesperides after binding Nereus, a typical shape-changing knowledgeable water-god. Of his various other performances, many concerned simply with sacking cities and deflowering young women, few are surprising, none profound. Among the more striking are his dealings with the Centaurs Cheiron, Pholus and Nessus that I have already described. After Heracles has sacked Oechalia to win his new flame Iole, his wife Deianeira uses Nessus's deadly philtre on him. Heracles has himself carried to the top of Mount Oeta and immolated on a pyre; that, with one or two of his other actions, might be connected with a ritual, since the casting of effigies into pyres on mountain-tops (among other locations) is a familiar fire-ritual connected with fertility.

How did Heracles come to dominate the heroic mythology of the Greeks? I wish we knew. His origin is disputed, but the old idea that he was simply a Dorian hero who imposed himself on Achaean cults is nowadays discredited. His associations are with Thebes as much as with the Argolid and Laconia, and his cult was ubiquitous. His monotonous feats against men, women and monsters are redeemed by a certain genuine nastiness on his part; yet along with prodigies of lust and gormandizing (he ate a whole ox at Lindos according to another of his myths that may have ritual implications) he has a more positive aspect, for example as founder of the Olympic Games, introducer of trees from the Hyperboreans, wrestler, above all, with death. Apart from the monster-encounters he is less encumbered with folktale activities than Theseus, Perseus, Jason or Peleus. One unusual motif is his enslavement, first to Eurystheus and then to Omphale, queen of Lydia, each time in requital for an act of murder. I conjecture that this motif was caused by a combination of intentional paradox (the strongest man becomes a slave, in the second case to a mere woman), narrative convenience (how to subject him to so many dangerous and distant quests), and historicizing reminiscence (for his city of Tiryns was probably a dependency of Eurystheus's Mycenae).

At this point the views of Angelo Brelich, one of the acutest of modern writers on these matters, are of interest. Brelich tried to show that the Greek heroes reveal a distinct morphology.[6] They all have some kind of association with the following: death, combat, athletic contests, prophecy, healing, mysteries, oracles, founding cities, and the initiation of young adults and the maintenance of clan groups. Heracles, more than most, has these associations; but H. J. Rose made the pertinent comment that to most of these subjects great aristocratic figures were bound to be related— notably the establishing of cities, games, mysteries, and oracles.[7] Combat is another obvious heroic activity; which only leaves initiation, healing, and death as in any way remarkable. Yet the association of local heroes with clan and tribal rituals is natural, and can be well documented; H. Jeanmaire was even persuaded that this is the origin of the Theseus myth.[8] One notes, however, that the part played by some of the greatest heroes in important festivals of initiation was quite minor, as with Heracles and the Apaturia at Athens.[9] Healing and medicine most obviously con- cern Asclepius (who like Heracles was treated as a god, not a hero, after a paradoxically discreditable death) and his master Cheiron, to a lesser degree Heracles himself; and it is through contact with them that a few other heroes have powers of healing. There remains the connexion with death. Admittedly most heroes die, often in peculiar ways: not only by accident or in war, but also by being burnt, torn to pieces, struck by lightning, or thrust into the earth. After their death they tend to receive a cult at their supposed tomb. Yet these attributes do not of themselves necessarily suggest any special connexion with death and the dead; which leaves us virtually with Heracles once more, and his attacks upon Hades. One of these attacks, if Geryon is a chthonic death-demon and his cattle are akin to the herds of Hades, may explain Heracles's association with healing; for hot springs, with which he is often connected, have been demonstrated by J. H. Croon to mark many of the traditional entrances to the underworld.[10]

The 'heroic morphology', although it deserves attention, is not so definite, complex or significant as Brelich maintains. One point he has usefully emphasized is that even the best of the heroes have

---

[6] *Gli Eroi Greci* (Rome, 1958), *passim*.
[7] *Classical Review*, N.S. x, 1960, 48–50.
[8] *Couroi et Courètes* (Lille, 1939), ch. 4.
[9] *Op. cit.*, 126; cf. L. Deubner, *Attische Feste* (Berlin, 1932), 226 f., 232–4.
[10] *The Herdsman of the Dead* (Diss., Amsterdam, 1952).

a violent and destructive side—even Aeacus, a son of Zeus, king of Aegina, and so renowned for his justice that he became a judge in Hades, was involved in the rape of Psamathe, a typically elusive sea-nymph. Perhaps that is not so bad; Heracles is certainly much worse. Is this because heroes represented some kind of mediation between order and disorder, just as some of them occupy a position, in terms of power and mortality, midway between men and the gods? It was the Giants, overwhelmed by Heracles himself, that in the art of the sixth and fifth centuries B.C. became the symbol of chaos, lawlessness and barbarism; in an important sense the heroes are their natural enemies and stand on the side of civilization and culture. And yet their seamier aspect might, after all, reflect an older and more ambivalent view. Or is their selfish violence little more than a projection of aristocratic materialism and love of power? On the whole I am inclined to see their ambiguity more as an accidental result of a complex tradition than as an intended contrast between order and disorder or nature and culture; although Heracles himself, as I suggested in chapter IV, represents an important exception.

The disconcerting fact remains that the greatest of Greek heroes, who has an unusually complex biography and finds his way into most of the cycles of myths, is for the most part an uninteresting performer, at least by the standards of fantasy and imagination that can be applied to the myths of other cultures, developed or undeveloped. To cover the remainder of Greek myth even at this length would be tedious and is in any case unnecessary. The sample given so far is adequate to demonstrate the thematic simplicity, almost shallowness, of most Greek myths. Instead of plodding through the rest, I prefer to present a bare list of the themes that occur repeatedly in the primarily heroic myths and occasionally in the primarily divine ones, and which between them account for much the greater part of their action; and to comment on their implications afterwards.

Commonest themes in Greek (mainly heroic) myths

1. *Tricks, riddles, ingenious solutions to dilemmas* (used by gods and heroes for all purposes: to disguise or unmask, catch a thief or adulterer, win a contest, delay pursuit, etc.)

2. *Transformations* (of men and women into birds, trees, animals, snakes, stars, as a punishment, or avoidance of an

impasse; of deities into humans, temporarily; of women to evade amorous attention, and of Zeus to further it; of water-deities into all shapes)

3. *Accidental killing of a relative, lover or friend*, often followed by flight to avoid vengeance or obtain purification (of Laius by Oedipus, Actaeon by his dogs, Cyzicus by the Argonauts, Electryon by Amphitryon, Hyacinthus by Apollo, Procris by Cephalus, Catreus by Althaemenes; cf. Megara by Heracles, Dryas by Lycurgus, Aigeus by Theseus, etc.)

4. *Giants, monsters, snakes* (as opponents of gods, guardians of treasure, ravagers to be destroyed by a hero; occasionally friendly (e.g. Hundred-handed giants, some Cyclopes, some Centaurs), sometimes of mixed animal and human shape (e.g. Sphinx, Minotaur, Centaurs, Satyrs))

5. *Attempts to get rid of a rival* by setting impossible and dangerous tasks

6. *Fulfilling a task or quest*, sometimes with help of a god or girl (killing a monster, gaining an inaccessible object, freeing (sometimes marrying) a princess)

7. *Contests* (for a bride, for kingship, for honour)

8. *Punishment for impiety* (of various graphic kinds; for attempting a goddess, boasting that one surpasses a deity; special kinds of death for opposing Dionysus)

9. *Displacement of parents or elders* (actual or feared displacement, often in accordance with an oracle)

10. *Killing, or attempting to kill, one's own child* (by exposure, to avoid displacement, cf. 9, or by accident, or to appease a deity; often in accordance with an oracle or prophecy)

11. *Revenge* by killing or seducing a man's wife or murdering his children

12. *Sons avenge mother* or protect her against an oppressor

13. *Disputes within the family*: sons fight each other, children oppressed by stepmother

14. *Deceitful wife*, vainly in love with young man, accuses him of rape

15. *Deceitful daughter*, in love with father's enemy, betrays father, is punished for it

16. *Incestuous relationships*

17. *Founding a city* (in accordance with an oracle, by following a certain animal or by other tokens)

18. *Special weapons* (needed to overthrow a particular enemy, cure a wound, etc.)

19. *Prophets and seers* (understand language of animals, propound riddles, cure childlessness, reveal way out of an impasse)

20. *Mortal lovers of goddesses and mistresses of gods*

21. *Perils of immortality* as a gift to men (danger of infinite old age if youth is not specified)

22. *External soul or life-token* (the life of a hero depends on a hair, a firebrand, etc.)

23. *Unusual births* (from the head or thigh of Zeus, from mother at point of death, by castrating father, etc.)

24. *Enclosure or imprisonment* in a chest, jar, or tomb

Of these themes, 1–4 are commonest of all; 5–7 concern heroic quests, tasks and adventures; 8, 20 and 21 concern relations between men and gods; 9–16 concern tensions and disputes within the family; the remainder are various, and more specific than many of the others. The categorization is inevitably personal and provisional, and certain changes might be introduced: mechanisms like oracles and curses might be given independent status, or certain of the themes, like 5 and 6 or 14 and 15, might be amalgamated under a more general title. Yet in general, and allowing for minor disagreement over details, I submit that the list accounts for the main episodic trends of most known heroic myths in Greece —and a considerable number of the divine ones also. Such an analysis varies in accordance with the specificity of the themes that can be distinguished and their total scope;[11] obviously any set of myths could be reduced to a small range of themes if these were made sufficiently general. But the present selection is not very general: even 1–4 have a certain precision (although they are, of course, familiar from the folktales of many cultures).

Such themes can be combined in groups of from two to five so as to form complex myths. A typical situation would be one in which a hero, after accidentally killing a friend or relative, becomes embroiled in a fight against a monster that he defeats by means of a trick. Some themes have particular structural importance in that they entail and motivate a change of place, relationship, or status:

[11] It is therefore continuous wih motif-analysis of the Aarne-Thompson kind. J. Fontenrose's analyses of themes in certain groups of myths, best exemplified in 'The Hero as Athlete' (*California Studies in Classical Antiquity*, 1, 1968, 73 ff.), point in the same direction.

for instance from a hero's birthplace to a different region with which he became associated in tradition or cult. So the accidental killing of a relative, etc. (3) is valuable, and tends to recur often, for the following reasons: it moves the hero into a second family and place, where he takes refuge or seeks purification; it alters (usually lowers) his status, and so makes it natural for him to be sent on quests; it is dramatic and deeply ironical in itself (since killing one's parent, for example, by mistake is horrible and futile); finally it often comes as fulfilment of a dream, prophecy, or oracle, which increases the irony as well as the complexity of the situation. *A* learns by dream or oracle that his son *B* will cause his death; *A* exposes the infant *B*, who is rescued by shepherds; *B* grows up elsewhere and does not know his true father; he kills a man who turns out to be *A*. This Oedipus plot is a special case of killing 'by mistake': the mistake is psychological (failing to recognize), rather than physical (for instance striking with an ill-aimed discus). Minor elements in this kind of plot remain constant just because they perform their function with greatest efficiency: it is nearly always a shepherd or goatherd who finds an exposed child, because they are the people most likely to be roaming around in the deserted uplands and least likely to be deterred by the cultural inhibitions of the city. The discus is the paradigm instrument for random killing, just because it is so easy to release it a fraction of a second too early or too late. These are the formulary elements of fictitious narrative, and in an essentially oral tradition they are varied no more than an analogous linguistic element would be needlessly varied in the formular language of Homer.

2: Basic concerns underlying the conventional structure

Some themes recur because of their mechanical usefulness, others because of a continuing taste for their style or content. The use of ingenuity or a trick to resolve a dilemma (1 in the preceding list) accords with the conciseness and formal neatness that Greek myths tended to assume—they do not sprawl or indulge in irrelevant detail or complication. But ingenuity must have been pleasing in itself, even apart from this general formal quality; the originators and transmitters of many of these myths must have found ingenious solutions intrinsically satisfying, which is why there are so many dilemma/solution sequences in Greek myths and, as was noted earlier, in many folktales all over the world.

This is a popular taste at quite a simple level—and not, for example, the reflexion of serious social problems, or the symbolic affirmation of an institutional norm. And yet certain persistent emphases seem to permeate the subject-matter even of these schematized and generally unfantastic heroic tales.

Giants and monsters (4) are both dramatic and useful. Slaying them creates a fundamental kind of suspense, in which danger and deprivation are satisfyingly replaced by safety and possession.[12] Monsters are the ideal enemy from the dramatic point of view, since, the more acute and apparently inhuman the danger, the greater the relief and satisfaction when it is overcome. The Greeks were relatively unimaginative in the development of monstrous forms, and remained content for the most part with basic Near-Eastern fantasies. Yet monsters were more than standardized motives for certain kinds of action, or excuses for the kind of ingenuity shown by Heracles over the Hydra and Geryon; they tend to have a symbolic value of their own. For different peoples in different lands they have represented the terrifying powers of nature, like earthquakes or thunderstorms, or the demons of death, or frightful human enemies beyond the borders, or elements of cosmic disorder, or the unknown powers of the unconscious mind. It is no longer possible to assign different Greek monsters to their appropriate categories with much precision, although certain reasonable conjectures can be made; such as that serpentine monsters are chthonic, of the earth, and so can represent the powers of the dead, or of earthquake, or even so tame a thing (in the case of the early Attic kings) as autochthony; that multi-bodied or multi-limbed monsters are so imagined simply to make them formidable opponents for a hero or an anthropomorphic god; and that winged monsters are mostly of Near-Eastern origin.

A third group (8, 20, 21) refers to men's relations with the gods. In Greece, as has been seen, the actions of developed gods and goddesses are often concerned with protecting or making love to a hero or heroine, or conversely persecuting or taking vengeance on them. These are some of the divine themes of myths: pursuit of a mortal love; support of a favourite in war, adventure, or kingship, as of Tydeus, Odysseus or Heracles by Athena, or Agamemnon by Zeus;

---

[12] There are, of course, several possible motives, whether psychological or practical, for combat-myths. To this extent Francis Vian, *Les Origines de Thèbes* (Paris, 1963), is correct as against J. Fontenrose's idea of *the* combat myth (*Python*, 99 ff., 465 f.).

persecution of a mortal for accidental or deliberate impiety, as Poseidon pursues Odysseus for blinding his son Polyphemus, or Artemis plagues Oeneus for forgetting her at a sacrifice, or Apollo and Artemis destroy Niobe's children because of her trivial boast that she had surpassed Leto herself in motherhood, or as Ixion is thrown into Tartarus for trying to rape Hera. Often enough the gods are little more than a convenient stimulus for heroic action; but certain myths are concerned to emphasize their absolute power, or alternatively the ambiguous borderline between gods and men: so for instance when a child is almost made immortal by a goddess (as Demophon by Demeter), or a man's life depends upon some physical appurtenance, his external soul, or a goddess has to discard a mortal husband (as Thetis abandons Peleus) when he grows old.

So far as gods and daemons are concerned the listing of common themes is misleading. The idea of Olympus as dwelling place for the greatest gods, or of a generation of dead heroes, some hovering close to their tombs and demanding worship, others as invisible daemons walking over the earth maintaining justice[13]—these ideas are in themselves genuinely imaginative, and this should not be forgotten through excessive preoccupation with the conventional, standardized and folktale aspects of Greek mythology. Admittedly, once their development and the assignment of their functions are complete, most of the gods engage in few actions that are unique and memorable, but perform those routine duties of protection, lust or persecution to which attention has been drawn. And yet the gods are always there, and this presence, so obvious that it can be overlooked, is a fundamental component of the Greek mythological conception. The heroes in their mythical world move and act in the aura of these numinous creations, whose combination of familiarity and unpredictability, even if their positive interventions are intermittent, repetitious or secondary, makes their presence continuously felt. It is the gods, ultimately, that make the heroes significant. One does not feel inclined to argue (to take a trivial instance) about whether Heracles could seduce fifty women in a night when one recalls that he is a son of Zeus—whereas the idea of an all-human superman is a self-contradictory bore. Moreover the very concept of the anthropomorphic gods, formulated in the remote past and certainly not exclusively Greek, was one of profound fantasy, far surpassing in importance the neatness

[13] Hesiod, *Works and Days*, 252 f., cf. 122 ff.

and rich detail that are the more obvious hallmarks of Greek myths as we perceive them. Once invented, the gods could never be entirely stripped of their imaginative implications, even though poems like the Theomachy in the twentieth and twenty-first *Iliad* did their best to trivialize them. Their essence provided a continuing commentary on human aspirations and limitations and the absurd conflicts between them.

The last conspicuous group of common themes (9–16) demonstrates that folktale motifs and convenient narrative devices can co-exist with more permanent social concerns. Stresses within the family operate between son and father and brother and brother, especially in a dynastic context; between husband and wife; between father and daughter (by incest, or through fear of displacement, or in a conflict of loyalties), or son and mother (Oedipus and Iocaste, Orestes and Clytemnestra) or stepmother. They result in lies, betrayal, counter-seduction and other forms of inhuman revenge. Only occasionally does the family act together as a unit to repel stresses from outside, as when sons protect or avenge their mother (like Perseus and Danae, or Zethus, with Amphion, and Antiope). The implicit drama of family stress is not confined to semi-realistic saga situations like those of the houses of Labdacus and Atreus. It permeates every kind of Greek myth, ranging from the theogonic succession myth of Ouranos, Kronos and Zeus to the folktale type of story of lusty and deceitful wives like Phaedra and Stheneboea or treacherous daughters like Medea and Comaetho. The wide distribution of this group of themes suggests that family stresses were a subject of deep personal interest—as well as great dramatic potentiality—both in the myth-forming period and in the subsequent tradition.[14] This interest exceeds that of ordinary folktales, yet one should not exaggerate it by too loose a comparison with the mythological concerns of many exotic societies. In a highly organized tribal structure particular tensions arise out of special conditions. A man may live, for example, in close proximity to his unmarried sister-in-law, a situation of proven danger. He does so as a result of the interaction of a set of practical needs: for the clan group to be concentrated, for the preservation of family property, for the use of women as articles of exchange, for the provision of secure

---

[14] To some extent, no doubt, complex family interrelationships were also a mechanical product of the unification of different regional traditions.

conditions for child-bearers, for avoidance of incest of the more remote kind. In Greece as we know it, and presumably at least as far back as the early Bronze Age, society was looser and less heavily schematized than that, matrilocal residence of the husband was not normal, and the chances of family stress, at least on the sexual level, were correspondingly less. Stresses, nevertheless, there obviously were. It is axiomatic that, whatever the social arrangements, men and women, and the old and the young, will always fight each other—as long, at least, as greed, jealousy and lust remain prominent among the hereditary qualities of men. The emphasis on family tensions in ancient Greece should be seen as a broad response to a continuing human characteristic rather than as a specific reaction to extreme social conditions.

The study of these ordinary themes, which in spite of their schematic qualities reveal certain underlying emphases, must be supplemented by that of themes that stand out as special, extraordinary, even bizarre, in subject and possibly in significance. These are the themes (some relatively frequent, and so also present in the first list, others infrequent, none unique) in which one might expect to find, most plainly preserved, speculative or seriously explanatory implications. Again it should be stressed that the selection is provisional and that not every theme will turn out on closer inspection to be unusually important.

Special, unusual or bizarre themes

1. *Fire*

　　(*a*) its gift or recovery (Phoroneus, Prometheus)

　　(*b*) needed for sacrifices (Zeus and Prometheus)

　　(*c*) makes immortal (Demophon, Achilles, cf. Meleagrus)

　　(*d*) and the cooking of children (Tantalus, Atreus, Procne and Philomela [for testing or revenge]; Ino and Melicertes [madness]), or of the old (Medea and Pelias, cf. Ixion and Eïoneus)

　　(*e*) as divine or cathartic (Zeus's lightning, stars as souls)

　　(*f*) renewed annually (women of Lemnos, Heracles on Oeta)

2. *Golden age*

　　(*a*) golden race in Hesiod's five-races myth

　　(*b*) reign of Kronos

　　(*c*) men dine with the gods (Tantalus; marriage of Peleus and Thetis, Cadmus and Harmonia; Mecone; cf. Apollo as servant of Laomedon, Admetus)

3. *Disappearing fertility-deities, and attempts at retrieval from the underworld*

(*a*) Kore/Persephone ravished by Plouton, retrieved for part of each year (cf. Dioscuri taking turns in underworld?)

(*b*) Adonis (cf. Mesopotamian and other Asiatic fertility-gods)

(*c*) (Cf. Orpheus and Eurydice, Heracles and Alcestis, etc.; mortal fertility-figures like daughters of Cecrops and Anius)

4. *Origin of old age and disease; perils of near-immortality*

(*a*) Pandora and the release of ills

(*b*) the end of the golden age

(*c*) punishment for trying to evade death (Sisyphus, Asclepius; Bellerophon?)

(*d*) immortality has its dangers (Cheiron, Peleus, Tithonus, Cumaean Sibyl; cf. Caeneus, Meleagrus)

5. *Displacement of elders*

(*a*) Ouranos, Kronos, Zeus (Heracles)

(*b*) suppression of children to avoid displacement (Zeus and Thetis's son, Laius and Oedipus, Priam and Paris, etc.)

(*c*) (Cf. family curses, Atreidae, Labdacids)

6. *Unusual births*

(*a*) earth (or sea) fertilized by divine seed or phallus (Kronos produces Typhoeus; Ouranos, Aphrodite; Hephaestus, Erichthonius; cf. Ixion, Nephele)

(*b*) men created from earth (Deucalion and Pyrrha; the Spartoi at Thebes; Prometheus made man out of clay)

(*c*) birth from a male god (Athena from Zeus; Dionysus from Zeus (in a second birth), cf. Asclepius removed from mother by Apollo; Zeus's brothers vomited up by Kronos)

(*d*) birth of twins (one mortal, the other divine: Polydeuces and Castor, cf. Heracles and Iphiclus)

7. *Enclosure*

(*a*) in chest, which is set afloat (Danae and Perseus, Auge and Telephus, Tenes and Hemithea, etc.)

(*b*) of fertility-object in chest (Adonis, put in chest by Aphrodite; Erichthonius, as snake; cf. Leda's egg, Meleagrus's soul)

(*c*) as imprisonment, in jar, tomb, or bronze room (of Ares by Aloadae (cf. of Eurystheus, or Cleomedes of Astypalaea, as refuge); of Polyidus, Danae; cf. of evils in Pandora's jar)

8. *Sex-change*

of Teiresias, of Caenis–Caeneus (cf. transvestism: Achilles, Dionysus, priest of Heracles in Cos, etc.)

Fire (1 in the above list) affects men on all sides: as instrument of cooking and other technology; of communication with the gods by means of sacrifice; as associated with the aither, the bright sky, place of gods and souls; as destructive—either negatively or, through purgation, positively. The myths not only reflect its importance, but also seem to perform something of their Lévi-Straussian function, in this case, of mediating a contradiction. There is a certain evident tension between the secular uses of fire (for cooking and manufacture, most notably) and its sacred use as a medium of sacrifice, ritual purgation, or divine punishment. This polarity is not stated directly, but is touched on implicitly in the dealings between Zeus and Prometheus. Prometheus tried to exaggerate the secular side of sacrifice (by giving men a proper meal, and the gods the useless portion); Zeus retaliated by removing fire altogether, which destroyed the dilemma, but to the detriment of gods as well as men. Analogous to this ambiguity of sacred and secular is another, of cathartic and destructive. This is reflected in the idea of goddesses who try to make human children immortal by holding them in the fire, as Thetis did Achilles, and Demeter Demophon (cathartic), as opposed to Ixion who achieved the opposite effect on his father-in-law Eïoneus (destructive: he cast him into a blazing pit). That mortal interveners, in the former instances, think that destruction, rather than catharsis, is being undertaken, and so frustrate the process, underlines the ambiguities in an almost Heraclitean idea of a tension of opposites that gods understand and humans do not. Secondly, Zeus burns up Semele by appearing to her in his true shape, as fire, and destroys Asclepius with his thunderbolt for reversing the natural order by trying to raise the dead (destruction); whereas the cremation of Heracles on Oeta ensures his passage to complete divinity by purging his mortal elements (catharsis).

The idea of a *golden age* (2) is probably based upon Near-Eastern models (rather than being derived from Egypt, where it also occurs); but there it is solely the gods who live in a land of perfect purity (see pp. 91 f. on the myth of Enki and Ninhursag), and men, created to be their servants, never experience anything similar. In the Greek conception men and gods used to feast together long ago—so according to Hesiod, *Ehoeae* 6 f. The gods and goddesses attended the weddings of Peleus and Thetis and Cadmus and Harmonia; Tantalus entertained the gods to dinner, and it was perhaps at a communal meal at Mecone or Sicyon that Prometheus tricked Zeus over the sacrifices (Hesiod, *Theogony*, 535 ff.). A slightly different conception is seen in *Works and Days*, where men of the golden race lived like gods (rather than with them), free from toil, grief and old age (109 ff.). The general picture is clear; in the distant past men lived like gods without toil, much as demi-gods still do in the Isles of the Blessed; but because of some presumptuous sin (by Prometheus on their behalf, or the crime of Tantalus, or the eating of flesh according to Empedocles's *Katharmoi*) they have lost all this and are entangled in toil, sorrow and sickness. Once again there seems to be a speculative or reflective background to this mythical topic, which is connected with the whole question of the inevitability of death.

Disappearing fertility-deities and attempts at retrieval from the underworld (3) are an almost obsessive motif in Near-Eastern myths— Sumerian, Akkadian, Hittite, and Canaanite. In the Greek canon the tale of Demeter and Persephone occupies a central place, and might be still more prominent in classical art and literature were it not restricted by its secret role in the Eleusinian mysteries. The seasonally reborn Adonis is an obviously Asiatic figure, but in the classical epoch, if not earlier, he made a powerful impression on the Greek imagination. In Greek myths it is the sequence of fertile and infertile seasons that is alluded to, rather than the years of drought that haunted the minds of western Asiatic peoples. The theme of disappearance is often associated with attempts at retrieval from the world of the dead—whether by the gods (as with Inanna/ Ishtar and Persephone) or by a hero, especially Heracles, but also Orpheus with Eurydice. Much must have disappeared. Eurydice may or may not have been a fertility-goddess in origin, and like Persephone connected with the dead. Ariadne presents a similar ambiguity. Ino's destruction of the seed-corn may have implications beyond temporary and local disaster. The daughters of Anius of Delos were called Oino, Spermo, and Elais (Wine, Seed, Olive-oil) and could produce these commodities at will; we should like to know more about them. Their grandmother Rhoio (Pomegranate, a fruit with associations both of fertility and of death) had

been launched in a chest, just like Danae and others, by a resent-
ful father. Curiously enough three other sisters with names suggesting fertility were associated with a chest; the daughters of
Cecrops, king of Athens, were Herse, Aglauros, and Pandrosos
(Dew, Shining, All-dewy), and Athena gave them charge of a
chest and told them not to look inside it. Naturally they did so; it
contained the snakish product of Hephaestus's seed (which fell on
the earth when he tried to rape Athena), later to become the
serpentine Erichthonius, and they went mad at the sight. Snakes,
as we all know, represent fertility, both because of their phallic
appearance and because their home is in the earth; and the
connexion with chests will be further discussed under the heading
'Enclosure'.

The *origin of old age and disease* (4) is closely associated with the
idea of a decline from the golden age. The Sumerian myth of Enki
and Ninhursag, although it concerned gods not men, still told of
the creation of diseases, to which, with death itself, certain Mesopotamian gods (who then became powers of the underworld) were
prone. The human preoccupation, there displaced on to the gods,
is clearer in Greek myths. Here men are never free from death, even
if Hesiod's golden race died swiftly, as though in sleep, and had
no old age (*Works and Days*, 113–16). In the preceding myth of the
first woman, before she released evils and diseases from the jar
men lived 'without evils and harsh toil and cruel diseases', whereas
now 'full is the earth of evils and full the sea, and diseases come
upon men by day, and others unprompted by night...' (91 f.,
101 ff.). The Greeks accepted the inevitability of death, and
myths like that of Sisyphus, who was punished for trying to escape
death by a trick, and Asclepius, who was thunderbolted for trying
to restore a dead man to life, demonstrate their feeling that death
is a natural and irreversible law. The Hesiodic myths, on the other
hand, show that the manner of men's death was not so easily
accepted: why did mortals have to undergo the humiliating and
wasteful process of old age and disease, if they could not achieve
the heroic ideal of death in battle?[15] Other Greek myths emphasize
that the gods are ageless, not merely immortal. It is not death, but
old age and its concomitants, that are cause for mortal resentment.
Tithonus and the Cumaean Sibyl, who were granted immortality
but not eternal youth, became obscene monsters, the one babbling

[15] See also pp. 226 ff.

from a locked room, the other a vocal heap in a bottle. Cheiron and Peleus are other instances of the futility of confusing mortality with immortality, of ambiguous positions between the two. The positive conclusion, that what men should pray for is a swift and honourable death, is implicit not in myths, curiously enough, but in the heroic ideal itself, and in exemplary tales like that of Cleobis and Biton (Herodotus, 1, 31).

The *displacement of elders* (5) also reflects the otiose and objectionable qualities of old age. Yet this idea is not specially emphasized, and moreover the motif is applied to gods as well as men. It must have arisen from the perception of stresses in human society, in the family as in the tribe, and was then imposed on the gods as part of their anthropomorphism and as a useful mechanism of proliferation and succession. But it was the thrusting ambition of the young, rather than the necessity for replacing the hopelessly old, that was the prime force. That is clearly implied in the Near-Eastern myths of which the Greek displacement accounts seem to be a reflexion. The removal of the elder gods, whether in the Babylonian Epic of Creation or in the Hurrian myth of Anu, Kumarbi, and the weather-god, has the special quality of involving strife, aggression and mutilation; the succession of primeval nature-gods by developed organizer-gods could, after all, have taken place without violence. Conceivably the violence reflects the historical clashes of tribal deities; or the older gods, like the monsters they produce in their defence, represent the chaotic disorder that must be subjected to the forces of order and coherence. More probably it reflects the cruelty and suppressed ruthlessness of human nature and its frustrated resentment of old age itself.

The divine displacement-myth includes an *unusual birth* (6) from Kumarbi, and less clearly from Kronos. I shall discuss this parallel later, in § 4. The theme is continued in the fertilization of earth (occasionally sea) by male divine seed so as to produce chthonic creatures, whether a monster like Typhoeus or an early Attic king like Erichthonius. Here the fertility of the earth itself is closely related to that of men and gods, just as in the Demeter and Kore myth or in Demeter's lying with Iasion in the thrice-ploughed furrow, and as in many Asiatic myths. Birth from a male god, on the other hand, may be allegorical (as when Zeus swallows Metis, Counsel, and gives birth to the wise Athena from his head), or of Indo-Iranian origin (since Indra sewed Soma into his thigh as

Zeus did Dionysus). It might also be a relic of a primitive pre-occupation with the generative and childbearing functions themselves, and with the odd and apparently arbitrary roles played by the two sexes (p. 216). Other and non-divine types of unusual birth, of men from stones or dragon's teeth, or of twins, probably reflect other relatively simple ideas: that men originally came out of the earth (as in Amerindian and other myths) and are a mixture of hard (male) and soft (female); that twins are a prodigy—normally a father sires one child at a time, so that when two children emerge there must be two fathers, of whom one (so wives at least will argue) must be divine.

Enclosure (7), as has been seen, is also sometimes connected with fertility. The tomb and the bronze room or tower are adequately accounted for by the special circumstances of Polyidus and Danae; but frequent enclosure in a chest is more difficult. For Freudians the reason is simple: chests are unconscious symbols of the womb, and the waters on which the chest is set adrift, as Danae was set adrift with the infant Perseus, represent the amniotic fluid surrounding the embryo. Another place of mythical imprisonment or refuge is the *pithos*, the huge storage jar, commonest in the Bronze Age, that was a conspicuous article in any substantial house or palace. Surely an obvious place for hiding or confinement, without further implications? And could not the same argument apply to the chest or *larnax*? We do not happen to have such things around in our houses, except in the almost unrecognizable form of the tallboy or chest-of-drawers, but the Greeks did, and the *larnax* must have been as conspicuous in a Greek palace as the *cassone* in an Italian. Yet this explanation does not cover all the facts—launching on water, the association with fertility, the occurrence of the chest in myths of simpler societies. Floating chests may be less odd than they at first seem. Deucalion's ark was a *larnax* according to Apollodorus; Odysseus's raft, too, was probably chest-shaped, and so was Noah's ark in Genesis, which measured 300 cubits by 50 by 50. Admittedly these could be the dimensions of a tapering boat, but Utnapishtim's craft in the Epic of Gilgamesh was certainly box-like, since each of its edges was 120 cubits.[16] It is just conceivable that in the Near-Eastern mythical tradition, starting from the widely dispersed myth of the great flood, a

[16] Apollodorus, I, 7, 2; Homer, *Odyssey* v, 244 ff.; Genesis 6. 15; Epic of Gilgamesh, XI, 58 (*ANET*², 93).

chest-like raft became standard for any impromptu floating refuge. That would still fail to explain the association with fertility—which is marked although not, of course, invariable. The Eleusinian mysteries may suggest an answer: if symbols of fertility, such as an ear of corn or representations of human sexual organs, are to be hidden and then revealed, a box or chest is as good a place for them as any; although we know that a basket was also used. This series of rationalizing suggestions still leaves something unexplained.

Finally *sex-change* (8): an uncommon theme, virtually restricted among earlier myths to the cases of Teiresias and Caenis who became Caeneus. Teiresias changed into a woman after he had struck at two coupling snakes with his staff, and then back into a man when the incident repeated itself; he was thus able to settle a divine dispute about which sex derived most pleasure from intercourse. The motif of the snakes, apart from anything else, suggests that sex-change is here connected with fertility. So, too, transvestite practices in occasional Greek cults (possibly reflected in the tale of the young Achilles brought up as a girl in Skyros—although judging by results he did not forget his true sex) seem to be associated with rites of passage, in which the reversal of the normal order of dress and behaviour reflects a passage from secular to sacral time as well as a drastic change in the status of the initiate or subject. The myth of Caenis is more complicated, but still the connexion with fertility, again in its phallic aspect, is probable. She was a Lapith girl who was loved by Poseidon and for some reason did not like it; granted a wish, she asked to be made *atrōtos*, unwoundable, and to be changed into a man. I suppose that *atrōtos* originally meant 'impenetrable' in a physiological sense, and that the transformation of sex was the best way to achieve that end. But it was also understood at an early date as 'invulnerable', its literal meaning, and may have given rise to the myth that Caeneus, in fighting against the Centaurs, could only be killed by being battered into the earth with the Centaurs' fir-branches. He was, after all, the son of Elatus, fir-tree; and another odd thing about him, probably phallic in implication, is that he had set up his spear to be worshipped.

Looking back over these unusual themes one sees that one or two are, after all, merely picturesque, attractive rather than of underlying significance. Other aspects, notably the association of chests with fertility and water, remain rather mysterious. Nevertheless three emphases can be traced. Fire is associated with *the relations between, and relative valuation of, men and gods, or mortality and immortality*; and so is the idea of a golden age and, to some extent, the origin of old age and disease, itself depending on the golden age's disappearance. *Fertility* is the second emphasis. It seems to be the underlying interest not only in disappearing-deity myths but also in certain unusual births, enclosures in chests, and myths about sex-changes; and it is also related to the idea of a golden age when fertility was automatic. Finally *the displacement of elders* also links men and gods, and is a consequence of the origin of old age and debility.

In the commonest themes, on the other hand, if we leave aside for the moment the predominant aspects of purely narrative and dramatic interest, these four preoccupations stood out: contests and quests, particularly involving monsters; the relations between men and gods, whether of love, protection, or oppression; the presence in the background of the gods themselves; and stresses within the family, leading to acts of vengeance and displacement. The second and third of these interests are obviously related, and the first and fourth both exemplify the important general idea of competitiveness and strife.

The result of amalgamating the two surveys—they already overlap at certain points, since the displacement of elders and various kinds of enclosure are both striking themes and frequent ones—is that the relations of men and gods, and hostility between generations, are broad interests common to both; whereas the idea of heroic contest and strife obtrudes itself by sheer frequency, as does the presence of the gods, assumed when not explicit. Problems of fertility in nature and the origins of old age and disease come into prominence in a few evidently speculative myths rather than by frequency; although the latter topic may be seen as a special aspect of the broader ones of relations between men and gods and hostility between generations. Fertility comes mainly in striking and unusual myths. It is surprisingly inconspicuous, by comparison with the myths of other cultures (especially the Western Asiatic), in the commoner and more folktale-influenced types.

To the result of these surveys must be added the theogonical ideas considered earlier. Some aspects of the early history of the gods, notably the succession-myth, Demeter and Persephone, and

Zeus and Prometheus, quite apart from the general presence of the gods, have already entered the lists of common and striking themes. Two important ideas, beyond the process of theogony itself, remain. First, the whole concept of nature-gods—Ouranos the sky, Gaia the earth, Okeanos the surrounding river, and so on. Greek myths do not carry it to the lengths of its probable Near-Eastern models, but its effects persist, even after the first stages of cosmogony, in Zeus's power over thunder and lightning, in Helios as the all-seeing sun-god, in associations like that of Hecate with the moon and Poseidon with earthquakes, and in the personification of storm-winds and other meteorological phenomena. Second is the idea of a developed and detailed eschatology, reflected not only in occasional disappearing-deity myths of Near-Eastern pattern but also in heroic penetrations of the underworld, especially by Heracles, and in the whole pervasive conception of Hades as the world of the dead.

Certain themes may have been overemphasized and others undervalued in what is bound to be an incompletely objective assessment. Yet I wonder whether the inclusive result, in so far as it affects the identification of the main preoccupations of Greek myths, would be seriously altered by the detailed corrections and subjective readjustments that might be made. More questionable is the crude amalgamation of implications drawn from frequency with those drawn from striking appearance. Yet, when one descends to individual cases, the possible distortion does not seem too great. Only fertility, among major preoccupations, is at present excluded from the list of common themes. That is admittedly misleading, because the myth of Demeter and Persephone, although different in quality from most of the common motifs—and relatively lacking, incidentally, in folktale character—is commonly assumed in wider mythological contexts and was one of the most familiar of all individual Greek myths. It remains an important truth, and one that distinguishes most Greek myths from most Near-Eastern ones, that the theme of fertility did not find in Greece many different forms of mythical, as distinct from ritual, expression.

A further limiting factor is that the unusual themes tend to come in Hesiod; and some of Hesiod's myths, particularly that of the five races, are presented in a partly rationalized form. Here is certainly a point at which discrimination must be exercised, even

in a survey that intentionally keeps clear of *Quellenforschung*. Yet
from the five-races myth only the idea of the golden age has been
used, and that is guaranteed by non-Hesiodic allusions as well as
by his own non-rationalizing *Ehoeae*; while the origin of evil and
old age, dependent on the first woman, survives in two separate
versions (in *Theogony* and *Works and Days*) whose basic structure
appears mythical in essence and was certainly so taken by all
subsequent Greeks.

The assessment also ignores interesting but unique or relatively
inconspicuous themes, for example that of Deucalion's flood or the
bronze Cretan giant Talos; also the more or less unparalleled
cosmogonical concepts preserved by Alcman and Pherecydes of
Syros. The flood-myth, although well known, is of palpably
Near-Eastern derivation and was not markedly conspicuous in
its Greek variants; the Talos myth, picturesque as it is, did not
make much impact on the Greeks before Apollonius of Rhodes;
and the two fascinatingly unusual cosmogonical accounts must at
present be counted as idiosyncratic. Such considerations reduce
the value of these unique myths as indices of general mythical
quality. Broader in their implications, but also composing a
special class, are what one might call applied myths: minor
aetiological tales and myths of certainly ritual origin. The former
give reasons, for example, for fireless sacrifices at Lindos in
Rhodes or for Amphiaraus's underground oracle, for striking
geographical features like the Bosporus or Mount Etna, for the
special characteristic of a flower like the hyacinth or a bird like
the nightingale, or for names like Epaphus, Myrmidons, or
Mount Nysa. The latter type is closely connected with, and again
offers *aitia* for, phenomena like the rituals of new fire held on
mountain-tops (Heracles on Oeta), or ritual cursing (again at
Lindos), or the curious annual passage of offerings to Apollo from
the far north in the Delian myth of the Hyperborean maidens.

With these reservations and limitations the results of the survey
may be broadly valid. They are far from obvious in certain respects, although banal in others, since by concentrating on the
heroic aspect of Greek myths, or on the prominence of gods, or on
the obviously most striking and memorable themes, one tends to
miss the importance of eschatology, the relation between mortality
and immortality, and the problem of old age and disease, as well as
to overrate the place and function of the gods in some respects

and undervalue them in others. In schematic terms, then, the implications of mythical themes may be represented as follows:

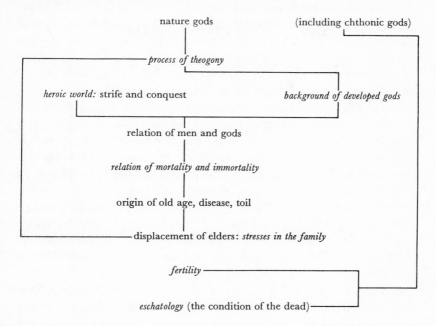

(italics indicate the more prominent interests; connecting lines represent direct relationships).

Finally I should stress that the assessment has temporarily suppressed the strongly dramatic and folktale tone of most Greek myths—the tone emphasized in §1. What the diagram symbolizes is a pattern of preoccupations that seem to have persisted through the schematizing process that the myths in their surviving format presuppose. Before the problem of the relation of Greek myths to fantasy and speculation is further pursued in §§7 and 8, I diverge to make some comparisons with other ancient sets of myths, together with one medieval set. The result will be to emphasize the unusual status of Greek myths, even in spite of their debt to Asiatic models.

3: A comparison with Germanic, Egyptian and Hindu mythology

No other mythology known to us—developed or primitive, ancient or modern—is marked by quite the same complexity and systematic quality as the Greek, by the same prominence of non-legendary heroes, and by a similar preponderance of folktale themes. The Germanic tradition might seem at first to be closely comparable. Yet there the heroic tales are mainly of saga type—that is, they are historical and realistic in tone. The Norse heroes, although they may be inspired by Odin or Thor and fight fantastic monsters like Grendel, do not live in a semi-divine world, are not the offspring of gods, and are not involved in situations like those of Pentheus and Dionysus, Aeneas and Aphrodite, or Odysseus and Calypso. There is a real distinction here. At the same time the cultural similarities between Mycenaean Greece, Germany in the era of migrations from the fourth to the sixth centuries A.D., and late pagan Scandinavia, summed up in the broad contention that each underwent a 'Heroic Age', are certainly significant for the origin of the Greek conception of heroes. The Greeks seem to have combined saga-type heroes, who survive more or less intact in the Homeric epic tradition, with another and more nearly divine type variously represented by Peleus, Jason, Heracles and Asclepius. Such figures can only rarely be paralleled in other mythologies: by Rama and Krishna, for example, who are incarnations of Vishnu, or by Gilgamesh, Adapa, and Etana, who have some historical status as king or priest but are more than mere saga figures. Other cultural sets primarily concerned with cosmogony and theogony, like the Egyptian or the Japanese, have occasional heroes, but these are involved in primarily folktale situations. Only the Greeks possessed a heroic mythology that blended all these three elements—saga, folktale, and divine myth—into an elaborate and superficially self-consistent system.

Apart from the limited resemblance in the heroic tales there are other broad similarities between Germanic and Greek myths (which, I repeat, may have affected the Germanic at several points)—but they are also common to Mesopotamian, for instance. Partial nature gods like Thor, the importance of fertility deities, the extreme interest in the fate of the dead, and the division of the world into definite regions inhabited by different classes of human or divine being (in spite of the un-Greek idea of the World Tree), are general points in common. More specific is the predominance of giants and their equivocal relationship with the gods. Yet there are also profound differences between the two mythologies. Germanic myths about the developed gods and their involvement in different episodes and actions are richer than the Greek. The gods themselves, even so, are less completely anthropomorphized in many respects—more ambiguous, also, in that they are eventually overwhelmed in the fiery cataclysm of Ragnarök, only to be reborn, in a sense, in their sons under the leadership of Balder. That is quite distinct from the Greek idea of everlasting divinity. Conversely the Teutonic and Norse tradition has little idea of a golden age in the past, contrary to Greek and other ancient mythologies. Perhaps as a corollary, the dilemma presented by old age and death is a different one: not all can go to Valhalla, and there is a special place for those who die from old age and disease, but that is all. Finally there is no Greek analogue closer than Prometheus to the trickster-god Loki, who is an important figure in Germanic myth and resembles other tricksters, notably those of the North-American Indians, in his strange combination of benevolence, harmless mischief and destructive malice.

The similarities and differences between Greek myths and Germanic are occasionally instructive, more often irrelevant. The comparison with other, ancient mythologies in Asia and Egypt is likely to be more productive. And yet it is heavily limited, in the case of Egypt, by the peculiarity of the country and its ancient inhabitants: a factor more significant than contacts between Egypt and Crete in the Late Bronze Age, or the predilection of classical Greeks for attributing their oldest ideas and institutions to Egyptian origin, or the hold that the worship of Isis, and the myth of her search for the scattered body of Osiris, exercised upon Greeks from the late fifth century B.C. down to the time of Plutarch and beyond. The special circumstances of Egypt as a country—its vast length and the resulting difficulty of communication between upper and lower Egypt, its total dependence on the Nile for fertility and the special social consequences that this produced, not to speak of its isolation from other cultures—encouraged the formation of a quite unique civilization. Among its most striking characteristics were early literacy (from about 3000 B.C. on) and an extraordinary domination by king and priesthood. All these resulted in a highly organized ritualistic religion and a very curious and circumscribed mythology. It is here, if anywhere, that the connexion of myth and ritual can be found at its strongest; and here, if anywhere, that it is least likely to be exemplary for other cultures.

Egyptian myths—most of which do not exist in the form of continuous accounts, either tales or epics, but have to be reconstituted from prolific but fragmentary allusions in funerary formulas—

revolve around the question of the king's divinity and the fate of his soul, on which the fate of every other individual depends. There are, it is true, local and functional gods, often animal-headed and of pre-dynastic origin, such as Anubis the jackal-headed god of the graveyards or Thoth the ibis-headed protector of scribes; there are cosmic gods like Re, the god of the sun-disk, himself hawk-headed, and abstract gods like Ptah of Memphis, who created the world by becoming the 'heart and tongue' of the divine Ennead. But the anthropomorphic Osiris and Amon became paramount. Amon became the national god in upper Egypt when Thebes rose to power around 1600 B.C., but he was soon amalgamated with the sun-god Re, who belonged to the Delta, in a typical process of religio-historical syncretism. Osiris, in origin a vegetation-god, represented the soul of the dead king in the third millennium but was generalized as the deified personality of every dead man by the time of the Coffin texts around 2000 B.C. The drama of his murder and dismemberment by Seth, his piecemeal discovery by Isis and the birth and revenge of Horus became the centre of popular Egyptian religion, ritual and mythology.

Summarizing gives an unjustified impression of uniformity and the orderly evolution of ideas. On the contrary, the development of Egyptian religious and mythological beliefs was random and inconsistent, the result of accidental forces like the establishment of a unified kingdom of Egypt, the irruption of Asiatic invaders, the conflict between conservatism and innovation, and above all the learned habits of literate priests partial to exegesis on the worst possible etymological principles.[17] Shu and Tefnut, the male and female deities who separate Geb (earth) and Nut (sky) in the Heliopolis cosmogony, are said to be 'spat out' by Atum because these names resemble words meaning 'spit'; and men are seen as the tears of the sun-god Re by another feeble etymology. Still other, non-etymological, accounts were given, and were not held to be inconsistent: in the Coffin texts Shu becomes 'command' and 'intelligence' rather than a kind of sneeze; he introduces Light and Time; but he also blows along the boat of the sun. This liberalism of interpretation, amounting at times to a chaotic in-

----

[17] Among recent treatments of Egyptian ideas see R. T. Rundle Clarke, *Myth and Symbol in Ancient Egypt* (London, 1959), as well as J. A. Wilson in *IA*. The Egyptian chapter in *Mythologies* is rather obscure—unlike that on the mythology of India, by W. Norman Brown, to which I am greatly indebted.

difference to consistency and meaning, is characteristic of Egyptian thought. It arose partly from the syncretizing of different local traditions in the interests of political unity, partly from the energetic pedantry of priests, but also from the feeling that the details of cosmology and creation were relatively unimportant. What were important were the maintenance of the order of nature and the establishment of the king's divinity, and under his guidance the divinity of all the dead. Enabling the sun-god to defeat each day the dragon Apophis by the recitation of a simple myth and the performance of a somewhat trivial ritual, seeing that the dead could carry out the elaborate instructions by which they, too, could become Osiris regenerated—these were the things that mattered, rather than the proliferation of many different stories about the secular activities of minor deities.

Inevitably a few resemblances to Greek myths (and Asiatic) can be found—the concept of a primeval separation of sky and earth, the idea of a golden age (whether it be set in the 'time' of Re, Osiris, or Horus), yet an age in which men escaped death altogether; the idea of a resurrected god (Osiris) who also represents the vegetation. But the differences, even apart from odd concepts like that of the 'Eye' of Horus or Re, are enormous: the cheerful eschatology, the lack of heroes (except for pure folktale or legendary characters in definitely literary compositions), the absence of myths reflecting social preoccupations, the ubiquity of rituals, the aggregation of gods of fundamentally divergent types (sun-disks, moral qualities, crocodiles...)—those things set the Egyptian myths quite apart from the Greek. Egyptian influence on Greek mythological thought seems for these reasons to be negligible.

Another ancient civilization with an *a priori* claim to have influenced Greece is that of India. That there is some connexion between Hindu and Greek mythology is inevitable; Greek is, after all, an Indo-European language closely related to Sanskrit, and Zeus is a congener of the Indic sky-god Dyaus. The trouble is that Indo-Iranian mythology and religion themselves seem to have been affected by Mesopotamian ideas during the second millennium B.C., before the separation of the Indian and Iranian strands and the penetration of the Aryans into the Indian peninsula. The effects are chiefly to be seen in the cosmogonical myths of the Rig-Veda, a collection of hymns compiled probably by about 1000 B.C. Moreover the Harappa civilization of the Indus valley,

which flourished during the third and second millennia, cultivated a goddess of Great Mother type who seems to have passed
into Hindu myth as Parvati, the consort of Shiva, later to be
known as the Divine Mother of the universe; so any resemblances
between Indian and Greek fertility goddesses could depend on the
widespread influence of this Great Mother type.

The claims for Indian influence on Greek myth—which in the
last century were colossal—must rest either on a number of isolated
thematic similarities outside the cosmogony of the Rig-Veda
(bearing in mind that occasional striking similarities even in
apparently quite separate myth-systems are a recurrent feature of
comparative mythology), or on a special theory that has been
energetically advanced by the French scholar Georges Dumézil.
Essentially he argues that the myths and institutions of all Indo-
European cultures reflect a tripartite division of functions in
society into those of priests, warriors, and producers (the last being
farmers, herdsmen, and craftsmen). A useful summary of Dumézil's
copious writings has been produced by C. S. Littleton under the
optimistic title of *The New Comparative Mythology* (Berkeley, 1966).
Unlike Dr Littleton I am not convinced that Dumézil has proved
his case. That many societies of the Indo-European language-
group reflect such a division of function is undeniable: but the
division is hardly surprising in itself, and indeed the Sanskritist
John Brough has recently pointed out that it applies likewise to the
Semitic societies portrayed in the Old Testament.[18] Moreover the
most prominent Indo-European culture, and that with which we
are directly concerned, is the Greek, and this is an embarrassing
exception to the tripartite division of functions. The division
simply does not occur, at least in any form specific enough to be
significant, in Greek culture and mythology, with the possible
exception of Boeotia. M. Dumézil and his follower Francis Vian
have devoted valuable attention to the foundation myth of
Thebes, to the place in Theban society occupied by the descendants
of the Sown Men, to the Giants, and to the Phlegyans of Orcho-
menus. The damaging fact remains that Greece as a whole does
not seem to manifest that specific structure which is claimed to be
the heritage of all cultures derived from the Indo-Iranian.

The Rig-Veda reveals a pre-cosmic hostility between the
Adityas or 'releasers' and the Danavas or 'restrainers'. Indra,

[18] *Bulletin of the School of Oriental and African Studies, London,* XXIII (1959), 69–85.

described as a 'son of might', agrees to attack the Danava serpent called Vritra or 'covering', on condition that he becomes king of the gods—rather like Marduk in the Babylonian Creation Epic. A special weapon, the lightning-bolt, is forged for him, and by an exclusively Indian touch he drinks *soma*, an alcoholic nectar, and swells up so much as to separate his parents, earth and sky. Vritra, coiled around the mountains, is split open like Tiamat in the Babylonian account (where, however, earth and sky were formed from the two parts of her body), and releases the waters that have been dammed up inside him. From these waters, now seen as cattle, is born the sun. Further cosmology is overseen by Varuna, leader of the Adityas; finally man is created from the sun in order to perform sacrifices and help the gods ward off evils and keep the world running smoothly, especially by ensuring the sun's safe diurnal passage and the regular recurrence of rain.

In giving as the motive for human creation the need to serve and help the gods, an idea absent from surviving Greek myths, this account accords with the Mesopotamian and even more closely with the Egyptian, which likewise underwent some Asiatic influence in the third and second millennia. Egyptian myths also stress the need to help the gods, by ritual means, in overcoming the dragon of darkness. The release, by a god, of fertile waters from the mountains corresponds loosely with ideas in the Babylonian myths about irrigation. What distinguishes the Indian cosmogony from the Babylonian and Greek is its abstract background—the concept of restraint being overwhelmed by release, and still more the interrelating of Sat and Asat, Being and Not-being, in subsequent stages of cosmogony. This interest in allegorical abstraction is a persistent and characteristic element in Indian thought, present in the Vedas but later finding its fullest expression in the learned speculations of the Upanishads.

The main non-cosmogonical deities are Vishnu and Shiva. Vishnu, associated with the sun, acts mainly in the form of his thirty-two incarnations or avatars (who, being in a sense part divine and part human, have a certain loose correspondence with the Greek heroes). The chief of these avatars are Rama and Krishna. Rama is a vegetation-god; his wife is Sita, meaning 'furrow'—he wins her, incidentally, by bending a great bow, like Odysseus or the Hurrian Gurparanzakh; he is also a culture-god and a symbol of the ideal aristocratic ruler. He is incarnated to fight Ravana, a terrible Ceylonese demon who interrupts the sacrifices to the gods. Rama and Sita underwent a fourteen-year term of rustic exile, and then Sita was abducted by Ravana. She was eventually recovered after many fantastic adventures (some of folktale type, though with no strong thematic resemblance to the Greek) by Rama aided by the monkeys; Ravana grew new heads as his were sliced off, rather like the Hydra, but was eventually despatched in a different manner with a divine arrow. Rama now ruled throughout a golden age in which there was no death, being similar in this respect to the Egyptian 'time of Re' and so on. Yet domestic problems were not entirely absent; Rama sent Sita into exile because of gossip about her relations with Ravana, who had touched her but no more; she had already had to indulge in one dramatic 'truth act' to convince Rama, and now she had had enough and was swallowed up by the earth—the action may remind one of Persephone, but the motivation is uniquely Hindu.

Krishna, on the other hand, has two different aspects united by the concept of love, ideal and physical. He is a great warrior, but one who in the *Bhagavad Gita* describes the whole organization and underlying principles of the world; he is also a rustic hero of a charming and irresistible kind. He is incarnated to overcome Kansa, wicked king of Mathura. Kansa learns by prophecy, in a motif already familiar to us, that he will be slain by the son of his sister (or cousin); he first wants to kill her, but then consents just to kill her children as they are born—there is an obvious parallel here to the Kronos theme. The first six succumb, but the seventh and the eighth, who is Krishna, survive by trick and miracle respectively. As he grows up the child overcomes many fantastic dangers, and when his foster-parents go to live in the forests he reveals another side of his nature by his erotic exploits with the *gopis*, the divine milkmaids, and especially with Radha.

Shiva, like Krishna, has erotic associations, but of a more solemn kind. His name means 'kindly' and his symbol is the *lingam* or phallus, whereas that of his consort Parvati (whose prototype existed, as we have seen, in the Harappa culture) is the *yoni* or vulva. But Shiva is not only the god of generative power and lord of the dance: he is guardian of morality, also a god of the mountains and desert places, a contemplative and ascetic; it is noticeable that Rama and Krishna, too, are associated for part of their careers with the wilderness or the countryside. His mythology is thinner and less varied than theirs, in part because he is more abstract and, with his four arms and feet (a bit like Marduk) less anthropomorphic. Yet all these gods are fascinating for their combination of at first sight irreconcilable qualities—the result in origin, possibly, of syncretism, but gradually taking on meaning and becoming assimilated to the serene universalism of Indian thought. Rama is both magnanimous and, towards Sita, tragically conventional; Krishna is a warrior and a philosopher as well as a perpetual lover of women: Shiva is the god of sexual power itself, yet he also wanders around graveyards in an abnegation of life and physical action; while his consort Parvati (also known as Devi, the lotus goddess, and as Shakti or 'power'), in her aspect of Kali can be vicious and destructive.

For certain of these ideas the sources are relatively late; but throughout Hindu mythology (only a small part of which, incidentally, is plausibly ritual in origin) there runs a contemplative, abstract streak that has its closest parallel in Egypt—and partly for the same reason, that in both cases the tradition is fully literate and subject to learned exegesis and elaboration by an established priesthood. Even the simplest folktales tend to be given a new dimension; yet there is an imaginative quality that is not just learned speculation but is truly mythical. When his foster-mother looked in the infant Krishna's mouth she saw there the three whole 'towns' of earth, air, and sky; and when he dances with the *gopis* each of them thinks she holds the real Krishna, whereas all except Radha hold mere illusory extensions of his body—a symbol of the relations of the individual mortal to god. Through all these myths a lesson is being taught. The later the source, the more explicit it is, but it is implicit even in the Vedas: that worldly affairs are unimportant in relation to the whole of time, that men will be reborn, that reality is equivocal, that the gods are superior, that sex and fertility are good, but that destruction is also necessary. How utterly different is much of this from the assumptions behind Greek myths!

4: The myths of Western Asia—Hurrian Kumarbi and Greek Kronos

Comparisons with Egyptian and Indian myths have been largely unfruitful in revealing profound influences on Greek myths. Certain isolated themes confirm what history and geography suggest, that there must have been the occasional idea that passed from one culture to the other—or, in the case of Indic myth, passed into both cultures from a common ancestor. The underlying principles and tone of the myths are distinct, and suggest that cross-cultural influences were otherwise slight. On the other hand the Egyptian and Indian style of myth provides an excellent example of abstract allegory developed to an extreme form.

In any event it is from western Asia that we should expect influence chiefly to come; Greece, as has been seen, cannot have remained untouched by the powerful diffusion of mythical themes and ideas from Mesopotamia, a diffusion that covered the whole of Asia Minor and the Near East in the second millennium B.C. Surviving Mesopotamian myths do not suggest many detailed thematic influences on the Greeks, although a whole mythical background is common to the two cultures. It is to myths that spread into Asia Minor that the most remarkable and specific similarities have been found. Even here it is only in two cases— the succession of the first gods, and the fight against a monster who presents a last challenge to the eventually supreme god—that the resemblance has been complex enough to make derivation from a common source extremely probable. Even that is questioned (usefully, although as I think unconvincingly) by P. Walcot, for example, who argues that the correspondences between Greek cosmogonical myths and the Babylonian Epic of Creation are at least as marked as those between Kronos and Kumarbi on the one hand and Typhoeus and Ullikummi on the other.[19]

Kumarbi and Ullikummi are figures of Hurrian myths, although as it happens they are known to us through Hittite sources.[20] The Hurrians were a rather mysterious non-Indo-European people who dominated northern Syria, northern Mesopotamia and part of Asia Minor around the middle of the second millennium B.C. Apart from epic or legendary tales like that of king Gurparanzakh, who has certain similarities to Odysseus, only two of their myths are known to us, and they form part of a single theogonical sequence. The mutilation of Anu by Kumarbi, the 'father of the gods', the subsequent displacement of Kumarbi by the storm-god (equivalent to the thunder-and-lightning god Zeus, and ultimate

---

[19] P. Walcot, *Hesiod and the Near East* (Cardiff, 1966), e.g. 24–6, 32 ff.
[20] See *ANET²*, 120–5.

ruler of the Hurrian pantheon), and Kumarbi's attempt to foster rebellion through the monster Ullikummi (corresponding with Kronos's attempt to foster rebellion through the monster Typhoeus), are too familiar to require a whole fresh evaluation from me. They have tended, indeed, to pre-empt too much of classical scholars' attention to links between the Mediterranean world and the Near East. Yet one part of the comparison responds to more careful examination than has yet been accorded it, and that is Kumarbi's pregnancy and Kronos's swallowing of his children. Kumarbi displaced his father Anu from the throne of the gods by biting off and swallowing his phallus, an action roughly parallel to Kronos's displacement of his father Ouranos by cutting off his phallus from within Gaia's body. Kronos simply threw the severed organ away; it and the blood fell on earth and sea and gave birth to certain deities. Kumarbi's case was more drastic since he swallowed the fertile member, with the result that he himself became pregnant, as Anu maliciously tells him, with either three or five 'terrible gods', including the storm-god himself, the river Tigris and the storm-god's helper Tasmisu. Kumarbi spits out some at least of the impregnating material, with the apparent result that all except the storm-god were born from the earth as in the Greek version; but he cannot abort the storm-god and has to give birth to him from himself.

There follows a debate between Anu and the storm-god inside Kumarbi about the best mode of egress from Kumarbi's body. The storm-god wants to split Kumarbi's *tarnassa*, presumably his fundament, but Anu deters him; eventually he comes out of what is cryptically described as 'the good place', after various other possibilities have been considered and rejected. It is necessary to cast prudery aside and discover what this 'good place' is. It is not the mouth, since the mouth and the 'good place' are mentioned by Anu as alternatives. It is not the ear, because the storm-god seems to suggest that being born from different parts of Kumarbi's body would defile corresponding parts of his own, and he separately mentions being defiled at the ear. Unfortunately the other places mentioned are missing, although one of them would cause the storm-god's mind to be defiled—something to do with the head, therefore, not the ear or mouth but possibly the nose (unless an Athena-type birth from the top of the head itself is envisaged). Once the upper orifices are excluded, and probably the fundament too, that leaves the navel and the phallus. A useful clue is given by the storm-god's objecting that 'if I came forth from the "good place", a woman will [...] me' (translation by Goetze, *ANET*², 121). He is obviously claiming that his own 'good place' will be defiled, and that this will have some effect on a woman. It looks as though the meaning should be loosely supplemented as 'a woman will ⟨be defiled by⟩ me', and therefore that the 'good place' is the phallus and not the navel. That seems quite probable in itself, since the phallus corresponds most closely to the female vagina and therefore to the normal (the 'good'?) place for childbirth; incidentally midwives are known in Hurrian as 'good women'. In the end we hear definitely that the storm-god came forth from the 'good place'; obviously he and Anu working in concert then managed to depose Kumarbi.

What is the point of this debate about the exact mode of birth— for it is not just accidental, or a bit of realistic detail, or meant to be shocking (I guess that the Hurrians and Hittites would tolerate much worse than that)? It has some of the elements of an exercise in comparative sex, showing some of the interest of primitive tribes in the mechanics of sexual generation.[21] Yet, if it were only that, we should expect far more physiological detail, and perhaps less emphasis on defilement. More important, I would guess, is this: that the storm-god is also a fertility-god, as is shown clearly from a Hittite rather than a Hurrian myth, in which Telepinu's father the storm-god is also a disappearing deity like his fertility-god son.[22] The emphasis on his birth from another god's phallus may well be intended to stress this aspect, perhaps to motivate it. His desire to split the *tarnassa*, presumably to give himself an easier passage at birth, would presumably have frus-

[21] In a Sherenté myth from South America about the origin of women, men practised homosexuality before women existed; one of them became pregnant, was unable to give birth, and so died (C. Lévi-Strauss, *CC*, 119 ff.). This was a theoretical problem that seems to have aroused considerable interest. A widespread Amerindian myth of the birth of Hare (e.g. among the Winnebago and Kwakiutl) makes him quarrel with his brother in the womb; eventually they agree to be born simultaneously, from different places, which kills the unfortunate mother. The Norse trickster Loki bore children as a passive homosexual (*Lokasenna*, str. 23). There are many other myths about the piercing of the first vagina, the overcoming of the mythical hazard of *vagina dentata*, and the establishment of a reasonable length for the phallus. Children, as well as 'primitives' like the Mohave Indians, are 'prone to develop theories of anal birth' according to George Devereux, *Mohave Ethnopsychiatry and Suicide* (Washington, D.C., 1961), 287, n. 41.

[22] See H. G. Güterbock in *Mythologies*, 144–80.

trated his fertility functions by associating him with natural wastes rather than with productiveness and human fertility.

The corresponding Greek myth about Kronos is a paler affair. Kronos simply swallows his children, and the attenuated 'birth' that terminates this milder pregnancy—although one that takes place in the belly just as with the storm-god—involves vomiting them up through the mouth, preceded by the stone offered in place of the infant Zeus.[23] There is no probability, as we saw, of the 'good place' of the Hurrian version being the mouth; and Kumarbi did not merely swallow babies first born by a female, but he brought the storm-god to his first and final birth by himself. The two versions cannot be entirely reconciled; yet there can be little doubt about their close parallelism at certain points, as the following tabulation suggests:

Hurrian version	Greek versions
	Ouranos keeps his children in Gaia by persistent mating
Anu is castrated by Kumarbi as he flees up to the sky	Ouranos is castrated by Kronos from within Gaia's vagina
Kumarbi swallows Anu's phallus, is made pregnant by it; has embryos in his belly	Kronos swallows his children as they are born from Gaia; has children in his belly
spits out some of them, which are brought to birth (probably) by earth	blood from Ouranos's wound impregnates earth with Erinyes, Giants, Melian nymphs; phallus falls in sea, engenders Aphrodite
Storm-god discusses with Anu how to be born from Kumarbi	
(Kumarbi wants to eat his son?)	Kronos is persuaded by Rhea to swallow stone instead of infant Zeus
Storm-god is born from 'good place'	Kronos vomits up children through his mouth
(something about a stone in the text?)	stone comes up first, is worshipped at Delphi
Storm-god rules, Kumarbi is displaced, but foments new rebellion using Ulli-kummi, product of his seed and a rock	Zeus rules, Kronos is displaced to Tartarus with Titans, but Gaia bears Typhoeus, source of new rebellion—product of Kronos's seed according to the B-scholium on *Iliad* ii, 783, or of Tartarus according to Hesiod.

[23] Hesiod, *Theogony*, 492 ff.; ἐπιπλομένων ἐνιαυτῶν, 'when the seasons had come round' (493), is the language of childbirth after a season of pregnancy.

Among possible special motives for this theme of displacement as applied to the first gods may be mentioned the following: the reflexion of general tensions between old and young, and of particular disputes over the succession to the kingship (which seems to have been a problem in Mesopotamia in the Sumerian and early Akkadian period); and the distinction of two stages of development, in which cosmogony is felt to be the function of nature-deities of the Anu, Ouranos, or Tiamat type, whereas organization of the human world and the establishment of fertility belong to other and more fully anthropomorphic types like Enki or Zeus.[24]

The Greek version, viewed in an abstract and semi-structuralist way, reveals a careful and symmetrical sequence, and this may be more important than possible dynastic or theogonical motives. Ouranos displays excessive sexual activity—he will not stop copulating with his wife even when she is pregnant—and is punished by the drastic diminution of sex in his castration by Kronos. Kronos, after being prevented from normal birth and kept inside his mother, and after an unnatural emergence by cutting off his father's phallus, then infringes the natural birth of his own children by swallowing them, immediately after their emergence from their mother, and subjecting them to a kind of second pregnancy in his belly. This is counterbalanced, not by castration this time, since he is behaving like an over-possessive mother and not like an over-sexual father, but by abortion or rather quasi-abortion, the forcible termination of quasi-pregnancy. Seen in this light the myth seems to convey an underlying message, that excesses and unnatural acts in the realm of sex and childbirth give rise to counterbalancing and deterrent excesses in the other direction. That would be remarkably similar to one underlying implication suggested in chapter III for the Sumerian myth of Enki and Ninhursag and its congeners.

It is important to notice that this pattern applies only to the Greek version and not to the Hurrian; the Greek has the necessary balancing theme of Ouranos's repression of his children, which the Hurrian lacks. I do not suppose the Greeks made this up; it is a theme that happens not to have survived in our Hurrian version, although it is essential to this particular pattern. On the other

---

[24] This last explanation works rather well for the Greek theogony, but the Babylonian Creation Epic does not operate quite so neatly. The first stage of cosmogony is there carried out by the older gods, by birth and consequent differentiation; but later gods, Enlil or Marduk, are still found performing vital divisions of the cosmos, not by birth but by separating the body of an older goddess, Tiamat.

hand the Hurrian explicit-pregnancy theme is not essential to it, since Kronos's act of swallowing (putting inside himself, as a match to Ouranos's keeping inside his wife) suffices. It is also unnecessary for the stone to have a counterpart in Hurrian, although the text is uncertain about that.[25]

The Hurrian version, for its part, manifests a different *schema*. Swallowing his father's phallus makes Kumarbi pregnant, that is, punishes him appropriately—he unnaturally takes and absorbs what should be a woman's, therefore he unnaturally assumes the woman's role of child-bearer. This presents a problem: exactly how is he to give birth? The choice is between homosexual and sterile or pseudo-heterosexual and fertile means, and Anu sees that the latter is necessary. So the storm-god, conceived by the severed phallus of his mutilated father, is born from the distended phallus of his father's assailant. In all this the phallus is all-important, whereas in the Greek version its relevance was entirely confined to the preceding episode in which Ouranos blocked Gaia.

So understood, each version has a different emphasis and presents a clearly defined structure peculiar to itself. The plain conclusion is that neither borrowed from the other, but each is a distinct form or portion of a complex set of mythical themes. Therefore even an apparently cautious judgement like Fontenrose's, that 'The Hurrian myth resembles an earlier and cruder version of the Greek myth', will not really do.[26] This is a genuinely important point, not merely a pedantic distinction, since the interpretation I am offering—and which seems clearly implicit in the material itself—suggests that the Greek version may be ultimately derived from a pre-Hurrian *koine* account. Such an account would presumably have remained available after the development of the special Hurrian pattern, so that the different pattern represented in the Greek version could itself theoretically be post-Hurrian. That depends on factors impossible to assess. I am not convinced, in any event, that the means of transfer usually suggested for the passage of western Asiatic mythical ideas to the Greeks have much to be said for them. Transfer in Cyprus or Al Mina/Poseideion and northern Phoenicia in the early Iron

[25] According to Goetze, *ANET*[2], 121, Kumarbi tells Ayas/Ea that he wants to devour his own son (II, 39–54); other commentators do not seem persuaded. But it may be relevant that in the Sumerian 'Enki and Ninhursag' Enki devours his plant-children, and that this is an important part of the apparent pattern: p. 97.

[26] Joseph Fonterose, *Python* (Berkeley, 1959), 212.

Age is probably too late, although there certainly were Greco-Levantine contacts in those places. Ugarit towards the end of the Bronze Age is naturally a possibility, but I should expect greater Canaanite influence to be detectable in Greek myths had that been the case. The time of transfer I suspect to be somewhat earlier, around the middle of the second millennium; on its method and exact place I have no specific suggestion to offer, on the basis of the evidence now available.

5: The myths of Western Asia—Hittite and Canaanite

That only leaves Hittite myths (as opposed to Hurrian myths recorded in Hittite) and Canaanite ones to be briefly surveyed before a compendious assessment of Asiatic mythology can be attempted.[27] Hebrew mythology, which had virtually no influence on Greek, is deliberately omitted. True Hittite myths from Anatolia are very simple in structure and expression, and the few that have survived have done so because of their connexion with rituals—which is different from saying that all Hittite myths were derived from rituals. They consist mainly of the Disappearing God myth (in two versions, one concerning the storm-god, the other his son Telepinu), and the battles between the storm-god and the Illuyanka-serpent. Telepinu disappears and vegetation withers, animal fertility sinks; the gods are concerned; Telepinu is furious for some reason, continues so when he is discovered and stung by a bee who has offered to find him, but is eventually mollified. In the Illuyanka myth the storm-god is first defeated by the dragon, then the goddess Inara with the help of a mortal lover makes the dragon drunk; the mortal binds him, the storm-god kills him. The mortal is then slain by Inara for breaking her injunction not to set eyes on his wife or children—all sorts of parallels spring to mind for this essentially folktale theme, not least Eurydice with Orpheus and Odysseus with Calypso. In another version the dragon captures the storm-god's heart and eyes; the storm-god marries a mortal woman, their son marries the dragon's daughter and obtains his father's heart and eyes as dowry; the storm-god then kills the dragon, but has to kill his own son as well. Common to both versions is the indispensable mortal help; the motive is uncertain, but

---

[27] On Hittite and Canaanite (Ugaritic) myths see A. Goetze and A. L. Ginsberg respectively in *ANET*[2], 120–55; and H. G. Güterbock and Cyrus H. Gordon in *Mythologies*, 141 ff. and 183 ff.

is probably connected with the strong folktale involvement in each version. The folktale theme of the stolen organs is closely paralleled in a story in Apollodorus (1, 6, 3) that the monster Typhon, Hesiod's Typhoeus, stole Zeus's sinews by seizing his sickle in close combat and cutting them out. He then placed both Zeus and his sinews under guard in the Corycian cave in Cilicia, but the sinews were restored by Hermes and Aegipan. Typhon was chased by Zeus to Mount Nysa, where he tasted 'the ephemeral fruits' (τῶν ἐφημέρων καρπῶν)—the Fates had persuaded him that he would be strengthened thereby, but the reverse happened and this led to his downfall. In spite of its probably late elements (Aegipan, the intervention of the Fates) this tale obviously goes back to Near-Eastern sources. Indeed the original encounter took place on Mount Casius in northern Syria, near Ugarit, which is specifically mentioned in the Hurrian myth about the monster Ullikummi; and the offering of the 'ephemeral fruits' that have the opposite effect to what had been implied is closely related to the theme of the food of life and death in the Akkadian myth of Adapa (pp. 123–5).

Canaanite myths, known through Late Bronze Age tablets excavated at Ugarit, are characterized by their extreme prolixity; no doubt the literary tradition is chiefly at fault, but even so the myths that have survived are relatively uninteresting in content except for one point. That is their heavy concentration on matters of fertility and the theme of the disappearing fertility-god. This theme, familiar throughout Asia since Sumerian times and exemplified in the myth of Inanna's visit to the nether world (pp. 108–12), finds its most emphatic expression in the Canaanite Baal and Anath cycle (it is really a long repetitive tale rather than a cycle). Baal is the god of rain, and one of the chief gods of fertility. With the help of Anath, the warrior-goddess, he manages to displace Yamm, the sea-god, whom the supreme elder god El has made king and rewarded with a palace and an honorific name. Anath and Baal protest about this, but Yamm manages to make Baal his slave; finally, however, Baal smites him with two special clubs made for him by the dual craftsman-god. There is a good deal of argument about Baal's palace; he feels deprived because he does not have one; eventually El allows him one, and the craftsman-god builds it. The builder wants to put in a window, but Baal refuses; eventually he feels so secure, has subdued all his enemies so thoroughly (with the help of Anath, who runs amok deep in blood), that he has one installed. This seems to be his downfall, lets in his enemy Mot, the god of death, who slays and devours him. All fertility vanishes; moreover the gods cannot find another to take Baal's place on the throne. Then Anath manages to kill Mot; she grinds him like corn and plants him in the earth, and Baal comes to life again in triumph. Yet this is only one phase in the recurring conflict between fertility and infertility and in the alternating fortunes of Baal in his sovereignty over Mot, Yamm, and Yamm's serpent Tannin, the equivalent of the Biblical Leviathan. C. H. Gordon has argued convincingly that the alternation of fertility and infertility in Canaanite myths is not seasonal but rather 'sabbatical', and refers to seven-year cycles of comparative rainfall and comparative drought.[28] This is, no doubt, a special application of the generic Near-Eastern idea of a disappearing god who represents fertility. In the Tammuz and Adonis versions the cycle is certainly intended to be seasonal, and that is the interpretation that the Greeks used in the development of their Demeter and Persephone myth. The Canaanite *nuance* seems to have made little impression on them, presumably because Greece was less liable than Syria to years of drought.

A second Canaanite myth that can be more or less reconstructed concerns Aqhat, born as a successor to the kingship; Anath hankers after his bow and kills him by means of the vulture Yatpan in order to get it. This causes infertility, for Aqhat turns out to be yet another fertility figure; the end is missing and his revival uncertain. A third myth, whose fragments have been interpreted in the most divergent ways, concerns king Krt (often spelled Keret). His wife and children die, and he too, it appears, is worried about succession to the kingship. El instructs him to march against king Udum and marry his daughter. This he does; queen Hurriya is a great success and bears him a large family. But then Krt falls ill; even El and all the gods cannot cure him, until El fashions a special healing goddess out of clay. Surprisingly, as the tablet breaks off, another claimant to the throne is accusing him of neglecting his duties. Thus the succession to the kingship, as well as fertility, seems to be a continuing Canaanite preoccupation. These themes are broadly represented, of course, in Greece; but little if anything of the peculiar Canaanite style and tone is to be found in Greek myths, and Asiatic influences on them are likely to be primarily from elsewhere.

[28] E.g. in *Mythologies*, 184.

6: Greek and Asiatic myths: a summary

Hittite and Canaanite myths are relatively unimportant for Greek mythology. They differ profoundly from each other in form and scale, since the former are thin and naive, akin to folktales, the latter verbose and excessively literary; but the Hittite myths provide a number of specific folktale-type parallels to Greek myths, whereas the Canaanite merely repeat *ad nauseam* the themes of succession and the disappearance of fertility. Hurrian myths are much more interesting, and one longs for more of them; at present they consist mainly of the succession-story featuring Kumarbi, and the defeat of the monster Ullikummi, each paralleled in the early history of the Greek gods. Yet we discovered that the Greek version of Kumarbi must have been selected from a fuller complex, not from the Hurrian form of the myth or any direct heir. Incidentally the Hurrian tablets are neither extremely literary nor jejune, but roughly similar in their approach and degree of detail to the versions given by Hesiod.

It is the Mesopotamian myths that provide the main corpus of comparative material, although not of a very specific kind. The aims of Sumerian myths, in particular, were often closely related to the character of the intense urban civilization of the great valleys, especially to its vital problems of irrigation. Fertility, a preoccupation that Greek mythology shared with all these other cultures, took a special form in Mesopotamia—much as it did, indeed, in Egypt (likewise heavily dependent on man-made irrigation), although Egyptian myths envisaged fertility as incidental to the fate of the dead Osiris. We shall not expect to find in Greek myths the careful exploration of problems about how far irrigation should be carried into the desert; nor do they manifest such a marked emphasis on the relation between sexual and vegetable fertility. Complex structural parallels are virtually confined to the Hurrian examples. There are certain specific similarities, of course, although most of them belong to the narrative or folktale aspect of Mesopotamian myths rather than to their fantastic side. There is, for example, a possibly significant parallel between Gilgamesh and Achilles: both are sons of divine mothers and performers of valiant deeds; both lose a close companion whose ghost appears to them briefly from the world of the dead. Monster-fights are too widespread, too universal a form of myth, to signify special connexions by themselves, but there are specific aspects of Marduk's fight against Tiamat that have suggested another possible influence on the Greek theogony. Historically it seems unlikely that such an enormously influential work as the Epic of Creation did not achieve some indirect influence on the Greeks, given the kinds of contact presupposed by the succession-motif. Yet in any event such resemblances of details are less striking than those in the general organization of the mythical cosmos as accepted both in Mesopotamia and in Greece.

In both sets of myths the nature-gods come first, and effect the initial stages of cosmological development by the device of mating and producing more specifically differentiated children. There is an important deviation here in that, despite Okeanos, Greek myths do not lay such stress on originative water as either the Mesopotamian or Egyptian; again, this probably reflects the difference between riverine and non-riverine cultures. The ultimate tripartition into sky (dwelling-place of the gods), earth, and underworld (dwelling-place of the dead) is too obvious and too widespread to be a specially significant point of contact—for example it occurs in India as well as among American Indians; but the close attention to the detailed geography of the world below, in Greek as in Mesopotamian myths, is a different matter. In both cases a river at the borders of the underworld has to be crossed by the newly dead, and the ferryman who takes Enlil across in his boat in the Sumerian 'Enlil and Ninlil' corresponds closely with the Greek Charon. The poisonous waters of death that Gilgamesh must negotiate in order to reach Utnapishtim are not quite consistent with the Greek underworld river, but have their parallel in Odysseus's voyage across Okeanos to reach the entrance to Hades in the eleventh *Odyssey*. The Mesopotamian picture of the world of the dead as a 'house of dust', with its equipment of terrifying rulers and demons, has been toned down in the Greek idea of the realm of Hades; but the pursuit of a miserable half-life by the dead, and the grading of dead souls according to their deeds in life and the regularity of their burial and their funerary offerings, are common to both. I have already referred to the remarkable parallel between Enkidu's ghost and that of Patroclus, both of which escape temporarily from the world of the dead to report on conditions there.

Babylonian myths reveal much greater interest than Greek in

the disposition of the heavenly bodies in the process of cosmogony, and this reflects a continuing astrological preoccupation; but the emergence of the supreme ruler by overcoming, with the aid of a special weapon, first the older gods, then one special monster, is common to the Greek and the western Asiatic imagination. At first the earth is occupied only by the gods, but men appear on the scene earlier in Greek than in Mesopotamian myths; less emphasis is placed on their manner of creation, and they are not created simply to serve the gods. The Greek golden age under the reign of Kronos is most closely reproduced in Sumerian myths by the life of the gods in Dilmun before men appeared. Egypt provides some parallel for the golden-age concept, and also for the idea, attenuated by the Greeks, that the gods indulge in periodic destructions of men. The theme of a great flood (which can only have originated in the conditions of the Tigris–Euphrates valley, and certainly not in Egypt) is taken over by the Greeks, and Zeus's plan to reduce the population of the teeming earth, a motif which in its most general form is widely distributed, is the starting-point of the *Iliad*; but there is no Greek equivalent to the blood-baths initiated by warrior-goddesses like Inanna/Ishtar, her Canaanite equivalent Anath, or the Egyptian goddess Hathor or Sekhmet.[29]

The Mesopotamian pantheon, once the initial upheavals are over, functions rather like the Greek, with Enlil or Marduk in supreme command and a number of great but subordinate gods with specific, but more exclusive, local attachments. Zeus, like Enlil or Anu, is protector of the institution of kingship, but Greek myths as they survive reveal less concern with this subject and with the problems of lawful succession. The structure of the Mesopotamian cities and their cults was, after all, very different, and we naturally find little equivalent in Greek myths to the tales of competition among the great city-gods for possession of the divine Ordinances; although the concept of fate itself is somewhat similar. A more far-reaching difference is the absence from Mesopotamian myths of a complex world of heroes. Gilgamesh is an almost unique exception, but his actions are closely concerned with demarcation problems concerning mortality and immortality, and in this respect there is a certain similarity to Heracles, much as

[29] *ANET²*, 94, 136, 11. The theme of the destruction of mankind is best exemplified, in its Mesopotamian form, in the Atrahasis epic, 1, 352 ff.: W. G. Lambert and A. R. Millard, *Atra-hasīs* (Oxford, 1969), 67 ff.

Adapa and Etana find some parallel in Bellerophon. Certainly the relation between life and death is an important common preoccupation that is not shared, in anything like this form, by the myths of either Egypt or India. Yet Greek mythology broke away from Mesopotamian in its strong concern'with tensions in the family. This is a natural concomitant of its vast development on the heroic side, and perhaps also of its strong folktale character (which seems to find some parallel in the native myths of Hittite Anatolia)—a character no doubt accentuated in the course of a long schematizing tradition.

The general conclusion, that many of the basic assumptions of the mythical world-view in Greece were held in common with, and probably in various ways derived from, those of ancient Mesopotamia, adds enormous importance to the study by classical scholars of Mesopotamian myths. One aim must be the further definition of the speculative element in those myths; indeed this remains a problem with myths in general since, the more complete the literate interference, the slighter the speculative implications usually become. I hope to have shown that even in Greek myths, notwithstanding their long and complex literary development, certain underlying preoccupations continued to make themselves felt. So far, however, I have held at arm's length the most explicitly speculative myths known from a Greek source: the Hesiodic myths of Prometheus, Pandora, and the five races or generations of men. The consideration of these, whose Asiatic affinities are probable if unknown in detail, will form a suitable introduction to the concluding assessment in § 8 of the rationalizing tendencies of Greek myths as a whole.

7: Mythical speculation in Hesiod

The order of events envisaged by Hesiod is systematic enough. Originally earth provided fruits in abundance and without toil (*Works and Days*, 42 ff.); then Zeus hid this easy livelihood because Prometheus had deceived him over sacrifices (48 f.). He also hid fire, which men must have possessed during the golden age when Kronos reigned. Prometheus stole it back in a hollow stalk, and Zeus retaliated once again by promising to make an evil in which all would rejoice (57 f.). This is Pandora. Up to this time mankind had lived free from evil, distress, and disease, but the woman released them all from the jar that contained them (90–104). Now follows the myth of the five races with which Hesiod claims to crown his account. The golden race, in the time of Kronos, had

neither toil nor disease—corresponding therefore with the stage
before Prometheus deceived Zeus over the sacrifices—but its
members were still mortal, even though they died painlessly and
swiftly and became daemons above the earth (113–23). The silver
race, by contrast, were immature; they manifested *hybris*, selfish
indulgence, to each other, and impious neglect to the gods. Their
folly brought them grief, and after a short adult life Zeus hid them
beneath the earth, where they became chthonic daemons. The
bronze race are different again: they pursue Ares and *hybris*; they
eat no (cereal?) food, but are hard and huge; they go down to
Hades without leaving a name. The heroic race are better, but
kill each other off in the famous wars; some go to Hades, some to
the Islands of the Blessed (where Kronos, according to verse 169,
omitted by some manuscripts, is their ruler). As for the iron race,
they will not cease by night or day from grief and destruction, and
they too will eventually be destroyed by Zeus. It is to this race that
Hesiod and we belong.

Man's progressive degradation begins with Prometheus's provo-
cative action over the sacrifices. He was not behaving like an en-
lightened culture-hero, he simply annoyed Zeus by trying to show
that he, Prometheus, was the cleverer. In Hesiod's words (at
Theogony, 534), he was punished because he ἐρίζετο βουλάς, entered
into a contest of counsel, with Zeus. This is what happened: at the
time when men and gods ἐκρίνοντο, were making a settlement
together (*Theogony* 535) at Mecone, Prometheus prepared two
portions from a great bull that had been slaughtered. One contained the best meat and the tripes, but was unattractively
wrapped in skin and stomach; the other was a tempting affair
covered in the rich fat that the Greeks enjoyed so much, but contained mere bones. Zeus commented on the unfair outward
appearance, and Prometheus invited him to take his pick. Zeus
chose the worse portion—knowingly according to Hesiod, but
that may be a pious gloss. That is why men burn only the bones
for the gods in their sacrifices, and keep all the best bits for their
own consumption. The aetiological motive is obvious, and is
openly expressed by Hesiod: here is a paradox, that men, in
professing to pay respect to the gods, give them the worst portions
of their sacrifices. Why is this not impiety? The answer is that it
was so fixed, once and for all, at Mecone, the arrangement being a
trick by Prometheus, who subsequently paid for it. Not many

Greek myths were explicitly aetiological, at least before the Hellenistic poets and mythographers decided to remedy the defect; here is one that was.[30]

Presumably the tale goes back long before Hesiod, and we can recognize some possible Near-Eastern prototypes, especially in the myth of Adapa. Adapa was subjected to a Promethean choice in reverse: he was offered the food and water of life, but had been misled by Ea into thinking they were the opposite and so made the wrong choice by refusing them (pp. 123-5). The idea of the deceitful person, divine or otherwise, who offers a misleading choice is world-wide in its currency. A folktale theme in essence, it has been widely used to explain why men are mortal. The Greeks were apparently not interested in such a use, but the aetiology of sacrifices is made, in Hesiod's version, to have important consequences; for men suffer, as well as Prometheus. Their permanent loss is a life without toil, age and disease. What precisely was happening at Mecone remains obscure; no other reference is made to this settlement in any source except Callimachus, for whom the settlement seems to have been of prerogatives among the gods alone. Presumably it brought to an end the period when men and gods dined together: they met at Mecone for the last time to arrange how the food should be apportioned in future.[31] Their decision to separate must have been caused by the end of the golden age, the displacement of Kronos and the new rule of Zeus. Prometheus was perhaps testing Zeus's power, and as a result men not only suffered the temporary loss of fire but also reaped the need to work, to sample the 'strife' that Zeus had placed in the roots of the earth (*Works and Days*, 18 f.). Fire is restored, as it has to be; Prometheus is acting for the gods, as well as for men, although he may not know it; since why should the gods permanently deprive themselves of any burnt offerings whatever? Perhaps this part of the myth once explained the origin of fireless offerings, or is a relic of the first gift of fire to men, whether by Prometheus himself or by the obscure antediluvian Phoroneus (who lived at Argos, not far from Mecone, if that is really an old name for Sicyon).[32] Here, at least, it has

[30] Yet is it quite true (as M. L. West claims, *Hesiod, Theogony* (Oxford, 1966), 305) that 'The Prometheus myth [*sc.* including fire and Pandora] is aetiological through and through'? The retrieval of fire, at least, is not strictly aetiological, nor is it quite the case that 'we learn how men come to have fire'.

[31] So M. L. West, *op. cit.*, 318, with further references.

[32] Pausanias, II, 19, 5.

been fitted into the two intertwined narratives of Prometheus's continuing contest of wits with Zeus, and men's progressive decline.

Men lose the conditions of the golden age; Kronos is in Tartarus, or alternatively presiding more comfortably over the Isles of the Blessed, while they themselves have to sweat in the fields and are on uncertain terms with their old friends the gods. There is more to the end of the golden age than we know. At least Hesiod's relative chronology is roughly consistent so far; although other myths, for example of the wedding of Peleus and Thetis, attended by the gods but only just preceding the Trojan War, are a different matter. In one respect, however, even Hesiod's arrangement is puzzling: for if Pandora is the first woman (and her unnamed equivalent in the *Theogony* version of this myth is certainly that), and she was created on Zeus's orders as punishment for the theft of fire, then men had no women during the golden age.

The two Hesiodic versions of the first-woman theme vary significantly in their implications. In the *Theogony*, probably the earlier of the two poems,[33] the name Pandora is not used, but at Zeus's bidding the divine craftsman Hephaestus makes out of earth the first woman, who is given beauty by Athena. Men and gods gaze upon her in wonder—but she is a paradoxical creature, a 'beautiful evil', a 'drastic deceit' (585, 589): 'from her is the destructive race of women, who dwell as a great source of woe among mortal men, fit companions not for destructive poverty but for surfeit of wealth' (591–3). That is the real objection to women in the *Theogony*: they are drones, they consume a man's substance and do nothing in return. And yet they do after all perform one service; for Zeus established a counterbalancing evil for the man who stays single, that he has no one to look after him in his old age, and after his death his substance will be divided among distant kin. Hesiod ends by saying that the man who has a good sensible wife gets a mixture of good and evil (*Theogony*, 608 f.)—here we can surely see his own views moderating, as well as being moderated by, the rather severe mythical theme.[34]

[33] Since the idea of the two kinds of strife in *Works and Days* (11 ff.) looks like a conscious correction of the single strife of the *Theogony* (225).

[34] At *Works and Days*, 695 ff. Hesiod stated categorically that a man should look around for a wife when he is close on thirty, and that there can be no better acquisition than a good wife, just as there can be no worse than a bad one. Of course a wife costs a bit, needs feeding, but Hesiod was a practical man who would accept that something has to be laid out to gain greater returns.

16   KSA

Women as an expensive and deceitful luxury, suborning men by flaunting their attractions, are a folktale-type motif; for the idea is widespread and traditional, involves no special fantasy, and arises out of everyday experience. Yet the *Theogony* myth goes much deeper. It can be seen as stating a typical dilemma implicit in the relations of man with nature and culture. On the one hand women are expensive and wasteful, and therefore it is better to be without them; on the other they look after their doddering husbands and produce heirs, and therefore it is better to have them around. The myth suggests no Lévi-Straussian mediation, although the form of the dilemma is itself a palliation of unmitigated evil. Obviously even a speculative myth need not suggest a solution, and there are many palpable myths that work round a problem without solving it. The origin of diseases, as we shall see, calls forth from Hesiod two separate treatments, of which one simply states the situation in mythical terms, the other suggests an explanation, but in terms that are only intermittently mythical.

The *Works and Days* version (57 ff.) is no less interesting. Hephaestus is told in much the same way to make a creature out of earth and water, in appearance like the immortal goddesses. Athena teaches her useful accomplishments, how to work the loom and so on, Aphrodite gives her charm and sexual desirability, and Hermes inserts into her a shameless mind and a deceitful character. She is called Pandora, 'All-gifts', according to Hesiod because all the gods gave her something. Then Zeus sends her off, led by Hermes, to Prometheus's feckless brother Epimetheus, who receives her in spite of his brother's firm instruction to accept no gift from Zeus. Up to this time men lived on earth without evil, harsh toil, or painful and fatal diseases (90 ff.); but then this woman took the great lid off the jar and scattered them all around—only hope was left inside. The rest, ten thousand griefs, wander among men; the earth and sea are full of evils; diseases come upon men by day and silently by night. In short, this is primarily a tale (and a defective one: what was this jar, and what was Pandora doing with it?) of the origin of diseases, while the *Theogony* version concerns the invention of women and the great curse they are to men. There is nothing about diseases in that version, nothing about the expensive wastefulness of women in this one. Yet women's deceitfulness is equally stressed in both. This is no doubt because the two descriptions of the actual creation and adornment of the woman, which are in places closely similar, are derived from a single source. Deceitfulness happens to be mentioned in both versions, although it is not particularly germane to the *Works and Days* version as it stands. Here, the opening of the jar seems to be due to female curiosity and meddling (another common folktale motif), although it cannot be ruled out that in a fuller version Pandora might have promised not to open the jar, much as the daughters of Cecrops agreed not to open the box given them by Athena. Conversely the woman's specifically sexual attractions are emphasized in *Works and Days* but not even mentioned in the *Theogony*, where Aphrodite has no part in the preparations. This might be accidental; sexual lure is relevant to both versions, since Epimetheus would be more understandable if he were susceptible as well as silly, and the marital role of women can hardly be assessed without some mention of their more pleasurable aspects. Moreover the hypothetical source might have continued with a double reason for men's sufferings—first Pandora released evils and diseases, then she went on, by mating with Epimetheus, to become the ancestress of women in general, with all their faults. There is a basic structural similarity between the two variants that may well be compatible with the idea of a single but complex original: in the *Theogony* women are all bad but are palliated by one important compensation, that they look after their old husbands and give them offspring; in *Works and Days* the objects released from the jar are all bad but are similarly palliated by one important compensation, namely hope, which is trapped under the lid and remains behind.

The Greeks did not waste time in trying to explain death away or make it somehow palatable. In so far as the Epic of Gilgamesh describes a hero probing the boundaries between mortal and immortal, it has no Greek counterpart. Not that the Greeks were silent on the subject: the elaborate mythology of the world below, the dismal view of the condition of the dead that is given its most vivid expression by Achilles in the underworld scene of the eleventh *Odyssey*, the theme of the vegetation-deity who disappears to Hades—all these show that Greek myths took full cognizance of death as a fact. But there is little evidence of questioning the need for death, of being angry with fate or the gods because death is universal or inescapable; and that was the apparent implication of the Gilgamesh poem. On the contrary, Greek literature is full of a direct and unequivocal acceptance of man's mortality, and

Homer, Pindar, and the tragedians stress repeatedly that in this respect there is an unbridgeable gap between gods and men. Man will surely die, and what after-life he may have will be a wretched one. This, at least until the spread of the mystery religions, is the view implied both in myths and in literature as a whole, and its freedom from illusion is one of the qualities for which the Greeks are most often admired.

And yet the longing is there in the background, expressed in mythical form not only in occasional heroic retrievals from the dead but also in the idea of a golden age. Even here the ultimate realism persists—for what men escaped under the reign of Kronos was not death itself, but toil, disease, and old age: 'beforetime on earth lived the tribes of men / far away from evils and without harsh toil / and without grievous diseases, which give doom to men' (*Works and Days*, 90–2). Then Pandora ends the age of paradise: 'Full of evils is the earth and full the sea, / and diseases come upon men by day, and others by night / wander of their own accord...' (101–3). The emphasis is on old age and disease rather than on other evils; certainly not on death as such. All men must die—that is accepted without question. Death is a melancholy topic, to see the daylight for the last time is a matter for lamentation; but even the most privileged of men, those of the golden race, underwent death. What is significant is the manner of their dying: not only did they live 'like gods with hearts free from care, / without toil and grief', but 'No miserable old age / came upon them, but with limbs that suffered no change / they rejoiced in festivities, apart from all evils; / *and they died as though subdued by sleep...*' (112–16).

At what stage, exactly, in this myth of the successive conditions of men, do diseases intervene? The silver race never reach old age, since after an abnormal state of immaturity lasting a hundred years they live only a short while longer, 'possessing griefs because of their folly' (133 f.). Zeus was angry with them and brought about their death, yet there is no mention of disease and suffering at this point. Moreover they too, like those of the golden race, become daemons or spirits, albeit of the underparts of the earth. The next two species, the bronze men and the heroes, neither reach old age nor succumb to disease, simply because they perish in battle or adventure. Only with the race of iron are diseases implicitly mentioned, and then they are a prominent part of a deplorable condition: 'neither by day / shall they ever cease from weariness and grief, nor by night / from being destroyed, but the gods shall give them harsh cares' (176–8). And in the final phase of iron, which for Hesiod lay in the future, men shall be grey-templed as soon as they are born (181), a bizarre detail which clearly means that men will have neither childhood nor maturity but will move straight into the dread condition of sickness, old age and imminent death. These grey-headed babies, mentioned in a single verse of Hesiod that uncomprehending critics have often wished to suppress, are one of the most potent and terrifying symbols to have survived among the desiccated remains of Greek mythology. Even here we cannot be absolutely sure that it is not due to the rationalizing imagination of Hesiod himself—although the Graeae, the mythical personifications of old age, provide some confirmation in that they, too, were grey-haired from birth.

This myth of the five races, which is strongly consequential in its arrangement, and in which the heroic race is notoriously a relatively new element, responds favourably to a kind of structural analysis applied to it by V. Goldschmidt and especially by J.-P. Vernant.[35] An important question is whether the iron generation is really divided into two phases—a present one, to which Hesiod himself belongs, and an even worse stage that lies in the near future and will culminate in the grey-headed babies and the destruction of the race by Zeus. I have already implied my acceptance of Vernant's argument that two such stages are envisaged, although the general lines of my interpretation do not depend wholly on that view.[36]

If this is right, then the five stages represented by the five generations become six; these six fall into three pairs, each of which contains a relatively better and a relatively worse member:

| relatively better: | gold | heroes | iron (1) |
| relatively worse: | silver | bronze | iron (2) |

There is also, of course, a progressive deterioration from pair to pair. What makes the second element of each pair worse is the addition of *hybris*, anti-social arrogance or selfish insolence. The

[35] Cf. J.-P. Vernant, *Mythe et pensée chez les Grecs* (Paris, 1965), 19–47.

[36] The decision is complicated by Hesiod's use of the future tense throughout: he proceeds from 'they will not ever cease from toil and grief' (177), implying the continuation of a present state, to the completed act of 'Zeus will destroy this generation also' (180), and then the ambiguous 'they will dishonour their ageing parents' (185). On the whole, however, it is plain that things are going to become distinctly worse.

golden race is free of this quality, but it is typical of the silver; the
race of heroes is above it, and in this respect is analogous to the
golden race, but the bronze race is riddled with it; both phases of
the race of iron have it, but the future phase, when Aidōs and
Nemesis (a sense of shame, and respect for the opinion of others
and of the gods) are forced to leave the earth, is much the worse.
In addition the central pair is vitiated by the pursuit of war, the
'groaning works of Ares' (145 f.).

The golden race manifests *dike*, justice, and no *hybris*; the
silver, only *hybris*. As yet there is no warfare, although strife is
beginning to intrude. Earlier in the poem Hesiod had distinguished
two kinds of strife (11 ff.), a good (healthy competitiveness) and a
bad (quarrelling and warfare); and not even the first of these is
relevant to generations that either have good things in abundance
and without toil, or depend on their mothers for nurture. The next
pair exemplifies the bad strife (although curiously enough the
term *eris* is not used in the course of this myth; which may suggest
that its present formulation was not primarily due to Hesiod
himself?); in addition the bronze men are full of *hybris*, while the
heroes who fought at Thebes and Troy are 'better and more just'
(158). In the third pair Hesiod contemplates a world dominated
by injustice, hatred, and envy, which will grow worse and worse
until Zeus destroys this generation like its predecessors. Whether it
will be followed by a cyclical reversion to a second golden age is
debated; I disagree with Vernant in thinking not, and that either
mankind will come to an end or that Hesiod or his source simply
did not consider the matter.

A dichotomy is being drawn here not only between types of men
and society but also between justice on the one hand and selfish
arrogance on the other. It may be said that a degree of mediation
between these polarities is achieved, in that their true relations
are made more comprehensible. Yet behind this *schema* there seems
to lie another, which depends on a contrast between immaturity,
maturity, and hypermaturity or old age. This emerges better
from some of the myth's curious details than from its overt plan—
from its mythical rather than its quasi-rationalized aspect.[37] We
have seen that the golden race do not fall sick or grow old, but
die as though falling asleep. The silver race, on the other hand,

[37] A similar connexion with an underlying structure was provided by the at first
sight irrelevant details of Enki and Ninhursag and the Epic of Gilgamesh.

are always children. Their infancy lasts for a hundred years—
during this period they cling to their mothers, and then after a
brief and impious youth, full of grief which they create for themselves by their arrogance, they perish. The men of the bronze and
heroic generations have no old age, for they kill each other first;
and childhood seems no less irrelevant to them. They are all
maturity, like the golden race, but their maturity is frustrated by
warfare and self-destruction. In the present phase of the iron race
wretchedness is everywhere, and men are hounded by toil, grief,
and disease—for the 'destruction by night' of 177 f. is a reminder
of the diseases that kill silently by night, released by Pandora at
102 ff. (here the language used in the myth seems to be Hesiod's
own). Men are at odds with their children, their brothers, their
ageing parents, and shall be so even more. Old age, always
regrettable, becomes even worse, since the old are neglected by
children who refuse to pay back the cares and costs of their up-
bringing, the θρεπτήρια that represented an unusually humane
concept in ordinary Greek culture. Then old age spreads to the
grey-haired children themselves and maturity is finally squeezed
out.

In all this one may detect a polarity between total maturity, no
grief or toil, no old age or disease (in the golden generation),
and no maturity, all grief and toil, all old age and disease (in the
final phase of the iron generation). The other races intervene, in
part to make up a logical and even historical progression, but in
part to provide a kind of mediation by exemplifying the effects of
adding certain moral and social ingredients to the extreme conditions. Full maturity is useless if it is dominated by strife, as with
the bronze race, although it can be relieved by justice or the
comparative absence of *hybris* in the heroic race; and the absence
or avoidance of toil, disease and old age is useless if there is no
settled maturity, as with the silver race. Moreover the second pair,
of which the common quality is war, intervenes between the first
and the third, whose common qualities are respectively the lack of
old age and disease, and their disastrous presence. It would be easy
to construct a Lévi-Straussian mediation here, for example by
adducing analogies of war-twins as mediators in North-American
Indian cultures. I believe that would be illegitimate; yet there is a
mediation of a kind, as I have already suggested. Whether under
the present aspect it is more than a historical one (for there are

obvious references to history and legend in the bronze and heroic generations) is debatable; although it may well be so. [In the *Theogony* Hesiod associated old age with strife and made them, like Grief and Death itself, children of Night (212, 214, 225). Death is unavoidable; but strife and old age seem theoretically unnecessary. [Why, then, are they so prominent in men's experience? Why cannot men live in peace and die 'as in sleep', like those of the golden generation? The myth of Pandora, in the *Works and Days* version, accounts for this state of affairs as a punishment by Zeus for an act of *hybris*, not directly by men but by their protector Prometheus. The myth of the five races makes a similar point, but more elaborately and in a less completely mythical fashion. Yet not only are old age and disease associated there with a moral decline of the whole human race, but they are also seen to be the result of a regular succession. Warfare no doubt seemed a natural part of life to all Greeks down to Hesiod's time and beyond; the heroic race showed that it could be substantially free of *hybris*, although their bronze predecessors had demonstrated that *hybris* and war tend to go together. Thus the 'conclusion' of the myth, if we choose to put it that way, is that the responsibility for the extension of death into life, for the degrading aspects of increasing maturity, lies partly with fate, the natural destiny of man to make war, which is in some ways good; but partly also with men themselves—for neither toil nor war demands *hybris* and precludes justice, yet this is what has come about.

These Hesiodic myths are the most obviously speculative of all Greek myths, which, as has been seen, are generally weak in this respect, at least in the form in which we know them. Yet the tales of Prometheus, of the first woman, of the five generations, are obviously either fragmentary and allusive, or incompletely mythical, or both. I could conjecture about their earlier history, but refrain from doing so—for it would be an exercise in academic ingenuity rather than a positive contribution to solving a real problem; except to repeat that, if Asiatic models lay behind them, as they probably did, then they remain largely invisible to us. In this respect the succession myth of Ouranos, Kronos and Zeus is quite different. But that, it may be objected, was a real mythical narrative; these others are more or less strongly infected by rational statement and logical ordering, and the so-called myth of the five generations does not even have a story. That is all true; but the deceit over the sacri-

fices, and Pandora's release of diseases, although strongly aetiological, and to that extent possessed of a kind of logic, are aetiological in a manner familiar from thousands of genuine myths
from other lands; and the five-races sequence includes fantastic
and imaginative concepts (the conditions of the golden race, the
hundred-year infancy of the silver, the metallic culture and restricted diet of the bronze, the grey-headed babies of the iron) that
belong to a mythical and not a rationalistic approach. Myths, as
surviving Mesopotamian instances showed, can vary from apparently pointless but gripping narratives to deliberate cultural
analyses loosely appended to mythical characters. Nor is order-
liness necessarily absent from genuine myths. Irregular and
fantastic connexions between events are admittedly more typical;
but order and a kind of logic, even beyond the minimal requirements of a story, are possible. They may have been elicited and
formalized by generations of literary transmission; but the order
was sometimes implicit in the first place. I very much doubt
whether Hesiod himself was capable of injecting into the account
of the five races that subtle progression from maturity to immaturity
to hypermaturity, or from justice to aggressive selfishness by the
medium of warfare, which seems to be present in the final result.
What he has transmitted reflects either the work of a more careful
thinker than he set out to be, or—and in view of the flashes of
mythical fantasy this seems the more probable—a longer and more
obviously mythological account, itself dependent on a tradition
incorporating a general feeling about the nature of mortality and
immortality, old age and disease.

Curiously enough the mythical implications of Pandora's jar are
in some ways more puzzling. Does it offer any implied reason for
the ultimate origin of diseases, apart from the quarrel between
Zeus and Prometheus or the conceivable motif of female curiosity?
What is the exact significance of the jar—a natural place for
hiding or imprisonment, but also a receptacle for evil and pollution in Near-Eastern myths and in Homer (*Iliad* xxiv, 527 ff.)?
Is there any serious connexion between women and the origin of
disease—do primitive associations between menstruation and
pollution lie in the background? These and other questions remind
us that the formation of myths was an enormously complex process, into which many factors, both conscious and unconscious,
entered. The Hesiodic myths are no exception, and they should not

for this reason, and because of their unusual speculative colouring, be disparaged and discounted, or wholly demoted to the level of proto-philosophy.

8: Mythical and rational thought

The modern tendency to see those Hesiodic versions as a kind of incipient philosophy introduces the final section of this consideration of Greek myths. At last, ponderously and a little tediously, their qualities and their relation to other mythologies have been pinned down. Their colours have temporarily faded in the process, and I regret that; especially because the question to be asked now is even more colourless and abstract—although it is an important, even an unusual one.

Did Hesiod, as is commonly asserted and almost universally assumed, really come at the point of transition from mythopoeic to rational modes of thought? Are the myths of Prometheus, Pandora and the five races permeated by a degree of direct expression and consequentiality because Hesiod himself stood precisely at the watershed? Let me cite F. M. Cornford again, not because he represents that view in its crudest form, but rather because he offers an unusually refined statement of it: 'After the primitive stage of genuine myth-making, there is a transitional period, in which the old images and symbols are retained, but with a nascent consciousness that they do go beyond the meaning proper. In Hesiod himself they are on the way to becoming metaphor and allegory...Pherecydes is a good example of the transitional phase ...Finally there may come a time when rational thinking consciously asserts itself, and the foremost intellects of the race awaken out of the dream of mythology...This happened in sixth-century Ionia, and what the Western world calls philosophy or science was born.'[38] At first sight this statement is unexceptionable; yet it manages to imply that the stage of 'genuine myth-making' lay relatively close behind Hesiod himself, just as the final awakening out of the dream into the full daylight of reason came very soon after him. The same sort of assumption lies behind the assertion of another unusually perceptive (although on this point less well-informed) critic, Lévi-Strauss, that the *bouleversement* by which mythical thought passes beyond concrete images is known to be

[38] F. M. Cornford, *The Unwritten Philosophy* (Cambridge, 1950), 42. Cf. also H. Fränkel, *Dichtung und Philosophie des frühen Griechentums*[2] (Munich, 1962), 108 ff.

situated 'at the frontiers of Greek thought, at the point where mythology desists in favour of a philosophy that emerges as the essential condition of scientific speculation'.[39] Once again there is a strong implication that truly mythical thought gives way to rational thought after a single, limited and definable transitional stage which lies just beyond the Presocratics.

A more specific analysis of the process is offered by yet another erudite and influential critic, W. K. C. Guthrie: 'The birth of philosophy in Europe, then, consisted in the abandonment, at the level of conscious thought, of mythological solutions to problems concerning the origin and nature of the universe and the processes that go on within it. For religious faith there is substituted the faith that was and remains the basis of scientific thought...that the visible world conceals a rational and intelligible order...'[40] Instead of a *bouleversement*, a birth—the process is still a rapid one, which leaves behind it a consistent stage of religious faith and mythological thought. But was the assumption that 'the visible world conceals a rational and intelligible order' so utterly foreign to the mythical view? Zeus's gradual triumph over the powers of obstruction and disorder surely represents the emergence of a principle of systematic and, in a way, even intelligent control of the world; and that is a conception that certainly preceded any kind of philosophic 'birth'. That Guthrie is inclined to play down this aspect of the Homeric gods, for instance, can be seen in the following extract: 'To the mind of a pre-philosophical man, there is no special difficulty in accounting for the apparently haphazard nature of much that goes on in the world. He knows that he himself is a creature of impulse and emotion...What more natural than that the ways of the world around him should have a similar explanation?... Everything there [*sc.* in the Homeric poems] has a personal explanation, not only external and physical phenomena like rain and tempest, thunder and sunshine, illness and death, but also those overmastering psychological impulses... [*sc.* like passion, folly, boldness].'[41] In my own view this greatly exaggerates the irrational qualities, not necessarily of some of the Homeric characters, but of the unknown poets who developed them. It is easy to point to Athena tugging Achilles's hair to restrain his

---

[39] C. Lévi-Strauss, *MC*, 407.
[40] W. K. C. Guthrie, *A History of Greek Philosophy*, 1 (Cambridge, 1962), 29.
[41] *Op. cit.*, 26 f.

anger or Aphrodite prodding Helen into the bedroom; it is equally easy to cite scores of passages where human actions are determined by reasonable processes of decision, and natural events by the operation of consistent principles. The *Iliad* and *Odyssey* are not a sort of mythopoeic jungle, and many of their quaint personifications and impulses are more likely to be part of a longstanding and archaistic literary convention than to represent the state of Homer's assumptions on causation in the late eighth century B.C.[42]

I am not questioning (to return to Cornford) that Hesiod, and perhaps Pherecydes too, mingled myth with allegory and literal statement with both. The implication that he thought neither wholly rationally nor wholly mythically is certainly correct. What I am questioning is whether an entirely mythical stage really lay just behind him—whether, because he represents a transition of a kind, at least in terms of literature, he represents *the* transition, the neat Zellerian turning-point at which mythopoeia was overthrown by reason. What I have in mind as a possible, indeed a probable, alternative to this convenient model is the much less precise one whereby any 'mythical' stage of Greek thought lay in the far distant past, not in the eighth century B.C. or the ninth, not even in the Mycenaean age or perhaps the Bronze Age as a whole, but possibly far back in the Neolithic Age, at a time, indeed, when the term 'Greek' has almost no meaning.

The reason for this conjecture is, of course, the quality of the myths as they appear in their earliest surviving forms—in Homer and Hesiod, who, whatever the exaggerations of Herodotus's assertion that they formulated for the Greeks their whole theogony,[43] undoubtedly represented a view of the mythical past that was not seriously altered until after Alexander the Great. It is not so much the gods that prompt the conjecture as the rest of the mythology, particularly its heroic parts, and the conventionalized and folktale aspect that was emphasized earlier and constitutes one of the most striking characteristics of Greek myths. This, with its obverse aspect of the rarity of deeply imaginative fantasy, and of the submergence of speculative and operative functions that are so important in other cultures, makes it improbable that the

[42] See also E. R. Dodds, *The Greeks and the Irrational* (Berkeley, 1951), ch. 1, especially pp. 13 ff. Dodds approaches the problem of rationality and irrationality primarily from the side of religion.

[43] Herodotus, II, 53.

process of rational attrition began only a relatively short time, generations rather than centuries or millennia, before Hesiod.

At present very little is known about Mycenaean mythology beyond Nilsson's observation that the surviving cycles of myth are centred on Mycenaean cities, and therefore probably existed in some form in Mycenaean times, together with the information of the Linear B tablets that some of the main Greek gods and goddesses were known in the Late Bronze Age. I have been assuming that Mycenaean mythology would have looked quite like much of the Greek mythology known from alphabetic sources; even that assumption presupposes that any different and more imaginative kind of myth must have lain in the pre-Mycenaean past. If we knew more about the intellectual development of the Greeks in its earlier stages this question of the chronology of mythical thought, and the point at which its adulteration by reason began, would be of crucial importance. As it is we should still do better, in composing our lamentably fragmentary picture of the second millennium B.C. in Greece, to omit from it the element of mythopoeic thought as an exclusive mode of conceptualizing and discovery. What we see in Hesiod—that mixture of personification, allegory, speculative myth, fable, literal statement, loose association, intermittent logic, and native shrewdness—was probably around in Greece for a very long time before him; and the stage when virtually all theorizing unconsciously took narrative and purely mythical form may have lain thousands of years in the past.

If Greek mythology as we know it is seriously short of the qualities of imaginative unreason that are normally associated with myths, if its most prominent characteristics are a highly developed complexity of essentially folktale themes and a sophisticated apparatus of rather unepisodic gods, then a clear choice is presented: either this mythology is a censored, derivative and literary affair, or the Greeks and their forebears never possessed any important body of fantastic myths, and the controls on the wilder kinds of imagination detectable from Homer and Hesiod on (with Old Comedy as a single glorious exception) reflect a permanent quality of the Greek mind.

This second alternative may appear to be framed merely as an absurdity to strengthen the first. On the contrary: it is the seriously held opinion of at least two, and I suspect the great majority, of the more prominent exponents of Greek mythology and religion over the last fifty years. The books on Greek religion by Martin Nilsson, so valuable in other respects, and the widely used handbook of Greek mythology by H. J. Rose have done much to perpetuate an essentially Victorian view about the clear air of Greece and its tonic effect on the Greek mind that Gilbert Murray and Jane Harrison laboured in vain to overthrow.

Nilsson's view is advanced in the section on Mythology in the first volume of his *Geschichte der griechischen Religion*.[44] After stressing the important role in Greek myths of *Märchenmotive* or folktale motifs, he goes on to assert that a systematic analysis will show 'how the special talent of the Greeks, their rationalism, led to selection, elimination and remoulding of the excessively fantastic folktale motifs' (18). He proceeds to make it plain that in his view this rationalism was innate, so much so that the Greeks were able to keep substantially clear of 'the primitive and fantastic ideas' of folktale and aetiological tale—with the result that 'Greek myth thus became something different from the folktales, aitia and sagas of other peoples, and justifiably bears a special name: Myth' (35); or, in the words of the earlier book, 'The Greek myth has thus become something other than the ordinary folktale, and rightly bears a separate name'.[45] In other words, Nilsson refuses the very name of myth to 'primitive' fantastic tales that have not been purged and pervaded by rationalism, the 'special talent' of the Greeks.

This attitude shows up no less clearly in the following amazing passage by the usually well-balanced H. J. Rose:[46] 'Another and a more important point to be remembered in the case of Greek myths is the way they reflect the national character. The Greeks at their

[44] *GgrR³*, 13–35. This section still retains a great deal from his much earlier *A History of Greek Religion* (Oxford, 1925), chapter II, from which the following extract is taken: 'Their marvellous qualities of mind, their rationalism and clarity of thinking, could brook no ambiguity or confusion. Hence was born among them that independent searching after truth which is Science, the greatest offspring of the spirit of Greece. We have seen that the same quality in a lower form, for which I should perhaps use the term rationalism, gave to Greek myths their peculiar character, in contradistinction to the primitive tale and folk-tale out of which they sprang. An outgrowth of the same kind is the humanizing of the myths, the anthropomorphism characteristic of Greek mythology. It is due not only to the plastic imagination of the Greeks, with its power of intuition, but also to their antipathy to the primitive and fantastic ideas and characteristics of the folk-tale, which led them to clear away all that too sharply contradicted the experiences of human life' (*op. cit.*, 75).

[45] *A History of Greek Religion* (Oxford, 1925), 75.

[46] *A Handbook of Greek Mythology* (5th ed., London, 1953), 14.

best were sane, high-spirited, clear-headed, beauty-loving optimists
and not in the least other-worldly. Hence their legends are almost
without exception free from the cloudiness, the wild grotesques,
and the horrible features which beset the popular traditions of
less gifted and happy peoples. Even their monsters are not very
ugly or uncouth, nor their ghosts and demons paralysingly dreadful. Their heroes, as a rule, may sorrow, but are not broken-
hearted...they meet with extraordinary adventures, but there is
a certain tone of reasonableness running through their most
improbable exploits. As for the gods and other supernatural
characters, they are glorified men and women, who remain extremely human, and on the whole neither irrational nor grossly
unfair in their dealings. Such tales as contain savage and repulsive
elements tend to drop into the background or be modified.'

It is no doubt possible to find in this passage one or two propositions that are true and even helpful. As a whole, however, it at best
glosses over an immensely important problem; at its worst it
propagates a view of the Greeks that is both naive and sentimental
and can only bring Greek studies into disrepute with the rest of the
world, which by and large has progressed beyond the methods and
values of J. C. Stobart, Edith Hamilton and Lowes Dickinson. As
a matter of fact Rose's expression of the view seems to owe a good
deal to one of the real masters of the history of Greek thought,
Eduard Zeller; I cite the relevant passage in the 1881 English
translation of Zeller's *History of Greek Philosophy* by S. P. Alleyne
(I, 49), which conveys the appropriate Victorian flavour: 'the
philosophic science of the Greeks is fully explained by the genius,
resources, and state of civilisation of the Hellenic tribes. If ever
there was a people capable of creating its own science, the Greeks
were that people. In the most ancient records of their culture, the
Homeric Poems, we already meet with that freedom and clearness
of spirit, that sobriety and moderation, that feeling for the beautiful and harmonious, which place these poems so distinctly above
the heroic legends of all other nations without exception. Of
scientific endeavour, there is nothing as yet; no necessity is felt to
investigate the natural causes of things; the writer is content to
refer them to personal authors and divine powers, the explanation
that comes uppermost in the childhood of mankind.'

That last sentence is echoed in the earlier quotations from
Guthrie and Cornford; but it is to the 'sobriety and moderation',

Nilsson's innate talent of rationalism and Rose's freedom from wild, grotesque and horrible features, that I want to return. For is it really true that Greek monsters 'almost without exception' lack the bizarre characteristics of those of other mythologies? Typhoeus, with his hundred snake-heads each giving tongue in a different way, is no less horrid than his Hurrian cousin Ulli-kummi, the huge stone monster rooted in the sea, although perhaps a little less imaginative. Admittedly Greek myths are freer of 'horrible features' than some, and relatively lacking in the franker and more inquisitive type of sexual and excretory des-cription—but not entirely so, as the tale of Ouranos permanently copulating with Gaia demonstrates; and that suffices to dispose of the theory that any crude elements that entered from outside were systematically purged. Judging from the number of references to that myth in classical literature, it was one the Greeks particularly enjoyed. Plato found it unedifying, but that is another matter. I do not want to deny that for some time before Hesiod many Greeks may have exercised a taste to which the stronger fantasies were unattractive; that is different from claiming that Greeks always had that taste, or had always applied a kind of clear-headed beauty-loving censorship. It is also quite removed from the conception common to both Nilsson and Rose that 'unreasonable' fantasy is somehow bad, that imaginative if crude myths are all right for savages but not for Greeks at any period in their develop-ment, and that Greek mythology is the better for being free of it. I suppose I have already made it plain that in my view Greek mythology is not the better but the worse for its lack of fantasy, its highly conventionalized form, and its diminution of the specula-tive functions of myth. And yet I, like Nilsson and Rose, admire the Greeks and am temperamentally disposed to see the best in them. For me, however, this prejudice takes the form not of claiming that they never had any real myths, but of supposing that they must have had them, at some time in the irrecoverable past; that they could never have become the people they were if they had been deprived of this essential element in the for-mation of a coherent, developed, and yet deeply imaginative culture.

That is an overtly emotional argument; at least it can stand as a point of view that is worth placing on record for maturer con-sideration; it is, by the nature of things, difficult to substantiate by concrete arguments and evidence. The best evidence is, precisely, the occurrence of certain pieces of genuinely mythical fantasy that for one reason or another have survived the operation of a very long tradition. The Ouranos and Gaia tale has already been cited. Others concern amazing births and sexual couplings (Dionysus, Athena, Kronos, the Minotaur); strange but largely indigenous mixtures like the Centaurs; the Cretan myths about Talos and Daedalus and Icarus; the clashing rocks, floating islands and other marvels concentrated in the adventures of Odysseus in the *Odyssey*. It is customary to dismiss most of the *Odyssey* as folktale; much of it is, but the type of folktale, and the varied imagination it exemplifies, still reveal something about the Greek mythical tradition in its broadest sense. The point is that if the Greeks had never been capable of anything but the emasculated kind of invention so admired by Nilsson and Rose, they would never have evolved these and a dozen other themes; or, if they had always been prone to remove improbable fantasies from the myths that came into their ken, they would never have allowed, over so long and selective a tradition, even the slightest crude fantasy to penetrate their net.[47] Nilsson further argues that the absence of variants like the casting of mountains or rivers in the path of a pursuer betokens a systematic resistance to certain kinds of imagination. Yet that particular kind is as much whimsical as genuinely primitive, and I am not surprised that the Greeks, with their evidently deep-rooted attachment to the ingenious, preferred to delay a pursuer with Atalanta's apples or Medea's scattering of bits of her young brother. One can accept that the Greeks exercised certain restraints at certain stages of the mythical tradition without committing oneself to the argument that they were always innately rational, naturally immune to the supposedly pointless, crude and wasteful fantasies of myth.

One further doubt may be cast on the passage of Cornford from which we started. In the transitional period that he envisaged, 'the old images and symbols are retained, but with a nascent consciousness that they do go beyond the meaning proper'; they are 'on their way to becoming metaphor and allegory' in Hesiod.[48] Images and symbols transformed into metaphor may or

---

[47] Unless, perhaps, it were protected by strong religious associations—which are unlikely, incidentally, to apply to the Ouranos and Kronos myth.

[48] F. M. Cornford, *The Unwritten Philosophy* (Cambridge, 1950), 42.

may not thereby become non-mythical or only quasi-mythical; but I am not sure that allegory is necessarily to be removed to a stage of transition, or that a nascent consciousness that images and symbols have some external reference is necessarily incompatible with a basically mythical way of viewing the world. A decision on this point depends on one's whole view of the nature of myth, and I shall be discussing these problems from a more theoretical standpoint in the next chapter. But when Ernst Cassirer applauded the nineteenth-century writer Schelling because he 'replaces the allegorical interpretation of the world of myths by a tautegorical interpretation, i.e. he looks upon mythical figures as autonomous configurations of the human spirit',[49] he was himself adopting an attitude that depends on a romantic idea of primitive thought as well as on a one-sided and exaggerated definition of allegory. The idea of myths that have no other reference except themselves, of people who think symbols rather than in terms of symbols, has in its contemporary form a dual pedigree. The theory of a special kind of 'primitive mentality', replete with strange magical associations and random imagistic concepts and utterly devoid of anything we should recognize as reason or logic, goes back in its most extreme form to Lucien Lévy-Bruhl, whose views on this topic came to be regarded as excessive even by himself. Claude Lévi-Strauss's picture of a *pensée sauvage* that is far from totally naive is based on a closer study of the conceptual operations of savage peoples, and is clearly much nearer the truth than Lévy-Bruhl's.[50] Secondly, the idea of non-referent symbols draws support from psychological theories of archetypes, of autonomous tendencies to formulate universal symbols that are claimed by Jung and his followers to play a special part in myths. It suffices at present to say that this theory, in spite of its vogue, is devoid of adequate evidential support.

It is not the nascent awareness that myths sometimes have an implication beyond their own terms, that in a wide sense they are allegorical, that shows Hesiod to represent a transitional phase; rather it is his reduction (for example) of the mythical golden and silver generations to a pseudo-historical *schema*, or his employment of personification and naked allegory in the idea that Dreams are the children of Sleep, or his quite assured use of genealogy as a

---

[49] *The Philosophy of Symbolic Forms*, II (Eng. tr., New Haven, 1955), 4.
[50] See also p. 264 and n. below.

logical tool.[51] At the same time such procedures do not show that he subjected myths to sophisticated treatment on every occasion and in every respect. As we have seen, certain myths reported by him are probably as mythical in their essentials as we can reasonably expect to find in a Greek context. Moreover even the use of logical schemes for relating different myths (and Hesiod himself was notoriously erratic in applying such schemes) may well have been common for many generations before his; after all, such schemes are no different in kind from progressive narrative structures that we should hesitate to confine to brief transitional periods on the very borders of philosophy. In short, Hesiod does indeed exemplify the quasi-rationalizing deployment of myth, is very probably a great organizer of the tradition, and happens to be the first surviving example of this kind of thing in Greece. But that does not mean that he was an entirely new phenomenon, that mixed uses of myth did not stretch back a long way into the past, or that even in what one might hypothetically call a true mythopoeic stage no connexion was implied and perceived between the content of myths and the content of life. The underlying concerns that emerged from the analysis in §§1 and 2 of the present chapter are surely much older than Hesiod.

Such a readjustment of the chronology of the development of mythical thought, together with the less stringent view I have suggested of its purity even in the 'truly' mythical past, would have important consequences for what came later. The emergence of the earliest Ionian philosophers would not be quite so simple and cataclysmic as is often thought. Their retention of a degree of personification, animism, and mythological language, and their redeployment of mythical concepts like those of *Eros*, love, and *Eris*, strife, at the same time as they were replacing many mythical explanations and procedures by rational ones, would not be so neatly accounted for by a kind of Hesiodic Revolution as we have been prone to imagine. My own conjecture would be that mythology had provided a conceptual language, long before Hesiod, for some sort of systematic discussion about, and ordering of, society and the outside world. Hesiod himself gave a startling demonstration of the possibilities of this language. Yet the rise of Ionian philosophy may have been stimulated at least as much by other

[51] On which cf. H. Fränkel, *Dichtung und Philosophie des frühen Griechentums*[2] (Munich, 1962), 112 ff.

factors: for example the recent spread of literacy, and the perception of both common and distinctive features in three different sets of myths—Egyptian, Asiatic, and Greek.

It has not, I think, often been remarked that for several generations early Greek philosophy left alone, or took entirely for granted, just those subjects that (if my interpretation of the general preoccupations of Greek mythology is correct) are subsumed by myths—the specific nature of deity, the relation of mortality and immortality, the status of suffering, old age, and disease, the fate of the dead, and the relation of nature and culture. The Ionian thinkers were, admittedly, chiefly concerned with the problem of the physical world outside men; yet men were sometimes used as a model, and the Ionians would have done well to leave less in this respect to the traditional province of myth. By the time of Heraclitus in the east and Empedocles in the west it had become clear that human limitations and concerns could not be left out. Had they been distinctively treated from the beginning, Ionian natural philosophy might have achieved even more than it did.

The myths themselves offered only an incomplete answer to these problems, even by their own standards. Fantasy and speculation, although certain relics can still be seen, were attenuated in the course of the tradition in favour of the positive qualities that strike one most forcibly: narrative interest, and the complex development of a system based on a restricted range of themes. And yet it is also important to recognize that there is more to this positive side, in the end, than interest and complexity—or rather, that those qualities acquire, in the context of Greek mythology as a whole, an emotional value that transcends mere narrative appeal. It is arguable that the myths of ancient India, as well as those of medieval Europe, were formed into systems as complicated and far-ranging as the Greek. Personally I believe that the Greek tradition probably outdoes them in this respect, but that is unimportant. What is undeniable is that Greek myths are unusually rich in characters, in personnel. Each region of Greece had its own mythical genealogies, concentrated on the ruling house of its main centre during the Mycenaean age; and a complex interrelating of the different regions themselves was achieved by individual displacements as well as by migration and war. The thematic base of the episodes involving this large number of mythical characters may be narrow, but the manifold combinations of themes, and their varying application to strikingly different local circumstances, produce a sense of both richness and realism. That is remarkable in itself, and that children and adults can still find in the myths an autonomous and deeply evocative world is no accident of modern taste. Even if their historical and sentimental appeal is discounted, they seem to lay hold on the emotions—and, through their neatness, their rounded-off quality, on the intellect—and did so too upon those of the Greeks themselves. That is a legitimate deduction from the fact that the culture of Greece in the classical age, and as far back at least as Homer and Hesiod, continued to be dominated by these myths, so that philosophers, poets and playwrights chose to express themselves in their terms. Direct statement or *logos* only gradually replaced *muthos*, and then with heavy travail, in the course of the fifth and fourth centuries B.C.

Theoretically a different deduction is possible: that the mythical tradition had established itself so firmly in the culture of late Bronze-Age and early Iron-Age Greece, and was so powerfully reinforced by Homer and Hesiod, that there was no escaping it; that the men of the seventh, sixth and fifth centuries expressed themselves in its terms not through emotional involvement in its variety and realism but because they could not combat its sterile omnipresence. There is an element of truth in this, and undoubtedly the persistence of the tradition delayed and inhibited the development of new forms of expression—written prose, for instance—that might provide some real substitute for it. Yet it is inconceivable that poets from Archilochus and Stesichorus to Pindar and the tragedians used such vast masses of mythical material simply because they did not know how to extricate themselves from it, or could not excogitate anything different. The vigour and imagination of their own writing show them to be deeply immersed, emotionally and intellectually, in the traditional world of myth. Only occasionally did that tradition clearly become an incubus. It is no accident, for instance, that one of Sappho's least successful surviving poems is a routine exercise on the wedding of Hector and Andromache—because Sappho, almost uniquely, really had escaped, in her main artistic interest, into a new genre of personal poetry for which the emotional and intellectual resources of the epic and mythic tradition provided no adequate expression.[52]

---

[52] Sappho, fr. 44 (Lobel-Page). The survival in her poems of elements of epic diction does not seriously affect this judgement.

Meanwhile politics, ethnography and philosophy were evolving different and incompatible interests. Parmenides's proem is replete with goddesses, gates, horses, a chariot, a road, and all sorts of other mythical allegory, but the main content of his *Way of Truth* belongs to a different world from that of Hesiod.[53] When rationalism, working with special force through the Sophists, had finally undermined belief in the mythical world of the past—at least among the educated classes—the domination by myth of the forms of literature became sterile and restrictive, and the whole delicately balanced system collapsed. Plato, although he abused the poets, temporarily reasserted the role of myth in his own practice; but it was not long before the Alexandrians discovered for myths a new and wholly artificial, and therefore destructive, role.

In a sense the history of Greek culture is the history of its attitudes to myth; no other important western civilization has been so controlled by a developed mythical tradition. That is a vast topic that lies outside the scope of this book. Yet one point remains to be made, since it reflects on the essence of Greek mythology as a whole, the elusive and complex quality that I set out to discover. In referring to the varied complexity of the mythical tradition I meant the tradition as it stood in, say, the seventh century B.C. Normally when people mention Greek mythology they are thinking, partly of Homer, but partly of the forms given to myths by Greek tragedy—forms that would be even more striking and definite if more than a fragment of tragedy survived. Literate reinterpretation of the myths reached a climax in the drama of the fifth century, when a fresh version of the mythical world was constructed, profounder and more subtle in thought and action than it had been for centuries, perhaps ever before. And yet it was predominantly a literary creation, quite separate in form, method and intention either from spontaneous myths of the preliterate past or from their transitional descendants. This kind of creation might be taken just as an extreme form of the self-conscious elaboration brought about by any passage of oral myths into a literate tradition, however unsophisticated; but the process is essentially different from those that produced the Gilgamesh Epic or *Works and Days*—the approach to underlying problems has become direct and explicit. The myths themselves, however, still carry fragmentary overtones of the past; and this,

[53] Parmenides, fr. 1 (Diels-Kranz).

combined with the poetic side of the dramatic vision, as well as with the direct application of mythical situations to contemporary problems, produces a very remarkable effect: a kind of new mythology.

The result was that Greek mythology, which had already gained in systematic complexity something to balance what it had lost by the gradual diminution of its imaginative and speculative aspects, now acquired a fresh dimension. The genuine mythopoeic urge lay in the hidden past; even Homer and Hesiod were working with a long, selective and formalized tradition; and with the poetry and drama of the fifth century the ingredients were altered once again. And so there may be said to be two separate stages of conscious manipulation of Greek myths: the long stage of selection and codification culminating in Homer and Hesiod, and the stage of reinterpretation carried through especially by the great trage-dians of the fifth century. They took the transitional and schema-tized mythology as a datum, and with new interests and tech-niques constructed out of it an erratic but vivid new world of myths, in which the preoccupations of contemporary society were re-flected against the background of traditional narrative situations. Neither of these two stages of manipulation should be underrated. Both were subtle and intelligent, and required a sensitive response to the old vision; both resulted in a new mythical dimension. But neither was what one loosely calls mythopoeic; the new mythical qualities came in more or less by accident, and the nature of the primary mythical imagination remains as a continuing problem— for which the next, concluding chapter will attempt to offer, not a solution, but certain essential delimitations.

VI

Tales, Dreams, Symbols: towards a fuller understanding of Myths

1: A suggested typology of functions

The time has come to draw together what has been discovered from examining the myths of several different cultures, and as a consequence to make certain suggestions about the myth-making process itself, including the kind of imagination it involves and the relation of myths to dreams. There is no single type of myth—that has been amply confirmed in earlier chapters—and unitary theories of mythical function are largely a waste of time; but that does not mean that there may not be a primary mode of mythical imagination or expression which is then applied in different ways and to different ends.

First, the conclusions reached so far on the basis of a primarily historical approach have been briefly as follows. There is no invariable connexion between myths and gods or rituals; folktales form a special genre in which narrative values and ingenious solutions are conspicuous (chapter I). Myths can possess significance through their structure, which may unconsciously represent structural elements in the society from which they originate or typical behaviouristic attitudes of the myth-makers themselves. They may also reflect specific human preoccupations, including those caused by contradictions between instincts, wishes, and the intransigent realities of nature and society (chapter II). Consideration of Mesopotamian myths suggested that the development of nature-gods into city-gods, although in one way a simple narrative reaction, may also have had special motives: to emphasize the limitations of human institutions and relate them to the natural environment as a whole, to establish the natural and social order as products of inevitability and divine mastery, and to elicit new conclusions about natural and human fertility, nature and culture, life and death, by the juxtaposition of separate mythical episodes (chapter III). Chapter IV showed that preoccupations can be deepened rather than destroyed in an elaborated literary form like that of the Epic of Gilgamesh, and that a basic questioning of the relations between nature and culture underlies advanced formulations like those of Gilgamesh and, in Greece, the Cyclopes and Centaurs, almost as clearly as through primitive myths of the kind examined by Lévi-Strauss. In chapter V it emerged that Greek mythology as we know it must have been heightened in its purely narrative aspects as it was diminished, in the course of a long tradition, in its imaginative and speculative content. Even so certain recurrent concerns show through; and it may be added that ideas connected with cosmogony and nature-gods, perhaps because of their strong Asiatic sanction, remain substantially unmodified. Moreover the variety and systematic complexity of Greek myths, even if their original speculative or functional elements have been suppressed, create a new kind of realistic fantasy that is derivative but still mythic in essence.

This restatement brings out an emphasis on the narrative and speculative aspects of myth at the expense of their practical and ceremonial ones. That is because I have consistently been concerned to show the error of universalist theories, like those of Malinowski or the myth-and-ritual school, that deny any problem-reflecting aspects beyond what is implied by trivial aetiology. In this respect the account may be held complementary to most anthropological ones, which are biased in the other direction—for the ceremonial circumstances in which myths are most conspicuously recited naturally make the deepest impression on the direct observer.

The following might be suggested as a simplified working typology of mythical functions.[1] The first type is primarily narrative

---

[1] On the probability of a multiple overlap of functions see Percy S. Cohen, *Man*, N.S. IV, 1969, 351.

and entertaining; the second operative, iterative, and validatory; and the third speculative and explanatory. I shall say something about these three objective types in turn, and only then consider the subjective modes of imagination and expression that allow the formation of myths in the first place. That order of investigation, in a primarily inductive examination, seems permissible.

That the typology is schematic is obvious enough, and is clearly shown in the first type; for all myths are stories and depend heavily on their narrative qualities for their creation and preservation. Yet myths that are exclusively narrative, and seem to have no speculative or operative content whatever, are rare—or rather they belong to the special genres of folktales and legends, preserved through their appeal either as neat and simple tales or as elaborated relics of the past. In fact legendary myths are not only told for entertainment, and can belong rather to the second type— they glorify famous leaders and tribal history by telling of wars and victories, like parts of the Homeric *Iliad*, or disguise contradictions between national ideals and actuality, as E. R. Leach showed for ancient Israel in his article 'The Legitimacy of Solomon'.[2] At times, however, they simply use traditional memories as the basis for dramatic narrative—much of the *Iliad*, again, is obviously of this kind—or elaborate a kind of historical fiction or ethnic fantasy. Greek myths again provide an example of this kind of mythical history, and Hesiod's poem *Ehoeae*, known only in fragments and built around the description of famous heroines, is one of its clearest instances. Starting from the eponymous ancestors of the main ethnic and tribal divisions (Graecus, Hellen, Aeolus, Ion, and so forth), it proceeded to trace their descendants through more specialized local eponyms down to the heroes and heroines of the full heroic age—those involved in the legendary *gestes* of the Argonauts, the Seven against Thebes and their successors, and the Achaeans who fought at Troy. The incidents in which these legendary and often rather abstract personages are involved are usually dynastic in implication (as with Danaus and Aegyptus and their children in the events described in Aeschylus's *Supplices*), and make use of folktale situations to show how X, the prince of M, moved to N and married Y's daughter.

The operative, iterative and validatory type is a broad category, as its description shows. The myths it includes tend to be repeated

[2] *AES*, vii, 1966, 58 ff.

regularly on ritual or ceremonial occasions; and their repetition is part of their value and meaning. Sometimes it will be magical in intention, part of a ritual designed to be efficacious, to bring about a desirable continuity in nature or society. Many fertility myths are of this kind. The reversal of the sun's passage at the solstices, or the beginning or ending of seasonal rains, is aided and confirmed by the performance of imitative actions at the crucial time of year, and often by the accompaniment of myths stating the first occasion, the originative and paradigmatic occurrence, of the desired event. Just as the performance of the ritual actions is felt to impose a sympathetic compulsion on the event (or at least to inhibit its interruption) by a symbolic rehearsal of regularity, so the reciting of the myth and the re-creation of the event's mythical origins help to ensure its repetition. Mircea Eliade has given many examples of the purposeful re-establishment of this 'first time', although in making that the function of virtually all myths he has greatly exaggerated its probable scope at the expense of other aspects;[3] and Theodor H. Gaster, in his *Thespis* (New York, 1950), has sufficiently emphasized the function of some myths in some rituals of the ancient Near East. Two familiar examples neatly illustrate the genre and its implications: the repelling of the dragon Apophis in Egypt and the recital of the Creation Epic in Babylon.[4] Each night the boat of the sun-god Re, as he passes under the earth, is threatened by the serpent Apophis; each day prayers, spells and rituals are spoken and performed in the temples to avert this nightly danger, and as part of the ritual the myth of the sun-god's ancestry and creation and his archetypal defeat of his enemy is recited—as it was by the souls of the dead, and recorded on papyrus in their coffins, to help them enter the blessed

---

[3] Especially in *The Myth of the Eternal Return* (Eng. tr., New York, 1954) and *Myths, Dreams, and Mysteries* (Eng. tr., New York, 1961). The uncritical nature of much of Eliade's work is illustrated by his assumption (p. 3 of the former work) that the aboriginal Australians, as well as the ancient Mesopotamians, must in all likelihood have possessed concepts of 'being', 'non-being', 'real', and 'becoming', even if they did not have words for them; or (pp. 33, 39 ff., 171 f. of the latter) that the idea of a creative 'first time' accounts for the constancy of heroic types like the braggart, for the concept of the noble savage, and for the love-making of Dido and Aeneas. Such extravagances, together with a marked repetitiousness, have made Eliade unpopular with many anthropologists and sociologists. Percy S. Cohen, for example, outlines a theory of myth as 'anchoring the present in the past' (*Man*, N.S. IV, 1969, 343 and 349 ff.) in apparent unawareness of Eliade's not dissimilar development of Malinowski.

[4] *ANET*[2], 6 f. and 11 f. (Egypt); 332 (Babylon).

land of the west. We have already noticed the priest in the New Year festival in Babylon retire into an inner shrine to tell over to his god the myth of Marduk's rise to power and establishment of the universe. That was likewise part of a ritual, whose purpose was to ensure the continuance of that primordial disposition and the power of the king as Marduk's representative on earth.

Other myths recited in a religious context had a different purpose: to rehearse the origins and past benevolence of a particular deity in order to win his support for the present—a use that merges with that of the hymn, and is exemplified in the narrative aspects of the Homeric Hymns in Greece. But it is myth as a model or charter that constitutes the second main subdivision of iterative myth. The main practical purpose of such myths is to confirm, maintain the memory of, and provide authority for tribal customs and institutions—the whole clan system, for example, or the institution of kingship and the rules for succession; and to re-affirm and institutionalize tribal beliefs. When the Trobriand islanders tell each other myths about clan origins, they are not only instructing the adolescents in the essentials of the tribal tradition; they are also restating, often on a solemn and regular occasion, their claim to particular ancestral lands and objects. Their tribal ancestors were literally autochthonous; according to the origin myths they emerged from the earth at the very spot at which the tribe is still centred. Somewhat similarly did the ancient Athenians claim to be autochthonous, always to have belonged to Attica, never to have migrated or been displaced, and never to have under-gone ambivalent changes of territory such as their northern neighbours the Boeotians had experienced, which tended to lead to trouble with later claimants and intruders. It is significant that we know of no Athenian myth of an actual emergence from the earth. It was the migrant Boeotians who had the greater need to possess such a mythical charter to their land, and that is one reason for the elaborate tradition of the foundation of Thebes by Cadmus and the emergence of its first warriors, born from the dragon's teeth, from its very soil.

Obviously this charter use of myths overlaps legendary types whose purpose is primarily just narrative and patriotic. It also has an aetiological aspect, more noticeable in the myths of the North-American Indians (for instance) than those of the ancient cultures. If a stranger asks about the nature and purpose of a tribal custom or ceremonial object, or about the name of a local landmark, he is apt to be regaled with a mythical account of its origin, often perfunctory and sometimes of doubtful relevance.[5] Things are accepted because their genealogy can be stated; they are related to the mythical time when everything was placed in order and achieved once and for all its proper nature. Those kinds of aetiology are in a sense a charter for the rightful existence of an object or custom. This is not entirely a question of resacralizing by invoking the creative first time, as Eliade implies. There are cases for which that is true, most of them explicitly concerned with religious beliefs and rituals; but in secular instances it is more often a matter of simply fixing something in the tradition in order to establish its relevance and true entity. Such minor explanatory myths often contain little in the way of narrative but merely emphasize a mythical relationship, for instance that the moon is the wife or child of the sun. Their repetition need not be ceremonial, and the tradition is maintained and confirmed by frequent informal reminiscence.

Finally charter myths may take on a more theoretical aspect in providing emotional support for an attitude or belief. For some instances these words of Malinowski are penetrating and true: 'Myth warranting the belief in immortality, in eternal youth, in a life beyond the grave, is not an intellectual reaction upon a puzzle, but an explicit act of faith born from the innermost instinctive and emotional reaction to the most formidable and haunting idea.'[6] There certainly are myths that reflect a concern or a conviction without trying to explain it. Such myths are speculative in a limited sense; but because they are not themselves explanatory, that does not mean that explanatory myths of a speculative kind cannot exist.

Indeed the third type of mythical function, an important one by any standards, is precisely the speculative and explanatory. It is true that explicit aetiologies, of the names, origins and functions of plants, animals, men, cults, rituals, customs, institutions, cliffs, caves, mountains, rivers, tend to be superficial; in savage societies they are often appended to a myth as a matter of routine, and without touching its essential character. This kind of aetiology

---

[5] Cf., e.g., A. W. Bowers, *Mandan Social and Ceremonial Organization* (Chicago, 1950), 340 f.

[6] *Myth in Primitive Psychology* (London, 1926), 43.

overlaps (as I suggested) the function of iterative and operative myths and is part of the process of binding the volatile present to the traditionally and divinely sanctioned regularity of the past. Complex and elaborate myths, on the other hand, especially if they are strongly imaginative and fantastic, rarely have as their purpose just the provision of a concrete and specific aetiology. The more complex the myth, the more fundamental and abstract the paradox or institution it tends to explain or reflect. Its explanatory function becomes significantly wider than that of the 'just-so' story—a favourite phrase with anthropologists, and justifiably, since the more trivial kind of aetiology usually has exactly the degree of artificiality and lack of seriousness that Kipling reproduced. What is totally misleading is the application of the 'just-so' description to more serious kinds of mythical explanation. In these, problems (or less directly the preoccupations they cause) are reflected in mythical narratives. Sometimes, as we saw, their mere reflexion or expression seems to serve as an outlet or incentive for the makers of the myth, without doing much more, and touches a response in successive audiences. More frequently the myth offers an apparent way out of the problem, either by simply obfuscating it, or making it appear abstract and unreal, or by stating in affective terms that it is insoluble or inevitable, part of the divine dispensation or natural order of things, or by offering some kind of palliation or apparent solution for it. Such a solution must itself be mythical. If the problem could be resolved by rational means (in terms of the accepted belief-system of the community, however strange that might seem to us), then its solution would take the form not of a myth but of a revised terminology, an altered institution or a direct statement.

The Epic of Gilgamesh is a good example of the kind of myth, in this case in a highly elaborated form, that palliates a dilemma by revealing its divine and ineluctable origin. Gilgamesh is told on higher and higher authority that mortals cannot evade death, that it is part of the human condition even for a king with a measure of divine blood. Explicit statements of this truth are supported by a story that shows the futility of Gilgamesh's striving —that confronts him with the desert, the life of untamed nature, then with the magical world inhabited by the sole exception to the rule of mortality, Utnapishtim and his wife, an exception never to

be repeated. Myth often behaves thus even when its main persuasive technique is to reveal, in dramatic circumstances, the irreversible order of nature or decree of the gods; for it tends to
substantiate the dogma by a practical demonstration of the
impossibility of evading it. The Greek myth of Orpheus and
Eurydice is another example, additionally conditioned by fertility
tale and folktale motif. That mortals cannot as a rule be retrieved
from the dead is demonstrated by the tale of how the law was
once nearly controverted; yet in the end human frailty asserted
itself, and frailty means death.

Myths in which dilemmas are apparently resolved, rather than
being sanctified or overlaid, seem more exciting to modern critics,
since they appear to exemplify a possible approach to problems of
the kind that even we, with greater resources of knowledge and
logic, cannot begin to solve. Yet this is, of course, an illusion.
When philosophers like Plato have recourse to myth, at those
crucial points at which pure reason seems unable to advance
further, the kind of myths they choose are not those that faintly
foreshadow, or short-circuit, the methods of philosophy. They are
purely evocative and imagistic, asserting the truth of immortality
and the like by reference to jewel-studded hills or lands flowing
with milk and honey. In a way the Epic of Gilgamesh, and genuine
myth in general, does better. It is rarely just wish-fulfilment, and
the primary myth-maker may be said to stand closer to reality than
does the philosopher who uses myth as second-best.

The kinds of solution that speculative myths can offer are these:
the removal of the problem, or its effective disguise, by a tale
that implies it to be irrelevant or simply pretends that it is not
there; the resolution of a contradiction after the manner indicated
by Lévi-Strauss, which entails the introduction of a mythical
factor that serves to mediate polar extremes; the domestication,
by reducing impersonal forces to personal and thereby more
comprehensible forms, of repellent or unassimilable aspects of
nature, as indicated by Tylor and Jacobsen; and the use of other
kinds of allegory in which the transposition of a problematic
situation into a fresh set of terms seems to reveal new associations
and relationships that make the problem less severe.

To these modes of explanatory and speculative myth should be
appended the evaluative mode, which is speculative in a way. A
myth may present two commodities like gold and copper, or two

activities like farming and herding, side by side, with the primary purpose of arguing for a particular relative valuation. Common in early Mesopotamia and many savage societies, but rare in Greece, such tales represent a genre of folk-literature, like animal-fables, rather than a separate type of mythical function.[7]

Finally, one category that is not particularly well served by this suggested typology is that of eschatological myths, narratives of the imaginary world of the dead: how gods or defunct mortals pass beneath the earth, what they see on their way, the geography of the underworld and the aspect of its rulers and their subjects, the sufferings caused to the dead by neglect of their funerary rituals on earth, and so on. More conspicuous in the mythologies of the ancient world than in most others, but still represented in Norse myths and many savage complexes, the eschatological myth need be neither strongly narrative, nor speculative and explanatory (since the world of the dead is in many cases simply accepted), nor even invariably operative and practical. In Egypt, admittedly, a practical function was almost universal; the soul of the deceased had to know how to enter the world of the dead and the ritual observances and declarations to be made—that was the purpose of the Coffin texts, the Book of the Dead, and all the other funerary aide-mémoire. Similar beliefs were occasionally held in Greece, although at no very early date. The tablets buried in 'Orphic' graves in Magna Grecia etc. from the late fourth century B.C. on reminded the dead of the topography of Hades, of the springs of remembering and forgetting and of what the soul must say to prove its purity. Plato gave hints of similar Orphic beliefs, and in the fifth century Herodotus connected this kind of eschatological myth and ritual with Egypt, a not unlikely origin. Yet it can also be traced in Mesopotamia itself. Enkidu is given certain instructions before descending to the nether world to try and regain Gilgamesh's drum and drumstick, and by failing to obey them he loses any chance of a safe return (p. 108). So the concept of eschatological myths as enshrining information for the dead is known from earliest times. Conceivably this was the origin

---

[7] In the Japanese myth of Fireshine and Fireshade, for example, the former, who lives from the sea, and the latter, who lives from the land, decide to exchange their luck, which leads not only to standard folktale adventures but also to a mythical evaluation of the two ways of life and modes of hunting (E. Dale Saunders in *Mythologies*, 429 ff.). The most familiar Sumerian example is 'Dumuzi and Enkimdu', *ANET*², 41 f.; see also p. 113.

of the whole genre, and to that extent these myths might be classified with the operative and iterative type. Yet in many cases the degree and kind of detail far exceed what is needed for these purposes, and the intention seems to be simply the vivid depiction of the condition of the dead. The nature of death as a state tended to call forth a special kind of mythical imagination, not necessarily operative or truly speculative, but reflecting, without trying to cure or explain, a universal obsession or fear or wish. There are also, of course, attempts to circumvent the 'problem' of death in mythical terms, but they are distinct. They are not eschatological as such, and do not dwell lovingly, or with horrified fascination, on images of what lies ahead for all mankind; rather they recount imaginary episodes in which death is heroically or ingeniously overcome.

2: Theories of mythical expression: Cassirer and others

So far the discussion has concerned appearance and function; but myths differ as much in their inner causation as in their outward effects. In theory one should be able to establish a second typology, of motives and expressive modes, that would subsume all the subjective aspects of myths. In practice that turns out to be confusing and precarious, and I have found it more fruitful to work towards a similar result by considering in more general terms the relevance to mythical creation of certain aspects of mental and emotional activity: the use and nature of fantasy, symbols, and dreams, and unconscious and infantile modes of thought. As a preliminary, three specific suggestions about the source of mythical expression may usefully be cleared away.

The first suggestion, already encountered in a different form, is that myths are about gods, are part of religion, and therefore emerge from the same sources as religion. The nature of those sources is notoriously controversial, and E. E. Evans-Pritchard has shown the fallibility of all the confident theories that have been showered upon it.[8] That, together with the demonstration in the first chapter that myths and religion are in any event far from co-extensive, disposes of any possible utility in suggestion number one.

The second idea is part of the 'general theory' of myths and rituals advanced by Clyde Kluckhohn and likewise rather sharply

[8] In his *Theories of Primitive Religion* (Oxford, 1965).

18

criticized in the first chapter.[9] Kluckhohn was primarily concerned to establish a common psychological origin for both myths and rituals, and did so, it may be remembered, by claiming that they constitute 'a cultural storehouse of adjustive responses for individuals'. No precise indication was offered of how this store is drawn upon in the case of myths; but the 'responses' have the effect of alleviating anxiety (primarily by the comforting repetition and traditionalism of myths) and directing antisocial feelings into safe channels, presumably by a kind of Aristotelian catharsis of pity, terror and so on. Myths are originated, therefore, for the primary purpose of acting as a socially sanctioned palliative of the mental ills to which individual members of a society are prone. Kluckhohn showed that the Navaho Indians tended to be deeply anxious about physical illness, and that their myths as well as their rituals are heavily directed towards the topic of curing.[10] If one is constantly hearing traditional tales about successful cures by witch-doctors or other means, a certain relief from hypochondriacal phobias probably accrues, and it is not hard to believe that in this kind of society (in which myths and rituals do tend to work closely together) myths often have this kind of operative function. Yet that is no justification for setting up this function and its implied aetiology as part of a 'general theory'. In other kinds of society the operative function is relatively much less important, and the speculative and explanatory functions are more so.

There is a certain similarity between the theory of myths as alleviators of anxiety and aggression and another favoured by anthropologists, in particular, since the time of Boas: that myths are partly shaped by wish-fulfilment. Both theories were affected by Freudian ideas; both have their uses in that they draw attention to a not irrelevant psychological factor in some myths; both are at fault in exaggerating this factor and diverting attention from other important aspects of myths, in particular the special kind of imagination they seem to deploy. The irrelevance of both wish-fulfilment fantasy and adjustive or adaptive responses to the whole class of origin and emergence myths is just one example of the non-generality of such theories. Yet at least wish-fulfilment is implicit in many folktales, and therefore closely connected with the

---

[9] 'Myths and Rituals: a General Theory', *HTR*, xxxv, 1942, 35 ff.; see pp. 23-5 above.

[10] *Op. cit.*, 72 f.

narrative function of many myths in the broadest sense. Kluck-hohn's theory is particularly defective in that respect, but it has one compensating advantage: in reinterpreting an essentially Durkheimian view of myths and rituals in terms of personal psychology, it lays stress on the important duality of myths as both traditional, and therefore in a sense collective, and individual.

The third theory to be rejected requires a longer digression. Ernst Cassirer, who devoted more time and thought to the philosophy of myth than anyone else, held that one could achieve 'systematic insight into the "inner forms" of mythology' not by explaining its origin or identifying its special objects or motives,[11] but by determining its sources of expression and the type of consciousness that actually produces myths.[12] That is precisely the aspect that concerns us here.

There seems to me to be two main currents in Cassirer's concept of myth, both developed from earlier thinkers; for he is essentially eclectic.[13] The first involves emphasizing 'an underlying *structural* form of the mythical fantasy and mythical thinking';[14] it is because of this form that any 'factual unity of the basic mythical configurations' exists. Superficially, at least, this resembles Jung on the one hand, Lévi-Strauss on the other. The 'underlying *structural* form' is akin to Jung's archetypes, and moreover seems to be supported by a similar assumption that there are such things as 'basic mythical configurations'—the existence of which, beyond common story-patterns and common human experiences, is far from established. Yet Cassirer's conclusion is reached by a different

[11] The ethnological approach is directed to the objects of myth, for example by finding it to be concerned with natural forces or tribal totems, whereas its motives are explored by psychologists (and are held to be primarily sexual by Freudians): E. Cassirer, *Essay*, 75. Cassirer had little use for Freud, since the heavy stress on sexuality conflicted with his own conception of the dignity of culture; but Susanne K. Langer pointed out how close some of Cassirer's ideas about the nature of mythic expression were to Freud's conception of the working of the unconscious mind, and in particular of the 'dreamwork' (*The Philosophy of Ernst Cassirer* (Evanston, 1949), ed. P. A. Schilpp, 394–400).

[12] *PSF*, xviii and 20 ff.

[13] Which is fair enough, perhaps, for one who sets out to create a philosophy of culture. Yet his approach is limited even by these standards: 'Cassirer's approach to mythology is that of the neo-Kantian phenomenologist; he is not interested in mythology as such, but in the processes of consciousness which lead to the creation of myths' (M. F. Ashley Montagu in *The Philosophy of Ernst Cassirer* (Evanston, 1949), ed. P. A. Schilpp, 367).

[14] *PSF*, 19.

route from that followed by Jung. It depends on a development of Kant's views about transcendental form as the means by which the human *esprit* (to use Lévi-Strauss's word) constructs the physical world. Kant himself emphasized the relevance of the structure of language to this conception, and language is the model that led both Cassirer and Lévi-Strauss to their distinct developments of the Kantian position. For Cassirer it was the symbolic aspect of language that was primarily significant, and only then its structural aspect; for Lévi-Strauss the order is reversed.

The emphasis on symbolism is one current of Cassirer's thought about myths. The other emanates rather from the sociological and ethnological theories of Durkheim, Mauss, and Lévy-Bruhl.[15] When Cassirer tries to say how the 'mythical consciousness' forms its symbols—when he tries to describe the actual mode of mythical expression—he falls back on a modified form of the idea of 'primitive mentality' outlined by Lévy-Bruhl. This is the part of Cassirer's thesis that concerns us at present: roughly how mythical concepts, ideas, symbols (whatever we may call them) are formed.[16]

Myth is not intellectual, according to Cassirer; it is tautegorical, not allegorical—'the "image" does not represent the "thing"; it *is* the thing'.[17] Myth belongs to the sphere of affectivity and will. Just as, according to von Humboldt, man surrounds himself with words to assimilate the world of objects, so 'To the factual world which surrounds and dominates it the spirit opposes an independent image world of its own—more and more clearly and consciously it confronts the force of the "impression" with an active force of "expression"'.[18] 'The mythic mind never perceives passively, never merely contemplates things; all its observations spring from some act of participation, some act of emotion and will. Even as mythic imagination materializes in permanent forms, and presents

[15] Especially in Durkheim's *Les Formes élémentaires de la vie religieuse* (1912) and Lévy-Bruhl's *Les Fonctions mentales dans les sociétés inférieures* (Paris, 1910; translated as *How Natives Think* (London, 1926)), and *La Mentalité primitive* (Paris, 1922; translated as *Primitive Mentality* (London and New York, 1923)).

[16] His dependence on Lévy-Bruhl, whose combination of ambiguous ethnological information and 'If-I-were-a-horse' intuitionism is largely discredited, is one that he tended to deny, since he withheld credence from 'mystic causes' and, most commendably and acutely, from the idea, now refuted by Lévi-Strauss in *La Pensée sauvage*, that primitive man is incapable of *empirical* analysis: see especially E. Cassirer, *Essay*, 80–2; also p. 30 above.

[17] *PSF*, 38.   [18] *PSF*, 23.

us with definite outlines of an "objective" world of beings, the significance of this world becomes clear to us only if we can still detect, underneath it all, that dynamic sense of life from which it originally arose. Only where this vital feeling is stirred from within, where it expresses itself as love or hate, fear or hope, joy or sorrow, mythic imagination is roused to the pitch of excitement at which it begets a definite world of representations.'[19] Cassirer tried to elaborate this process of forming the mythical image in a short essay translated by Susanne Langer as *Language and Myth* (New York, 1946): 'When on the one hand, the entire self is given up to a single impresssion, is "possessed" by it and, on the other hand, there is the utmost tension between the subject and its object, the outer world; when external reality is not merely viewed and contemplated, but overcomes a man in sheer immediacy, with emotions of fear or hope, terror or wish fulfilment: then the spark jumps somehow across, the tension finds release, as the subjective excitement becomes objectified and confronts the mind as a god or a demon' (33). What Cassirer had in mind at this point is best described by Susanne Langer herself: 'The earliest products of mythic thinking are not permanent, self-identical, and clearly distinguished "gods"; neither are they immaterial spirits. They are like dream elements—objects endowed with demonic import, haunted places, accidental shapes in nature resembling something ominous—all manner of shifting, fantastic images which speak of Good and Evil, of Life and Death, to the impressionable and creative mind of man. Their common trait is...the quality of *holiness*.'[20]

One cannot help admiring the passion and confidence of Cassirer's vision and the poetical vigour of its expression. Yet it is purely conjectural, and rather improbable at that. Cassirer knew no more than anyone else about how myths are created—no more than can be inferred from the procedures of poets and medieval mystics or the necessarily defective observations of anthropologists. Moreover what he was describing seems to be primarily his idea of religious rather than specifically mythical thinking. That is strongly suggested by the 'god or demon' that confronts the excited mind in the last quotation from him above. Susanne Langer's summary widens the scope to include strange and

[19] *PSF*, 69.
[20] *The Philosophy of Ernst Cassirer* (Evanston, 1949), ed. P. A. Schilpp, 387.

sacred-seeming places, and we recognize even more clearly that we are moving within the purlieus of the old 'animistic' view of the origins of religion. According to that view, developed from the time of E. B. Tylor onwards, everything that made a deep impression on 'primitive man' was taken as a spirit; and it is really that conception that underlies Cassirer's vivid description of the 'symbol' that is 'expressed' as a god or demon when the mind is in a high state of emotion. Cassirer himself may have thought it legitimate to work on the basis of a theory of the origins of religion, since he considered mythical thought (although according to him it originates from magic rather than religion itself, and is strongly affected by dream experience and ritual) to be 'continuous' with religious thought.[21] I have already suggested reasons for doubting that.

Cassirer's attempt to describe in detail the formation of mythico-religious images only emphasizes still more the improbability of the suggested process, or at least its arbitrary nature. We are asked to visualize a person detecting the 'dynamic sense of life' from which the world arose, being stirred from within by some strong emotion (love or hate, fear or hope, and so forth), then becoming so excited that his imagination 'confronts the force of the "impression" with an active force of "expression"' by begetting a 'definite world of representations'. That may or may not explain why a 'savage' sees a terrifying spirit at work in a thunderstorm; it certainly does not explain many of the essential qualities of myths, either in their objects (giants, heroes, supernatural animals, and so on) or, more to the point, in their actions. As I implied earlier (pp. 30 f.), there is no overwhelming reason for believing that an Amerindian emergence myth, a Mesopotamian fertility myth, or a prototypical Greek hero myth, should be created under conditions of extreme excitement, indeed solely in response to that excitement and a feeling of the world's vitality. This whole conception is a myth in a different sense, compounded of Tylorian animism and a keen but in many ways nineteenth-century imagination.

Cassirer also denies that myths have any intellectual component. Presumably he is reacting against intellectualist and specifically allegorical types of interpretation; and it is probably true that, although allegorical aspects cannot be discounted, they are secondary, not part of the mythical imagination as such. Yet

[21] Magic, *PSF*, 16; dream, *ibid.*, 36; ritual, *Essay*, 79; religious thought, *ibid.*, 87.

Lévi-Strauss's structural interpretation and Freud's idea of 'dreamwork' equally emphasize the danger of absolutely excluding unconscious forms of intellection from primarily imaginative processes; and even Cassirer seems to allow them in, although in a much less probable way. According to him, the images projected by the mythical imagination may themselves imply a special kind of understanding. Again Susanne Langer gives a convenient exposition: 'mythic symbols do not give rise to discursive understanding; they do beget a kind of understanding, but not by sorting out concepts and relating them in a distinct pattern; they tend, on the contrary, merely to bring together great complexes of related ideas, in which all distinctive features are merged and swallowed'.[22] The products of mythic expression are 'images charged with meaning, but the meanings remain implicit, so that the emotions they command seem to be centred on the image rather than on anything it merely conveys; in the image, which may be a vision, a gesture, a sound-form (musical image) or a word as readily as an external object, many meanings may be concentrated, many ideas telescoped and interfused, and incompatible emotions simultaneously expressed'.[23]

Again, all this seems exaggerated. In terms of 'understanding', a symbol is *of* something—possibly of a complex of ideas and emotions, but not an indefinite and self-contradictory one. Its meanings are conditioned by those of other symbols or subjects with which it is associated; a myth is, after all, and unlike a religious feeling, a statement about action. Cassirer himself recognized this: the vital principle of myth is dynamic, not static, and 'is describable only in terms of action'.[24] Yet in describing the act of mythical imagination he concentrates on the static symbol, and assigns to this the multiplicity of meanings that ought rather to be looked for in the whole structure of a myth and in the mutual relations of its subjects—just as the meaning of language cannot be sought in its static word-symbols but depends on their dynamic relations with each other.

Cassirer's positive contribution to the study of mythical forms of imagination and expression lies primarily, as it seems to me, in his emphasis on their emotional nature. Most of his description of the act of myth-making is pure fiction; yet it is permeated, like

---

[22] *The Philosophy of Ernst Cassirer* (Evanston, 1949), ed. P. A. Schilpp, 388.
[23] *Op. cit.*, 395 f.   [24] *Essay*, 79.

all his work, by flashes of acute diagnosis. One such perception, that mythical thinking is distinguished 'as much by its *concept of causality* as by its *concept of the object*',[25] may suitably lead to a more positive examination of the relation of myth to imagination and fantasy.

3: Fantasy and dreams

Throughout this investigation it has become steadily clearer that myths, unless they have been reduced to the more straight-forward kind of folktale, or never risen much above it, make use of a special kind of imagination that I have called, with no great precision or subtlety, 'fantasy'. Fantasy deals in events that are impossible by real-life standards; but in myths it tends to exceed the mere manipulation of the supernatural and express itself in a strange dislocation of familiar and naturalistic connexions and associations. That is what Cassirer meant by referring to the mythical concept of causality. At the same time mythical fantasy does operate, to some extent, upon the static objects, the things, personages and places of myths. It is useful, for the purposes of analysis, to separate this faculty from that which manipulates these objects in such unpredictable ways. Apart from anthropo-morphic deities, in which the element of fantasy is relatively low, the fantastic figures of myths tend to be giants, ogres, monsters, animals with supernatural powers (whether of help and advice, prophecy, hostility, creativity, or transformation), heroes who can fly, or become invisible, or otherwise change their appearance, or climb up to the sky. To these must be added fantastic objects like magical rings, talismanic or doom-laden heirlooms, branches or brands that contain a man's soul, and natural phenomena full of mysterious power. In some cases the whole of the fantasy is focused on magic itself and the imaginative power is lessened (for magic is a kind of system); but usually the invention is less circum-scribed. Certain fantasies, like ogres, may be projections of child-hood terrors and imaginings, just as heroes who can fly through the air, and easily defeat terrible opponents, reflect subconscious aspirations to absolute power and freedom. Most of the recurrent figures of myth carry a load of psychological implications of this kind, as well as other less personal associations acquired in the narrative tradition itself.

The dynamic aspect of mythical fantasy is both more revealing

[25] *PSF*, 43.

and more typical. It includes more than causality; indeed, *all* the rules of normal action, normal reasoning and normal relationships may be suspended or distorted. The hero suddenly becomes the villain or vice versa; minor actions turn out to have profound consequences; transformations of humans into trees, animals, natural substances or stars require no more explanation than, and seem just as arbitrary as, the sudden shifts in time and space. Yet not everything is arbitrary. Quite often the process of events is regular for a time; or a special kind of logic, rather like that of the Mad Hatter's tea-party, shows itself to be at work: a logic that often depends on unusual categorizations or verbal discriminations. Above all there is no consistency of tone or action, and many problems are left unanswered; how, for example, did men perpetuate themselves, in the imaginations of those whose myths asserted that women were created later or only subsequently acquired sexual organs and the power of childbirth? The mythical fantasy finds that kind of question irrelevant, or at least it provides, often enough, no answer.

An important pair of questions must be interjected. Is what is being described as mythical fantasy simply identical with what Lévi-Strauss means by 'la pensée sauvage'? And in describing it as permeated by strange dislocations, and so on, am I merely applying the standards of Aristotelian logic to other logical or para-logical systems to which they are irrelevant? To take the second question first, I do not think so; although it may be conceded that there is a great deal in this concept of 'fantasy' that is undefined and potentially misleading. In writing of strange dislocations I am intentionally using my own cultural and logical standards as part of a descriptive analysis directed towards others who share them. As to whether this 'fantasy' is simply a manifestation of the ordinary thought-processes of 'savage' or tribal peoples: in a sense, so far as *their* myths are concerned, it obviously is. Yet a myth that includes such 'fantasy' can occur in other cultures, like the ancient Mesopotamian, where ordinary thinking seems to bear little resemblance to Lévi-Strauss's 'pensée sauvage'. Indeed his diagnosis of this *pensée* does not really accord with my suggested summary of the distinguishing qualities of many myths, except in the negative quality of strangeness by Aristotelian standards; for example he emphasizes the systematic nature of savage thought in general, whereas myths, although by the structuralist view systematic in a way, are in many respects quite definitely unsystematic.

To some extent in their objects, but more conspicuously in their dislocation of normal associations and connexions, myths are strongly reminiscent of dreams.[26] Dreams, like myths, present us with a fantastic *mélange* of subjects, places, periods, sequences and styles. Their emotional tone is liable to change disconcertingly from tranquillity to terror, from deep involvement to passionless observation.[27] Like myths they have an odd propensity for switching from minute detail, or a kind of visual brilliance and heightened realism, to a colourless detachment and abstraction.[28] Such similarities between myths and dreams have impressed themselves on people of many different cultures, most clearly on the simplest and least sophisticated. The primitive Australians with their creative Dreamtime, and North-American Indians like the Pima, the Yuma, the Mohave, the Hopi and the Navaho, with their conviction that myths are dreamed, that this is how they occur, testify to the similar appearance of the two modes of imagination or expression—an appearance that has given rise to the unproductive idea, bandied from Reik, Abraham and Rank to Freud and Jung, that myths are in some sense the collective dreams of the tribe.

There is no point in exaggerating this illogical character of myths. Some of them, even among primitive tribes (where the progressive rationalizing of fantastic elements is least to be expected), are no more than rather spasmodic in their action. Myths, after all, are stories, and that imposes a degree of consequentiality on their development. Even dreams can occasionally appear as straightforward narratives: for example Maury's famous dream of being guillotined. Yet it remains true that most myths that have

---

[26] The rearrangement or reversal of temporal and logical sequences in myths as in dreams was noted by Otto Rank (e.g. *The Myth of the Birth of the Hero* (1909, Eng. tr. 1913, 72), and accepted by Freud.

[27] When we describe certain myths as having a 'dream-like quality' the conception is probably slightly different, of a vague aura of pleasurable indistinctness.

[28] Dreams are also unpredictable in their *mode* of expression. One subject or image may give rise to another by a determinable form of connexion, but the second subject may take a quite different form from that of the first, and for no clear reason: not as a visual picture, for example, but as a written word, or a point on a map, or something overheard in a conversation. It may be indirectly represented, by a verbal similarity or a metaphor, or grotesquely disguised by normally incompatible characteristics. The selection of one mode of expression rather than another often seems random; and something of the same quality is detectable in many myths.

not been obviously tamed and domesticated possess this quality of dislocation. Among instances considered earlier, the Sumerian myth of Enki and Ninhursag, the Bororo myth of Geriguiaguiatugo and the Aborigine myth of the ogre Guruwelin are clear examples. Even the Greek myths concerning Prometheus, and especially the creation of the first woman, strike one as curiously arbitrary in places. That may represent an original quality in the tale, or it may be an accident of the literary tradition—a tradition that has had time to lose the emotional emphases of living myth but not time enough to complete the process of rationalization. On the other hand the probably archaic myth of the rape of Persephone as she gathered flowers, and her detention in the underworld palace of Hades for part of each year after she had eaten the seed of pomegranate, is logical enough in its sequences of thought once certain basic assumptions are granted: that there is an underworld, that it has an anthropomorphic ruler, that sharing someone's food creates an obligation, and so on.

Certain mythical motifs are probably drawn from the dreams of individuals; but can we accept the view of the Hopi or Mohave that all myths are so derived? My first reaction is to agree with Cassirer, who found that although 'the whole life and activity of many primitive peoples, even down to trifling details, is determined and governed by their dreams', yet 'the animistic theory which attempts to derive the whole content of myth from this one source, which explains myth primarily as a confusion and mixture of dream experience and waking experience, is unbalanced and inadequate in this form, given it primarily by Tylor'.[29] Yet in making this kind of judgement we depend on our own experience of dreams and myths, which is likely to be heavily defective in both respects. We know almost nothing about the real effects of myths, and we are not good at remembering dreams. Recent research reveals that most human beings dream each night for much of the time. Westerners seem to have up to ten separate dreams a night, most of which they forget, or fail to bring into their consciousness, on waking.[30] That means that a considerable proportion of our total mental experience is undergone as dreaming and is largely

---

[29] *PSF*, 36.

[30] See e.g. William C. Dement, 'The Psychophysiology of Dreaming', *The Dream and Human Societies* (Berkeley, 1966), ed. G. E. von Grunebaum and Roger Caillois, 77 ff., with bibliography.

devoid of waking logic. The more practised at remembering dreams an individual or society is—and that will depend on an awareness of the importance of dreams—the more he or it is likely to be affected by dream modes of thought in waking life. Aboriginal Australians who talk of the creative past as 'Dreamtime', who consider that that was the real world, are not incapable of distinguishing dreams from waking experience, but they are aware of the former as equally important to them as the latter. People like this are quite likely to depend heavily on dreams for the formation of their myths; whereas other primitive tribal groups (or more developed cultures), being less skilled in remembering dreams, will depend upon them less.[31]

Substantial claims are being made at present for the new research on dreams, based on the discovery that the act of dreaming reveals itself by rapid eye movements and a fast-wave encephalograph reading.[32] At present it seems that going short of dreaming impairs the mental stability of the individual. The reason may be physiological, for example because dreaming somehow stimulates production of a chemical necessary for other functions of the brain, rather than physio-psychological, for example because dreaming clears the brain of useless and clogging memories.[33] In any event it seems probable that earlier psychological explanations of the functions of dreams, namely that they serve to release repressions, or to compensate for deficiencies of the waking personality, or to vent subconscious anxieties and aspirations, or even to protect sleep, will be swamped in the near future by mechanistic explanations in terms of the electrical or chemical operation of the brain.

[31] There is, of course, an enormous Freudian literature on the derivation of myths from dreams. Géza Róheim's *The Gates of the Dream* (New York, 1951) is typical of the arbitrary use of evidence in which this literature abounds; but see Alan Dundes, *American Anthropologist*, LXIV, 1962, 1032–51.

[32] In a more sinister kind of activity, cats are being reduced by the thousand to sleepless gibbering wrecks to convince the rather slow minds of some young research workers of the obvious—or alternatively to save a little time and trouble. It appears, for instance, that if you want to be sure of having a non-seeing cat for a few hours, it is easier to remove its eyes than temporarily to paralyse its optic nerve. A great deal of this work seems to the layman both needlessly cruel and pointlessly repetitious. In the end, no doubt, it will succeed in throwing a little new light on the physiological and psychological function of dreaming.

[33] For this last idea see Christopher Evans, 'Sleeping and Dreaming—a new "Functional" Theory', *Trans-action*, V (2), 1967, 45–7. If the activity is interrupted and the dream is recognized as such the memory is not erased, according to this theory, but is made more permanent.

And yet certain of those psychological operations will, I suspect, remain an important part of the emotional functioning of the whole personality, even if they are not primary in nature but to some extent a product of social evolution. It is hard to believe that Freud, for all his excesses, did not establish certain general truths about the emotional effects of unconscious intellection.

I return to consider an older idea that is still widespread in its effects and cannot be passed over: that in some sense myths are the dream-thinking of the people. It was Otto Rank who seems to have originated this formulation, first in his *Der Künstler* of 1907. According to his *The Myth of the Birth of the Hero* (1909, Eng. tr. 1913, 6), the myth is 'a dream of the masses of the people'. In the same year Karl Abraham stated in his *Dreams and Myths* (1909, Eng. tr. (New York, 1913), 72) that the myth is 'a fragment preserved from the infantile psychic life of the race, and dreams are the myths of the individual'. These men belonged to the circle of Freud, and Freud himself had sown the germ of the idea as early as the first edition of his *The Interpretation of Dreams* (1900; standard ed., London, 1953, v, 345), although it is more clearly expressed in his brief *On Dreams* of the following year: 'Dream-symbolism extends far beyond dreams: it is not peculiar to dreams, but exercises a similar dominating influence on representations in fairy-tales, myths and legends, in jokes and in folklore. It enables us to trace the ultimate connections between dreams and these latter productions' (standard ed., v, 685). This lacks the idea of myths as collective dreams—an idea that Freud seems to have accepted from Rank, and eventually developed into his bizarre theory of the growth of the Oedipus myth from a myth-maker's account of strange events in the primal horde. In 'The Relation of the Poet to Day-Dreaming' (1908) Freud wrote that 'it seems extremely probable that myths, for example, are the distorted vestiges of the wish-phantasies of whole nations—the age-long dreams of young humanity'.[34]

It was from Freudian writers that Jane Harrison derived the same idea, expressed in her *Epilegomena to the Study of Greek Religion* (Cambridge, 1921) as follows: 'The myth is a fragment of the soul-life, the dream-thinking of the people, as the dream is the myth of the individual.'[35] This kind of language still finds

[34] S. Freud, *Collected Papers*, IV (London, 1925), 182.
[35] *Op. cit.*, 32. The words are virtually Abraham's.

a reflexion in Cornford: 'Finally there may come a time when rational thinking consciously asserts itself, and the foremost intellects of the race awaken out of the dream of mythology.'[36] More important, Carl Jung (originally, of course, a member of the Freudian circle) accepted the idea in its essentials, although with an obscure modification: 'The conclusion that the myth-makers thought in much the same way as we still think in dreams is almost self-evident. . . But one must certainly put a large question-mark after the assertion that myths spring from the "infantile" psychic life of the race. They are on the contrary the most mature product of that young humanity.'[37]

One trouble about all these statements is their assumption that 'the people' has a collective mind, and one that could have dreams. At least Durkheim had evaded this difficulty with his idea of 'collective representations', for, as E. E. Evans-Pritchard neatly put it, 'religious ideas are produced by a synthesis of individual minds in collective action, but once produced they have a life of their own'.[38] It is true that collective ritual behaviour, mass-hysteria or other kinds of emotive social action can impress their participants with new ideas that belong to the occasion. These ideas then persist—but in the minds of individuals. Nevertheless they are in a sense collective. What the Freudians were hinting at, and what Jung eventually made explicit, was the different concept of a collective *unconscious*—a concept that could derive no support in logic from Durkheim's theory. Moreover the Freudians seemed to imply that the race is like an individual who grows up from infancy to adulthood; myths are crude and chaotic because they are remembered relics of the psychic life of the race in its infancy, according to Abraham, and they are remembered much as you or I might remember an incident of our childhood.[39]

[36] F. M. Cornford, *The Unwritten Philosophy* (Cambridge, 1950), 42.

[37] C. G. Jung, *Symbols of Transformation* (1911; Eng. tr. of the 4th ed., New York and London, 1956, 24).

[38] *Theories of Primitive Religion* (Oxford, 1965), 63.

[39] This approach is only a little less naive than that of J. A. MacCulloch in his once-popular *The Childhood of Fiction* (London and New York, 1905), 1: '"Tell me a story", cries the child; and in the childhood of the race there was heard the same cry.' The result, of course, was a myth!

4: Archetypes and symbols

It must be said to Jung's credit that in the end he extricated himself from this particular fallacy. Whether or not his emendation of infantile memory to 'the most mature product' of young humanity was intended to point in this direction, he was in the process of formulating a more serious theory of the 'collective unconscious' —a theory which, although he confused himself and everyone else by the term 'archetype', deserves our consideration. The theory, most plainly summarized in his last work,[40] is in short that all human beings possess similar inborn tendencies to form certain general symbols, and that these symbols manifest themselves through the unconscious mind in myths, dreams, delusions and folklore. The positive evidence advanced by Jung is that such general symbols—wise old man, earth-mother, divine child, the self, god, the sun, the animus and anima (idea of man in a woman and vice versa), the number four, the cross, the mandala, and a few others—do as a matter of experience constantly recur in myths and dreams, and therefore must have some general collective origin.

It is on this point of actual occurrence that it is simplest to refute Jung. Although his numerous books, and those of followers like K. Kerényi, are replete with assertions that these symbols are of frequent and universal occurrence, no convincing statistical evidence has ever been presented or even attempted. In the words of Jean Piaget, 'Jung has an amazing capacity for construction, but a certain contempt for logic and rationality, which he contracted through daily contact with mythological and symbolic thought, has made him inclined to be content with too little in the way of proof. The better to understand the reality of which he speaks, he adopts an anti-rationalist attitude, and the surprising comparisons of which he has the secret cannot fail sometimes to disturb the critical reader.'[41] Jung has somehow succeeded in persuading many people that his general symbols are of universal occurrence; but the probability is that they are nothing of the sort. Analysis of any of the cultural sets of myths considered in this

[40] That is, in his contribution (the first chapter), written in 1960, to *Man and his Symbols* (London, 1964), of which he was the main editor.

[41] J. Piaget, *Play, Dreams and Imitation in Childhood* (Eng. tr., New York and London, 1951), 196.

book is sufficient to dispose of the idea. The earth-mother, the divine child, the anima, and so on, simply do not occur often (or specifically) enough to make a general theory necessary or acceptable; and neither do the typical myth-sequences (swallowing by a sea-monster, betrayal of the hero, and so on) that are implied, rather puzzlingly, to enshrine these symbols.

In so far as such ideas or images do occur they may just as probably, or more probably, arise out of the common experience of all humanity during the early years of life; the wise old man (but is he really a frequent element of myths and dreams?) obviously being a memory of one's father at a certain stage, the sun being a force that impresses every human being without the invocation of racial memory, and so forth. Piaget's life-work has been to show how children progressively formulate the concepts of space, time, objective existence, causation, and the working of the outside world in general, from infancy upwards. His observations of infants and young children have demonstrated the progressive distinction of the self from the outside world, and shown how simple infantile imitation is gradually developed, first into the use of symbols, then into the capacity for generalization and abstraction. His opinion that Jung's general symbols could in theory be the result of common processes of symbolic assimilation in childhood, and in practice are, is going to take a great deal of refuting.[42]

As for Jung's 'contempt for logic and rationality', a typically Jungian use of argument permeates the book which he wrote in

---

[42] Piaget considers that symbolic thought is pre-logical thought, in the sense that a growing child proceeds from images and symbols to intuitions to conceptions. Only at the last stage does he reach the world of logic. Piaget supports this idea by an adaptation of the Freudian view that symbols are condensed and displaced, and by the Jungian conception of 'non-directed thought'. The theory may be too neat, but it leads to a more than usually acceptable version of the 'childhood of the race' idea. Piaget considers that some of the concepts of the Presocratic thinkers in Greece correspond with those of children between the ages of seven and ten today: for instance their explanation of stars as made out of air or mist (explanation by identification of substance). 'The more primitive a society, the more lasting the influence of the child's thought on the individual's development' (op. cit., 198): in this way Piaget avoids comparing the Presocratic stage with the 'infancy' of the race, but rather suggests that, as a more complex logic than was available to them developed, so it would be adopted in later generations by children after the age of ten. The Presocratics, who did not have this logic, remained in a stage of 'childish' symbolism and intuition. I cite this view as a comparatively reasonable development of the 'childhood of the race' idea, not because I am entirely convinced by it in relation to the Presocratics.

association with Kerényi, called *Introduction to a Science of Mythology* (Eng. tr., London, 1951)—the very title, with its amazing implication that the study of myths can ever be a science, takes one back to Max Müller's *Contributions to the Science of Mythology* of 1897. The work purports to deal with the Eleusinian myth and the nature of Kore/Persephone, and in its second section, on the child archetype (by which he here means the symbol itself), Jung includes the following statements: 'Today we can hazard the formula that the archetypes appear in myths and fairy-tales just as they do in dreams and in the products of psychotic fantasy' (100); 'the child-motif represents the pre-conscious, childhood aspect of the collective psyche' (111); 'the mythological idea of a child is emphatically not a copy of the empirical child, but a *symbol* clearly recognizable as such: it is a wonder-child, a divine child...and not—this is the point—a human child' (111 n.); 'The "child" is born out of the womb of the unconscious, begotten out of the depths of human nature, or rather out of living Nature herself' (123). These extracts suggest that this work has certain limitations as a practical demonstration of the applicability of a general theory.

And yet Jung was a master of intuition. Nothing in his arguments makes it probable that ideas or symbols actually are inherited; but it is important to concede that no particular reason is so far known why they should not be. One of Jung's successes, indeed, has been his reiteration of the analogy of instinct. 'The archetype is a tendency to form...representations of a motif—representations that can vary a great deal in detail without losing their basic pattern...They are, indeed, an instinctive *trend*, as marked as the impulse of birds to build nests, or ants to form organised colonies.'[43] At first it might seem easy to refute such a simple parallelism between mind and body, concepts that seem to be in our heads and instincts that seem to be in our bones. Yet the mind has a physiological basis, and there may be no obvious reason why modes of thinking should not be inherited just as much as modes of behaving (even apart from those that arise from the morphology of the body itself)—such as those that cause fish to force their way up long and dangerous rivers to spawn. Neurologists disagree about whether the chromosomes can contain enough genetic information to determine the connexions of many millions

[43] *Man and his Symbols*, 67 and 69.

of nerve cells in the brain. Professor M. Jacobson, at least, thinks that some cells are so determined, whereas others are able to make new connexions and so account for freshly acquired memory.[44] But if some cells were genetically determined, might they not carry instructions leading to the formation of mental concepts no less than of physical structure and instinctual behaviour? If so, certain of these concepts could be common to all or most human beings. That might conceivably explain how certain motifs (like the separation of earth and sky), not apparently explicable by similar environmental factors or common experiences in growing up, tend to recur in the myths and folklore of quite separate societies— for that, unlike Jung's collective symbols, is a proved phenomenon, and one that has given rise to endless controversy about the probabilities of the diffusion of myths as against their separate evolution.

It may be felt that Jung's idea of basic mythical symbols is useful, even if the rest of the theory of inherited and collective archetypes has to be drastically remodelled in order to keep it alive, or totally abandoned for lack of supporting evidence. I have already outlined a loose distinction between static and dynamic fantasy—between imaginative *subjects* like hostile giants or jewel-studded landscapes and fantastic *actions* involving strange relationships and the dislocation of everyday experience. It is tempting to replace the word 'subjects' in this context by 'symbols'; linguists talk about words as symbols, and using their example Lévi-Strauss refers to the agents and objects of myths, the subjects of relationships, as symbols. But Jung means something different, and adheres to a much older usage (seen also in Freud's theory of dream-symbols) by which symbols are static subjects that bear some indirect reference outside themselves. Using 'symbol' in this sense, then (so that a walking-stick in a dream would be held by Freud to represent, be a symbol of, the phallus), can it be said that all or most of the emphasized subjects of dreams or myths are symbols? Freud thought so; modern psychologists assign greater weight to other, possibly random elements in dreams; but even so it would still be generally agreed that dreams tend to be symbolic for much of the time. Yet are they statically or dynamically symbolic? In the latter case, an episode or action in a dream would refer by some metaphorical means to an action or

[44] *Science*, 7 February 1969, 543–7.

idea (or a group of such actions or ideas) outside the dream, probably belonging to waking experience, personal in nature and relative in value. In the former, dreams would consist of more or less unimportant transitions between significant static symbols, and the meaning of the dream would be derived mainly from separate and absolute implications of each of these symbols. That is no doubt an exaggerated formulation of the distinction; even Freud thought that the circumstances in which dream-symbols occurred were relevant, as were the particular associations of the patient. Yet his belief that some symbols have a broadly universal meaning whenever they occur in dreams has tended to confirm a similar view about myths.[45]

An analogous idea was independently developed by Cassirer who, as we saw, believed that religious fantasies and myths are created by the expressing of symbols that are somehow concentrations of meanings and emotions. For Jung, likewise, the static image or mythological motif produced by an archetype could have complex implications: for example 'The child-motif is a picture of certain *forgotten* things in our childhood'. There is some similarity, indeed, between his idea and Cassirer's of how a myth is formed: 'The primitive mentality does not *invent* myths, it *experiences* them. Myths are original revelations of the pre-conscious psyche, involuntary statements about unconscious psychic happenings.'[46]

My purpose in citing these particular theories, which can hardly be described as very convincing accounts of the origins or nature of myths, is to draw attention to the concept of the static symbol, or more strictly the static symbol with dynamic potentialities. This conception has been accepted by many more than would subscribe to the whole theory of a Jung or a Cassirer. For many people, statements like 'myths make use of symbols' imply that a myth derives any significance it may possess from its inclusion of one or more special symbols, each of which in itself represents some important and complex emotion or some widespread but not easily expressible intuition about the world. I believe this way of

[45] Freud's view is exemplified by this passage from *On Dreams* (§ xii, added in 1911; standard ed., v, 683 f.): 'There are some symbols which bear a single meaning almost universally...rooms represent women and their entrances and exits the openings of the body...Sharp weapons, long and stiff objects, such as tree-trunks and sticks, stand for the male genital; while cupboards, boxes, carriages or ovens may represent the uterus.'

[46] C. G. Jung and K. Kerényi, *Introduction to a Science of Mythology*, 111 and 101.

understanding the symbolic aspect of myths to be largely erroneous. It is undeniable that certain myths do contain static symbols of this kind—some of those adduced by Freud and Jung, even. More important, recurrent subjects like ogres may carry with them special psychological associations of terror, revulsion, or other strong emotion, and therefore have a symbolic value independent of the actions in which they are involved. Yet many myths do not contain, or at least do not emphasize, such symbols—most of the myths considered in earlier chapters, for example. Many of them have a symbolic reference or set of references, but the reference is dynamic and allegorical in a complex way; it implies the transposition of whole episodes or situations on to different semantic and emotional levels. Most of the operative and speculative functions of myth entail a degree of this kind of transference, and even the structural interpretation of myths sees their meaning as implicit in relationships, not static subjects.

Beyond emphasizing once again that myths, like dreams, vary enormously in their mode and scope of symbolic meanings I do not want to labour this point any further. Yet it is important, if valid, since it disposes of the idea that myths are created by the emission of pregnant symbols, rather like a rabbit having babies. My own view of the possible origin of myths lays much more stress on the gradual development of narrative structures, of stories, with complex symbolic implications coming in almost incidentally.

5: Possibilities of origin

Most investigations of the mode of mythical expression are based on the premise that one can determine the origin of myths. Yet perhaps the best one can do is discover how myths seem to have been used in those cultures of the past for which sufficient documentation exists. This has been the primary aim of the present enquiry. Nevertheless the problem of origin keeps obtruding itself, because function, growth and origin are all interconnected. The study of the nature of religions has been seriously hindered in the past by theories of origin; and that study is clearly analogous at many points to the study of myths. Yet what was wrong about those theories was their dogmatism, together with the assumption that one single type of origin could be clearly identified. It was against this position that the strictures of E. E. Evans-Pritchard were most damaging. The consideration of *possibilities* of origin is another matter; and in my opinion the understanding of religion would have been the poorer if, in the interest of epistemological perfectionism, that kind of consideration had never been undertaken. Similarly, while it is certain that how a myth originates in a non-literate culture can never be determined, and doubtful whether in any case all myths originate in the same manner, it seems theoretically justifiable and practically useful to make certain suggestions about possible alternatives. One must naturally remain aware, in so doing, of the limitations of *a priori* arguments in a field about which so little is known, and of the restricted value of personal intuitions on the part of literate, demythologized and Aristotelianized academics.

Some critics have found it more probable that myths started life as simple tales, which then acquired the special characteristics of myths, than that those characteristics, as revealed by different ultimate functions (validatory, explanatory, and so on), shaped the tales from the very beginning. Their preference, attractive as it might seem at first sight, rests on a hypothetical model that may be too simple and is certainly quite conjectural, whereby story-telling for its own sake follows relatively quickly upon the development of language itself, and its earliest subjects are actual experiences or simple constructions based upon them.[47] I do not believe one can usefully generalize about the relative chronology of practical, as distinct from merely gratifying, communication. Some stories in some cultures may very well have performed some useful function (like embodying a lesson or preserving a necessary piece of information) from the very beginning; and again I emphasize that cultures could have varied in this respect.

It is certainly more prudent to assume that the narrative and functional aspects of myths tended in many cases to develop side by side, rather than to rely on uncertain analogies with language, or systems of communication in general, and end with the conviction that mere narratives always preceded functional myths, or conversely that the very idea of story-telling must have been determined by specific functional needs. No kind of evidence I can imagine could finally settle the choice, even for a single culture. There are virtually no cultures left that have not been affected,

[47] Cf., e.g., Joseph Fontenrose, *The Ritual Theory of Myth* (Berkeley, 1966), 57. The opposite opinion is implicit in the idea, influentially propagated by the Grimm brothers, that folktale is a kind of detritus of myth.

indirectly at least, by literacy; if there are, they already possess myths of some kind and are therefore conditioned in relation to the possible development of new ones. In any case, as is well known, such a development could not be studied by anthropologists without further distorting the whole experiment.

Myths are at the very least tales that have been passed down from generation to generation, that have become traditional. For them to be more than transitory, the kind of tale that is forgotten almost as soon as told, they must possess certain special qualities. So must their tellers, and that further complicates the issue. It may be significant that the development and preservation of tales in modern non-literate cultures in which oral epics flourished until recently were strongly affected by the singers' techniques and by their relation to their particular society. Mostly, singers acquired songs from other, more experienced, singers, and they seem to have introduced innovations mainly by selection and rearrangement, sometimes almost accidentally. Whether or not a song or a tale becomes traditional—that is, enters the repertory maintained among more or less professional exponents—depends not only on *its* own qualities but also on *their* tastes, methods, ambitions, and limitations. *Mutatis mutandis* this is likely to apply to the tellers of tales in other and simpler societies. The story-teller himself must have been an important and largely unknown factor in the formation of tales and in their preservation over the vital first two generations—more broadly, up to the point at which they became firmly traditional.

The qualities that make a tale traditional, that establish it in a culture, are either narrative or functional or both together, and I have stressed the impossibility of determining a specific, let alone a universal, formula for the process. It may be more useful to ask at what point the special, fantastic quality that we have seen to be the distinguishing mark of many myths might have entered the tradition. I am doubtful if, unless that kind of fantasy is part of the whole way of life of the society in question, it can have belonged to tales in their very first development, or have entered them fully fledged as part of their earliest operational applications —even if it is often in those fantastic dislocations that the underlying usefulness of a developed myth most clearly reveals itself. I have pointed out that fantasy and dislocation are not qualities that Lévi-Strauss implies to be essential to the thought-processes of tribal cultures; neither are there reasons for seeing them as innately rooted in the mental operations of early Mesopotamians. There are admittedly certain cultures, notably of the ancient Egyptians and the aboriginal Australians, in which fantasy and dislocation seem to have been almost a regular part of life. In the former, at least, this was due to priestly and ritual syncretism at least as much as to any innate mode of thought.

Supposing, then, that fantasy and dislocation affected tales gradually: how and why might they have done so? All one can do, once again, is to list possibilities. It is possible, for example, that these qualities occasionally arose as an incident of the tradition of story-telling itself, whereby themes were displaced or carelessly amalgamated in ways that seemed somehow effective, and so were preserved, or that stimulated the teller to unplanned flights of the imagination. It is possible, too, that certain tales made use of material derived from dreams, and reproduced their imaginative and chaotic qualities. I have already suggested that the obvious similarities between some dreams and some myths imply a degree of interdependence, at least in societies that are particularly dream-conscious. The reason for such similarities might also be the dependence of each manifestation (dreams, myths) on the sub-conscious mind, so that fantasy and dislocation would enter myths directly from that source. Again, however, it may be easier to believe in a gradual moulding of narrative material, a progressive extension of imagination and the unreal by the incorporation of dream-sequences (in accordance with unconscious or only partly conscious preferences and responses), than to accept the essentially romantic idea of myths as simply welling up directly out of the unconscious.

A third possible factor is a concern with the supernatural for its own sake—with beings or forces outside the range of ordinary human experience. Since stories take the unusual, the remarkable, as their subject-matter, and since the behaviour and events associated with supernatural forces tend to be remarkable, it is inevitable that many stories include supernatural subjects. That is simply on the narrative level; but it is also obvious that, as stories begin to reflect individual concerns or tribal values, they incorporate elements of religion itself. It was argued in the first chapter that not by any means all of what we commonly call myths are primarily and essentially concerned with religion, or gods, or the supernatural; but many are, and these topics, since on the one hand they are by nature related to fantasy, and on the other they are of deep human concern, form part of the background of most myths. Yet we have seen that mythical fantasy and dislocation are not predominantly restricted to religious ideas. Rather these constitute a special if limited genre of fantasy (divine actions, like magic, are rarely unpredictable); they must have enormously strengthened and encouraged the fantastic development of myths, but quite probably did not initiate it.

Throughout this book I have been concentrating especially on the speculative aspects of myths, on the role of many myths as embodying responses to problems. I do not believe, like Lévi-Strauss, that all myths behave so, or that they all reflect problems in the same way. It is that kind of doctrinaire oversimplification that first gave explanatory theories of myths a bad name—that caused Malinowski and his followers to react by claiming that no myth whatever, at least in tribal cultures, was concerned with abstract explanation. Lévi-Strauss has demonstrated that this, at least, is false. I have expressed certain reservations about his analysis of Amerindian myths, but find it hard to believe that any informed critic can now reject a serious speculative or preoccupation-reflecting undertone to much of this material. Moreover I claim to have shown that many of the extant Mesopotamian tales, not to speak of other tribal myths or even a few of the relics of Greek mythology, are most plausibly and completely interpreted as attempting, in part at least, to deal with matters of confusion and concern. If so, what kind of relation exists between the fantasy-and-dislocation aspect of many myths and their problem-reflecting aspects?

Obviously, if what I have suggested above is well founded, there is unlikely to be an essential and invariable relation between them. Moreover one might argue that a problem could be reflected by means of a strictly allegorical and non-fantastic story. But this leads straight to the point: could a problem be in any sense resolved or palliated by such means? Mere transposition into a different code would not achieve it, as I suggested earlier; perhaps the code, or the mythical or allegorical model, might carry its own implication of a solution—but at this point we are going beyond strict allegory. Some of the dislocation, at least, is likely to be relevant to the problematic function. In two-stage Mesopotamian myths, for example, it looks as though separate tales were sometimes juxtaposed (sometimes, initially, as an accident of the tradition?), in a way which caused some dislocation, and which is then used as a means of refracting one situation upon another. This question, in particular, needs much fuller discussion.

According to the weighting of possibilities that has been provisionally suggested, the speculative and operative functions of myths may often develop gradually out of their narrative ones; the needs of the community impress themselves on story-telling, among other aspects of social life, as a basic mode of communication; and the most fantastic elements of myths, reflecting the demand for the remarkable in stories as well as the importance of the irrational and supernatural both in waking and in sleeping experience, are gradually and erratically accreted. Such an assessment would be seriously different from those that see myths solely as charters, or as attempts to describe nature, or as reflexions of rituals; also from those that concentrate on a particular mythical mode of expression, seen perhaps as a special kind of emotional reaction to the world and depending on the emission of pregnant symbols.

Even such a provisional picture would be heavily defective. More would be needed before the process of making a myth could be even dimly apprehended—not least a fuller understanding of mythical fantasy as something attractive for its own sake, as providing a different and more luminous view of the world. More tangible tasks remain, for example the fuller study of the story-teller in non-literate communities, especially in those least affected by what we call civilization. And in the end the firmest part of our study will continue to be the careful and sympathetic analysis of actual documents, surviving myths themselves. In this respect the cultures of the ancient world are at least as important as those of modern tribal societies.

General Index

DATE DUE